NATIONAL SAFETY COUNCIL ™

INJURY FACTS

2002 Edition

FORMERLY
ACCIDENT FACTS®

The National Safety Council, chartered by an act of Congress, is a nongovernmental, not-for-profit, public service organization devoted solely to educating and influencing society to adopt safety, health, and environmental policies, practices, and procedures that prevent and mitigate human suffering and economic losses arising from preventable causes.

Injury Facts®, the Council's annual statistical report on unintentional injuries and their characteristics and costs, was prepared by:

Research and Statistics Department
Mei-Li Lin, Director
Alan F. Hoskin, Manager
Kevin T. Fearn
Kathleen T. Porretta, Production Manager

Fleet accident rates were prepared by:

Carolanne Haase

Questions or comments about the content of *Injury Facts*® should be directed to the Research and Statistics Department, National Safety Council, 1121 Spring Lake Drive, Itasca, IL 60143, or telephone 630-775-2322, or fax 630-285-0242, or E-mail rssdept@nsc.org.

For price and ordering information, write Customer Relations, National Safety Council, 1121 Spring Lake Drive, Itasca, IL 60143, or telephone 1-800-621-7619, or fax 630-285-0797.

Acknowledgments
The information presented in *Injury Facts*® was made possible by the cooperation of many organizations and individuals, including state vital and health statistics authorities, state traffic authorities, state workers' compensation authorities, state and local safety councils, trade associations, Bureau of the Census, Bureau of Labor Statistics, Consumer Product Safety Commission, Federal Highway Administration, Federal Railroad Administration, National Center for Health Statistics, National Fire Protection Association, National Highway Traffic Safety Administration, National Transportation Safety Board, National Weather Service, and Mine Safety and Health Administration. Specific contributions are acknowledged in footnotes and source notes throughout the book.

Visit the National Safety Council's website:

http://www.nsc.org

Suggested citation: National Safety Council. (2002). *Injury Facts*®, *2002 Edition*. Itasca, IL: Author.

Library of Congress Catalog Card Number: 99–74142

Printed in U.S.A.   ISBN 0–87912–246–3   NSC Press Product No. 02302–0000

TABLE OF CONTENTS

FOREWORD

Unintentional-injury deaths were up 2% in 2001 compared to the revised 2000 total. Unintentional-injury deaths were estimated to total 98,000 in 2001 and 96,000 in 2000.

The resident population of the United States increased 1% from 2000 to 2001.

The death rate in 2001 was 35.3 per 100,000 population—1% greater than the rate in 2000 and 4% greater than the lowest rate on record, which was 34.0 in 1992.

A more complete summary of the situation in 2001 and recent trends is given on page 2.

The graph on the opposite page shows the overall trends in the number of unintentional-injury deaths, the population, and the death rate per 100,000 population.

It is important to note that the final 1999 death certificate data used in many tables in *Injury Facts®* is now based on the tenth revision of the *International Classification of Diseases.* The implications of this change are noted, where appropriate, throughout the book and especially in the Technical Appendix.

Changes in the 2002 Edition

For the third year in a row, eight pages have been added to *Injury Facts®* to provide more usable information to readers. The book has grown from 108 pages to 178 pages over the past decade. Pages have been added to the All Unintentional Injuries, Work, State Data, and Other Sources chapters. Several pages with state-level data have been moved to the State Data chapter.

Look for *new* data on …

• U-I deaths and rates by sex and age

• Years of potential life lost

• Part of body (work)

• U-I deaths by race and Hispanic origin

• Terrorism

• Forklifts

• Health promotion and productivity at work

• Teen safety belt use

• Electrocutions at home

• Child drownings

• Child deaths in unattended vehicles

and *updated* or *expanded* data on …

• Emergency department visits for injuries

• Occupational injury and illness incidence rates

• Workers' compensation claims and costs

• Industry Division profile data

• State traffic laws

• Highway work zones

• Sports injuries

• Consumer product-related injuries

• Home fires

• Environmental health issues

• State-level injury mortality

UNINTENTIONAL-INJURY DEATHS, DEATH RATES, AND POPULATION, UNITED STATES, 1903–2001

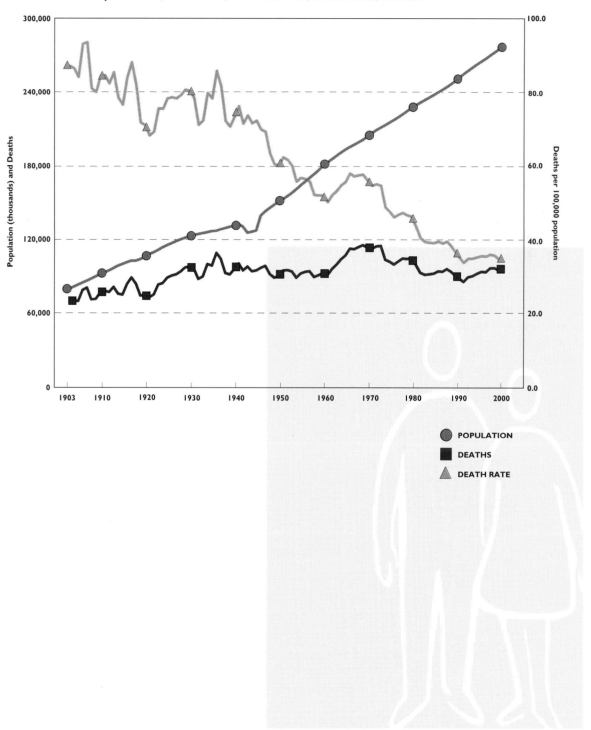

POPULATION
DEATHS
DEATH RATE

ALL UNINTENTIONAL
INJURIES

ALL UNINTENTIONAL INJURIES, 2001

Unintentional-injury deaths were up 2% in 2001 compared to the revised 2000 total. Unintentional-injury deaths were estimated to total 98,000 in 2001 and 96,000 in 2000. The 2001 estimate is virtually unchanged from the 1999 final count of 97,860. The 2001 figure is 13% greater than the 1992 total of 86,777 (the lowest annual total since 1924) but 16% below the 1969 peak of 116,385 deaths.

The death rate in 2001 was 35.3 per 100,000 population—4% greater than the lowest rate on record, which was 34.0 in 1992. The 2001 death rate was 1% greater than the 2000 revised rate of 34.9.

Comparing 2001 to 2000, public deaths decreased while home, work, and motor-vehicle deaths increased. The population death rate in the public class declined, in the motor-vehicle class it was unchanged, and the rate increased in the work and home classes.

The motor-vehicle death total was up 1% in 2000. The motor-vehicle death rate per 100,000,000 vehicle-miles was 1.54 in 2001, down 1% from the 2000 revised rate (1.55) and down 3% from the 1999 revised rate of 1.58.

According to the latest final data (1999), unintentional injuries continued to be the fifth leading cause of death, exceeded only by heart disease, cancer, stroke, and chronic lower respiratory diseases. Preliminary death certificate data for 2000 indicate that unintentional injuries will remain in fifth place.

Nonfatal injuries also affect millions of Americans. In 2000, about 2.5 million people were hospitalized for injuries; about 40.4 million people were treated in hospital emergency departments, and about 9.5 million in outpatient departments; and about 89.9 million visits to physicians' offices were due to injuries. In 1997, about 34.4 million people—more than one in eight—sought medical attention because of an injury.

The economic impact of these fatal and nonfatal unintentional injuries amounted to $516.9 billion in 2001. This is equivalent to about $1,900 per capita, or about $5,000 per household. These are costs that every individual and household pays whether directly out of pocket, through higher prices for goods and services, or through higher taxes.

Beginning with 1999 data, which became available in September 2001, deaths are now classified according to the 10th revision of the *International Classification of Diseases*. Overall, about 3% more deaths are classified as due to "unintentional injuries" under the new classification system than under the 9th revision. The difference varies across causes of death. See the Technical Appendix for more information on comparability. Caution should be used in comparing data classified under the two systems.

ALL UNINTENTIONAL INJURIES, 2001

Class	2001 Deaths	Change from 2000	Deaths per 100,000 Persons	Disabling Injuries[a]
All Classes[b]	98,000	+2%	35.3	20,400,000
Motor-vehicle	42,900	+1%	15.4	2,300,000
Public nonwork	*40,500*			*2,200,000*
Work	*2,200*			*100,000*
Home	*200*			*(c)*
Work	5,300	+6%	1.9	3,900,000
Nonmotor-vehicle	*3,100*			*3,800,000*
Motor-vehicle	*2,200*			*100,000*
Home	33,200	+7%	12.0	8,000,000
Nonmotor-vehicle	*33,000*			*8,000,000*
Motor-vehicle	*200*			*(c)*
Public	19,000	-5%	6.8	6,300,000

Source: National Safety Council estimates (rounded) based on data from the National Center for Health Statistics, Bureau of Labor Statistics, state departments of health, state traffic authorities, and state industrial commissions. The National Safety Council adopted the Bureau of Labor Statistics' Census of Fatal Occupational Injuries count for work-related unintentional injuries retroactive to 1992 data. See the Glossary for definitions and the Technical Appendix for revised estimating procedures.

[a] Disabling injuries are not reported on a national basis, so the totals shown are approximations based on ratios of disabling injuries to deaths developed by the National Safety Council. The totals are the best estimates for the current year. They should not, however, be compared with totals shown in previous editions of this book to indicate year-to-year changes or trends. See the Glossary for definitions and the Technical Appendix for estimating procedures.

[b] Deaths and injuries above for the four separate classes add to more than the All Classes figures due to rounding and because some deaths and injuries are included in more than one class. For example, 2,200 work deaths involved motor vehicles in transport and are in both the work and motor-vehicle totals, and 200 motor-vehicle deaths occurred on home premises and are in both home and motor-vehicle. The total of such duplication amounted to about 2,400 deaths and 100,000 injuries in 2001.

[c] Less than 10,000.

UNINTENTIONAL-INJURY DEATHS BY CLASS, UNITED STATES, 2001

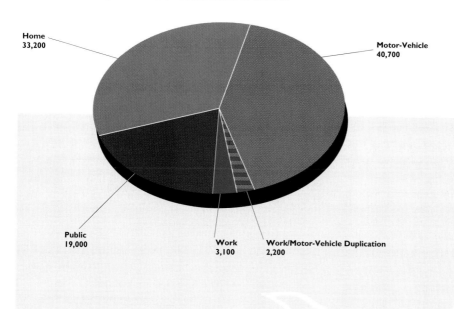

Home
33,200

Motor-Vehicle
40,700

Public
19,000

Work
3,100

Work/Motor-Vehicle Duplication
2,200

UNINTENTIONAL DISABLING INJURIES BY CLASS, UNITED STATES, 2001

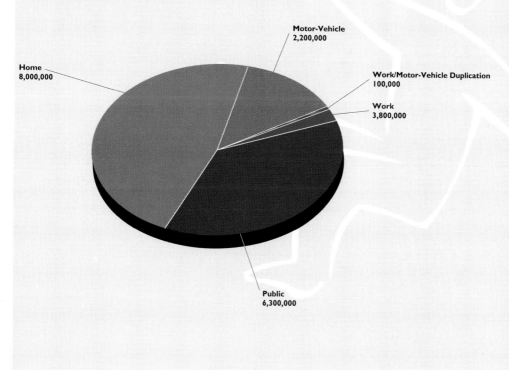

Motor-Vehicle
2,200,000

Work/Motor-Vehicle Duplication
100,000

Home
8,000,000

Work
3,800,000

Public
6,300,000

COSTS OF UNINTENTIONAL INJURIES
BY CLASS, 2001

The total cost of unintentional injuries in 2001, $516.9 billion, includes estimates of economic costs of fatal and nonfatal unintentional injuries together with employer costs, vehicle damage costs, and fire losses. Wage and productivity losses, medical expenses, administrative expenses, and employer costs are included in all four classes of injuries. Cost components unique to each class are identified below.

Motor-vehicle costs include property damage from motor-vehicle accidents. Work costs include the value of property damage in on-the-job motor-vehicle accidents and fires. Home and public costs include estimated fire losses, but do not include other property damage costs.

Besides the estimated $516.9 billion in economic losses from unintentional injuries in 2001, lost quality of life from those injuries is valued at an additional $1,172.3 billion, making the comprehensive cost $1,689.2 billion in 2001.

Cost estimating procedures were revised extensively for the 1993 edition of *Accident Facts*®. New components were added, new benchmarks adopted, and a new discount rate assumed (see the Technical Appendix). In general, cost estimates are not comparable from year to year. As additional or more precise data become available, they are used from that point forward. Previously estimated figures are not revised.

CERTAIN COSTS OF UNINTENTIONAL INJURIES BY CLASS, 2001 ($ BILLIONS)

Cost	Total[a]	Motor-Vehicle	Work	Home	Public Nonmotor-Vehicle
Total	**$516.9**	**$199.6**	**$132.1**	**$118.1**	**$82.1**
Wage and productivity losses	266.8	73.2	69.2	75.5	52.7
Medical expenses	95.2	24.9	24.6	26.9	20.2
Administrative expenses[b]	74.1	50.4	21.7	5.4	4.0
Motor-vehicle damage	49.2	49.2	2.0	(c)	(c)
Employer cost	21.4	1.9	11.8	4.5	3.6
Fire loss	10.2	(c)	2.8	5.8	1.6

Source: National Safety Council estimates. See the Technical Appendix.
[a] *Duplication between work and motor-vehicle, which amounted to $15.0 billion, was eliminated from the total.*
[b] *Home and public insurance administration costs may include costs of administering medical treatment claims for some motor-vehicle injuries filed through health insurance plans.*
[c] *Not included; see comments above.*

COST OF UNINTENTIONAL INJURIES BY CLASS, 2001

TOTAL COST $516.9 BILLION

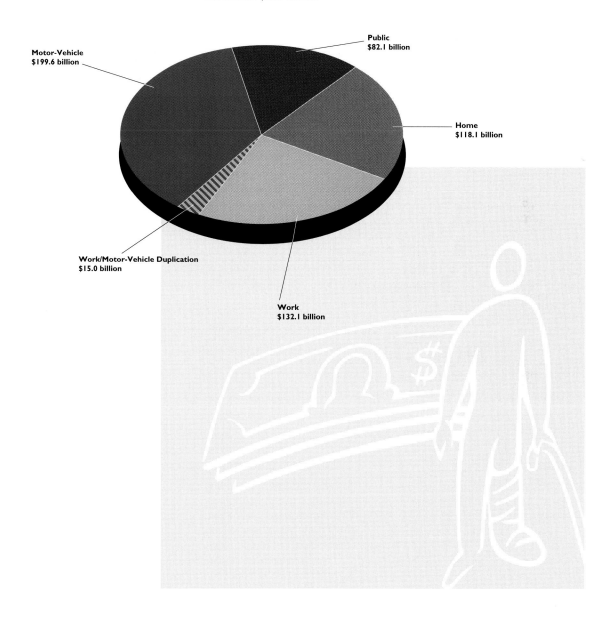

Public
$82.1 billion

Motor-Vehicle
$199.6 billion

Home
$118.1 billion

Work/Motor-Vehicle Duplication
$15.0 billion

Work
$132.1 billion

COSTS OF UNINTENTIONAL INJURIES BY COMPONENT

Wage and Productivity Losses

A person's contribution to the wealth of the nation usually is measured in terms of wages and household production. The total of wages and fringe benefits together with an estimate of the replacement-cost value of household services provides an estimate of this lost productivity. Also included is travel delay for motor-vehicle accidents.

Medical Expenses

Doctor fees, hospital charges, the cost of medicines, future medical costs, and ambulance, helicopter, and other emergency medical services are included.

Administrative Expenses

Includes the administrative cost of public and private insurance, and police and legal costs. Private insurance administrative costs are the difference between premiums paid to insurance companies and claims paid out by them. It is their cost of doing business and is a part of the cost total. Claims paid by insurance companies are not identified separately, as every claim is compensation for losses such as wages, medical expenses, property damage, etc.

Motor-Vehicle Damage

Includes the value of property damage to vehicles from motor-vehicle accidents. The cost of normal wear and tear to vehicles is not included.

Employer Costs

This is an estimate of the uninsured costs incurred by employers, representing the dollar value of time lost by uninjured workers. It includes time spent investigating and reporting injuries, giving first aid, hiring and training of replacement workers, and the extra cost of overtime for uninjured workers.

Fire Loss

Includes losses from both structure fires and nonstructure fires such as vehicles, outside storage, crops, and timber.

Work–Motor-Vehicle Duplication

The cost of motor-vehicle crashes that involve persons in the course of their work is included in both classes, but the duplication is eliminated from the total. The duplication in 2001 amounted to $15.0 billion and was made up of $3.8 billion in wage and productivity losses, $1.4 billion in medical expenses, $7.4 billion in administrative expenses, $2.0 billion in vehicle damage, and $0.4 billion in uninsured employer costs.

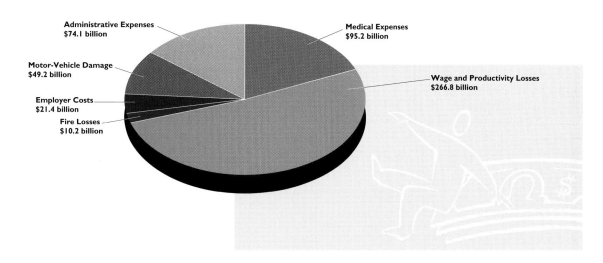

TOTAL COST $516.9 BILLION

Administrative Expenses
$74.1 billion

Medical Expenses
$95.2 billion

Motor-Vehicle Damage
$49.2 billion

Wage and Productivity Losses
$266.8 billion

Employer Costs
$21.4 billion

Fire Losses
$10.2 billion

COST EQUIVALENTS

The costs of unintentional injuries are immense—billions of dollars. Since figures this large can be difficult to comprehend, it is sometimes useful to reduce the numbers to a more understandable scale by relating them to quantities encountered in daily life.

The table below shows how the costs of unintentional injuries compare to common quantities such as taxes, corporate profits, or stock dividends.

COST EQUIVALENTS, 2001

The Cost of ...	Is Equivalent to ...
...All Injuries ($516.9 billion)	...52 cents of every dollar paid in federal personal income taxes, **or** ...52 cents of every dollar spent on food in the United States.
...Motor-Vehicle Crashes ($199.6 billion)	...purchasing 590 gallons of gasoline for each registered vehicle in the United States, **or** ...more than $1,000 per licensed driver, **or** ...nearly 11 times greater than the combined profits reported by ExxonMobil and ChevronTexaco.
...Work Injuries ($132.1 billion)	...32 cents of every dollar of corporate dividends to stockholders, **or** ...19 cents of every dollar of pre-tax corporate profits, **or** ...exceeds the combined profits reported by the top 15 Fortune 500 companies.
...Home Injuries ($118.1 billion)	...a $94,000 rebate on each new single-family home built, **or** ...46 cents of every dollar of property taxes paid.
...Public Injuries ($82.1 billion)	...a $9.1 million grant to each public library in the United States, **or** ...a $99,600 bonus for each police officer and firefighter.

Source: National Safety Council estimates.

DEATHS DUE TO UNINTENTIONAL INJURIES, 2001

All Unintentional Injuries

The term "unintentional" covers most deaths from injury and poisoning. Excluded are homicides (including legal intervention), suicides, deaths for which none of these categories can be determined, and war deaths.

	Total	Change from 2000	Death Rate[a]
Deaths	98,000	+2%	35.3

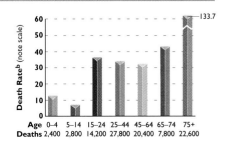

Age	0–4	5–14	15–24	25–44	45–64	65–74	75+
Deaths	2,400	2,800	14,200	27,800	20,400	7,800	22,600

Motor-Vehicle Accidents

Includes deaths involving mechanically or electrically powered highway-transport vehicles in motion (except those on rails), both on and off the highway or street.

	Total	Change from 2000	Death Rate[a]
Deaths	42,900	+1%	15.4

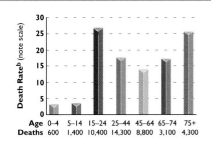

Age	0–4	5–14	15–24	25–44	45–64	65–74	75+
Deaths	600	1,400	10,400	14,300	8,800	3,100	4,300

Poisoning

Includes deaths from drugs, medicines, other solid and liquid substances, and gases and vapors. Excludes poisonings from spoiled foods, salmonella, etc., which are classified as disease deaths.

	Total	Change from 2000	Death Rate[a]
Deaths	14,500	+14%	5.2

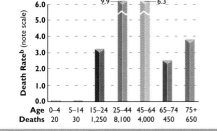

Age	0–4	5–14	15–24	25–44	45–64	65–74	75+
Deaths	20	30	1,250	8,100	4,000	450	650

Falls

Includes deaths from falls from one level to another or on the same level. Excludes falls in or from transport vehicles, or while boarding or alighting from them.

	Total	Change from 2000	Death Rate[a]
Deaths	14,200	+10%	5.1

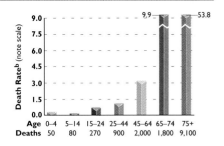

Age	0–4	5–14	15–24	25–44	45–64	65–74	75+
Deaths	50	80	270	900	2,000	1,800	9,100

Suffocation by Ingested Object

Includes deaths from unintentional ingestion or inhalation of food or other objects resulting in the obstruction of respiratory passages.

	Total	Change from 2000	Death Rate[a]
Deaths	4,200	–2%	1.5

See footnotes on page 9.

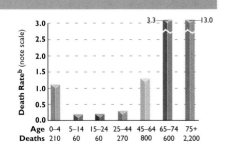

Age	0–4	5–14	15–24	25–44	45–64	65–74	75+
Deaths	210	60	60	270	800	600	2,200

Fires, Flames, and Smoke

Includes deaths from exposure to fires, flames, and smoke, and from injuries in fires—such as falls and being struck by falling objects. Excludes burns from hot objects or liquids.

	Total	Change from 2000	Death Rate[a]
Deaths	3,900	0%	1.4

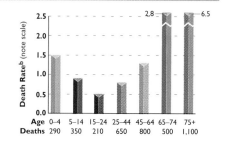

Drowning

Includes nontransport-related drownings such as those resulting from swimming, playing in the water, or falling in. Excludes drownings in floods and other cataclysms, which are classified to the cataclysm, and boating-related drownings.

	Total	Change from 2000	Death Rate[a]
Deaths	3,300	0%	1.2

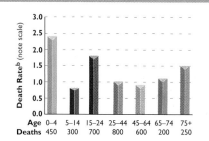

Mechanical Suffocation

Includes deaths from hanging and strangulation, and suffocation in enclosed or confined spaces, cave-ins, or by bed clothes, plastic bags, or similar materials.

	Total	Change from 2000	Death Rate[a]
Deaths	1,300	−13%	0.5

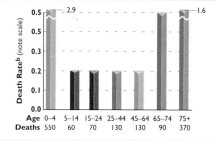

Natural Heat or Cold

Includes deaths resulting from exposure to excessive natural heat and cold (e.g., extreme weather conditions).

	Total	Change from 2000	Death Rate[a]
Deaths	1,100	+10%	0.4

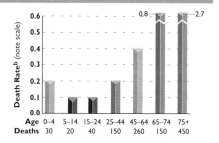

All Other Types

Most important types included are: firearms, struck by or against object, machinery, electric current, and air, water, and rail transport.

	Total	Change from 2000	Death Rate[a]
Deaths	12,600	−9%	4.5

Note: Category descriptions have changes due to adoption of ICD-10. See Technical Appendix for comparablity.
[a]*Deaths per 100,000 population.*
[b]*Deaths per 100,000 population in each age group.*

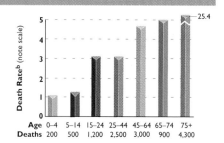

LEADING CAUSES OF DEATH

Unintentional injuries are the leading cause of death among persons in age groups from 1 to 34. Among persons of all ages, unintentional injuries are the fifth leading cause of death. See pages 14–17 for leading causes of death by single years of age.

Beginning with 1999 data, deaths are now classified according to the 10th revision of the International Classification of Diseases. See the Technical Appendix for comparability with prior years.

DEATHS AND DEATH RATES BY AGE AND SEX, 1999

Cause	Number of Deaths			Death Rates[a]		
	Total	Male	Female	Total	Male	Female
All Ages[b]						
All Causes	2,391,399	1,175,460	1,215,939	877.0	882.0	872.2
Heart disease	725,192	351,617	373,575	265.9	263.8	268.0
Cancer (malignant neoplasms)	549,838	285,832	264,006	201.6	214.5	189.4
Stroke (cerebrovascular disease)	167,366	64,485	102,881	61.4	48.4	73.8
Chronic lower respiratory diseases	124,181	62,415	61,766	45.5	46.8	44.3
Unintentional injuries	**97,860**	**63,535**	**34,325**	**35.9**	**47.7**	**24.6**
Motor-vehicle	42,401	28,552	13,849	15.5	21.4	9.9
Falls	13,162	7,109	6,053	4.8	5.3	4.3
Poisoning	12,186	8,887	3,299	4.5	6.7	2.4
Inhalation, ingestion of food, object	3,885	1,917	1,968	1.4	1.4	1.4
Drowning	3,529	2,794	735	1.3	2.1	0.5
All other unintentional injuries	22,697	14,276	8,421	8.3	10.7	6.0
Diabetes mellitus	68,399	31,150	37,249	25.1	23.4	26.7
Influenza and pneumonia	63,730	27,718	36,012	23.4	20.8	25.8
Alzheimer's disease	44,536	13,391	31,145	16.3	10.0	22.3
Nephritis and nephrosis	35,525	17,016	18,509	13.0	12.8	13.3
Septicemia	30,680	13,395	17,285	11.3	10.1	12.4
Under 1 Year						
All Causes	27,937	15,646	12,291	731.4	801.5	658.1
Congenital anomalies	5,473	2,875	2,598	143.3	147.3	139.1
Short gestation, low birth weight, n.e.c.	4,392	2,455	1,937	115.0	125.8	103.7
Sudden infant death syndrome	2,648	1,553	1,095	69.3	79.6	58.6
Maternal complications of pregnancy	1,399	791	608	36.6	40.5	32.6
Respiratory distress	1,110	655	455	29.1	33.6	24.4
Complications of placenta, cord, membranes	1,025	533	492	26.8	27.3	26.3
Unintentional injuries	**845**	**494**	**351**	**22.1**	**25.3**	**18.8**
Mechanical suffocation	409	244	165	10.7	12.5	8.8
Motor-vehicle	184	97	87	4.8	5.0	4.7
Drowning	68	39	29	1.8	2.0	1.6
Inhalation, ingestion of food, object	63	37	26	1.6	1.9	1.4
Fires and flames	41	21	20	1.1	1.1	1.1
All other unintentional injuries	80	56	24	2.1	2.9	1.3
Bacterial sepsis	691	397	294	18.1	20.3	15.7
Diseases of the circulatory system	667	360	307	17.5	18.4	16.4
Atelectasis	647	392	255	16.9	20.1	13.7
1 to 4 Years						
All Causes	5,249	2,975	2,274	34.7	38.5	30.8
Unintentional injuries	**1,898**	**1,127**	**771**	**12.6**	**14.6**	**10.4**
Motor-vehicle	650	366	284	4.3	4.7	3.8
Drowning	490	310	180	3.2	4.0	2.4
Fires and flames	302	173	129	2.0	2.2	1.7
Inhalation, ingestion of food, object	88	60	28	0.6	0.8	0.4
Mechanical suffocation	74	36	38	0.5	0.5	0.5
All other unintentional injuries	294	182	112	1.9	2.4	1.5
Congenital anomalies	549	310	239	3.6	4.0	3.2
Cancer (malignant neoplasms)	418	227	191	2.8	2.9	2.6
Homicide	376	194	182	2.5	2.5	2.5
Heart disease	183	104	79	1.2	1.3	1.1
Influenza and pneumonia	130	66	64	0.9	0.9	0.9
Certain conditions originating in the perinatal period	92	56	36	0.6	0.7	0.5
Septicemia	87	48	39	0.6	0.6	0.5
Benign neoplasms	63	33	30	0.4	0.4	0.4
Chronic lower respiratory diseases	54	30	24	0.4	0.4	0.3

See source and footnotes on page 12.

DEATHS AND DEATH RATES BY AGE AND SEX, 1999, Cont.

Cause	Number of Deaths			Death Rates[a]		
	Total	Male	Female	Total	Male	Female
5 to 14 Years						
All Causes	**7,595**	**4,492**	**3,103**	**19.2**	**22.2**	**16.1**
Unintentional injuries	**3,091**	**1,974**	**1,117**	**7.8**	**9.8**	**5.8**
Motor-vehicle	1,771	1,062	709	4.5	5.3	3.7
Drowning	369	275	94	0.9	1.4	0.5
Fires and flames	262	147	115	0.7	0.7	0.6
Mechanical suffocation	86	76	10	0.2	0.4	0.1
Firearms	76	60	16	0.2	0.3	0.1
All other unintentional injuries	527	354	173	1.3	1.8	0.9
Cancer	1,012	555	457	2.6	2.7	2.4
Congenital anomalies	428	215	213	1.1	1.1	1.1
Homicide	432	250	182	1.1	1.2	0.9
Heart disease	277	157	120	0.7	0.8	0.6
Suicide	244	194	50	0.6	1.0	0.3
Chronic lower respiratory diseases	139	93	46	0.4	0.5	0.2
Benign neoplasms	101	49	52	0.3	0.2	0.3
Influenza and pneumonia	93	53	40	0.2	0.3	0.2
Septicemia	77	36	41	0.2	0.2	0.2
15 to 24 Years						
All Causes	**30,656**	**22,414**	**8,242**	**81.2**	**115.9**	**44.7**
Unintentional injuries	**13,656**	**10,040**	**3,616**	**36.2**	**51.9**	**19.6**
Motor-vehicle	10,128	7,127	3,001	26.8	36.9	16.3
Poisoning	964	754	210	2.6	3.9	1.1
Drowning	647	592	55	1.7	3.1	0.3
Firearms	251	229	22	0.7	1.2	0.1
Falls	242	209	33	0.6	1.1	0.2
All other unintentional injuries	1,424	1,129	295	3.8	5.8	1.6
Homicide	4,998	4,191	807	13.2	21.7	4.4
Suicide	3,901	3,326	575	10.3	17.2	3.1
Cancer	1,724	1,023	701	4.6	5.3	3.8
Heart disease	1,069	664	405	2.8	3.4	2.2
Congenital anomalies	434	262	172	1.1	1.4	0.9
Chronic lower respiratory diseases	209	123	86	0.6	0.6	0.5
Human immunodeficiency virus infection	198	95	103	0.5	0.5	0.6
Stroke (cerebrovascular disease)	182	95	87	0.5	0.5	0.5
Influenza and pneumonia	179	90	89	0.5	0.5	0.5
25 to 34 Years						
All Causes	**41,066**	**28,276**	**12,790**	**108.3**	**150.2**	**66.9**
Unintentional injuries	**11,890**	**9,097**	**2,793**	**31.3**	**48.3**	**14.6**
Motor-vehicle	6,778	4,993	1,785	17.9	26.5	9.3
Poisoning	2,355	1,828	527	6.2	9.7	2.8
Drowning	446	397	49	1.2	2.1	0.3
Falls	343	294	49	0.9	1.6	0.3
Fires and flames	282	197	85	0.7	1.0	0.4
All other unintentional injuries	1,686	1,388	298	4.4	7.4	1.6
Suicide	5,106	4,194	912	13.5	22.3	4.8
Homicide	4,231	3,346	885	11.2	17.8	4.6
Cancer	4,005	1,959	2,046	10.6	10.4	10.7
Heart disease	3,066	1,988	1,078	8.1	10.6	5.6
Human immunodeficiency virus infection	2,729	1,914	815	7.2	10.2	4.3
Diabetes mellitus	582	319	263	1.5	1.7	1.4
Stroke (cerebrovascular disease)	580	299	281	1.5	1.6	1.5
Congenital anomalies	465	242	223	1.2	1.3	1.2
Chronic liver disease and cirrhosis	407	257	150	1.1	1.4	0.8
35 to 44 Years						
All Causes	**89,256**	**57,118**	**32,138**	**199.2**	**256.7**	**142.5**
Cancer	16,732	7,471	9,261	37.3	33.6	41.1
Unintentional injuries	**15,231**	**11,248**	**3,983**	**34.0**	**50.5**	**17.7**
Motor-vehicle	6,738	4,735	2,003	15.0	21.3	8.9
Poisoning	4,549	3,349	1,200	10.2	15.0	5.3
Falls	645	528	117	1.4	2.4	0.5
Drowning	475	402	73	1.1	1.8	0.3
Fires and flames	421	300	121	0.9	1.3	0.5
All other unintentional injuries	2,403	1,934	469	5.4	8.7	2.1
Heart disease	13,600	9,640	3,960	30.3	43.3	17.6
Suicide	6,466	5,019	1,447	14.4	22.6	6.4
Human immunodeficiency virus infection	6,232	4,706	1,526	13.9	21.1	6.8
Chronic liver disease and cirrhosis	3,302	2,314	988	7.4	10.4	4.4
Homicide	3,206	2,307	899	7.2	10.4	4.0
Stroke (cerebrovascular disease)	2,574	1,308	1,266	5.7	5.9	5.6
Diabetes mellitus	1,942	1,139	803	4.3	5.1	3.6
Influenza and pneumonia	1,063	592	471	2.4	2.7	2.1

See source and footnotes on page 12.

DEATHS AND DEATH RATES BY AGE AND SEX, 1999, Cont.

Cause	Number of Deaths			Death Rates[a]		
	Total	Male	Female	Total	Male	Female
45 to 54 Years						
All Causes	152,974	95,659	57,315	427.3	546.7	313.1
Cancer	46,681	23,634	23,047	130.4	135.1	125.9
Heart disease	34,994	25,489	9,505	97.7	145.7	51.9
Unintentional injuries	**11,639**	**8,602**	**3,037**	**32.5**	**49.2**	**16.6**
Motor-vehicle	4,972	3,473	1,499	13.9	19.8	8.2
Poisoning	2,844	2,106	738	7.9	12.0	4.0
Falls	824	661	163	2.3	3.8	0.9
Drowning	370	311	59	1.0	1.8	0.3
Fires and flames	368	254	114	1.0	1.5	0.6
All other unintentional injuries	2,261	1,797	464	6.3	10.3	2.5
Chronic liver disease and cirrhosis	6,368	4,829	1,539	17.8	27.6	8.4
Stroke (cerebrovascular disease)	5,563	2,996	2,567	15.5	17.1	14.0
Suicide	5,081	3,854	1,227	14.2	22.0	6.7
Diabetes mellitus	4,735	2,791	1,944	13.2	15.9	10.6
Human immunodeficiency virus infection	3,907	3,134	773	10.9	17.9	4.2
Chronic lower respiratory diseases	3,110	1,551	1,559	8.7	8.9	8.5
Influenza and pneumonia	1,697	1,059	638	4.7	6.1	3.5
55 to 64						
All Causes	238,979	142,724	96,255	1,021.8	1,280.0	786.5
Cancer	89,067	48,833	40,234	380.8	437.9	328.7
Heart disease	64,167	43,662	20,505	274.3	391.6	167.5
Chronic lower respiratory diseases	11,297	5,958	5,339	48.3	53.4	43.6
Stroke (cerebrovascular disease)	9,652	5,305	4,347	41.3	47.6	35.5
Diabetes mellitus	9,097	4,856	4,241	38.9	43.5	34.7
Unintentional injuries	**7,285**	**5,015**	**2,270**	**31.1**	**45.0**	**18.5**
Motor-vehicle	3,370	2,200	1,170	14.4	19.7	9.6
Falls	887	650	237	3.8	5.8	1.9
Poisoning	668	448	220	2.9	4.0	1.8
Fires and flames	319	194	125	1.4	1.7	1.0
Inhalation, ingestion of food, object	272	152	120	1.2	1.4	1.0
All other unintentional injuries	1,769	1,371	398	7.6	12.3	3.3
Chronic liver disease and cirrhosis	5,637	3,943	1,694	24.1	35.4	13.8
Suicide	2,896	2,255	641	12.4	20.2	5.2
Nephritis and nephrosis	2,864	1,530	1,334	12.2	13.7	10.9
Septicemia	2,714	1,412	1,302	11.6	12.7	10.6
65 to 74 Years						
All Causes	452,600	254,920	197,680	2,484.3	3,109.3	1,972.9
Cancer	152,338	84,544	67,794	836.2	1,031.2	676.6
Heart disease	129,253	78,836	50,417	709.5	961.6	503.2
Chronic lower respiratory diseases	32,644	17,477	15,167	179.2	213.2	151.4
Stroke (cerebrovascular disease)	24,092	12,220	11,872	132.2	149.0	118.5
Diabetes mellitus	16,908	8,279	8,629	92.8	101.0	86.1
Unintentional injuries	**8,208**	**4,992**	**3,216**	**45.1**	**60.9**	**32.1**
Motor-vehicle	3,276	1,931	1,345	18.0	23.6	13.4
Falls	1,663	1,027	636	9.1	12.5	6.3
Inhalation, ingestion of food, object	566	315	251	3.1	3.8	2.5
Fires and flames	416	244	172	2.3	3.0	1.7
Poisoning	300	172	128	1.6	2.1	1.3
All other unintentional injuries	1,987	1,303	684	10.9	15.9	6.8
Influenza and pneumonia	6,861	3,893	2,968	37.7	47.5	29.6
Nephritis and nephrosis	6,841	3,504	3,337	37.6	42.7	33.3
Septicemia	5,750	2,919	2,831	31.6	35.6	28.3
Chronic liver disease and cirrhosis	5,642	3,454	2,188	31.0	42.1	21.8
75 Years and Older						
All Causes	1,344,731	550,959	793,772	8,238.9	9,015.3	7,774.2
Heart disease	478,012	190,770	287,242	2,928.7	3,121.6	2,813.2
Cancer	237,784	117,544	120,240	1,456.9	1,923.4	1,177.6
Stroke (cerebrovascular disease)	124,507	42,140	82,367	762.8	689.5	806.7
Chronic lower respiratory diseases	75,468	36,599	38,869	462.4	598.9	380.7
Influenza and pneumonia	50,421	20,134	30,287	308.9	329.5	296.6
Alzheimer's disease	40,816	11,700	29,116	250.1	191.4	285.2
Diabetes mellitus	34,935	13,664	21,271	214.0	223.6	208.3
Unintentional injuries	**24,011**	**10,852**	**13,159**	**147.1**	**177.6**	**128.9**
Falls	8,434	3,651	4,783	51.7	59.7	46.8
Motor-vehicle	4,504	2,541	1,963	27.6	41.6	19.2
Inhalation, ingestion of food, object	2,330	992	1,338	14.3	16.2	13.1
Fires and flames	732	358	374	4.5	5.9	3.7
Natural heat/cold	490	212	278	3.0	3.5	2.7
All other unintentional injuries	7,521	3,098	4,423	46.1	50.7	43.3
Nephritis and nephrosis	23,097	10,459	12,638	141.5	171.1	123.8
Septicemia	18,876	7,212	11,664	115.6	118.0	114.2

Source: Adapted from Anderson, R.N. (2001). Deaths: Leading causes for 1999. National Vital Statistics Reports, 49(11), 14-20, 71; with additional unintentional injury data from CDC's WONDER and WISQARS systems.
[a]*Deaths per 100,000 population in each age group.*
[b]*Includes deaths where the age is unknown.*

LEADING CAUSES OF UNINTENTIONAL INJURIES TREATED IN HOSPITAL EMERGENCY DEPARTMENTS BY AGE GROUP, UNITED STATES, 2000[a]

Rank	All Ages	Age Group									
		< 1	1–4	5–9	10–14	15–24	25–34	35–44	45–54	55–64	65+
1	Falls 7,434,032	Falls 135,251	Falls 900,850	Falls 688,942	Falls 638,873	Struck by/against 1,103,864	Struck by/against 814,406	Falls 802,758	Falls 656,056	Falls 461,756	Falls 1,628,146
2	Struck by/against 4,970,710	Struck by/against 39,452	Struck by/against 440,984	Struck by/against 496,279	Struck by/against 605,991	Motor-vehicle occupant 1,032,905	Motor-vehicle occupant 718,054	Struck by/against 656,746	Struck by/against 411,840	Struck by/against 184,005	Struck by/against 217,035
3	Motor-vehicle occupant 3,354,553	Fire/burn 17,704	Other bite/sting[b] 146,945	Pedalcyclist 152,483	Over-exertion 269,895	Falls 813,206	Falls 706,512	Over-exertion 655,272	Over-exertion 377,397	Motor-vehicle occupant 182,050	Motor-vehicle occupant 197,431
4	Over-exertion 3,233,993	Foreign body 14,604	Foreign body 121,077	Cut/pierce 140,719	Pedalcyclist 180,428	Over-exertion 788,401	Over-exertion 699,342	Motor-vehicle occupant 582,489	Motor-vehicle occupant 358,124	Over-exertion 145,752	Over-exertion 149,275
5	Cut/Pierce 2,364,651	Motor-vehicle occupant 10,315	Cut/pierce 98,800	Other bite/sting[b] 110,223	Cut/pierce 165,920	Cut/pierce 535,688	Cut/pierce 465,147	Cut/pierce 427,281	Cut/pierce 272,633	Cut/pierce 140,244	Cut/pierce 111,758
6	Other bite/sting[b] 1,036,796	Other bite/sting[b] 9,947	Poisoning 80,447	Motor-vehicle occupant 88,296	Unknown/unspecified 139,315	Unknown/unspecified 204,764	Other bite/sting[b] 144,468	Other bite/sting[b] 142,989	Other bite/sting[b] 99,749	Other bite/sting[b] 59,217	Other bite/sting[b] 83,554
7	Unknown/unspecified 789,390	Poisoning 7,091	Over-exertion 65,234	Over-exertion 78,717	Motor-vehicle occupant 119,677	Other bite/sting[b] 164,703	Foreign body 127,895	Foreign body 122,461	Foreign body 69,743	Foreign body 37,010	Other transport[c] 38,124
8	Foreign body 735,214	Cut/pierce 6,368	Motor-vehicle occupant 63,595	Dog bite 60,923	Other bite/sting[b] 75,000	Other transport[c] 119,052	Unknown/unspecified 124,440	Unknown/unspecified 100,074	Fire/burn 59,484	Other transport[c] 33,479	Unknown/unspecified 36,994
9	Pedalcyclist 660,403	Inhalation/suffocation 5,857	Fire/burn 62,755	Foreign body 56,681	Other transport[c] 64,393	Foreign body 116,623	Other transport[c] 95,862	Fire/burn 91,488	Unknown/unspecified 56,208	Fire/burn 28,013	Foreign body 36,116
10	Other transport[c] 558,337	Unknown/unspecified 4,583	Unknown/unspecified 43,338	Unknown/unspecified 52,472	Dog bite 48,072	Pedalcyclist 116,246	Fire/burn 94,627	Other transport[c] 82,153	Other transport[c] 53,536	Unknown/unspecified 27,150	Fire/burn 21,688

Source: Office of Statistics and Programming, National Center for Injury Prevention and Control, CDC.
[a]Annualized national estimates based on emergency department visits from 7/1–12/31, 2000. Estimates may be affected by seasonality.
[b]Other than dog bite.
[c]Includes occupant of any transport vehicle other than a motor vehicle or motor cycle (e.g., airplane, rail car, boat, ATV, animal rider).

LEADING CAUSES OF UNINTENTIONAL-INJURY DEATH BY AGE, 1999

Motor-vehicle crashes, falls, poisonings, choking (inhalation or ingestion of food or other object), drownings, and fires and flames were the six leading causes of unintentional-injury death in the United States in 1999. The graph below depicts the number of deaths attributed to these causes by single years of age through age 84.

Motor-vehicle crashes were the leading cause of unintentional-injury death overall and the leading cause of unintentional-injury death from age 1 to 78 in 1999. The distribution of 1999 motor-vehicle fatalities shows a sharp increase for persons aged 13 to 18, rising from 192 for 13-year-olds to 1,325 for 18-year-olds. The greatest number of motor-vehicle fatalities occurred to persons aged 18 and 19 in 1999.

The second leading cause of unintentional-injury death overall in 1999 was falls. Falls were the leading cause of

unintentional-injury death of persons aged 79 and over and second leading cause from ages 58 through 78; deaths resulting from falls peaked at 503 for individuals age 84. Poisoning was the third leading cause of unintentional-injury death in the United States in 1999. Poisoning fatalities reached a high of 528 for 43-year-old individuals and were the second leading cause of unintentional-injury death for persons aged 19 to 57.

Choking was the fourth leading cause of unintentional-injury death in 1999. Choking fatalities reached a high of 137 for 83-year-olds. The fifth leading cause of unintentional-injury death was drowning, which peaked at 215 for 1-year-olds. Drowning was the second leading cause of unintentional-injury death for children and youths.

Source: National Safety Council tabulations of National Center for Health Statistics data. See the Technical Appendix for ICD-10 codes for the leading causes and comparability with prior years.

LEADING CAUSES OF UNINTENTIONAL-INJURY DEATH BY AGE, UNITED STATES, 1999

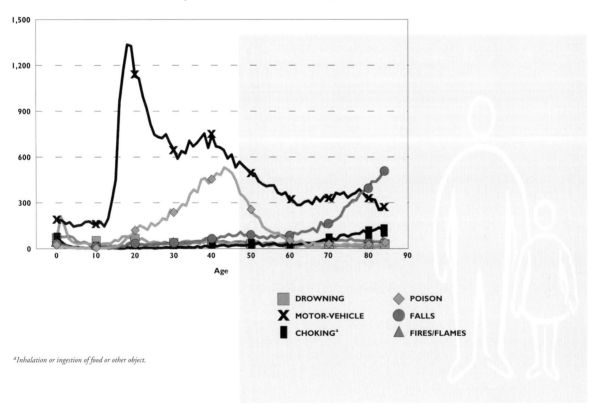

a Inhalation or ingestion of food or other object.

On a rate basis, motor-vehicle deaths by single year of age in 1999 rose to a high of 34.2 per 100,000 population for persons 18 years of age. This rate declined to an average of about 15.0 for those aged 30 to 70, then increased to another high at 33.0 for those 82 years of age.

While motor-vehicle crashes are a significant problem for all ages, deaths resulting from falls for certain older ages have even higher death rates. Beginning at about age 70, the death rate from falls increases dramatically. At age 79 the falls death rate surpasses that for motor-vehicle, with the death rate continuing to rise through 84 years of age where it reaches 62.6.

The death rates for drownings and fires both show peaks at very young ages. The death rate from fires also

increases for the elderly. The poisoning death rate remains low until about age 20 where it rises to its peak rate of 12.4 at 43 years of age then falls again.

Death rates due to choking on inhaled or ingested food or other objects are quite low for most ages. Rates are slightly elevated for infants and toddlers and rise rapidly beginning at about age 70.

The graph below depicts unintentional-injury death rates per 100,000 population for single years of age through age 84 in 1999.

Source: National Safety Council tabulations of National Center for Health Statistics data. See the Technical Appendix for ICD-10 codes for the leading causes and comparability with prior years.

DEATH RATES OF LEADING CAUSES OF UNINTENTIONAL-INJURY DEATH BY AGE, UNITED STATES, 1999

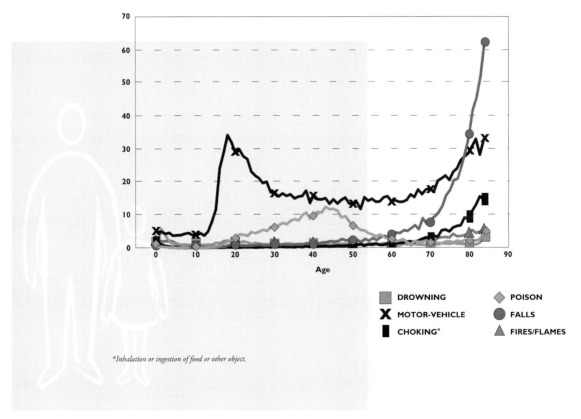

ᵃInhalation or ingestion of food or other object.

UNINTENTIONAL-INJURY DEATHS BY SEX AND AGE

Males incur more deaths due to unintentional injuries than females at all ages from under one year old to age 81.

The difference between the unintentional-injury death totals ranges from as little as 8 at age 83 to as much as 865 at age 19. The difference in the number of deaths for males compared to females is most evident from the late teenage years to the mid-forties, where the gap begins to narrow.

Unintentional-injury deaths are at their lowest level for both sexes from about age 4 to about age 13. For males

the highest number of deaths (1,294) occurs at age 19 and the totals remain high until the mid-forties. For females, however, the highest totals occur among the elderly from about age 75 and older.

The graph below shows the number of unintentional-injury deaths for each sex by single years of age from under one year old to age 84. It is based on death certificate data from the National Center for Health Statistics.

UNINTENTIONAL-INJURY DEATHS BY SEX AND AGE, UNITED STATES, 1999

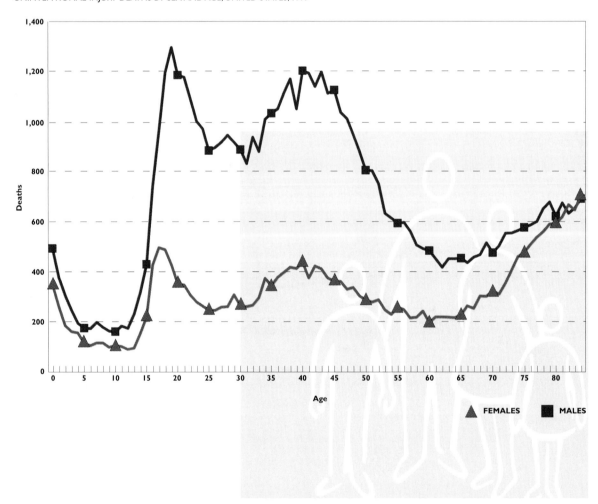

UNINTENTIONAL-INJURY DEATH RATES BY SEX AND AGE

Males have greater unintentional-injury death rates at every age from under one year old to age 84. The difference ranges from as little as 1.6 deaths per 100,000 population at age 4 to as much as 106.4 at age 84.

Death rates for both sexes are lowest from birth until the mid teenage years, where rates rise rapidly. Rates then remain fairly constant until the late sixties, where they again rise steadily with increasing age.

The graph below shows the unintentional-injury death rates for males and females by single years of age from under one year old to age 84. It is based on National Center for Health Statistics mortality data and U.S. Census Bureau population data.

UNINTENTIONAL-INJURY DEATH RATES BY SEX AND AGE, UNITED STATES, 1999

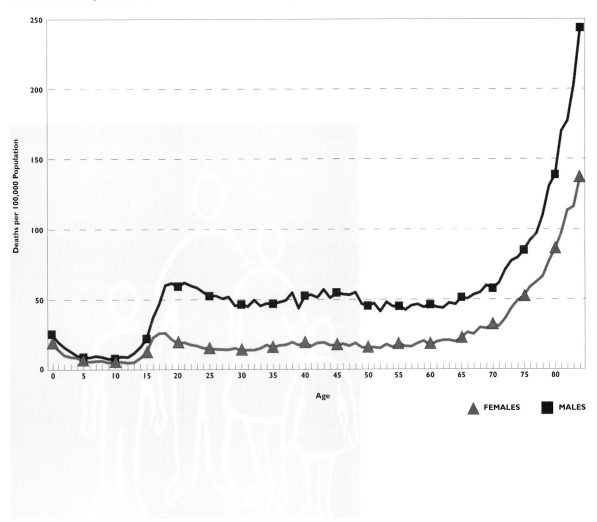

ALL DEATHS DUE TO INJURY

MORTALITY BY SELECTED EXTERNAL CAUSES, UNITED STATES, 1999

Type of Accident or Manner of Injury	1999[a]
All External Causes of Mortality, V01–Y98[b]	**151,109**
Deaths Due to Unintentional (Accidental) Injuries, V01–X59, Y85–Y86	**97,860**
Transport Accidents, V01–V99, Y85	**46,423**
Pedestrian, V01–V09	6,047
Pedalcyclist, V10–V19	800
Motorcycle rider, V20–V29	2,316
Occupant of three-wheeled motor vehicle, V30–V39	33
Car occupant, V40–V49	14,549
Occupant of pick-up truck or van, V50–V59	3,133
Occupant of heavy transport vehicle, V60–V69	422
Bus occupant, V70–V79	62
Animal rider or occupant of animal-drawn vehicle, V80	110
Occupant of railway train or railway vehicle, V81	54
Occupant of streetcar, V82	1
Other and unspecified land transport accidents, V83–V89	16,992
Occupant of special industrial vehicle, V83	*18*
Occupant of special agricultural vehicle, V84	*348*
Occupant of special construction vehicle, V85	*38*
Occupant of all-terrain or other off-road motor vehicle, V86	*603*
Other and unspecified person, V87–V89	*15,985*
Water transport accidents, V90–V94	679
Drowning, V90, V92	*501*
Other and unspecified injuries, V91, V93–V94	*178*
Air and space transport accidents, V95–V97	715
Other and unspecified transport accidents and sequelae, V98–V99, Y85	510
Other specified transport accidents, V98	*8*
Unspecified transport accident, V99	*6*
Nontransport Unintentional (Accidental) Injuries, W00–X59, Y86	**51,437**
Falls, W00–W19	13,162
Fall on same level from slipping, tripping, and stumbling, W01	*611*
Other fall on same level, W00, W02–W03, W18	*820*
Fall involving bed, chair, other furniture, W06–W08	*624*
Fall on and from stairs and steps, W10	*1,421*
Fall on and from ladder or scaffolding, W11–W12	*375*
Fall from out of or through building or structure, W13	*550*
Other fall from one level to another, W09, W14–W17	*772*
Other and unspecified fall, W04–W05, W19	*7,989*
Exposure to inanimate mechanical forces, W20–W49	2,739
Struck by or striking against object, W20–W22	*842*
Caught between objects, W23	*93*
Contact with machinery, W24, W30–W31	*622*
Contact with sharp objects, W25–W29	*68*
Firearms discharge, W32–W34	*824*
Explosion and rupture of pressurized devices, W35–W38	*33*
Fireworks discharge, W39	*7*
Explosion of other materials, W40	*166*
Foreign body entering through skin or natural orifice, W44–W45	*38*
Other and unspecified inanimate mechanical forces, W41–W43, W49	*46*
Exposure to animate mechanical forces, W50–W64	214
Struck by or against another person, W50–W52	*52*
Bitten or struck by dog, W54	*25*
Bitten or struck by other mammals, W53, W55	*69*
Bitten or stung by nonvenomous insect and other arthropods, W57	*10*
Bitten or crushed by other reptiles, W59	*45*
Other and unspecified animate mechanical forces, W56, W58, W60, W64	*13*
Accidental drowning and submersion, W65–W74	3,529
Drowning and submersion while in or falling into bath-tub, W65–W66	*320*
Drowning and submersion while in or falling into swimming-pool, W67–W68	*530*
Drowning and submersion while in or falling into natural water, W69–W70	*1,212*
Other and unspecified drowning and submersion, W73–W74	*1,467*
Other accidental threats to breathing, W75–W84	5,503
Accidental suffocation and strangulation in bed, W75	*330*
Other accidental hanging and strangulation, W76	*307*
Threat to breathing due to cave-in, falling earth, and other substances, W77	*47*
Inhalation of gastric contents, W78	*417*
Inhalation and ingestion of food causing obstruction of respiratory tract, W79	*640*
Inhalation and ingestion of other objects causing obstruction of respiratory tract, W80	*2,828*
Confined to or trapped in a low-oxygen environment, W81	*16*
Other and unspecified threats to breathing, W83–W84	*918*

See source and footnotes on page 19.

Type of Accident or Manner of Injury	1999[a]
Exposure to electric current, radiation, temperature, and pressure, W85–W99	479
Electric transmission lines, W85	127
Other and unspecified electric current, W86–W87	310
Radiation, W88–W91	0
Excessive heat or cold of man-made origin, W92–W93	18
High and low air pressure and changes in air pressure, W94	22
Other and unspecified man-made environmental factors, W99	2
Exposure to smoke, fire, and flames, X00–X09	3,348
Uncontrolled fire in building or structure, X00	2,676
Uncontrolled fire not in building or structure, X01	78
Controlled fire in building or structure, X02	56
Controlled fire not in building or structure, X03	32
Ignition of highly flammable material, X04	73
Ignition or melting of nightwear, X05	6
Ignition or melting of other clothing and apparel, X06	112
Other and unspecified smoke, fire, and flames, X08–X09	315
Contact with heat and hot substances, X10–X19	123
Contact with hot tap-water, X11	51
Other and unspecified heat and hot substances, X10, X12–X19	72
Contact with venomous animals and plants, X20–X29	61
Contact with venomous snakes and lizards, X20	7
Contact with venomous spiders, X21	6
Contact with hornets, wasps, and bees, X23	43
Contact with other and unspecified venomous animal or plant, X22, X24–X29	5
Exposure to forces of nature, X30–X39	1,488
Exposure to excessive natural heat, X30	594
Exposure to excessive natural cold, X31	598
Lightning, X33	64
Earthquake and other earth movements, X34–X36	46
Cataclysmic storm, X37	129
Flood, X38	15
Exposure to other and unspecified forces of nature, X32, X39	42
Accidental poisoning by and exposure to noxious substances, X40–X49	12,186
Nonopioid analgesics, antipyretics, and antirheumatics, X40	168
Antiepileptic, sedative-hypnotic, antiparkinsonism, and psychotropic drugs n.e.c., X41	671
Narcotics and psychodysleptics [hallucinogens] n.e.c., X42	6,009
Other and unspecified drugs, medicaments, and biologicals, X43–X44	4,307
Alcohol, X45	320
Gases and vapors, X46–X47	597
Other and unspecified chemicals and noxious substances, X48–X49	114
Overexertion, travel and privation, X50–X57	191
Accidental exposure to other and unspecified factors and sequelae, X58–X59, Y86	8,414
Intentional self-harm, X60–X84	**29,199**
Intentional self-poisoning, X60–X69	4,893
Intentional self-harm by hanging, strangulation, and suffocation, X70	5,427
Intentional self-harm by firearm, X72–X74	16,599
Other and unspecified means and sequelae, X71, X75–X84, Y87.0	2,280
Assault, X85–Y09	**16,889**
Assault by firearm, X93–X95	10,828
Assault by sharp object, X99	1,879
Other and unspecified means and sequelae, X85–X92, X96–X98, Y00–Y09, Y87.1	4,182
Event of undetermined intent, Y10–Y34	**3,917**
Poisoning, Y10–Y19	2,595
Hanging, strangulation, and suffocation, Y20	110
Drowning and submersion, Y21	243
Firearm discharge, Y22–Y24	324
Exposure to smoke, fire, and flames, Y26	70
Falling, jumping, or pushed from a high place, Y30	59
Other and unspecified means and sequelae, Y25, Y27–Y29, Y31–Y34, Y87.2, Y89.9	516
Legal intervention, Y35, Y89.0	**398**
Legal intervention involving firearm discharge, Y35.0	299
Legal execution, Y35.5	88
Other and unspecified means and sequelae, Y35.1–Y35.4, Y35.6–Y35.7, Y89.0	11
Operations of war and sequelae, Y36, Y89.1	**23**
Complications of medical and surgical care and sequelae, Y40–Y84, Y88.0–Y88.3	**2,823**

Source: National Center for Health Statistics. Deaths are classified on the basis of the Tenth Revision of "The International Classification of Diseases" (ICD-10), which became effective in 1999.
Note: n.e.c. = not elsewhere classified.
[a]*Latest official figures.*
[b]*Numbers following titles refer to External Cause of Injury and Poisoning classifications in ICD-10.*

DEATHS BY AGE, SEX, AND TYPE

Of the 97,860 unintentional-injury deaths in 1999, males accounted for 65% of all deaths. For women, the percentage was highest in the 75 and over age group. By type of accident, men accounted for 79% of all drowning deaths, but only 49% of deaths due to choking (inhalation or ingestion of food or other object obstructing breathing).

UNINTENTIONAL-INJURY DEATHS BY AGE, SEX, AND TYPE, UNITED STATES, 1999[a]

Age & Sex	All Types[b]	Motor-vehicle	Falls	Poisoning	Choking[c]	Drowning[d]	Fires, Flames	Mechanical Suffocation	Natural Heat/Cold	% Male, All Types
All Ages	**97,860**	**42,401**	**13,162**	**12,186**	**3,885**	**3,529**	**3,348**	**1,618**	**1,192**	**65%**
Under 5	2,743	834	67	46	151	558	343	483	24	59%
5–14	3,091	1,771	53	40	46	369	262	86	9	64%
15–24	13,656	10,128	242	964	41	647	201	98	25	74%
25–44	27,121	13,516	988	6,904	238	921	703	242	164	75%
45–64	18,924	8,342	1,711	3,512	513	589	687	209	297	72%
65–74	8,208	3,276	1,663	300	566	185	416	115	178	61%
75 & over	24,117	4,534	8,438	420	2,330	260	736	385	495	45%
Male	**63,535**	**28,552**	**7,109**	**8,887**	**1,917**	**2,794**	**2,025**	**1,040**	**725**	
Female	**34,325**	**13,849**	**6,053**	**3,299**	**1,968**	**735**	**1,323**	**578**	**467**	
Percent Male	65%	67%	54%	73%	49%	79%	60%	64%	61%	

Source: National Safety Council tabulations of National Center for Health Statistics mortality data.
[a] *Latest official figures.*
[b] *Includes types not shown separately.*
[c] *Inhalation or ingestion of food or other object.*
[d] *Excludes water transport drownings.*

UNINTENTIONAL-INJURY DEATH RATES BY TYPE AND SEX, UNITED STATES, 1999

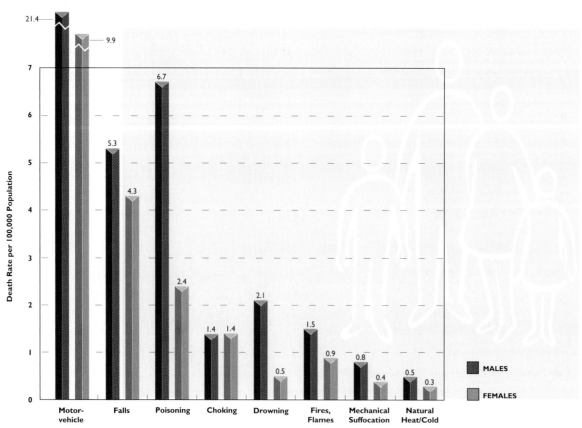

UNINTENTIONAL-INJURY DEATHS BY MONTH AND TYPE, UNITED STATES, 1999[a]

Month	All Types	Motor-vehicle	Falls	Poisoning	Choking[b]	Drowning[c]	Fires and Flames	Mechanical Suffocation	Natural Heat/Cold	Firearms	All Other Types
All Months	**97,860**	**42,401**	**13,162**	**12,186**	**3,885**	**3,529**	**3,348**	**1,618**	**1,192**	**824**	**15,715**
January	7,932	2,936	1,221	1,035	388	122	489	115	192	73	1,361
February	7,001	2,750	1,041	979	323	140	337	125	85	58	1,163
March	7,801	3,209	1,183	987	393	171	306	123	76	57	1,296
April	7,567	3,148	1,015	1,038	333	243	250	163	39	65	1,273
May	8,418	3,741	1,101	1,015	325	355	236	136	29	60	1,420
June	8,195	3,590	1,021	961	272	525	198	156	58	50	1,364
July	9,318	3,910	1,027	1,140	288	733	209	139	367	71	1,434
August	8,832	4,061	1,032	1,024	305	498	175	142	162	49	1,384
September	8,106	3,715	1,113	941	288	291	186	144	25	71	1,332
October	8,354	3,945	1,158	1,029	292	189	231	148	31	83	1,248
November	7,850	3,658	1,008	988	305	145	289	114	33	101	1,209
December	8,486	3,738	1,242	1,049	373	117	442	113	95	86	1,231
Average	**8,155**	**3,533**	**1,097**	**1,016**	**324**	**294**	**279**	**135**	**99**	**69**	**1,310**

Source: National Safety Council tabulations of National Center for Health Statistics mortality data.
[a] Latest official figures.
[b] Inhalation or ingestion of food or other object.
[c] Excludes water transport drownings.

UNINTENTIONAL-INJURY DEATHS BY MONTH, UNITED STATES, 1999

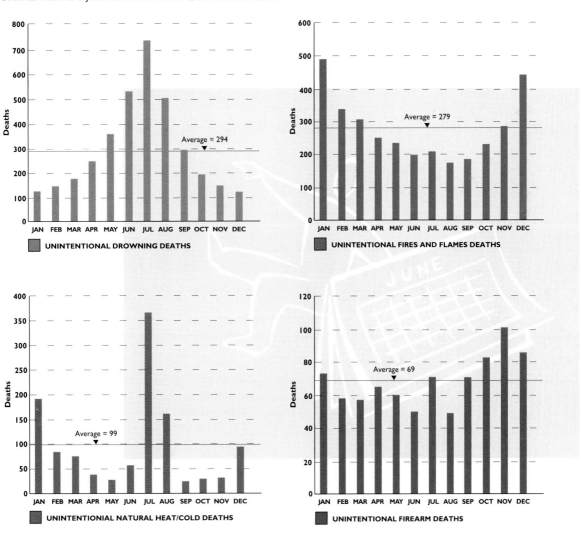

See page 98 for motor-vehicle deaths by month.

While unintentional injuries are the fifth leading cause of death in the United States, unintentional-injury victims tend to be younger than those for the four leading causes of death (heart disease, cancer, stroke, and chronic lower respiratory disease). Ranked by years of potential life lost (YPLL) before age 65, unintentional injuries were the leading cause of death, accounting for 2.0 million years lost in 1999.

Heart disease was the leading cause of death in 1999 and ranked third in terms of YPLL at 1.4 million years. Cancer ranked second in both number of deaths and YPLL. Stroke was the third leading cause of death and ranked ninth in YPLL.

Within unintentional-injury deaths, motor-vehicle crashes accounted for 43% of the deaths and 54% of the years of potential life lost in 1999. Poisoning accounted for 15% of the YPLL and 12% of the deaths. Falls, which were the second leading cause of unintentional-injury deaths, ranked sixth on YPLL.

Years of potential life lost before age 65 are calculated by subtracting the age at death from 65 and adding the result across all persons who died from a particular cause.

Source: Centers for Disease Control and Prevention, National Center for Injury Prevention and Control.

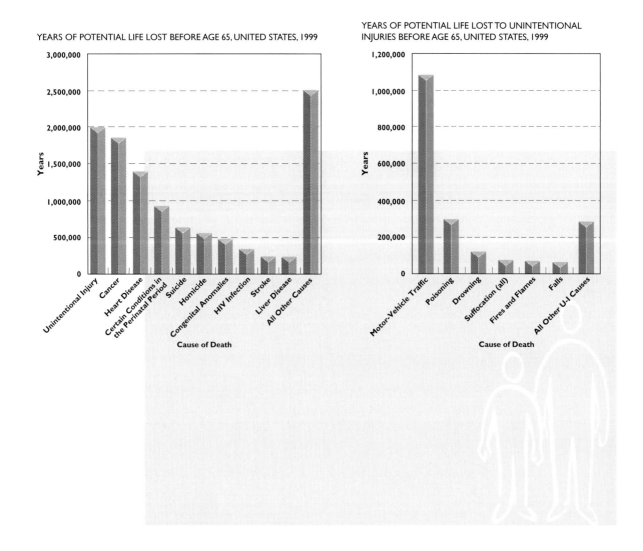

YEARS OF POTENTIAL LIFE LOST BEFORE AGE 65, UNITED STATES, 1999

YEARS OF POTENTIAL LIFE LOST TO UNINTENTIONAL INJURIES BEFORE AGE 65, UNITED STATES, 1999

THE   NATIONAL   HEALTH   INTERVIEW   SURVEY

The National Health Interview Survey, conducted by the National Center for Health Statistics, is a continuous, personal-interview sampling of households to obtain information about the health status of household members, including injuries experienced during the 3 months prior to the interview. Responsible family members residing in the household supplied the information found in the survey. Of the nation's 101,018,000 households in 1997, 39,832 households containing 103,477 persons were interviewed. See below for definitions and comparability with other injury figures published in *Injury Facts®*.

ANNUAL RATE[a] OF LEADING EXTERNAL CAUSES OF INJURY AND POISONING EPISODES BY SEX AND AGE, UNITED STATES, 1997[b]

Sex and Age		External Cause of Injury and Poisoning				
	Falls	Struck by or Against Person or Object	Transportation[c]	Overexertion	Cutting/Piercing Instruments	Poisoning
Both sexes	**42.4**	**19.6**	**16.7**	**13.9**	**10.0**	**7.3**
Under 12 years	45.7	17.3	8.6	[d]	8.0	13.0
12–21 years	45.5	49.1	23.8	12.3	15.4	5.6
22–44 years	30.6	18.9	22.9	20.3	13.4	6.7
45–64 years	32.1	11.5	11.2	17.6	5.5	5.5
65 years and over	86.2	4.0	11.5	7.8	4.4	5.4
Male	**36.9**	**27.6**	**19.3**	**15.1**	**13.3**	**6.9**
Under 12 years	47.7	21.9	13.8	[d]	10.7	11.3
12–21 years	49.1	75.3	28.2	17.1	25.7	[d]
22–44 years	29.9	27.0	26.1	22.5	15.7	7.6
45–64 years	25.0	11.3	9.8	17.5	6.6	[d]
65 years and over	47.2	[d]	12.3	[d]	[d]	[d]
Female	**47.7**	**11.9**	**14.1**	**12.7**	**6.9**	**7.7**
Under 12 years	43.7	12.5	[d]	[d]	[d]	14.7
12–21 years	41.7	21.7	19.2	[d]	[d]	[d]
22–44 years	31.3	11.0	19.7	18.1	11.2	5.9
45–64 years	38.7	11.6	12.6	17.8	[d]	5.8
65 years and over	114.5	[d]	11.0	10.2	[d]	[d]

NUMBER AND PERCENT OF INJURY EPISODES BY PLACE OF OCCURRENCE AND SEX, UNITED STATES, 1997[b]

Place	Both Sexes		Male		Female	
	Number of Episodes (000)	%	Number of Episodes (000)	%	Number of Episodes (000)	%
All injury episodes	**32,438**	**100.0**	**17,646**	**100.0**	**14,792**	**100.0**
All places mentioned[e]	**32,900**	**101.4**	**17,911**	**101.5**	**14,989**	**101.3**
Home (inside)	7,832	24.1	3,098	17.6	4,734	32.0
Home (outside)	5,760	17.8	3,074	17.4	2,686	18.2
Street/highway	4,220	13.0	2,293	13.0	1,927	13.0
Sport facility	2,369	7.3	1,716	9.7	653	4.4
Industrial/construction	2,191	6.8	1,866	10.6	325	2.2
School	1,991	6.1	1,315	7.5	676	4.6
Trade/service	1,986	6.1	1,095	6.2	892	6.0
Park/recreation area	1,289	4.0	866	4.9	423	2.9
Other public building	920	2.8	447	2.5	473	3.2
Other (specified)[f]	2,414	7.4	999	5.7	1,415	9.6
Other	1,603	4.9	981	5.6	622	4.2
Refused/don't know	324	1.0	161	0.9	163	1.1

Source: Warner, M., Barnes, P.M., & Fingerhut, L.A. (2000, July). Injury and poisoning episodes and conditions: National Health Interview Survey, 1997. Vital and Health Statistics, Series 10 (No. 202). Hyattsville, MD: National Center for Health Statistics.
[a] Per 1,000 population.
[b] Latest official figures.
[c] Transportation includes the categories "Motor vehicle traffic"; "Pedalcycle, other"; "Pedestrian, other"; and "Transport, other."
[d] Figure does not meet standard of reliability or precision.
[e] "All Places Mentioned" is greater than the total number of injury episodes because respondents could indicate up to two places.
[f] "Other (specified)" place includes child care center or preschool, residential institution, health care facility, parking lot, farm, river, lake, stream, ocean, swimming pool, and mine or quarry.

Injury definitions
National Health Interview Survey definitions. The National Health Interview Survey (NHIS) figures include injuries due to intentional violence as well as unintentional injuries. An injury or poisoning is included in the NHIS totals if it is *medically attended*. A *medically attended* injury or poisoning is one for which a physician has been consulted (in person or by telephone) for advice or treatment. Calls to poison control centers are considered contact with a health care professional and are included in this definition of medical attendance.

National Safety Council definition of injury. A disabling injury is defined as one that results in death, some degree of permanent impairment, or renders the injured person unable to effectively perform their regular duties or activities for a full day beyond the day of the injury. This definition applies to all unintentional injuries. All injury totals labeled "disabling injuries" in *Injury Facts®* are based on this definition. Some *rates* in the Work section are based on OSHA definitions of recordable cases (see Glossary).

Numerical differences between NHIS and National Safety Council injury totals are due mainly to the duration of disability. The Council's injury estimating procedure was revised for the 1993 edition of *Accident Facts®*. See the Technical Appendix for more information.

INJURY-RELATED HOSPITAL EMERGENCY DEPARTMENT VISITS, 2000

About 37% of all hospital emergency department visits in the United States were injury related, according to information from the 2000 National Hospital Ambulatory Medical Care Survey conducted for the National Center for Health Statistics. There were approximately 108.0 million visits made to emergency departments, of which about 40.4 million were injury related. This resulted in an annual rate of about 39.4 emergency department visits per 100 persons, of which about 14.8 visits per 100 persons were injury related.

Males had a higher rate of injury-related visits than females. For males, about 16.6 visits per 100 males were recorded; for females the rate was 13.0 per 100 females. Those aged 15 to 24 had the highest rate of injury-related visits for males, and those aged 75 and over had the highest rate for females.

Falls and motor-vehicle accidents were the leading causes of injury-related emergency department visits, accounting for about 20% and 12% of the total, respectively. In total, about 8.1 million visits to emergency departments were made in 2000 due to accidental falls, and about 5.0 million were made due to motor-vehicle accidents. The next leading types were struck against or struck accidentally by objects or persons with 4.7 million visits (nearly 12% of the total), and accidents caused by cutting or piercing instruments, which accounted for about 3.0 million visits (7% of the total).

Over 30% of all injuries resulting in emergency department visits occurred at home, the most common place of injury. Street or highway was the place of injury for about 13% of the total, while recreation/sport area and industrial place accounted for about 6% and 5%, respectively. Other public building and school were each the place of injury for over 2% of the total. However, over 41% of all injuries resulting in emergency department visits occurred in an "other or unknown place."

The table and charts on these pages show totals, rates, and percent distributions of injury-related visits to hospital emergency departments in 2000 by cause of injury, place of injury, age, and sex.

NUMBER AND PERCENT DISTRIBUTION OF EMERGENCY DEPARTMENT VISITS BY CAUSE OF INJURY, UNITED STATES, 2000

Cause of Injury and E-code[a]	Number of Visits (000)	%
All Injury-related Visits	**40,447**	**100.0%**
Unintentional Injuries, E800–869, E880–E929	**30,907**	**76.4%**
Accidental Falls, E880–E886, E888	8,053	19.9%
Total Motor Vehicle Accidents, E810–E825	4,974	12.3%
Motor vehicle traffic, E810–E819	4,563	11.3%
Motor vehicle, nontraffic, E820–E825(.0–5, .7–.9)	411	1.0%
Striking Against or Struck Accidentally by Objects or Persons, E916–E917	4,727	11.7%
Accidents Caused by Cutting or Piercing Instruments, E920	2,998	7.4%
Accidents Due to Natural and Environmental Factors, E900–E909, E928.0–E928.2	1,802	4.5%
Overexertion, E927	1,787	4.4%
Accidental Poisoning by Drugs, Medicinal Substances, Biologicals, Other Solid and Liquid Substances, Gases and Vapors, E850–E869	796	2.0%
Pedalcycle, Nontraffic and Other, E800–E807(.3), E820–E825(.6), E826.1, E826.9	482	1.2%
Accidents Caused by Fire and Flames, Hot Substances or Object, Caustic or Corrosive Material, and Steam, E890–E899, E924	392	1.0%
Machinery, E919	310	0.8%

Cause of Injury and E-code[a]	Number of Visits (000)	%
Other Transportation, E800–807(.0–.2, .8–.9), E826(.0, .2–.8), E827–E829, E831, E833–E845	(b)	—
Other Mechanism,[c] E830, E832, E846-E848, E910–E915, E918, E921–E923, E925–E926, E928.8, E929.0–E929.5	2,482	6.1%
Mechanism Unspecified, E887, E928.9, E929.8, E929.9	1,978	4.9%
Intentional Injuries, E950–E959, E960–E969, E970–E978, E990–E999	**2,299**	**5.7%**
Assault, E960–E969	1,881	4.7%
Unarmed Fight or Brawl and Striking by Blunt or Thrown Object, E960.0, E968.2	980	2.4%
Assault by Cutting and Piercing Instrument, E966	143	0.4%
Assault by Other and Unspecified Mechanism,[d] E960.1, E962–964, E965.5–E965.9, E967–E968.1, E968.3–E969	758	1.9%
Self-inflicted Injury, E950–E959	387	1.0%
Poisoning by Solid or Liquid Substances, Gases or Vapors, E950–E952	248	0.6%
Other and Unspecified Mechanism[e], E954–E955, E957–E959	139	0.3%
Other Causes of Violence, E970–E978, E990–E999	(b)	—
Adverse Effects of Medical Treatment, E870–E879, E930–E949	**1,169**	**2.9%**
Other and Unknown[f]	**6,072**	**15.0%**

Source: McCaig, L.F., & Ly, N. (2002). National Hospital Ambulatory Medical Care Survey: 2000 Emergency Department Summary (Advance Data, Number 326, April 22, 2002). Hyattsville, MD: National Center for Health Statistics.
Note: Sum of parts may not add to total due to rounding.
[a] Based on the International Classification of Diseases, 9th Revision, Clinical Modification (ICD-9-CM).
[b] Figure did not meet standard of reliability or precision.
[c] Includes drowning, suffocation, firearm missile, and other mechanism.
[d] Includes assault by firearms and explosives, and other mechanism.
[e] Includes injury by cutting and piercing instrument, suffocation, and other and unspecified mechanism.
[f] Includes all other major E-code categories where the estimate was too low to be reliable, as well as uncodable, illegible, and blank E-codes.

NUMBER AND PERCENT DISTRIBUTION OF EMERGENCY DEPARTMENT VISITS BY PLACE OF INJURY AND AGE, UNITED STATES, 2000

Place of Injury	All Ages		Under 18		18–64 Years		65 Years & Over	
	Number of Visits (000)	%	Number of Visits (000)	%	Number of Visits (000)	%	Number of Visits (000)	%
Total	40,447	100.0	11,383	100.0	24,690	100.0	4,374	100.0
Home	12,163	30.1	4,197	36.9	5,833	23.6	2,133	48.8
Street or Highway	5,404	13.4	1,213	10.7	3,908	15.8	283	6.5
Recreation/Sports Area	2,370	5.9	1,200	10.5	1,110	4.5	(a)	(a)
Industrial Places	1,960	4.8	(a)	(a)	1,909	7.7	(a)	(a)
Other Public Building	974	2.4	148	1.3	726	2.9	(a)	(a)
School	879	2.2	728	6.4	145	0.6	(a)	(a)
Other	1,686	4.2	253	2.2	1,290	5.2	143	3.3
Unknown	15,011	37.1	3,622	31.8	9,769	39.6	1,621	37.1

See source on page 24.
Note: Sum of parts may not add to total due to rounding.
[a]Estimate did not meet standard of reliability or precision.

RATE OF INJURY-RELATED VISITS TO EMERGENCY DEPARTMENTS BY PATIENT AGE AND SEX, 2000

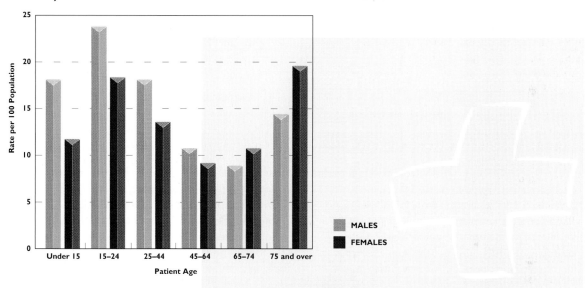

DISTRIBUTION OF INJURY-RELATED EMERGENCY DEPARTMENT VISITS BY INTENTIONALITY AND AGE, UNITED STATES, 2000

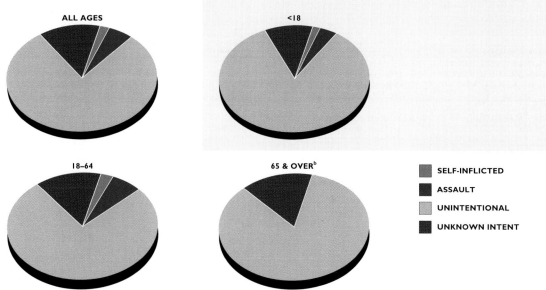

[b]Estimates for "self-inflicted" and "assault" did not meet standard of reliability or precision.

RACE AND HISPANIC ORIGIN

The rank of unintentional-injuries as a cause of death varies with race and Hispanic origin. While ranking fifth overall (following heart disease, cancer, stroke, and chronic lower respiratory diseases), unintentional injuries rank third for Hispanics after heart disease and cancer.

By race, unintentional injuries rank fifth for whites, fourth for blacks and Asians and Pacific Islanders (after heart disease, cancer, and stroke), and third for American Indians and Alaskan Natives (after heart disease and cancer).

UNINTENTIONAL-INJURY DEATHS RANK, NUMBER, AND RATE, UNITED STATES, 1999

| | Hispanic Origin | | | | | | | | |
| | Total | | | Non-Hispanic Origin | | | Hispanic Origin | | |
Race	Rank	Number	Rate	Rank	Number	Rate	Rank	Number	Rate
All Races	5	97,860	35.9	5	88,669	36.7	3	8,650	27.6
White	5	82,245	36.6	5	73,326	37.4	3	8,488	—
Black	4	12,728	36.5	4	12,533	37.9	3	94	—
American Indian & Alaskan Native	3	1,327	55.4	3	1,286	63.5	3	39	—
Asian & Pacific Islander	4	1,560	14.4	4	1,524	15.0	4	29	—

Source: National Center for Health Statistics, Centers for Disease Control and Prevention, and National Safety Council.
Note: Rates are deaths per 100,000 population in each race/Hispanic origin group. Dash (—) indicates data not available. Total column includes some deaths for which Hispanic origin was not determined.

The three leading causes of unintentional-injury deaths overall are motor-vehicle crashes, falls, and poisonings. The same is true for non-Hispanics of all races, whites overall, and whites of non-Hispanic origin. For Hispanics, the order is motor-vehicle crashes, poisoning, and falls. Among black non-Hispanics the three leading causes are motor-vehicle crashes, poisoning, and fires. For black Hispanics, the top three are motor-vehicle crashes, poisoning, and drowning. For American Indians and Alaskan Natives, motor-vehicle crashes, poisoning, and falls are the leading causes of unintentional-injury deaths, while for Asians and Pacific Islanders motor-vehicle crashes, falls, and drowning lead.

LEADING CAUSES OF UNINTENTIONAL-INJURY DEATHS BY RACE AND HISPANIC ORIGIN, UNITED STATES, 1999

| | Leading Causes of Unintentional-Injury Deaths | | |
Race / Hispanic Origin	First	Second	Third
All Races / Both	**Motor-vehicle crashes**	**Falls**	**Poisoning**
All Races / Non-Hispanic	**Motor-vehicle crashes**	**Falls**	**Poisoning**
All Races / Hispanic	**Motor-vehicle crashes**	**Poisoning**	**Falls**
White / Both	Motor-vehicle crashes	Falls	Poisoning
White / Non-Hispanic	Motor-vehicle crashes	Falls	Poisoning
White / Hispanic	Motor-vehicle crashes	Poisoning	Falls
Black / Both	Motor-vehicle crashes	Poisoning	Fires and flames
Black / Non-Hispanic	Motor-vehicle crashes	Poisoning	Fires and flames
Black / Hispanic	Motor-vehicle crashes	Poisoning	Drowning
American Indian & Alaskan Native	Motor-vehicle crashes	Poisoning	Falls
Asian & Pacific Islander	Motor-vehicle crashes	Falls	Drowning

Source: Centers for Disease Control and Prevention, National Center for Injury Prevention and Control.

UNINTENTIONAL-INJURY DEATH RATES BY HISPANIC ORIGIN, UNITED STATES, 1999

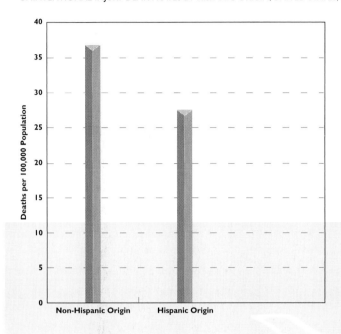

UNINTENTIONAL-INJURY DEATH RATES BY RACE, UNITED STATES, 1999

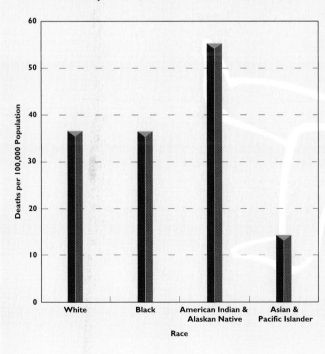

PRINCIPAL CLASSES BY STATE

The states listed below participate in the Injury Mortality Tabulations reporting system. Reports from these states are used to make current year estimates. See the Technical Appendix for more information.

The estimated total number of unintentional-injury deaths for 2001 increased 2% from 2000. The number of unintentional-injury deaths in the Public Nonmotor-Vehicle class was down 5%, while the Motor-Vehicle, Work, and Home classes showed increases of 1%, 6%, and 7%, respectively. The population death rate for the Public Nonmotor-Vehicle class decreased 6%, while the rates for the Total, Work, and Home classes showed increases of 1%, 6%, and 7%, respectively. The rate for the Motor-Vehicle class remained unchanged.

PRINCIPAL CLASSES OF UNINTENTIONAL-INJURY DEATHS BY STATE, 2001

State	Total[a]		Motor-Vehicle[b]		Work[c]		Home		Public Nonmotor-Vehicle	
	Deaths	Rate[d]	Deaths	Rate[d]	Deaths	Rate[d]	Deaths	Rate[d]	Deaths	Rate[d]
Total U.S.	**98,000**	**35.3**	**42,900**	**15.4**	**5,300**	**1.9**	**33,200**	**12.0**	**19,000**	**6.8**
Colorado	1,776	40.2	760	17.2	98	2.2	404	9.1	540	12.2
Delaware	243	30.5	139	17.5	8	1.0	64	8.0	36	4.5
Florida	6,850	41.8	2,582	15.7	299	1.8	1,677	10.2	2,037	12.4
Idaho	552	41.8	273	20.7	24	1.8	135	10.2	111	8.4
Kansas	1,056	39.2	505	18.7	68	2.5	268	9.9	237	8.8
Missouri	2,106	37.4	1,129	20.1	78	1.4	600	10.7	298	5.3

Source: Provisional reports of vital statistics registrars; deaths are by place of occurrence. U.S. totals are National Safety Council estimates.

[a] *The all-class total may not equal the sum of the separate class totals because Motor-Vehicle and other transportation deaths occurring to persons in the course of their employment are included in the Work death totals as well as the Motor-Vehicle and Public Nonmotor-Vehicle totals and also because unclassified deaths are included in the total.*

[b] *Differences between the figures given above and those on pages 162 and 163 are due in most cases to the inclusion of nontraffic deaths in this table.*

[c] *Work death totals may be too low where incomplete information on death certificates results in the deaths being included in the Public class. The Work totals may include some cases that are not compensable. For compensable cases only, see page 53.*

[d] *Deaths per 100,000 population, adjusted to annual basis where less than 12 months were reported.*

TERRORISM IN THE UNITED STATES

While the horrific death toll from the September 11, 2001, suicide hijackings in New York, Washington, and Pennsylvania is unprecedented—more than 3,000 people died in those incidents—terrorism is unfortunately not a new phenomenon in the United States. The terrorism statistics shown below were compiled by the Federal Bureau of Investigation and include incidents in the United States and its territories from acts of terrorism by both international and domestic groups or individuals. The data cover 1980 through 1999, which is the latest year available.

The FBI uses the following definitions of terrorism:

- Domestic terrorism is the unlawful use, or threatened use, of force or violence by a group or individual based and operating entirely within the United States or its territories without foreign direction committed against persons or property to intimidate or coerce a government, the civilian population, or any segment thereof, in furtherance of political or social objectives.

- International terrorism involves violent acts or acts dangerous to human life that are a violation of the criminal laws of the United States or any state, or that would be a criminal violation if committed

within the jurisdiction of the United States or any state. These acts appear to be intended to intimidate or coerce a civilian population, influence the policy of a government by intimidation or coercion, or affect the conduct of a government by assassination or kidnapping. International terrorist acts occur outside the United States or transcend national boundaries in terms of the means by which they are accomplished, the persons they appear intended to coerce or intimidate, or the locale in which the perpetrators operate or seek asylum.

The statistics shown below cannot be used to estimate an individual's risk of being killed or injured in a terrorist act for two reasons. First, unlike some unintentional injuries where the risk is relatively stable from year to year, the risk of terrorism is unknown and cannot be estimated using historical data, which makes it impossible to predict what the risk would be at any given time. Second, the overall statistical risk for a large population is not the same as the risk faced by an individual, which depends on his or her activities and where he or she lives, works, and travels.

TERRORISM IN THE UNITED STATES, 1980–1999

Year	Incidents	Injured	Killed
1980	29	19	1
1981	45	6	6
1982	52	41	8
1983	33	4	6
1984	16	0	1
1985	13	13	2
1986	27	19	1
1987	17	1	0
1988	14	0	0
1989	8	2	0

Year	Incidents	Injured	Killed
1990	7	0	0
1991	5	0	0
1992	3	0	0
1993[a]	4	1,042	6
1994	1	3	1
1995[b]	1	754	169
1996[c]	3	112	2
1997	4	5	0
1998	5	2	1
1999	10	15	3

Source: Federal Bureau of Investigation. (2000). Terrorism in the United States, 1999. Washington, DC: U.S. Department of Justice.
[a] Includes World Trade Center bombing.
[b] Includes Oklahoma City Federal Building bombing.
[c] Includes Centennial Olympic Park bombing.

MAJOR DISASTERS, 2001

Disasters are front-page news even though the lives lost in the United States are relatively few when compared to the day-to-day life losses from injuries. The National Safety Council tracks major disasters resulting in unintentional-injury deaths. Listed below are the three major U.S. disasters taking 25 or more lives during 2001. The terrorist attacks of September 11, 2001, which resulted in more than 3,000 deaths, are not included here because the acts were intentional, not unintentional.

Type and Location	No. of Deaths	Date of Disaster
Tropical storm Allison, Gulf Coast to southern New England	41	June 8–15, 2001
Heat wave in the Midwest	56	August, 2001
Crash of scheduled plane near Belle Harbor, N.Y.	265	November 12, 2001

Source: National Transportation Safety Board, National Climatic Data Center, and infoplease.com.

LARGEST U.S. DISASTERS, 1982–2001

Year	Date	Type and Location	No. of Deaths
		Air Transportation	
2001	November 12	Crash of scheduled plane near Belle Harbor, N.Y.	265
1996	July 17	Crash of scheduled plane near East Moriches, N.Y.	230
1987	August 16	Crash of scheduled plane in Detroit, Mich.	156
1982	July 9	Crash of scheduled plane in Kenner, La.	154
1985	August 2	Crash of scheduled plane in Ft. Worth/Dallas, Texas Airport	135
1994	September 8	Crash of scheduled plane in Aliquippa, Pa.	132
1989	July 19	Crash of scheduled plane in Sioux City, Iowa	112
1996	May 11	Crash of scheduled plane near Miami, Fla.	110
2000	January 31	Crash of scheduled plane near Point Mugu, Calif.	88
1986	August 31	Two-plane collision over Los Angeles, Calif.	82
1982	January 13	Crash of scheduled plane in Washington, D.C.	78
1990	January 25	Crash of scheduled plane in Cove Neck, N.Y.	73
1994	October 31	Crash of scheduled plane in Indiana	68
1994	July 2	Crash of scheduled plane in Charlotte, N.C.	37
		Weather	
1995	July 11–27	Heat wave in Chicago, Ill.	465
1993	March 12–15	Severe snowstorm in Eastern states	270
1999	July 22–31	Heat wave in the Midwest	232
1998	May–July	Drought and heat wave in South and Southeast	200[a]
1996	January	Snow storm and floods in Appalachians, Mid-Atlantic, and Northeast	187
1996	Jan–Feb	Cold wave in eastern two-thirds of the U.S.	100[a]
1993	June–July	Heat wave in Southeast	100[a]
1998	January 5	Winter storm and flooding in South and East	90[a]
1999	September 14–18	Hurricane Floyd, North Carolina and other states	78
1985	May 31	Storm and tornadoes in Pennsylvania and Ohio	74
1997	March	Tornadoes and flooding in South and Southeast	67
1985	November 4–5	Floods in W.Va., Va., Pa., and East Coast	65
1984	March 28–29	Storm and tornadoes in N.C., S.C., and East Coast	62
2001	August	Heat wave in Midwest	56
1999	May 3	Tornadoes in Oklahoma, Kansas, Texas, and Tennessee	54
1994	March 27	Tornado in Southeast	47
2000	July 8–20	Heat wave in Southeast	46
1998	February 22	Tornadoes across central Florida	42
2001	June 8–15	Tropical storm Allison from Gulf Coast to southern New England	41
1996	September 5	Hurricane Fran in North Carolina and Virginia	36
1998	April 8	Tornado in central Alabama	34
1997	May 27	Tornadoes in Texas	29
1994	July 4–17	Floods in Georgia	28
		Work	
1987	April 24	Collapse of apartment building under construction in Bridgeport, Conn.	28
1982	March 19	Military plane exploded and crashed near Chicago, Ill.	27
1984	December 21	Mine fire in Orangeville, Utah	27
1991	September 3	Fire at food processing plant in Hamlet, N.C.	25
		Other Disasters	
1994	January 17	Earthquake along San Andreas Fault, Calif.	61
1989	October 17	Earthquake in San Francisco, Calif., and surrounding area	61
1993	September 22	Bridge collapse under train, Mobile, Ala.	47

Source: National Safety Council, Accident Facts®, 1983–1998 editions, and Injury Facts®, 1999–2001 editions.
[a] *Final death toll undetermined.*

While you make a 10-minute safety speech, 2 persons will be killed and about 390 will suffer a disabling injury. Costs will amount to $9,850,000. On average, there are 11 unintentional-injury deaths and about 2,330 disabling injuries every hour during the year.

Deaths and disabling injuries by class occurred in the nation at the following rates in 2001:

DEATHS AND DISABLING INJURIES BY CLASS, 2001

Class	Severity	One Every—	Number per . . .			2001 Total
			Hour	Day	Week	
All	**Deaths**	**5 minutes**	**11**	**268**	**1,880**	**98,000**
	Injuries	**2 seconds**	**2,330**	**55,900**	**392,300**	**20,400,000**
Motor-Vehicle	Deaths	12 minutes	5	118	830	42,900
	Injuries	14 seconds	260	6,300	44,200	2,300,000
Work	Deaths	99 minutes	1	15	100	5,300
	Injuries	8 seconds	450	10,700	75,000	3,900,000
Workers Off-the-Job	Deaths	12 minutes	5	118	830	43,000
	Injuries	5 seconds	780	18,600	130,800	6,800,000
Home	Deaths	16 minutes	4	91	640	33,200
	Injuries	4 seconds	910	21,900	153,800	8,000,000
Public Nonmotor-Vehicle	Deaths	28 minutes	2	52	370	19,000
	Injuries	5 seconds	720	17,300	121,200	6,300,000

Source: National Safety Council estimates.

DEATHS EVERY HOUR . . .

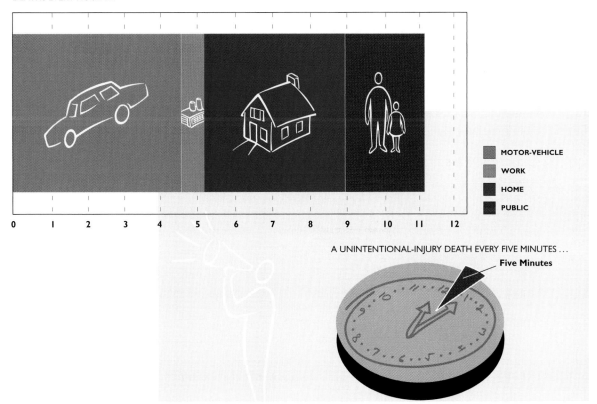

MOTOR-VEHICLE
WORK
HOME
PUBLIC

A UNINTENTIONAL-INJURY DEATH EVERY FIVE MINUTES . . .

Five Minutes

CHILDREN AND YOUTHS

For children and youths aged 1 to 24 years, unintentional injuries are the leading cause of death, accounting for 43% of the 43,500 total deaths of these persons in 1999. Overall, motor-vehicle crashes were the leading cause of unintentional-injury deaths for this age group, followed by drowning, poisoning, fires and flames, falls, and firearms.

While unintentional-injury deaths decrease fairly steadily for those aged 1 to 10, they increase markedly for teenagers—from 268 for those age 12 to 1,723 for those age 19. Motor-vehicle crashes account for most of this increase.

For infants under 1 year of age, unintentional injuries are the seventh leading cause of death, following congenital anomalies; short gestation and low birth weight; sudden infant death syndrome; maternal complications of pregnancy; respiratory distress; and complications involving the placenta, cord, and membranes (see page 10). Although unintentional injuries only account for about 3% of deaths for those under age 1, the number of unintentional-injury deaths for this age is greater than for any age from 1 to 15.

UNINTENTIONAL-INJURY DEATHS BY EVENT, AGES 0–24, UNITED STATES, 1999

Age	Population (000)	Total	Rates[a]	Motor-vehicle	Drowning	Poisoning	Fires, Flames	Falls	Firearms	Choking[b]	Mechanical Suffocation	All Other
Under 1 year	3,820	845	22.1	184	68	12	41	12	0	63	409	56
1–24 years	92,392	18,645	20.2	12,549	1,506	1,038	765	350	339	175	258	1,665
1 year	3,757	641	17.1	181	215	14	75	22	2	41	38	53
2 years	3,758	493	13.1	159	152	8	74	16	4	22	15	43
3 years	3,755	410	10.9	169	73	6	80	7	2	16	10	47
4 years	3,853	354	9.2	141	50	6	73	10	4	9	11	50
5 years	3,895	295	7.6	147	39	2	47	4	2	11	7	36
6 years	3,944	282	7.2	151	38	3	34	7	3	4	3	39
7 years	4,030	318	7.9	171	44	5	42	3	6	3	2	42
8 years	3,909	298	7.6	174	38	2	29	6	5	4	7	33
9 years	4,170	266	6.4	159	33	0	18	5	3	2	11	35
10 years	4,036	270	6.7	154	30	4	33	6	1	1	11	30
11 years	3,896	289	7.4	171	32	4	20	5	7	8	7	35
12 years	3,846	268	7.0	142	38	3	16	5	12	6	14	32
13 years	3,878	330	8.5	192	39	6	11	6	16	2	10	48
14 years	3,892	475	12.2	310	38	11	12	6	21	5	14	58
15 years	3,820	652	17.1	446	60	14	16	7	30	3	18	58
16 years	3,924	1,171	29.8	951	56	26	14	17	19	1	10	77
17 years	4,017	1,460	36.3	1,160	84	51	16	14	21	2	3	109
18 years	3,875	1,682	43.4	1,325	85	78	11	34	31	6	8	104
19 years	4,111	1,723	41.9	1,316	74	91	31	40	25	5	10	131
20 years	3,898	1,537	39.4	1,119	59	126	23	26	31	5	15	133
21 years	3,705	1,523	41.1	1,105	60	150	20	28	34	2	4	120
22 years	3,564	1,394	39.1	989	71	139	26	25	20	6	9	109
23 years	3,378	1,280	37.9	911	57	123	17	26	22	5	9	110
24 years	3,481	1,234	35.4	806	41	166	27	25	18	6	12	133
0–4 years	18,943	2,743	14.5	834	558	46	343	67	12	151	483	249
5–9 years	19,948	1,459	7.3	802	192	12	170	25	19	24	30	185
10–14 years	19,548	1,632	8.3	969	177	28	92	28	57	22	56	203
15–19 years	19,747	6,688	33.9	5,198	359	260	88	112	126	17	49	479
20–24 years	18,026	6,968	38.7	4,930	288	704	113	130	125	24	49	605

Source: National Safety Council tabulations of National Center for Health Statistics mortality data.
Note: Data does not include "age unknown" cases, which totaled 106 in 1999.
[a] Deaths per 100,000 population in each age group.
[b] Inhalation or ingestion of food or other object.

Falls account for one third of unintentional-injury deaths of the elderly.

More than 78,000 adults aged 25 and older died as a result of unintentional injuries in 1999, with motor vehicles accounting for about 38% of these deaths. Data for 10-year age groups indicate that motor-vehicle crashes are the most common type of unintentional-injury death through age 74. Poisoning is the second most common type for age groups 25 through 54, and falls are the second most common type from age 55 through age 74, at which point it becomes the primary cause of fatal injury for those aged 75 and older. Falls account for more than one third of the unintentional-injury deaths in this age group.

Death rates per 100,000 population are relatively stable for those aged 25–64, averaging about 32.2. Death rates then increase with age. The death rate for those aged 85 and older is nearly nine times higher than the average rate for those aged 25–64. All age groups older than 65 have death rates higher than the all-ages rate of 35.9.

UNINTENTIONAL-INJURY DEATHS BY EVENT, AGES 25 AND OLDER, UNITED STATES, 1999

| Age | Population (000) | Unintentional-Injury Deaths | | | | | | | | | | | |
		Total	Rates[a]	Motor-vehicle	Drowning	Poisoning	Fires, Flames	Falls	Firearms	Choking[b]	Mechanical Suffocation	Natural Heat/Cold	All Other
25–34	37,936	11,890	31.3	6,778	446	2,355	282	343	143	79	99	45	1,320
35–44	44,813	15,231	34.0	6,738	475	4,549	421	645	136	159	143	119	1,846
45–54	35,802	11,639	32.5	4,972	370	2,844	368	824	92	241	133	169	1,626
55–64	23,389	7,285	31.1	3,370	219	668	319	887	48	272	76	128	1,298
65–74	18,218	8,208	45.1	3,276	185	300	416	1,663	33	566	115	178	1,476
75–84	12,146	12,282	101.1	3,243	158	265	487	3,856	23	1,072	188	289	2,701
85 and older	4,175	11,729	280.9	1,261	68	143	245	4,578	10	1,258	197	201	3,768
25 and older	176,479	78,264	44.3	29,638	1,921	11,124	2,538	12,796	485	3,647	951	1,129	14,035
35 and older	138,543	66,374	47.9	22,860	1,475	8,769	2,256	12,453	342	3,568	852	1,084	12,715
45 and older	93,730	51,143	54.6	16,122	1,000	4,220	1,835	11,808	206	3,409	709	965	10,869
55 and older	57,928	39,504	68.2	11,150	630	1,376	1,467	10,984	114	3,168	576	796	9,243
65 and older	34,539	32,219	93.3	7,780	411	708	1,148	10,097	66	2,896	500	668	7,945
75 and older	16,321	24,011	147.1	4,504	226	408	732	8,434	33	2,330	385	490	6,469

Source: National Safety Council tabulations of National Center for Health Statistics mortality data.
Note: Data does not include "age unknown" cases, which totaled 106 in 1999.
[a] Deaths per 100,000 population in each age group.
[b] Inhalation or ingestion of food or other object.

TRENDS IN UNINTENTIONAL-INJURY DEATH RATES

Between 1912 and 2001, unintentional-injury deaths per 100,000 population were reduced 55% (after adjusting for the classification change in 1948) from 82.4 to 35.3. The reduction in the overall rate during a period when the nation's population nearly tripled has resulted in nearly 4,600,000 fewer people being killed due to unintentional injuries than there would have been if the rate had not been reduced.

Age-adjusted rates, which eliminate the effect of shifts in the age distribution of the population, have decreased 62% from 1912 to 2001. The adjusted rates, which are shown in the graph on the opposite page, are standardized to the year 2000 standard U.S. population. The break in the lines at 1948 shows the estimated effect of changes in the International Classification of Diseases (ICD). The break in the lines at 1992 resulted from the adoption of the Bureau of Labor Statistics Census of Fatal Occupational Injuries for work-related deaths. Another change in the ICD in 1999 also affects the trends. See the Technical Appendix for comparability.

The table below shows the change in the age distribution of the population since 1910.

The age-adjusted death rate for all unintentional-injuries increased and decreased significantly several times during the period from 1910 to 1940. Since 1940, there have been some setbacks, such as in the early 1960s, but the overall trend has been positive. The age-adjusted death rates for unintentional-injury deaths in the work and home classes have declined fairly steadily since they became available in the late 1920s, although the home class rates increased in the 1990s. The rates in the public class declined for three decades, rose in the 1960s, and then continued declining. The age-adjusted motor-vehicle death rate rose steadily from 1910 to the late 1930s as the automobile became more widely used. A sharp drop in use occurred during World War II, and a sharp rise in rates occurred in the 1960s, with death rates reflecting economic cycles and a long-term downward trend since then.

UNITED STATES POPULATION, SELECTED YEARS

Year	All Ages	0–14	15–24	25–44	45–64	65 & Older
Number (in thousands)						
1910	91,973[a]	29,499	18,121	26,810[a]	13,424	3,950
2000[b]	274,634	58,964	38,077	81,892	60,991	34,710
2001	277,803	58,715	39,077	81,756	63,190	35,063
Percent						
1910	100.0%	32.1%	19.7%	29.2%	14.6%	4.3%
2000[b]	100.0%	21.5%	13.9%	29.8%	22.2%	12.6%
2001	100.0%	21.1%	14.1%	29.4%	22.7%	12.6%

Source: For 1910: U. S. Bureau of the Census. (1960). Historical Statistics of the United States, Colonial Times to 1957. Series A 71-85. Washington, DC: U.S. Government Printing Office.
For 2000: Anderson, R.N., & Rosenberg, H.M. (1998). Age standardization of death rates: Implementation of the year 2000 standard. National Vital Statistics Reports, 47(3), 13.
For 2001: Population Projections Program, Population Division. (Internet Release Date: January 2000). Projections of the Total Resident Population by 5-year Age Groups, and Sex with Special
   Age Categories: Middle Series, 2001 to 2005. Washington, DC: U.S. Bureau of the Census. http://www.census.gov/population/www/projections/natsum-T3.html
[a] Includes 169,000 persons with age unknown.
[b] This is the population used for standardization (age-adjustment) and differs slightly from the actual 2000 population, which totaled 275,306,000.

AGE-ADJUSTED DEATH RATES BY CLASS OF INJURY, UNITED STATES, 1910–2001

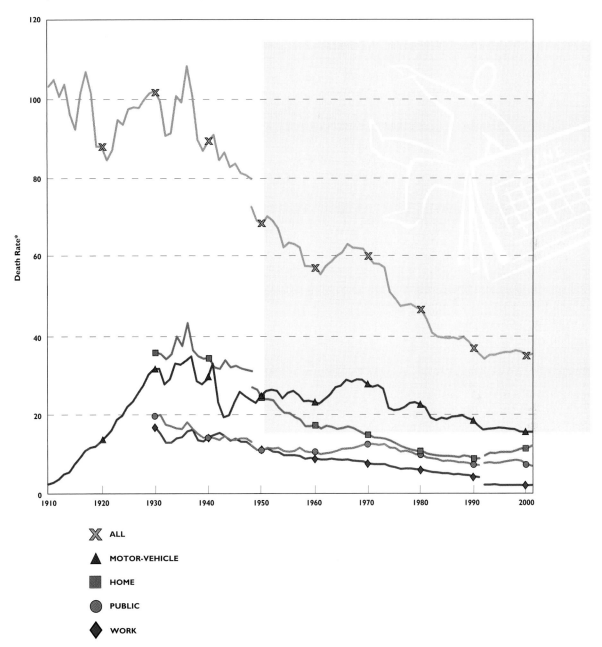

X ALL

▲ MOTOR-VEHICLE

■ HOME

● PUBLIC

◆ WORK

*Deaths per 100,000 population, adjusted to 2000 standard population. The break at 1948 shows the estimated effect of classification changes.
The break at 1992 is due to the adoption of the Bureau of Labor Statistics' Census of Fatal Occupational Injuries for work-related deaths.

PRINCIPAL CLASSES OF UNINTENTIONAL-INJURY DEATHS

PRINCIPAL CLASSES OF UNINTENTIONAL-INJURY DEATHS, UNITED STATES, 1903–2001

Year	Total[a] Deaths	Rate[b]	Motor-Vehicle Deaths	Rate[b]	Work Deaths	Rate[b]	Home Deaths	Rate[b]	Public Nonmotor-Vehicle Deaths	Rate[b]
1903	70,600	87.2	(c)	–	(c)	–	(c)	–	(c)	–
1904	71,500	86.6	(c)	–	(c)	–	(c)	–	(c)	–
1905	70,900	84.2	(c)	–	(c)	–	(c)	–	(c)	–
1906	80,000	93.2	400	0.5	(c)	–	(c)	–	(c)	–
1907	81,900	93.6	700	0.8	(c)	–	(c)	–	(c)	–
1908	72,300	81.2	800	0.9	(c)	–	(c)	–	(c)	–
1909	72,700	80.1	1,300	1.4	(c)	–	(c)	–	(c)	–
1910	77,900	84.4	1,900	2.0	(c)	–	(c)	–	(c)	–
1911	79,300	84.7	2,300	2.5	(c)	–	(c)	–	(c)	–
1912	78,400	82.5	3,100	3.3	(c)	–	(c)	–	(c)	–
1913	82,500	85.5	4,200	4.4	(c)	–	(c)	–	(c)	–
1914	77,000	78.6	4,700	4.8	(c)	–	(c)	–	(c)	–
1915	76,200	76.7	6,600	6.6	(c)	–	(c)	–	(c)	–
1916	84,800	84.1	8,200	8.1	(c)	–	(c)	–	(c)	–
1917	90,100	88.2	10,200	10.0	(c)	–	(c)	–	(c)	–
1918	85,100	82.1	10,700	10.3	(c)	–	(c)	–	(c)	–
1919	75,500	71.9	11,200	10.7	(c)	–	(c)	–	(c)	–
1920	75,900	71.2	12,500	11.7	(c)	–	(c)	–	(c)	–
1921	74,000	68.4	13,900	12.9	(c)	–	(c)	–	(c)	–
1922	76,300	69.4	15,300	13.9	(c)	–	(c)	–	(c)	–
1923	84,400	75.7	18,400	16.5	(c)	–	(c)	–	(c)	–
1924	85,600	75.6	19,400	17.1	(c)	–	(c)	–	(c)	–
1925	90,000	78.4	21,900	19.1	(c)	–	(c)	–	(c)	–
1926	91,700	78.7	23,400	20.1	(c)	–	(c)	–	(c)	–
1927	92,700	78.4	25,800	21.8	(c)	–	(c)	–	(c)	–
1928	95,000	79.3	28,000	23.4	19,000	15.8	30,000	24.9	21,000	17.4
1929	98,200	80.8	31,200	25.7	20,000	16.4	30,000	24.6	20,000	16.4
1930	99,100	80.5	32,900	26.7	19,000	15.4	30,000	24.4	20,000	16.3
1931	97,300	78.5	33,700	27.2	17,500	14.1	29,000	23.4	20,000	16.1
1932	89,000	71.3	29,500	23.6	15,000	12.0	29,000	23.2	18,000	14.4
1933	90,932	72.4	31,363	25.0	14,500	11.6	29,500	23.6	18,500	14.7
1934	100,977	79.9	36,101	28.6	16,000	12.7	34,000	26.9	18,000	14.2
1935	99,773	78.4	36,369	28.6	16,500	13.0	32,000	25.2	18,000	14.2
1936	110,052	85.9	38,089	29.7	18,500	14.5	37,000	28.9	19,500	15.2
1937	105,205	81.7	39,643	30.8	19,000	14.8	32,000	24.8	18,000	14.0
1938	93,805	72.3	32,582	25.1	16,000	12.3	31,000	23.9	17,000	13.1
1939	92,623	70.8	32,386	24.7	15,500	11.8	31,000	23.7	16,000	12.2
1940	96,885	73.4	34,501	26.1	17,000	12.9	31,500	23.9	16,500	12.5
1941	101,513	76.3	39,969	30.0	18,000	13.5	30,000	22.5	16,500	12.4
1942	95,889	71.6	28,309	21.1	18,000	13.4	30,500	22.8	16,000	12.0
1943	99,038	73.8	23,823	17.8	17,500	13.0	33,500	25.0	17,000	12.7
1944	95,237	71.7	24,282	18.3	16,000	12.0	32,500	24.5	16,000	12.0
1945	95,918	72.4	28,076	21.2	16,500	12.5	33,500	25.3	16,000	12.1
1946	98,033	70.0	33,411	23.9	16,500	11.8	33,000	23.6	17,500	12.5
1947	99,579	69.4	32,697	22.8	17,000	11.9	34,500	24.1	18,000	12.6
1948 (5th Rev.)[d]	98,001	67.1	32,259	22.1	16,000	11.0	35,000	24.0	17,000	11.6
1948 (6th Rev.)[d]	93,000	63.7	32,259	22.1	16,000	11.0	31,000	21.2	16,000	11.0
1949	90,106	60.6	31,701	21.3	15,000	10.1	31,000	20.9	15,000	10.1
1950	91,249	60.3	34,763	23.0	15,500	10.2	29,000	19.2	15,000	9.9
1951	95,871	62.5	36,996	24.1	16,000	10.4	30,000	19.6	16,000	10.4
1952	96,172	61.8	37,794	24.3	15,000	9.6	30,500	19.6	16,000	10.3
1953	95,032	60.1	37,955	24.0	15,000	9.5	29,000	18.3	16,500	10.4
1954	90,032	55.9	35,586	22.1	14,000	8.7	28,000	17.4	15,500	9.6
1955	93,443	56.9	38,426	23.4	14,200	8.6	28,500	17.3	15,500	9.4
1956	94,780	56.6	39,628	23.7	14,300	8.5	28,000	16.7	16,000	9.6
1957	95,307	55.9	38,702	22.7	14,200	8.3	28,000	16.4	17,500	10.3
1958	90,604	52.3	36,981	21.3	13,300	7.7	26,500	15.3	16,500	9.5
1959	92,080	52.2	37,910	21.5	13,800	7.8	27,000	15.3	16,500	9.3
1960	93,806	52.1	38,137	21.2	13,800	7.7	28,000	15.6	17,000	9.4
1961	92,249	50.4	38,091	20.8	13,500	7.4	27,000	14.8	16,500	9.0
1962	97,139	52.3	40,804	22.0	13,700	7.4	28,500	15.3	17,000	9.2
1963	100,669	53.4	43,564	23.1	14,200	7.5	28,500	15.1	17,500	9.3
1964	105,000	54.9	47,700	25.0	14,200	7.4	28,000	14.6	18,500	9.7
1965	108,004	55.8	49,163	25.4	14,100	7.3	28,500	14.7	19,500	10.1
1966	113,563	58.1	53,041	27.1	14,500	7.4	29,500	15.1	20,000	10.2
1967	113,169	57.3	52,924	26.8	14,200	7.2	29,000	14.7	20,500	10.4
1968	114,864	57.6	54,862	27.5	14,300	7.2	28,000	14.0	21,500	10.8
1969	116,385	57.8	55,791	27.7	14,300	7.1	27,500	13.7	22,500	11.2
1970	114,638	56.2	54,633	26.8	13,800	6.8	27,000	13.2	23,500	11.5
1971	113,439	54.8	54,381	26.3	13,700	6.6	26,500	12.8	23,500	11.4
1972	115,448	55.2	56,278	26.9	14,000	6.7	26,500	12.7	23,500	11.2
1973	115,821	54.8	55,511	26.3	14,300	6.8	26,500	12.5	24,500	11.6

See source and footnotes on page 37.

PRINCIPAL CLASSES OF UNINTENTIONAL-INJURY DEATHS, UNITED STATES, 1903–2001, Cont.

Year	Total[a] Deaths	Total[a] Rate[b]	Motor-Vehicle Deaths	Motor-Vehicle Rate[b]	Work Deaths	Work Rate[b]	Home Deaths	Home Rate[b]	Public Nonmotor-Vehicle Deaths	Public Nonmotor-Vehicle Rate[b]
1974	104,622	49.0	46,402	21.8	13,500	6.3	26,000	12.2	23,000	10.8
1975	103,030	47.8	45,853	21.3	13,000	6.0	25,000	11.6	23,000	10.6
1976	100,761	46.3	47,038	21.6	12,500	5.7	24,000	11.0	21,500	10.0
1977	103,202	47.0	49,510	22.5	12,900	5.9	23,200	10.6	22,200	10.1
1978	105,561	47.5	52,411	23.6	13,100	5.9	22,800	10.3	22,000	9.9
1979	105,312	46.9	53,524	23.8	13,000	5.8	22,500	10.0	21,000	9.4
1980	105,718	46.5	53,172	23.4	13,200	5.8	22,800	10.0	21,300	9.4
1981	100,704	43.9	51,385	22.4	12,500	5.4	21,700	9.5	19,800	8.6
1982	94,082	40.6	45,779	19.8	11,900	5.1	21,200	9.2	19,500	8.4
1983	92,488	39.6	44,452	19.0	11,700	5.0	21,200	9.1	19,400	8.3
1984	92,911	39.4	46,263	19.6	11,500	4.9	21,200	9.0	18,300	7.8
1985	93,457	39.3	45,901	19.3	11,500	4.8	21,600	9.1	18,800	7.9
1986	95,277	39.7	47,865	19.9	11,100	4.6	21,700	9.0	18,700	7.8
1987	95,020	39.2	48,290	19.9	11,300	4.7	21,400	8.8	18,400	7.6
1988	97,100	39.7	49,078	20.1	11,000	4.5	22,700	9.3	18,400	7.5
1989	95,028	38.5	47,575	19.3	10,900	4.4	22,500	9.1	18,200	7.4
1990	91,983	36.9	46,814	18.8	10,100	4.0	21,500	8.6	17,400	7.0
1991	89,347	35.4	43,536	17.3	9,800	3.9	22,100	8.8	17,600	7.0
1992	86,777	34.0	40,982	16.1	4,968[e]	1.9[e]	24,000[e]	9.4[e]	19,000[e]	7.4[e]
1993	90,523	35.1	41,893	16.3	5,035	2.0	26,100	10.1	19,700	7.6
1994	91,437	35.1	42,524	16.3	5,338	2.1	26,300	10.1	19,600	7.5
1995	93,320	35.5	43,363	16.5	5,018	1.9	27,200	10.3	20,100	7.6
1996	94,948	35.8	43,649	16.5	5,058	1.9	27,500	10.4	21,000	7.9
1997	95,644	35.7	43,458	16.2	5,162	1.9	27,700	10.3	21,700	8.1
1998	97,835	36.2	43,501	16.1	5,120	1.9	29,000	10.7	22,600	8.4
1999[f, g]	97,860	35.9	42,401	15.5	5,185	1.9	30,500	11.2	22,200	8.1
2000[g]	96,000	34.9	42,500	15.4	5,018	1.8	30,900	11.2	19,900	7.2
2001[h]	98,000	35.3	42,900	15.4	5,300	1.9	33,200	12.0	19,000	6.8
Changes										
1991 to 2001	+10%	(j)	−1%	−11%	(j)	(j)	(j)	(j)	(j)	(j)
2000 to 2001	+2%	+1%	+1%	0%	+6%	+6%	+7%	+7%	−5%	−6%

Source: Total and motor-vehicle deaths, 1903–1932 based on National Center for Health Statistics death registration states; 1933–1948 (5th Rev.), 1949–1963, 1965–1999 are NCHS totals for the U.S. Work deaths for 1992–2000 are from the Bureau of Labor Statistics, Census of Fatal Occupational Injuries. All other figures are National Safety Council estimates.
[a] Duplications between Motor-Vehicle, Work, and Home are eliminated in the Total column.
[b] Rates are deaths per 100,000 population.
[c] Data insufficient to estimate yearly totals.
[d] In 1948 a revision was made in the International Classification of Diseases. The first figures for 1948 are comparable with those for earlier years, the second with those for later years.
[e] Adoption of the Census of Fatal Occupational Injuries figure for the Work class necessitated adjustments to the Home and Public classes. See the Technical Appendix for details.
[f] In 1999 a revision was made in the International Classification of Diseases. See the Technical Appendix for comparability with earlier years.
[g] Revised.
[h] Preliminary.
[i] Change less than 0.5%.
[j] Comparison not valid for 1991-2001 because of change in estimating procedure (see footnote "e").

UNINTENTIONAL-INJURY DEATHS BY AGE

UNINTENTIONAL-INJURY DEATHS BY AGE, UNITED STATES, 1903–2001

Year	All Ages	Under 5 Years	5–14 Years	15–24 Years	25–44 Years	45–64 Years	65–74 Years	75 Years & Over[a]
1903	70,600	9,400	8,200	10,300	20,100	12,600	10,000	
1904	71,500	9,700	9,000	10,500	19,900	12,500	9,900	
1905	70,900	9,800	8,400	10,600	19,600	12,600	9,900	
1906	80,000	10,000	8,400	13,000	24,000	13,600	11,000	
1907	81,900	10,500	8,300	13,400	24,900	14,700	10,100	
1908	72,300	10,100	7,600	11,300	20,500	13,100	9,700	
1909	72,700	9,900	7,400	10,700	21,000	13,300	10,400	
1910	77,900	9,900	7,400	11,900	23,600	14,100	11,000	
1911	79,300	11,000	7,500	11,400	22,400	15,100	11,900	
1912	78,400	10,600	7,900	11,500	22,200	14,700	11,500	
1913	82,500	9,800	7,400	12,200	24,500	16,500	12,100	
1914	77,000	10,600	7,900	11,000	21,400	14,300	11,800	
1915	76,200	10,300	8,200	10,800	20,500	14,300	12,100	
1916	84,800	11,600	9,100	7,700	24,900	17,800	13,700	
1917	90,100	11,600	9,700	11,700	24,400	18,500	14,200	
1918	85,100	10,600	10,100	10,600	21,900	17,700	14,200	
1919	75,500	10,100	10,000	10,200	18,600	13,800	12,800	
1920	75,900	10,200	9,900	10,400	18,100	13,900	13,400	
1921	74,000	9,600	9,500	9,800	18,000	13,900	13,200	
1922	76,300	9,700	9,500	10,000	18,700	14,500	13,900	
1923	84,400	9,900	9,800	11,000	21,500	16,900	15,300	
1924	85,600	10,200	9,900	11,900	20,900	16,800	15,900	
1925	90,000	9,700	10,000	12,400	22,200	18,700	17,000	
1926	91,700	9,500	9,900	12,600	22,700	19,200	17,800	
1927	92,700	9,200	9,900	12,900	22,900	19,700	18,100	
1928	95,000	8,900	9,800	13,100	23,300	20,600	19,300	
1929	98,200	8,600	9,800	14,000	24,300	21,500	20,000	
1930	99,100	8,200	9,100	14,000	24,300	22,200	21,300	
1931	97,300	7,800	8,700	13,500	23,100	22,500	21,700	
1932	89,000	7,100	8,100	12,000	20,500	20,100	21,200	
1933	90,932	6,948	8,195	12,225	21,005	20,819	21,740	
1934	100,977	7,034	8,272	13,274	23,288	24,197	24,912	
1935	99,773	6,971	7,808	13,168	23,411	23,457	24,958	
1936	110,052	7,471	7,866	13,701	24,990	26,535	29,489	
1937	105,205	6,969	7,704	14,302	23,955	24,743	27,532	
1938	93,805	6,646	6,593	12,129	20,464	21,689	26,284	
1939	92,628	6,668	6,378	12,066	20,164	20,842	26,505	
1940	96,885	6,851	6,466	12,763	21,166	21,840	27,799	
1941	101,513	7,052	6,702	14,346	22,983	22,509	27,921	
1942	95,889	7,220	6,340	13,732	21,141	20,764	26,692	
1943	99,038	8,039	6,636	15,278	20,212	20,109	28,764	
1944	95,237	7,912	6,704	14,750	19,115	19,097	27,659	
1945	95,918	7,741	6,836	12,446	19,393	20,097	29,405	
1946	98,033	7,949	6,545	13,366	20,705	20,249	29,219	
1947	99,579	8,219	6,069	13,166	21,155	20,513	30,457	
1948 (5th Rev.)[b]	98,001	8,387	5,859	12,595	20,274	19,809	31,077	
1948 (6th Rev.)[b]	93,000	8,350	5,850	12,600	20,300	19,300	9,800	16,800
1949	90,106	8,469	5,539	11,522	19,432	18,302	9,924	16,918
1950	91,249	8,389	5,519	12,119	20,663	18,665	9,750	16,144
1951	95,871	8,769	5,892	12,366	22,363	19,610	10,218	16,653
1952	96,172	8,871	5,980	12,787	21,950	19,892	10,026	16,667
1953	95,032	8,678	6,136	12,837	21,422	19,479	9,927	16,553
1954	90,032	8,380	5,939	11,801	20,023	18,299	9,652	15,938
1955	93,443	8,099	6,099	12,742	29,911	19,199	9,929	16,464
1956	94,780	8,173	6,319	13,545	20,986	19,207	10,160	16,393
1957	95,307	8,423	6,454	12,973	20,949	19,495	10,076	16,937
1958	90,604	8,789	6,514	12,744	19,658	18,095	9,431	15,373
1959	92,080	8,748	6,511	13,269	19,666	18,937	9,475	15,474
1960	93,806	8,950	6,836	13,457	19,600	19,385	9,689	15,829
1961	92,249	8,622	6,717	13,431	19,273	19,134	9,452	15,620
1962	97,139	8,705	6,751	14,557	19,955	20,335	10,149	16,687
1963	100,669	8,688	6,962	15,889	20,529	21,262	10,194	17,145
1964	100,500	8,670	7,400	17,420	22,080	22,100	10,400	16,930
1965	108,004	8,586	7,391	18,688	22,228	22,900	10,430	17,781
1966	113,563	8,507	7,958	21,030	23,134	24,022	10,706	18,206
1967	113,169	7,825	7,874	21,645	23,255	23,826	10,645	18,099
1968	114,864	7,263	8,369	23,012	23,684	23,896	10,961	17,679
1969	116,385	6,973	8,186	24,668	24,410	24,192	10,643	17,313
1970	114,638	6,594	8,203	24,336	23,979	24,164	10,644	16,718
1971	113,439	6,496	8,143	24,733	23,535	23,240	10,494	16,798
1972	115,448	6,142	8,242	25,762	23,852	23,658	10,446	17,346
1973	115,821	6,037	8,102	26,550	24,750	23,059	10,243	17,080

See source and footnotes on page 39.

UNINTENTIONAL-INJURY DEATHS BY AGE, UNITED STATES, 1903–2001, Cont.

Year	All Ages	Under 5 Years	5–14 Years	15–24 Years	25–44 Years	45–64 Years	65–74 Years	75 Years & Over[a]
1974	104,622	5,335	7,037	24,200	22,547	20,334	9,323	15,846
1975	103,030	4,948	6,818	24,121	22,877	19,643	9,220	15,403
1976	100,761	4,692	6,308	24,316	22,399	19,000	8,823	15,223
1977	103,202	4,470	6,305	25,619	23,460	19,167	9,006	15,175
1978	105,561	4,766	6,118	26,622	25,024	18,774	9,072	15,185
1979	105,312	4,429	5,689	26,574	26,097	18,346	9,013	15,164
1980	105,718	4,479	5,224	26,206	26,722	18,140	8,997	15,950
1981	100,704	4,130	4,866	23,582	26,928	17,339	8,639	15,220
1982	94,082	4,108	4,504	21,306	25,135	15,907	8,224	14,898
1983	92,488	3,999	4,321	19,756	24,996	15,444	8,336	15,636
1984	92,911	3,652	4,198	19,801	25,498	15,273	8,424	16,065
1985	93,457	3,746	4,252	19,161	25,940	15,251	8,583	16,524
1986	95,277	3,843	4,226	19,975	27,201	14,733	8,499	16,800
1987	95,020	3,871	4,198	18,695	27,484	14,807	8,686	17,279
1988	97,100	3,794	4,215	18,507	28,279	15,177	8,971	18,157
1989	95,028	3,770	4,090	16,738	28,429	15,046	8,812	18,143
1990	91,983	3,496	3,650	16,241	27,663	14,607	8,405	17,921
1991	89,347	3,626	3,660	15,278	26,526	13,693	8,137	18,427
1992	86,777	3,286	3,388	13,662	25,808	13,882	8,165	18,586
1993	90,523	3,488	3,466	13,966	27,277	14,434	8,125	19,767
1994	91,437	3,406	3,508	13,898	27,012	15,200	8,279	20,134
1995	93,320	3,067	3,544	13,842	27,660	16,004	8,400	20,803
1996	94,948	2,951	3,433	13,809	27,092	16,717	8,780	22,166
1997	94,644	2,770	3,371	13,367	27,129	17,521	8,578	22,908
1998	97,835	2,689	3,254	13,349	27,172	18,286	8,892	24,193
1999[c,d]	97,860	2,743	3,091	13,656	27,121	18,924	8,208	24,117
2000[d]	96,000	2,700	2,800	13,800	26,800	19,100	7,700	23,100
2001[e]	98,000	2,400	2,800	14,200	27,800	20,400	7,800	22,600
Changes								
1991 to 2001	+10%	−34%	−23%	−7%	+5%	+49%	−4%	+23%
2000 to 2001	+2%	−11%	0%	+3%	+4%	+7%	+1%	−2%

Source: 1903 to 1932 based on National Center for Health Statistics data for registration states; 1933–1948 (5th Rev.), 1949–1963, 1965–1999 are NCHS totals. All other figures are National Safety Council estimates. See Technical Appendix for comparability.
[a] Includes "age unknown." In 1999, these deaths numbered 106.
[b] In 1948, a revision was made in the International Classification of Diseases. The first figures for 1948 are comparable with those for earlier years, the second with those for later years.
[c] In 1999, a revision was made in the International Classification of Diseases. See the Technical Appendix for comparability with earlier years.
[d] Revised.
[e] Preliminary.

UNINTENTIONAL-INJURY DEATH RATES[a] BY AGE, UNITED STATES, 1903–2001

Year	Standardized Rate[b]	All Ages	Under 5 Years	5–14 Years	15–24 Years	25–44 Years	45–64 Years	65–74 Years	75 Years & Over[b]
1903	99.4	87.2	98.7	46.8	65.0	87.4	111.7		299.8
1904	103.4	86.6	99.1	50.9	64.9	84.6	108.1		290.0
1905	98.4	84.2	98.6	47.0	64.1	81.4	106.2		282.5
1906	114.2	93.2	99.1	46.5	77.1	97.3	111.7		306.0
1907	112.4	93.6	102.7	45.5	78.0	98.8	117.8		274.2
1908	99.7	81.2	97.5	41.2	64.4	79.5	102.2		256.7
1909	97.4	80.1	94.2	39.6	59.9	79.6	101.0		268.2
1910	103.0	84.4	92.8	39.1	65.3	87.3	104.0		276.0
1911	104.7	84.7	101.9	39.3	62.1	81.4	108.7		292.1
1912	100.4	82.5	97.1	40.5	62.3	79.2	103.2		275.8
1913	103.5	85.5	88.4	37.4	65.2	85.6	112.5		281.7
1914	95.9	78.6	94.3	38.9	58.5	73.2	94.6		268.1
1915	92.1	76.7	90.8	39.7	57.3	69.0	92.1		268.8
1916	101.4	84.1	101.4	43.3	40.8	82.5	112.1		297.6
1917	106.7	88.2	108.4	45.3	62.1	79.8	113.8		301.2
1918	101.2	82.1	91.0	46.5	58.7	72.2	106.3		294.2
1919	87.7	71.9	87.2	45.9	55.3	60.1	81.8		262.0
1920	87.8	71.2	87.4	44.9	55.5	56.9	85.6		289.5
1921	84.3	68.4	80.8	42.4	51.4	55.5	79.4		259.8
1922	86.9	69.4	80.6	41.5	51.4	57.1	81.4		265.1
1923	94.5	75.7	82.0	42.4	55.6	64.5	92.6		282.8
1924	93.3	75.6	82.9	42.4	58.6	61.7	90.2		283.5
1925	97.2	78.4	78.6	42.3	59.7	64.7	97.8		293.9
1926	97.7	78.7	77.9	41.4	59.9	65.4	98.2		298.7
1927	97.5	78.4	75.9	41.0	60.2	65.2	98.0		295.4
1928	99.6	79.3	74.4	40.4	59.9	65.6	99.9		306.2
1929	101.2	80.8	73.3	40.0	63.1	67.7	102.1		308.9
1930	101.8	80.5	71.8	36.9	62.3	67.0	102.9		317.9
1931	99.2	78.5	69.9	35.2	59.7	63.0	102.1		313.3
1932	90.5	71.3	65.1	32.8	52.7	55.6	89.3		296.9
1933	91.1	72.4	65.5	33.4	53.6	56.3	90.8		295.3
1934	100.5	79.9	68.1	33.9	57.8	61.8	103.3		328.5
1935	97.9	78.4	68.5	32.2	56.9	61.6	98.0		319.8
1936	108.1	85.9	74.4	32.9	58.8	65.3	108.6		367.4
1937	100.7	81.7	69.6	32.7	60.9	62.1	99.3		333.4
1938	89.4	72.3	65.3	28.5	51.3	52.5	85.4		308.9
1939	86.7	70.8	62.9	28.2	50.7	51.2	81.0		300.0
1940	89.1	73.4	64.8	28.8	53.5	53.2	83.4		305.7
1941	90.7	76.3	65.0	29.7	60.9	57.2	84.8		297.4
1942	84.3	71.6	63.9	27.9	59.8	52.4	77.1		275.5
1943	86.3	73.8	66.9	29.0	69.7	50.3	73.6		287.8
1944	82.5	71.7	63.2	29.1	72.9	48.9	68.9		268.6
1945	83.4	72.4	59.8	29.5	64.5	50.5	71.6		277.6
1946	81.0	70.0	60.2	28.1	61.7	48.8	70.9		267.9
1947	80.5	69.4	57.4	25.8	59.6	49.0	70.6		270.7
1948 (5th Rev.)[d]	79.5	67.1	56.3	24.6	56.8	46.2	66.8		267.4
1948 (6th Rev.)[d]	72.5	63.7	56.0	24.5	56.8	46.2	65.1	122.4	464.3
1949	69.0	60.6	54.4	23.0	52.2	43.5	60.6	120.4	450.7
1950	68.1	60.3	51.4	22.6	55.0	45.6	60.5	115.8	414.7
1951	70.1	62.5	50.8	23.6	57.7	49.0	62.7	117.1	413.6
1952	69.0	61.8	51.5	22.5	60.9	47.7	62.7	111.1	399.8
1953	67.0	60.1	49.5	22.1	61.4	46.4	60.5	106.7	383.6
1954	62.2	55.9	46.7	20.5	56.4	43.0	55.9	100.7	354.4
1955	63.4	56.9	43.9	20.7	60.1	44.7	57.7	100.8	350.2
1956	63.0	56.6	43.3	20.2	63.3	44.7	56.7	100.6	335.6
1957	62.2	55.9	43.5	19.9	59.5	44.6	56.6	97.5	333.3
1958	57.5	52.3	44.5	19.6	56.2	42.0	51.7	89.3	292.6
1959	57.4	52.2	43.6	18.9	56.5	42.1	53.2	87.7	284.7
1960	57.3	52.1	44.0	19.1	55.6	42.0	53.6	87.6	281.4
1961	55.4	50.4	42.0	18.1	54.0	41.2	52.1	83.8	267.9
1962	57.5	52.3	42.6	18.0	55.0	42.7	54.6	88.5	277.7
1963	58.6	53.4	42.8	18.2	57.2	44.0	56.3	87.9	277.0
1964	60.0	54.9	43.1	19.1	59.9	47.3	57.6	88.9	263.9
1965	61.9	55.8	43.4	18.7	61.6	47.7	58.8	88.5	268.7
1966	63.0	58.1	44.4	19.9	66.9	49.6	60.7	89.8	267.4
1967	62.1	57.3	42.2	19.4	66.9	49.7	59.2	88.5	257.4
1968	62.0	57.6	40.6	20.5	69.2	50.1	58.5	90.2	244.0
1969	61.8	57.8	40.2	20.0	71.8	51.2	58.4	86.6	232.0
1970	59.8	56.2	38.4	20.1	68.0	49.8	57.6	85.2	219.6
1971	58.1	54.8	37.7	20.1	66.1	48.4	54.7	82.7	213.2
1972	58.0	55.2	35.9	20.6	67.6	47.5	55.2	80.8	214.2
1973	57.1	54.8	35.8	20.6	68.2	48.0	53.3	77.3	206.3

See source and footnotes on page 41.

UNINTENTIONAL-INJURY DEATH RATES[a] BY AGE, UNITED STATES, 1903–2001, Cont.

Year	Standardized Rate[b]	All Ages	Under 5 Years	5–14 Years	15–24 Years	25–44 Years	45–64 Years	65–74 Years	75 Years & Over[b]
1974	50.9	49.0	32.4	18.2	60.9	42.7	46.7	68.7	186.7
1975	49.3	47.8	30.7	17.8	59.5	42.3	44.9	66.2	175.5
1976	47.3	46.3	30.0	16.7	58.9	40.3	43.2	62.0	168.4
1977	47.6	47.0	28.7	17.0	61.3	40.9	43.4	61.5	164.0
1978	47.8	47.5	30.3	16.9	63.1	42.3	42.4	60.5	159.7
1979	47.0	46.9	27.6	16.1	62.6	42.7	41.3	58.8	154.8
1980	46.5	46.5	27.2	15.0	61.7	42.3	40.8	57.5	158.6
1981	44.0	43.9	24.4	14.2	55.9	41.2	39.0	54.4	147.4
1982	40.6	40.6	23.8	13.2	51.2	37.3	35.8	50.9	140.0
1983	39.6	39.6	22.8	12.7	48.2	36.0	34.7	50.8	142.8
1984	39.4	39.4	20.6	12.4	48.9	35.7	34.3	50.7	142.8
1985	39.2	39.3	21.0	12.6	47.9	35.3	34.2	50.9	143.0
1986	39.4	39.7	21.4	12.6	50.5	36.1	33.0	49.6	141.5
1987	39.0	39.2	21.4	12.4	48.1	35.7	33.0	49.8	141.6
1988	39.5	39.7	20.9	12.3	48.5	36.1	33.4	50.9	145.3
1989	38.4	38.5	20.4	11.8	44.8	35.7	32.8	49.3	141.5
1990	36.7	36.9	18.5	10.4	44.0	34.2	31.6	46.4	136.5
1991	35.3	35.4	18.9	10.2	42.0	32.3	29.3	44.5	136.7
1992	34.0	34.0	16.8	9.3	37.8	31.3	28.7	44.2	134.5
1993	35.0	35.1	17.7	9.4	38.8	33.0	29.1	43.6	139.9
1994	35.0	35.1	17.3	9.4	38.4	32.5	29.9	44.3	139.2
1995	35.4	35.5	15.7	9.3	38.2	33.2	30.6	44.8	140.6
1996	35.7	35.8	15.3	8.9	38.1	32.3	31.1	47.0	145.9
1997	35.7	35.7	14.5	8.7	36.5	32.5	31.6	46.3	146.2
1998	36.1	36.2	14.2	8.3	35.9	32.6	31.9	48.3	151.1
1999[e,f]	35.8	35.9	14.5	7.8	36.1	32.7	32.0	45.0	147.7
2000[f]	34.8	34.9	14.3	7.1	35.9	32.5	31.2	42.2	138.8
2001[g]	35.2	35.3	12.7	7.0	36.3	34.0	32.3	43.0	133.7
Changes									
1991 to 2001		([h])	−33%	−31%	−14%	+5%	+10%	−3%	−2%
2000 to 2001		+1%	−11%	−1%	+1%	+5%	+4%	+2%	−4%
2001 Population (Millions)									
Total		277.803[i]	18.899	39.816	39.077	81.756	63.190	18.155	16.908
Female		142.008	9.245	19.437	19.078	41.210	32.583	9.937	10.516
Male		135.795	9.654	20.381	19.998	40.545	30.606	8.218	6.391

Source: All figures are National Safety Council estimates. See Technical Appendix for comparability.
[a] Rates are deaths per 100,000 resident population in each age group.
[b] Adjusted to the year 2000 standard population to remove the influence of changes in age distribution between 1903 and 2001.
[c] Includes "age unknown."
[d] In 1948, a revision was made in the International Classification of Diseases. The first figures for 1948 are comparable with those for earlier years, the second with those for later years.
[e] In 1999, a revision was made in the International Classification of Diseases. See the Technical Appendix for comparability.
[f] Revised.
[g] Preliminary.
[h] Change less than 0.5%.
[i] Sum of parts may not equal total due to rounding.

PRINCIPAL TYPES OF
UNINTENTIONAL-INJURY DEATHS

PRINCIPAL TYPES OF UNINTENTIONAL-INJURY DEATHS, UNITED STATES, 1903–1998

Year	Total	Motor-Vehicle	Falls	Drowning[a]	Fires, Burns[b]	Ingest. of Food, Object	Firearms	Poison (Solid, Liquid)	Poison (Gas, Vapor)	All Other
1903	70,600	(c)	(c)	9,200	(c)	(c)	2,500	(c)	(c)	58,900
1904	71,500	(c)	(c)	9,300	(c)	(c)	2,800	(c)	(c)	59,400
1905	70,900	(c)	(c)	9,300	(c)	(c)	2,000	(c)	(c)	59,600
1906	80,000	400	(c)	9,400	(c)	(c)	2,100	(c)	(c)	68,100
1907	81,900	700	(c)	9,000	(c)	(c)	1,700	(c)	(c)	70,500
1908	72,300	800	(c)	9,300	(c)	(c)	1,900	(c)	(c)	60,300
1909	72,700	1,300	(c)	8,500	(c)	(c)	1,600	(c)	(c)	61,300
1910	77,900	1,900	(c)	8,700	(c)	(c)	1,900	(c)	(c)	65,400
1911	79,300	2,300	(c)	9,000	(c)	(c)	2,100	(c)	(c)	65,900
1912	78,400	3,100	(c)	8,600	(c)	(c)	2,100	(c)	(c)	64,600
1913	82,500	4,200	15,100	10,300	8,900	(c)	2,400	3,200	(c)	38,400
1914	77,000	4,700	15,000	8,700	9,100	(c)	2,300	3,300	(c)	33,900
1915	76,200	6,600	15,000	8,600	8,400	(c)	2,100	2,800	(c)	32,700
1916	84,800	8,200	15,200	8,900	9,500	(c)	2,200	2,900	(c)	37,900
1917	90,100	10,200	15,200	7,600	10,800	(c)	2,300	2,800	(c)	41,200
1918	85,100	10,700	13,200	7,000	10,200	(c)	2,500	2,700	(c)	38,800
1919	75,500	11,200	11,900	9,100	9,100	(c)	2,800	3,100	(c)	28,300
1920	75,900	12,500	12,600	6,100	9,300	(c)	2,700	3,300	(c)	29,400
1921	74,000	13,900	12,300	7,800	7,500	(c)	2,800	2,900	(c)	26,800
1922	76,300	15,300	13,200	7,000	8,300	(c)	2,900	2,800	(c)	26,800
1923	84,400	18,400	14,100	6,800	9,100	(c)	2,900	2,800	2,700	27,600
1924	85,600	19,400	14,700	7,400	7,400	(c)	2,900	2,700	2,900	28,200
1925	90,000	21,900	15,500	7,300	8,600	(c)	2,800	2,700	2,800	28,400
1926	91,700	23,400	16,300	7,500	8,800	(c)	2,800	2,600	3,200	27,100
1927	92,700	25,800	16,500	8,100	8,200	(c)	3,000	2,600	2,700	25,800
1928	95,000	28,000	17,000	8,600	8,400	(c)	2,900	2,800	2,800	24,500
1929	98,200	31,200	17,700	7,600	8,200	(c)	3,200	2,600	2,800	24,900
1930	99,100	32,900	18,100	7,500	8,100	(c)	3,200	2,600	2,500	24,200
1931	97,300	33,700	18,100	7,600	7,100	(c)	3,100	2,600	2,100	23,000
1932	89,000	29,500	18,600	7,500	7,100	(c)	3,000	2,200	2,100	19,000
1933	90,932	31,363	18,962	7,158	6,781	(c)	3,014	2,135	1,633	19,886
1934	100,977	36,101	20,725	7,077	7,456	(c)	3,033	2,148	1,643	22,794
1935	99,773	36,369	21,378	6,744	7,253	(c)	2,799	2,163	1,654	21,413
1936	110,052	38,089	23,562	6,659	7,939	(c)	2,817	2,177	1,665	27,144
1937	105,205	39,643	22,544	7,085	7,214	(c)	2,576	2,190	1,675	22,278
1938	93,805	32,582	23,239	6,881	6,491	(c)	2,726	2,077	1,428	18,381
1939	92,623	32,386	23,427	6,413	6,675	(c)	2,618	1,963	1,440	17,701
1940	96,885	34,501	23,356	6,202	7,521	(c)	2,375	1,847	1,583	19,500
1941	101,513	39,969	22,764	6,389	6,922	(c)	2,396	1,731	1,464	19,878
1942	95,889	28,309	22,632	6,696	7,901	(c)	2,678	1,607	1,741	24,325
1943	99,038	23,823	24,701	7,115	8,726	921	2,282	1,745	2,014	27,711
1944	95,237	24,282	22,989	6,511	8,372	896	2,392	1,993	1,860	25,942
1945	95,918	28,076	23,847	6,624	7,949	897	2,385	1,987	2,120	22,033
1946	98,033	33,411	23,109	6,442	7,843	1,076	2,801	1,961	1,821	19,569
1947	99,579	32,697	24,529	6,885	8,033	1,206	2,439	1,865	1,865	14,060
1948 (5th Rev.)[d]	98,001	32,259	24,836	6,428	7,743	1,315	2,191	1,753	2,045	19,611
1948 (6th Rev.)[d]	93,000	32,259	22,000	6,500	6,800	1,299	2,330	1,600	2,020	17,192
1949	90,106	31,701	22,308	6,684	5,982	1,341	2,326	1,634	1,617	16,513
1950	91,249	34,763	20,783	6,131	6,405	1,350	2,174	1,584	1,769	16,290
1951	95,871	36,996	21,376	6,489	6,788	1,456	2,247	1,497	1,627	17,395
1952	96,172	37,794	20,945	6,601	6,922	1,434	2,210	1,440	1,397	17,429
1953	95,032	37,955	20,631	6,770	6,579	1,603	2,277	1,391	1,223	16,603
1954	90,032	35,586	19,771	6,334	6,083	1,627	2,271	1,339	1,223	15,798
1955	93,443	38,426	20,192	6,344	6,352	1,608	2,120	1,431	1,163	15,807
1956	94,780	39,628	20,282	6,263	6,405	1,760	2,202	1,422	1,213	15,605
1957	95,307	38,702	20,545	6,613	6,269	2,043	2,369	1,390	1,143	16,233
1958	90,604	36,981	18,248	6,582[e]	7,291[e]	2,191[e]	2,172	1,429	1,187	14,523
1959	92,080	37,910	18,774	6,434	6,898	2,189	2,258	1,661	1,141	14,815
1960	93,806	38,137	19,023	6,529	7,645	2,397	2,334	1,679	1,253	14,809
1961	92,249	38,091	18,691	6,525	7,102	2,499	2,204	1,804	1,192	14,141
1962	97,139	40,804	19,589	6,439	7,534	1,813	2,092	1,833	1,376	15,659
1963	100,669	43,564	19,335	6,347	8,172	1,949	2,263	2,061	1,489	15,489
1964	105,000	47,700	18,941	6,709	7,379	1,865	2,275	2,100	1,360	16,571
1965	108,004	49,163	19,984	6,799	7,347	1,836	2,344	2,110	1,526	16,895
1966	113,563	53,041	20,066	7,084	8,084	1,831	2,558	2,283	1,648	16,968
1967	113,169	52,924	20,120	7,076	7,423	1,980	2,896	2,506	1,574	16,670
1968	114,864	54,862	18,651	7,372[e]	7,335	3,100[e]	2,394[e]	2,583	1,526	17,041
1969	116,385	55,791	17,827	7,699	7,163	3,712	2,309	2,967	1,549	16,368
1970	114,638	54,633	16,926	7,860	6,718	2,753	2,406	3,679	1,620	18,043
1971	113,439	54,381	16,755	7,396	6,776	2,877	2,360	3,710	1,646	17,538
1972	115,448	56,278	16,744	7,586	6,714	2,830	2,442	3,728	1,690	17,436
1973	115,821	55,511	16,506	8,725	6,503	3,013	2,618	3,683	1,652	17,610

See source and footnotes on page 43.

PRINCIPAL TYPES OF UNINTENTIONAL-INJURY DEATHS, UNITED STATES, 1903–1998, Cont.

Year	Total	Motor-Vehicle	Falls	Drowning[a]	Fires, Burns[b]	Ingest. of Food, Object	Firearms	Poison (Solid, Liquid)	Poison (Gas, Vapor)	All Other
1974	104,622	46,402	16,339	7,876	6,236	2,991	2,513	4,016	1,518	16,731
1975	103,030	45,853	14,896	8,000	6,071	3,106	2,380	4,694	1,577	16,453
1976	100,761	47,038	14,136	6,827	6,338	3,033	2,059	4,161	1,569	15,600
1977	103,202	49,510	13,773	7,126	6,357	3,037	1,982	3,374	1,596	16,447
1978	105,561	52,411	13,690	7,026	6,163	3,063	1,806	3,035	1,737	16,630
1979	105,312	53,524	13,216	6,872	5,991	3,243	2,004	3,165	1,472	15,825
1980	105,718	53,172	13,294	7,257	5,822	3,249	1,955	3,089	1,242	16,638
1981	100,704	51,385	12,628	6,277	5,697	3,331	1,871	3,243	1,280	14,992
1982	94,082	45,779	12,077	6,351	5,210	3,254	1,756	3,474	1,259	14,922
1983	92,488	44,452	12,024	6,353	5,028	3,387	1,695	3,382	1,251	14,916
1984	92,911	46,263	11,937	5,388	5,010	3,541	1,668	3,808	1,103	14,193
1985	93,457	45,901	12,001	5,316	4,938	3,551	1,649	4,091	1,079	14,931
1986	95,277	47,865	11,444	5,700	4,835	3,692	1,452	4,731	1,009	14,549
1987	95,020	48,290	11,733	5,100	4,710	3,688	1,440	4,415	900	14,744
1988	97,100	49,078	12,096	4,966	4,965	3,805	1,501	5,353	873	14,463
1989	95,028	47,575	12,151	4,015	4,716	3,578	1,489	5,603	921	14,980
1990	91,983	46,814	12,313	4,685	4,175	3,303	1,416	5,055	748	13,474
1991	89,347	43,536	12,662	4,818	4,120	3,240	1,441	5,698	736	13,096
1992	86,777	40,982	12,646	3,542	3,958	3,182	1,409	6,449	633	13,976
1993	90,523	41,893	13,141	3,807	3,900	3,160	1,521	7,877	660	14,564
1994	91,437	42,524	13,450	3,942	3,986	3,065	1,356	8,309	685	14,120
1995	93,320	43,363	13,986	4,350	3,761	3,185	1,225	8,461	611	14,378
1996	94,948	43,649	14,986	3,959	3,741	3,206	1,134	8,872	638	14,763
1997	95,644	43,458	15,447	4,051	3,490	3,275	981	9,587	576	14,779
1998	97,835	43,501	16,274	4,406	3,255	3,515	866	10,255	546	15,217

PRINCIPAL TYPES OF UNINTENTIONAL-INJURY DEATHS, UNITED STATES, 1999–2001

Year	Total	Motor-Vehicle	Falls	Poisoning	Ingest. of Food, Object	Drowning[f]	Fires, Flames, Smoke[b]	Mechanical Suffocation	Firearms	All Other
1999[g,h]	97,860	42,401	13,162	12,186	3,885	3,529	3,348	1,618	824	16,907
2000[h]	96,000	42,500	12,900	12,700	4,300	3,300	3,900	1,500	800	14,100
2001[i]	98,000	42,900	14,200	14,500	4,200	3,300	3,900	1,300	800	12,900
Changes										
1991 to 2001	+10%	−1%	(j)	(j)	+30%	(j)	−5%	(j)	−44%	(j)
2000 to 2001	+2%	+1%	+10%	+14%	−2%	0%	0%	−13%	0%	−9%

Source: National Center for Health Statistics and National Safety Council. See Technical Appendix for comparability.
[a] *Includes drowning in water transport accidents.*
[b] *Includes burns by fire, and deaths resulting from conflagration regardless of nature of injury.*
[c] *Comparable data not available.*
[d] *In 1948, a revision was made in the International Classification of Diseases. The first figures for 1948 are comparable with those for earlier years, the second with those for later years.*
[e] *Data are not comparable to previous years shown due to classification changes in 1958 and 1968.*
[f] *Excludes water transport drownings.*
[g] *In 1999, a revision was made in the International Classification of Diseases. See the Technical Appendix for comparability.*
[h] *Revised.*
[i] *Preliminary.*
[j] *Comparison not valid because of change in classifications (see footnote "g").*

UNINTENTIONAL-INJURY DEATH RATES FOR PRINCIPAL TYPES

UNINTENTIONAL-INJURY DEATH RATES[a] FOR PRINCIPAL TYPES, UNITED STATES, 1903–1998

Year	Total	Motor-Vehicle	Falls	Drowning[b]	Fires, Burns[c]	Ingest. of Food, Object	Firearms	Poison (Solid, Liquid)	Poison (Gas, Vapor)	All Other
1903	87.2	(d)	(d)	11.4	(d)	(d)	3.1	(d)	(d)	72.7
1904	86.6	(d)	(d)	11.3	(d)	(d)	3.4	(d)	(d)	71.9
1905	84.2	(d)	(d)	11.1	(d)	(d)	2.4	(d)	(d)	70.7
1906	93.2	0.5	(d)	11.0	(d)	(d)	2.4	(d)	(d)	79.3
1907	93.6	0.8	(d)	10.4	(d)	(d)	2.0	(d)	(d)	80.4
1908	81.2	0.9	(d)	10.5	(d)	(d)	2.1	(d)	(d)	67.7
1909	80.1	1.4	(d)	9.4	(d)	(d)	1.8	(d)	(d)	67.5
1910	84.4	2.0	(d)	9.4	(d)	(d)	2.1	(d)	(d)	70.9
1911	84.7	2.5	(d)	9.6	(d)	(d)	2.2	(d)	(d)	70.4
1912	82.5	3.3	(d)	9.0	(d)	(d)	2.2	(d)	(d)	68.0
1913	85.5	4.4	15.5	10.6	9.1	(d)	2.5	3.3	(d)	40.1
1914	78.6	4.8	15.1	8.8	9.1	(d)	2.3	3.3	(d)	35.2
1915	76.7	6.6	14.9	8.6	8.4	(d)	2.1	2.8	(d)	33.3
1916	84.1	8.1	14.9	8.7	9.3	(d)	2.2	2.8	(d)	38.1
1917	88.2	10.0	14.7	7.4	10.5	(d)	2.2	2.7	(d)	40.7
1918	82.1	10.3	12.8	6.8	9.9	(d)	2.4	2.6	(d)	37.3
1919	71.9	10.7	11.4	6.9	8.7	(d)	2.7	3.0	(d)	28.5
1920	71.2	11.7	11.8	5.7	8.7	(d)	2.5	3.1	(d)	27.7
1921	68.4	12.9	11.3	7.2	6.9	(d)	2.6	2.7	(d)	24.8
1922	69.4	13.9	12.0	6.4	7.5	(d)	2.6	2.5	(d)	24.5
1923	75.7	16.5	12.6	6.1	8.1	(d)	2.6	2.5	2.4	24.9
1924	75.6	17.1	12.9	6.5	8.4	(d)	2.5	2.4	2.5	23.3
1925	78.4	19.1	13.4	6.3	7.4	(d)	2.4	2.3	2.4	25.1
1926	78.7	20.1	13.9	6.4	7.5	(d)	2.4	2.2	2.7	23.5
1927	78.4	21.8	13.9	6.8	6.9	(d)	2.5	2.2	2.3	22.0
1928	79.3	23.4	14.1	7.1	7.0	(d)	2.4	2.3	2.3	20.7
1929	80.8	25.7	14.5	6.2	6.7	(d)	2.6	2.1	2.3	20.7
1930	80.5	26.7	14.7	6.1	6.6	(d)	2.6	2.1	2.0	19.7
1931	78.5	27.2	14.6	6.1	5.7	(d)	2.5	2.1	1.7	18.6
1932	71.3	23.6	14.9	6.0	5.7	(d)	2.4	1.8	1.7	15.2
1933	72.4	25.0	15.1	5.7	5.4	(d)	2.4	1.7	1.3	15.8
1934	79.9	28.6	16.4	5.6	5.9	(d)	2.4	1.7	1.3	18.0
1935	78.4	28.6	16.8	5.3	5.7	(d)	2.2	1.7	1.3	16.8
1936	85.9	29.7	18.4	5.2	6.2	(d)	2.2	1.7	1.3	21.2
1937	81.7	30.8	17.5	5.5	5.6	(d)	2.0	1.7	1.3	17.3
1938	72.3	25.1	17.9	5.3	5.0	(d)	2.1	1.6	1.1	14.2
1939	70.8	24.7	17.9	4.9	5.1	(d)	2.0	1.5	1.1	13.6
1940	73.4	26.1	17.7	4.7	5.7	(d)	1.8	1.4	1.2	14.8
1941	76.3	30.0	17.1	4.8	5.2	(d)	1.8	1.3	1.1	15.0
1942	71.6	21.1	16.9	5.0	5.9	(d)	2.0	1.2	1.3	18.2
1943	73.8	17.8	18.4	5.3	6.5	0.7	1.7	1.3	1.5	20.6
1944	71.7	18.3	17.3	4.9	6.3	0.7	1.8	1.5	1.4	19.5
1945	72.4	21.2	18.0	5.0	6.0	0.7	1.8	1.5	1.6	16.6
1946	70.0	23.9	16.5	4.6	5.6	0.8	2.0	1.4	1.3	13.9
1947	69.4	22.8	17.1	4.8	5.6	0.8	1.7	1.3	1.3	14.0
1948 (5th Rev.)[e]	67.1	22.1	17.0	4.4	5.3	0.9	1.5	1.2	1.4	13.3
1948 (6th Rev.)[e]	63.7	22.1	15.1	4.5	4.7	0.9	1.6	1.1	1.4	12.3
1949	60.6	21.3	15.0	4.5	4.0	0.9	1.6	1.1	1.1	11.1
1950	60.3	23.0	13.7	4.1	4.2	0.9	1.4	1.1	1.2	10.7
1951	62.5	24.1	13.9	4.2	4.4	1.0	1.5	1.0	1.1	11.3
1952	61.8	24.3	13.5	4.2	4.5	0.9	1.4	0.9	0.9	11.2
1953	60.1	24.0	13.0	4.3	4.2	1.0	1.4	0.9	0.8	10.2
1954	55.9	22.1	12.3	3.9	3.8	1.0	1.4	0.8	0.8	9.8
1955	56.9	23.4	12.3	3.9	3.9	1.0	1.3	0.9	0.7	9.5
1956	56.6	23.7	12.1	3.7	3.8	1.1	1.3	0.8	0.7	9.4
1957	55.9	22.7	12.1	3.9	3.7	1.2	1.4	0.8	0.7	9.4
1958	52.3	21.3	10.5	3.8[f]	4.2[f]	1.3[f]	1.3	0.8	0.7	8.4
1959	52.2	21.5	10.6	3.7	3.9	1.2	1.3	0.9	0.7	8.4
1960	52.1	21.2	10.6	3.6	3.9	1.3	1.3	0.9	0.7	8.2
1961	50.4	20.8	10.2	3.6	3.9	1.4	1.2	1.0	0.7	7.6
1962	52.3	22.0	10.5	3.5	4.1	1.0	1.1	1.0	0.7	8.4
1963	53.4	23.1	10.3	3.4	4.3	1.0	1.2	1.1	0.8	8.2
1964	54.9	25.0	9.9	3.5	3.9	1.0	1.2	1.1	0.7	8.4
1965	55.8	25.4	10.3	3.5	3.8	1.0	1.2	1.1	0.8	8.7
1966	58.1	27.1	10.3	3.6	4.8	0.9	1.3	1.2	0.8	8.1
1967	57.3	26.8	10.2	3.6	3.8	1.0	1.5	1.3	0.8	8.3
1968	57.6	27.5	9.4	3.7[f]	3.7[f]	1.6[f]	1.2[f]	1.3	0.8	8.4
1969	57.8	27.7	8.9	3.8	3.6	1.8	1.2	1.5	0.8	8.5
1970	56.2	26.8	8.3	3.9	3.3	1.4	1.2	1.8	0.8	8.7
1971	54.8	26.3	8.1	3.6	3.3	1.4	1.1	1.8	0.8	8.4
1972	55.2	26.9	8.0	3.6	3.2	1.4	1.2	1.8	0.8	8.3
1973	54.8	26.3	7.8	4.1	3.1	1.4	1.2	1.7	0.8	8.4

See source and footnotes on page 45.

UNINTENTIONAL-INJURY DEATH RATES[a] FOR PRINCIPAL TYPES, UNITED STATES, 1903–1998, Cont.

Year	Total	Motor-Vehicle	Falls	Drowning[b]	Fires, Burns[c]	Ingest. of Food, Object	Firearms	Poison (Solid, Liquid)	Poison (Gas, Vapor)	All Other
1974	49.0	21.8	7.7	3.7	2.9	1.4	1.2	1.8	0.7	7.8
1975	47.8	21.3	6.9	3.7	2.8	1.4	1.1	2.2	0.7	7.7
1976	46.3	21.6	6.5	3.1	2.9	1.4	0.9	1.9	0.7	7.3
1977	47.0	22.5	6.3	3.2	2.9	1.4	0.9	1.5	0.7	7.6
1978	47.5	23.6	6.2	3.2	2.8	1.4	0.8	1.4	0.8	7.3
1979	46.9	23.8	5.9	3.1	2.7	1.4	0.9	1.4	0.7	7.0
1980	46.5	23.4	5.9	3.2	2.6	1.4	0.9	1.4	0.5	7.2
1981	43.9	22.4	5.5	2.7	2.5	1.5	0.8	1.4	0.6	6.5
1982	40.6	19.8	5.2	2.7	2.2	1.4	0.8	1.5	0.5	6.5
1983	39.6	19.0	5.1	2.7	2.2	1.4	0.7	1.4	0.5	6.6
1984	39.4	19.6	5.1	2.3	2.1	1.5	0.7	1.6	0.5	6.0
1985	39.3	19.3	5.0	2.2	2.1	1.5	0.7	1.7	0.5	6.3
1986	39.7	19.9	4.8	2.4	2.0	1.5	0.6	2.0	0.4	6.1
1987	39.2	19.9	4.8	2.1	1.9	1.5	0.6	1.8	0.4	6.2
1988	39.7	20.1	4.9	2.0	2.0	1.6	0.6	2.2	0.4	5.9
1989	38.5	19.3	4.9	1.9	1.9	1.4	0.6	2.3	0.4	5.8
1990	36.9	18.8	4.9	1.9	1.7	1.3	0.6	2.0	0.3	5.4
1991	35.4	17.3	5.0	1.8	1.6	1.3	0.6	2.3	0.3	5.2
1992	34.0	16.1	5.0	1.4	1.6	1.2	0.6	2.5	0.2	5.4
1993	35.1	16.3	5.1	1.5	1.5	1.2	0.6	3.1	0.3	5.5
1994	35.1	16.3	5.2	1.5	1.5	1.2	0.5	3.2	0.3	5.4
1995	35.5	16.5	5.3	1.7	1.4	1.2	0.5	3.2	0.2	5.5
1996	35.8	16.5	5.6	1.5	1.4	1.2	0.4	3.3	0.2	5.7
1997	35.7	16.2	5.8	1.5	1.3	1.2	0.4	3.6	0.2	5.5
1998	36.2	16.1	6.0	1.6	1.2	1.3	0.3	3.8	0.2	5.7

UNINTENTIONAL-INJURY DEATH RATES[a] FOR PRINCIPAL TYPES, UNITED STATES, 1999-2001

Year	Total	Motor-Vehicle	Falls	Poisoning	Ingest. of Food, Object	Drowning[g]	Fires, Flames, Smoke[c]	Mechanical Suffocation	Firearms	All Other
1999[h,i]	35.9	15.5	4.8	4.5	1.4	1.3	1.2	0.6	0.3	6.3
2000[i]	34.9	15.4	4.7	4.6	1.6	1.2	1.4	0.5	0.3	5.2
2001[j]	35.3	15.4	5.1	5.2	1.5	1.2	1.4	0.5	0.3	4.7
Changes										
1991 to 2001	([l])	−11%	([k])	([k])	+15%	([k])	−13%	([k])	−50%	([k])
2000 to 2001	+1%	0%	+9%	+13%	−6%	0%	0%	0%	0%	−10%

Source: National Safety Council estimates. See Technical Appendix for comparability.
[a] *Deaths per 100,000 population.*
[b] *Includes drowning in water transport accidents.*
[c] *Includes burns by fire, and deaths resulting from conflagration regardless of nature of injury.*
[d] *Comparable data not available.*
[e] *In 1948, a revision was made in the International Classification of Diseases. The first figures for 1948 are comparable with those for earlier years, the second with those for later years.*
[f] *Data are not comparable to previous years shown due to classification changes in 1958 and 1968.*
[g] *Excludes water transport drownings.*
[h] *In 1999, a revision was made in the International Classification of Diseases. See the Technical Appendix for comparability.*
[i] *Revised.*
[j] *Preliminary.*
[k] *Comparison not valid because of change in classifications (see footnote "h").*
[l] *Change less than 0.5%.*

WORK

WORK, 2001

Between 1912 and 2001, unintentional work deaths per 100,000 population were reduced 90%, from 21 to 2. In 1912, an estimated 18,000 to 21,000 workers' lives were lost. In 2001, in a work force nearly quadrupled in size and producing nine times the goods and services, there were only an estimated 5,300 work deaths.

The National Safety Council adopted the Bureau of Labor Statistics' Census of Fatal Occupational Injuries (CFOI) figure, beginning with the 1992 data year, as the authoritative count of work-related deaths. The Technical Appendix discusses the change in the Council's estimating procedures.

The CFOI system counts intentional as well as unintentional work injuries. Each year between 850 and 1,300 homicides and suicides are identified and counted. These fatal injuries are not included in the unintentional-injury estimates below. In 2001, more than 3,000 intentional-injury deaths, mostly work-related, resulted from the events of September 11. As with other homicides, they are not included below.

Note: The table of fatal occupational injuries by state and event or exposure has been moved to the State Data section which begins on page 150.

Unintentional-Injury Deaths	**5,300**
Unintentional-Injury Deaths per 100,000 Workers	**3.9**
Disabling Injuries	**3,900,000**
Workers	**136,246,000**
Costs	**$132.1 billion**

UNINTENTIONAL INJURIES AT WORK BY INDUSTRY, UNITED STATES, 2001

Industry Division	Workers[a] (000)	Deaths[a]		Deaths per 100,000 Workers[a]		Disabling Injuries
		2001	Change from 2000	2001	Change from 2000	
All industries	**136,246**	**5,300**	**+6%**	**3.9**	**+3%**	**3,900,000**
Agriculture[b]	3,209	700	+1%	21.3	+6%	130,000
Mining, quarrying[b]	566	180	+18%	31.8	+8%	20,000
Construction	9,125	1,210	+9%	13.3	+7%	470,000
Manufacturing	18,898	630	+1%	3.3	+6%	600,000
Transportation and public utilities	8,131	930	+7%	11.4	+6%	410,000
Trade[b]	27,563	470	+5%	1.7	+6%	740,000
Services[b]	48,441	690	+7%	1.4	+6%	950,000
Government	20,313	490	+7%	2.4	+7%	580,000

Source: National Safety Council estimates based on data from the Bureau of Labor Statistics, National Center for Health Statistics, state vital statistics departments, and state industrial commissions.
[a]*Deaths include persons of all ages. Workers and death rates include persons 16 years and older.*
[b]*Agriculture includes forestry, fishing, and agricultural services. Mining includes oil and gas extraction. Trade includes wholesale and retail trade. Services includes finance, insurance, and real estate.*

UNINTENTIONAL WORK-INJURY DEATHS AND DEATH RATES, UNITED STATES, 1992–2001

Year	Deaths	Workers[a]	Death Rate[b]
1992	4,965	119,168	4.2
1993	5,034	120,778	4.2
1994	5,338	124,470	4.3
1995	5,015	126,248	4.0
1996	5,069	127,997	4.0
1997	5,160	130,810	3.9
1998	5,117	132,772	3.9
1999[c]	5,184	134,688	3.8
2000[c]	5,017	136,402	3.7
2001[d]	5,300	136,246	3.9

Source: Deaths through 2000 are from the Bureau of Labor Statistics, Census of Fatal Occupational Injuries. Employment is from the Bureau of Labor Statistics and is based on the Current Population Survey. All other data are National Safety Council estimates. Deaths include persons of all ages. Workers and death rates include persons 16 years and older.
[a] In thousands. Workers are persons ages 16 and older gainfully employed, including owners, managers, other paid employees, the self-employed, unpaid family workers, and active-duty resident military personnel. Due to changes in procedures, estimates of workers from 1992 to the present are not comparable to prior years.
[b] Deaths per 100,000 workers.
[c] Revised.
[d] Preliminary.

WORKERS, UNINTENTIONAL-INJURY DEATHS, AND DEATH RATES, UNITED STATES, 1992–2001

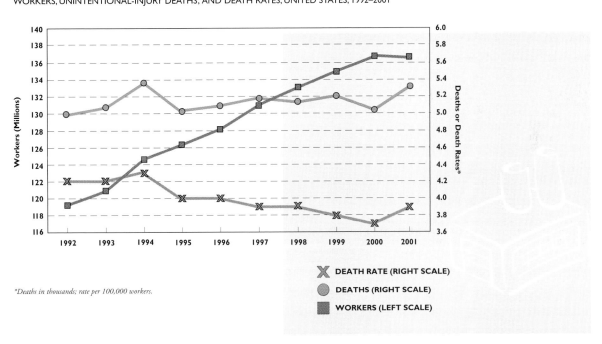

*Deaths in thousands; rate per 100,000 workers.

X DEATH RATE (RIGHT SCALE)

● DEATHS (RIGHT SCALE)

■ WORKERS (LEFT SCALE)

OCCUPATIONAL-INJURY DEATHS AND DEATH RATES, UNITED STATES, 1992–2001

Year	Total	Homicide & Suicide	Unintentional								
			All Industries[a]	Agri-culture[b]	Mining, Quarrying[c]	Construc-tion	Manufac-turing	Transpor-tation & Public Utilities	Trade[d]	Services[e]	Govern-ment
Deaths											
1992	6,217	1,252	4,965	779	175	889	707	767	415	601	586
1993	6,331	1,297	5,034	842	169	895	698	753	450	631	527
1994	6,632	1,294	5,338	814	177	1,000	734	819	492	676	534
1995	6,275	1,260	5,015	769	155	1,021	640	784	461	608	528
1996	6,202	1,133	5,069	762	151	1,025	660	883	451	615	321
1997	6,238	1,078	5,160	799	156	1,075	678	882	451	593	504
1998	6,055	938	5,117	808	143	1,136	631	830	443	634	465
1999[f]	6,054	870	5,184	776	122	1,168	671	918	425	623	451
2000[f]	5,935	898	5,017	693	153	1,113	624	872	447	643	458
2001[g]	—	—	5,300	700	180	1,210	630	930	470	690	490
Deaths per 100,000 Workers											
1992	5.2	1.0	4.2	23.1	26.4	13.7	3.6	11.5	1.7	1.6	3.0
1993	5.2	1.0	4.2	26.0	25.3	13.3	3.6	11.0	1.8	1.6	2.6
1994	5.3	1.0	4.3	22.8	26.5	14.4	3.7	11.6	1.9	1.7	2.7
1995	4.9	1.0	4.0	21.4	24.8	14.3	3.1	11.0	1.8	1.5	2.7
1996	4.8	0.9	4.0	21.2	26.6	13.7	3.2	12.2	1.7	1.4	1.6
1997	4.8	0.8	3.9	22.5	24.7	13.7	3.3	11.6	1.7	1.3	2.6
1998	4.5	0.7	3.9	22.7	23.1	14.1	3.1	10.8	1.6	1.4	2.4
1999[f]	4.5	0.6	3.8	22.6	21.7	13.8	3.4	11.5	1.5	1.3	2.2
2000[f]	4.3	0.7	3.7	20.1	29.4	12.4	3.1	10.8	1.6	1.4	2.3
2001[g]	—	—	3.9	21.3	31.8	13.3	3.3	11.4	1.7	1.4	2.4

Source: Deaths are from Bureau of Labor Statistics, Census of Fatal Occupational Injuries, except 2001 which are National Safety Council estimates. Rates are National Safety Council estimates based on Bureau of Labor Statistics employment data. Deaths include persons of all ages. Death rates include persons 16 years and older. A dash (—) indicates data not available.
[a] *Includes deaths with industry unknown.*
[b] *Agriculture includes forestry, fishing, and agricultural services.*
[c] *Mining includes oil and gas extraction.*
[d] *Trade includes wholesale and retail trade.*
[e] *Services includes finance, insurance, and real estate.*
[f] *Revised.*
[g] *Preliminary.*

OCCUPATIONAL UNINTENTIONAL-INJURY DEATHS AND DEATH RATES BY INDUSTRY, UNITED STATES, 2001

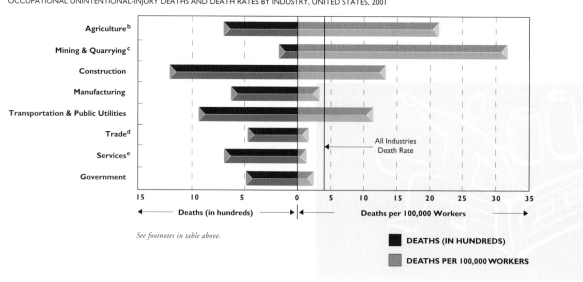

See footnotes in table above.

DEATHS (IN HUNDREDS)

DEATHS PER 100,000 WORKERS

The true cost to the nation, to employers, and to individuals of work-related deaths and injuries is much greater than the cost of workers' compensation insurance alone. The figures presented below show the National Safety Council's estimates of the total economic costs of occupational deaths and injuries. Cost-estimating procedures were revised for the 1993 edition of *Accident Facts*®. In general, cost estimates are not comparable from year to year. As additional or more precise data become available, they are used from that year forward. Previously estimated figures are not revised.

Total Cost in 2001 . . . . $132.1 billion
Includes wage and productivity losses of $69.2 billion, medical costs of $24.6 billion, and administrative expenses of $21.7 billion. Includes employer costs of $11.8 billion such as the monetary value of time lost by workers other than those with disabling injuries, who are directly or indirectly involved in injuries, and the cost of time required to investigate injuries, write up injury reports, etc. Also includes damage to motor vehicles in work injuries of $2.0 billion and fire losses of $2.8 billion.

Cost per Worker $970
This figure indicates the value of goods or services each worker must produce to offset the cost of work injuries. It is not the average cost of a work injury.

Cost per Death $1,020,000

Cost per Disabling Injury $29,000
These figures include estimates of wage losses, medical expenses, administrative expenses, and employer costs, and exclude property damage costs except to motor vehicles.

T I M E   L O S T   B E C A U S E   O F   W O R K   I N J U R I E S

                                                    DAYS LOST
TOTAL TIME LOST IN 2001 130,000,000

Due to Injuries in 2001 85,000,000
Includes primarily the actual time lost during the year from disabling injuries, except that it does not include time lost on the day of the injury or time required for further medical treatment or check-up following the injured person's return to work.

Fatalities are included at an average loss of 150 days per case, and permanent impairments are included at actual days lost plus an allowance for lost efficiency resulting from the impairment.

Not included is time lost by persons with nondisabling injuries or other persons directly or indirectly involved in the incidents.

                                                    DAYS LOST
Due to Injuries in Prior Years 45,000,000
This is an indicator of the productive time lost in 2001 due to permanently disabling injuries that occurred in prior years.

                                                    DAYS LOST
**TIME LOSS IN FUTURE YEARS FROM
2001 INJURIES.** 65,000,000
Includes time lost in future years due to on-the-job deaths and permanently disabling injuries that occurred in 2001.

WORKER DEATHS AND INJURIES ON AND OFF THE JOB

Nearly 9 out of 10 deaths and about three fifths of the disabling injuries suffered by workers in 2001 occurred off the job. The ratios of off-the-job deaths and injuries to on-the-job were 8.1 to 1 and 1.7 to 1, respectively. Production time lost due to off-the-job injuries totaled about 165,000,000 days in 2001, compared with 85,000,000 days lost by workers injured on the job. Production time lost in future years due to off-the-job injuries in 2001 will total an estimated 415,000,000 days, more than six times the 65,000,000 days lost in

future years from 2001's on-the-job injuries. Off-the-job injuries to workers cost the nation at least $184.0 billion in 2001.

The basis of the rates shown in the table below was changed from 1,000,000 hours to 200,000 hours beginning with the 1998 edition. This change was made so that the rates would be on the same basis as the occupational injury and illness incidence rates shown elsewhere in *Injury Facts®*.

ON- AND OFF-THE-JOB INJURIES, UNITED STATES, 2001

Place	Deaths		Disabling Injuries	
	Number	Rate[a]	Number	Rate[a]
On- and off-the-job	**48,300**	**0.012**	**10,700,000**	**2.7**
On-the-job	5,300	0.004	3,900,000	2.7
Off-the-job	43,000	0.016	6,800,000	2.6
Motor-vehicle	22,900	0.084	1,200,000	4.4
Public nonmotor-vehicle	7,800	0.018	2,600,000	6.2
Home	12,300	0.006	3,000,000	1.6

Source: National Safety Council estimates. Procedures for allocating time spent on and off the job were revised for the 1990 edition. Rate basis changed to 200,000 hours for the 1998 edition. Death and injury rates are not comparable to rate estimates prior to the 1998 edition.
[a] Per 200,000 hours exposure by place.

WORKERS' ON- AND OFF-THE-JOB INJURIES, 2001

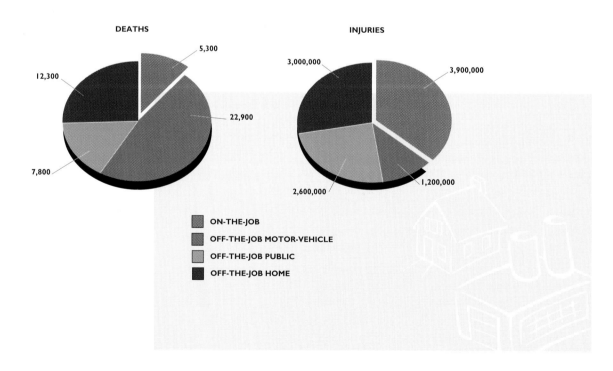

WORKERS' COMPENSATION CASES

According to the National Academy of Social Insurance, an estimated $45.9 billion, including benefits under deductible provisions, was paid out under workers' compensation in 2000 (the latest year for which data were available), an increase of about 6.4% from 1999. Of this total, $25.9 billion was for income benefits and $20.0 billion was for medical and hospitalization costs. Private carriers paid about $25.7 billion of the total workers' compensation benefits in 2000. In 2000,

approximately 126.6 million workers were covered by workers' compensation—an increase of 2.3% over the 123.8 million in 1999.

The table below shows the trend in the number of compensated or reported cases in each reporting state. Due to the differences in population, industries, and coverage of compensation laws, comparison among states should not be made.

WORKERS' COMPENSATION CASES, UNITED STATES, 1999–2001

State	Deaths[a]			Cases[a]			2000 Compensation Paid ($000)
	2001	2000	1999	2001	2000	1999	
Arizona	93	113	75	138,936	154,177	156,083	481,520
Arkansas	66	79	100	12,391	12,738	13,218	187,825
Colorado	—	114[b]	109	—	33,520[b]	32,706	768,758
Delaware	10	13	14	21,485	22,661	20,564	100,251
Dist. of Columbia	6	4	9	11,160	13,108	12,072	77,682
Georgia[c]	—	252	268	—	43,851	45,561	881,848
Idaho	—	—	—	46,243	45,283	44,763	167,664
Iowa[c]	42	69	76	25,427	34,452	34,527	328,854
Kansas	52	70	68	87,969	88,966	96,274	341,505
Maryland	45	54	66	28,685	28,463	28,390	1,194,629
Massachusetts	—	95	111	40,490	41,162	41,404	666,455
Minnesota[c]	36	34	48	—	—	—	798,100
Missouri	119	122	127	159,327	173,488	177,197	525,553
Montana	23	21	35	32,503	33,776	32,155	150,269
Nebraska	38	54	53	67,011	68,057	67,339	179,988
New Mexico	26	14	24	22,852	19,105	16,238	136,830
North Carolina	163	227	161	63,318	66,871	86,469	788,369
North Dakota	10	21	13	20,320	20,045	20,034	85,767
Ohio	155	175	194	263,911	280,873	288,242	2,091,992
Oregon[c]	34	45	47	24,645	25,365	25,802	412,710
South Carolina	105	133	116	28,986	30,705	30,159	596,526
Utah	51	50	51	72,307	76,795	74,956	159,283
Vermont	5	4	4	24,247	24,556	24,855	114,393
Virginia	188	144	145	202,564	134,450	130,557	534,014
Washington	82	87	82	232,718	247,112	248,084	1,499,070
Wisconsin[d]	64	77	67	46,608	52,860	58,620	703,299

Source: Deaths and Cases—State workers' compensation authorities for calendar or fiscal year. States not listed did not respond to the survey. Compensation Paid—Mont, D., Burton, J. F., Jr., Reno, V., & Thompson, C. (June, 2002). Workers' compensation: benefits, coverage, and costs, 2000 new estimates. *Washington DC: National Academy of Social Insurance.*
Note: Dash (—) indicates data not available.

Definitions:
Reported case—a reported case may or may not be work-related and may not receive compensation.
Compensated case—a case determined to be work-related and for which compensation was paid.

[a] *Reported cases involving medical and indemnity benefits, unless otherwise noted.*
[b] *Preliminary.*
[c] *Closed or compensated cases.*
[d] *Cases first closed in the calendar year involving Indemnity benefits only.*

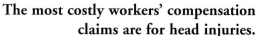

The most costly workers' compensation claims are for head injuries.

WORKERS' COMPENSATION CLAIMS COSTS, 1999–2000

The data in the graphs below and on the opposite page are from the National Council on Compensation Insurance's (NCCI) Detailed Claim Information (DCI) file, a stratified random sample of lost-time claims in 41 states. Total incurred costs consist of medical and indemnity payments plus case reserves on open claims, and are calculated as of the second report (18 months after the initial report of injury). Injuries that result in medical payments only, without lost time, are not included. For open claims, costs include all payments as of the second report plus case reserves for future payments.

Cause of Injury. The most costly lost-time workers' compensation claims by cause of injury, according to the NCCI data, are for those resulting from motor-vehicle crashes. These injuries averaged nearly $21,900 per workers' compensation claim filed in 1999 and 2000. The other types with above-average costs were those involving cumulative trauma ($15,301), a fall or slip ($13,829), struck by ($12,359), and caught

in or between objects or equipment ($12,058). The average cost for all claims combined was $12,055.

Nature of Injury. The most costly lost-time workers' compensation claims by the nature of the injury are for those resulting from amputation. These injuries averaged $26,459 per workers' compensation claim filed in 1999 and 2000. The next highest costs were for injuries resulting in fracture ($17,030), carpal tunnel syndrome ($16,308), and "other trauma" ($14,411). The average cost for all natures of injury combined was $12,055.

Part of Body. The most costly lost-time workers' compensation claims are for those involving the head or central nervous system. These injuries averaged $27,627 per workers' compensation claim filed in 1999 and 2000. The next highest costs were for injuries involving multiple body parts ($17,470); neck ($17,235); and leg ($14,460). The average cost for all parts of body combined was $12,055.

AVERAGE TOTAL INCURRED COSTS PER CLAIM BY CAUSE OF INJURY, 1999–2000

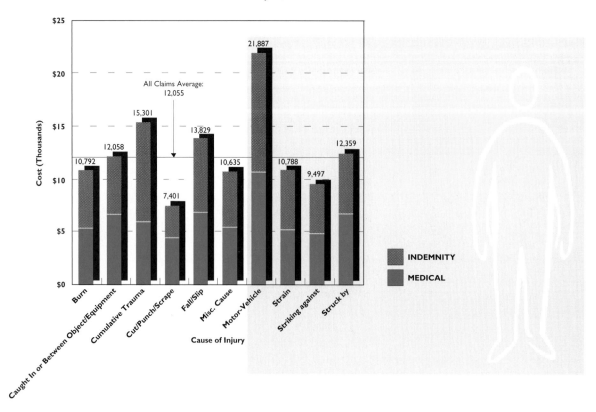

AVERAGE TOTAL INCURRED COSTS PER CLAIM BY NATURE OF INJURY, 1999–2000

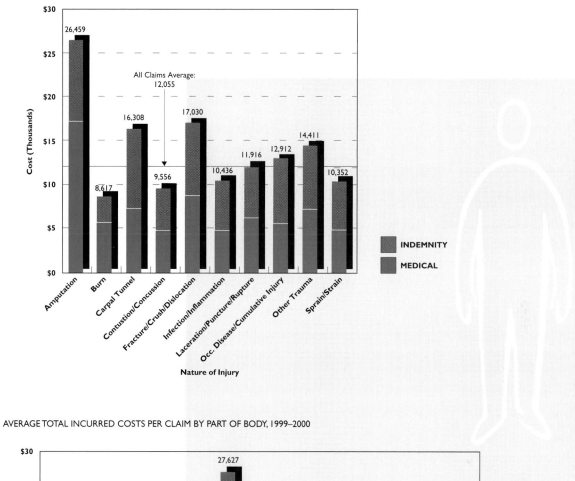

AVERAGE TOTAL INCURRED COSTS PER CLAIM BY PART OF BODY, 1999–2000

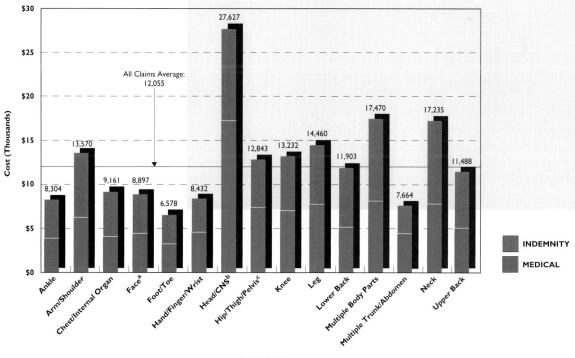

^aIncludes teeth, mouth, and eyes.
^bCentral nervous system.
^cIncludes sacrum and coccyx.

FORKLIFTS

Fatal occupational injuries with forklift as the primary source of injury numbered 75 in 1997, increased to 90 in 1998, and increased yet again to 105 in 1999 before falling slightly to 96 in 2000. The table below shows the percent distribution of forklift fatalities with forklift as the primary and secondary source of injury by industry division for the period 1997-2000. Forklift fatalities are most prevalent in the manufacturing industry, accounting for nearly one-third of the total forklift fatalities. The construction industry accounted for the next highest portion of forklift fatalities, followed by transportation and public utilities.

The number of nonfatal forklift injuries involving days away from work averaged 18,399 over the seven-year period from 1994-2000, exhibiting a generally downward trend with moderate increases in 1997 and 2000. As with the fatal forklift injuries just described, manufacturing had the highest number of nonfatal forklift injuries. Wholesale trade had the second-highest number of nonfatal injuries, followed by transportation and public utilities.

FATAL OCCUPATIONAL INJURIES WITH FORKLIFT AS THE SOURCE OF INJURY, BY INDUSTRY DIVISION, UNITED STATES, 1997–2000

| Industry Division | Year | | | | | | | |
| | 1997 | | 1998 | | 1999 | | 2000 | |
	Forklift as Primary[a] Source	Forklift as Secondary[b] Source	Forklift as Primary[a] Source	Forklift as Secondary[b] Source	Forklift as Primary[a] Source	Forklift as Secondary[b] Source	Forklift as Primary[a] Source	Forklift as Secondary[b] Source
Total	**100.0%**	**100.0%**	**100.0%**	**100.0%**	**100.0%**	**100.0%**	**100.0%**	**100.0%**
Agriculture, forestry, and fishing[c]	5.3	8.1	4.4	—	6.7	—	—	—
Mining	—	—	—	—	—	—	—	—
Construction	16.0	16.2	17.8	33.3	13.3	22.2	9.4	16.1
Manufacturing	32.0	27.0	28.9	28.2	33.3	37.8	38.5	28.6
Transportation and public utilities	17.3	21.6	16.7	7.7	13.3	15.6	16.7	19.6
Wholesale trade	10.7	13.5	7.8	10.3	11.4	—	15.6	10.7
Retail trade	6.7	—	7.8	12.8	6.7	—	5.2	14.3
Finance, insurance, and real estate	—	—	—	—	—	—	—	—
Services	5.3	—	11.1	—	9.5	—	8.3	—

Source: Bureau of Labor Statistics (**www.bls.gov**).
Percentages may not add to totals because of rounding. Dashes (—) indicate no data reported or data that do not meet publication guidelines.
[a] The primary source of injury identifies the object, substance, or exposure that directly produced or inflicted the injury. For transportation incidents, the source identifies the vehicle in which the deceased was an occupant.
[b] The secondary source of injury, if any, identifies the object, substance, or person that generated the source of injury or that contributed to the event or exposure. For vehicle collisions, the deceased's vehicle is the primary source and the other object (truck, road, divider, etc.) is the secondary source.
[c] Excludes farms with fewer than 11 employees.

NUMBER OF NONFATAL OCCUPATIONAL INJURIES INVOLVING DAYS AWAY FROM WORK[a] WITH FORKLIFT AS THE SOURCE OF INJURY, BY INDUSTRY DIVISION, UNITED STATES, 1994–2000

| Industry Division | All Sources | Forklift Injuries | | | | | | |
	2000	1994	1995	1996	1997	1998	1999	2000
Total	**1,664,018**	**20,146**	**19,749**	**17,389**	**18,754**	**18,329**	**16,667**	**17,757**
Agriculture, forestry, and fishing[b]	37,256	296	200	258	412	297	269	232
Mining	14,084	22	32	25	18	90	26	22
Construction	194,410	832	889	687	969	1,183	1,322	1,565
Manufacturing	376,574	7,437	6,821	6,444	6,619	6,436	5,924	5,811
Transportation and public utilities	207,037	3,241	3,585	2,441	3,303	2,596	2,978	3,176
Wholesale trade	125,554	4,751	4,684	3,099	3,309	3,848	3,582	3,804
Retail trade	281,253	2,392	2,489	2,711	3,256	2,999	1,877	2,706
Finance, insurance, and real estate	39,549	48	37	83	124	42	99	—
Services	388,300	1,127	1,013	1,641	745	839	591	429

Source: Bureau of Labor Statistics (2002). Occupational Injuries and Illnesses in the United States—Profiles Data 1992–2000. (CD-ROM, National and Boston, Philadelphia, and Chicago Regions, Version 8.0).
Because of rounding and data exclusion of nonclassifiable reponses, data may not sum to total. Dashes (—) indicate no data reported or data that do not meet publication guidelines.
[a] Days away from work include those that result in days away from work with or without restricted work activity.
[b] Excludes farms with fewer than 11 employees.

According to the Bureau of Labor Statistics, the back was the body part most frequently affected in injuries involving days away from work in 2000, accounting for about a quarter of the total 1,664,018 injuries in private industry. Multiple-part injuries were the second most common, followed by finger, knee, and head injuries. Overall, the service and manufacturing industries had the highest number of injuries, combining to make up nearly 46% of the total.

NUMBER OF NONFATAL OCCUPATIONAL INJURIES INVOLVING DAYS AWAY FROM WORK[a] BY PART OF BODY AFFECTED AND INDUSTRY DIVISION, PRIVATE INDUSTRY, UNITED STATES, 2000

Part of Body Affected	Private Industry[b]	Goods Producing				Service Producing				
		Agri-culture[b, c]	Mining[c]	Construc-tion	Manufac-turing	Trans. & Public Utilities	Wholesale Trade	Retail Trade	Finance, Insurance, & Real Estate	Services
Total[d]	**1,664,018**	**37,256**	**14,084**	**194,410**	**376,574**	**207,037**	**125,554**	**281,253**	**39,549**	**388,300**
Head	110,251	3,189	1,168	15,090	28,391	12,453	7,833	17,631	2,369	22,127
Eye	*53,816*	*1,484*	*266*	*8,136*	*18,020*	*4,501*	*3,799*	*7,108*	*918*	*9,584*
Neck	28,615	450	259	2,401	5,643	5,555	2,021	3,996	693	7,597
Trunk	618,307	10,917	5,521	67,123	131,069	82,264	50,593	96,625	12,538	161,657
Shoulder	*96,118*	*1,549*	*528*	*10,487*	*23,906*	*13,793*	*7,141*	*14,873*	*2,215*	*21,627*
Back	*411,143*	*7,125*	*3,240*	*42,695*	*79,385*	*54,417*	*34,641*	*64,550*	*8,601*	*116,489*
Upper extremities	382,735	10,299	3,006	44,499	115,520	33,213	27,090	71,834	9,581	67,694
Wrist	*85,192*	*1,597*	*477*	*6,945*	*24,602*	*8,351*	*6,356*	*14,481*	*4,102*	*18,281*
Hand, except finger	*69,464*	*2,228*	*538*	*10,325*	*19,668*	*5,440*	*5,103*	*14,633*	*1,228*	*10,302*
Finger	*138,325*	*4,211*	*1,235*	*16,253*	*48,184*	*9,265*	*9,135*	*27,370*	*2,011*	*20,662*
Lower extremities	347,742	8,790	3,040	46,363	66,127	49,587	26,446	60,913	8,148	78,328
Knee	*130,063*	*2,758*	*1,158*	*17,937*	*23,909*	*19,129*	*7,989*	*22,601*	*2,271*	*32,311*
Foot, except toe	*58,104*	*1,909*	*569*	*8,131*	*12,665*	*6,950*	*5,287*	*11,760*	*1,362*	*9,471*
Toe	*18,240*	*325*	*71*	*2,599*	*4,156*	*2,272*	*1,729*	*3,746*	*540*	*2,802*
Body systems	20,986	488	66	1,395	4,469	2,721	1,241	2,551	1,607	6,448
Multiple parts	145,558	2,893	998	15,805	23,597	19,897	9,836	26,533	4,328	41,672

Source: Bureau of Labor Statistics (2002). Occupational Injuries and Illnesses in the United States—Profiles Data 1992–2000, *CD-ROM Disk 1 (National and Boston, Philadelphia, and Chicago Regions), Version 8.0.*
[a]*Days-away-from-work cases include those that result in days away from work with or without restricted work activity.*
[b]*Excludes farms with less than 11 employees.*
[c]*Agriculture includes forestry and fishing; mining includes quarrying and oil and gas extraction.*
[d]*Data may not sum to column totals because of rounding and exclusion of nonclassifiable responses.*

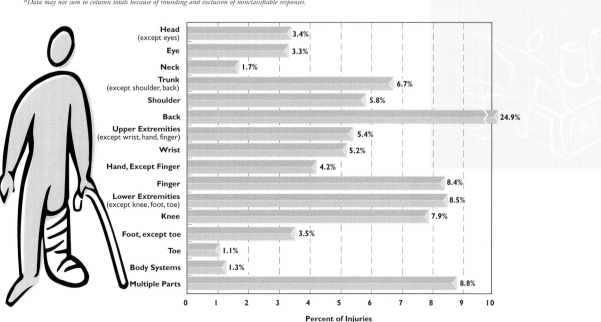

Head (except eyes) 3.4%
Eye 3.3%
Neck 1.7%
Trunk (except shoulder, back) 6.7%
Shoulder 5.8%
Back 24.9%
Upper Extremities (except wrist, hand, finger) 5.4%
Wrist 5.2%
Hand, Except Finger 4.2%
Finger 8.4%
Lower Extremities (except knee, foot, toe) 8.5%
Knee 7.9%
Foot, except toe 3.5%
Toe 1.1%
Body Systems 1.3%
Multiple Parts 8.8%

Percent of Injuries

BENCHMARKING

Safety professionals in business and industry often want to compare, or benchmark, the occupational injury and illness incidence rates of their establishments with a national average. The only national averages available are the incidence rates compiled by the U.S. Bureau of Labor Statistics (BLS) through its annual Survey of Occupational Injuries and Illnesses.[a] The incidence rates published on the following pages and available on the BLS Internet site are for 2000 or earlier years and as such were compiled under the OSHA record-keeping requirements in effect at the time. Incidence rates compiled under the revised OSHA record-keeping requirements that went into effect in 2002 will not be published until December 2003.

Step 1.

The first step in benchmarking is to calculate the incidence rates for the establishment. The basic formula for computing incidence rates is $(N \times 200,000)/EH$, where N is the number of cases, EH is the number of hours worked by all employees during the time period, and $200,000$ is the base for 100 full-time workers (working 40 hours per week, 50 weeks per year). Because the BLS rates are based on reports from entire establishments, both the OSHA 200 Log and the number of employee hours (EH) should cover the whole establishment being benchmarked. In addition, both the hours worked and the log should cover the same time period (e.g., a month, quarter, or full year).

There are four rates that are most often benchmarked.

(a) Total Cases—defined as the incidence rate of total OSHA-recordable cases per 200,000 hours worked. For this rate, N is the count of the number of cases with check marks in columns 2, 6, 9, and 13 of the OSHA 200 Log.

(b) Total Lost Workday Cases—defined as the incidence rate of cases with either days away from work, days of restricted work activity, or both. For this rate, N is the count of cases with entries in columns 2 and 9 of the OSHA 200 Log.

(c) Cases with Days away from Work—defined as the incidence rate of cases with days away from work (with or without days of restricted activity). For this rate, N is the count of cases with entries in columns 3 and 10 of the OSHA 200 Log.

(d) Cases Without Lost Workdays—defined as the incidence rate of cases with neither days away from work nor days of restricted work activity. For this rate, N is the count of cases with entries in columns 6 and 13 of the OSHA 200 Log.

Step 2.

After computing one or more of the rates, the next step is to determine the Standard Industrial Classification (SIC) code for the establishment.[b] This code is used to find the appropriate BLS rate for comparison. A convenient way to find SIC codes is to use the search feature on the OSHA Internet site (http://www.osha.gov/oshstats/sicser.html).

Otherwise, call a regional BLS office for assistance.

Step 3.

Once the SIC code is known, the comparable BLS rates may be found by (a) consulting the table of rates on pages 62–64, (b) visiting the BLS Internet site (http://www.bls.gov/iif/), or (c) by calling a regional BLS office. Note that some tables on the Internet site provide incidence rates by size of establishment and rate quartiles within each SIC code. Quartiles divide the reporting establishments into four equal parts. One fourth of the establishments had rates lower than the first quartile rate; one fourth had rates between the first quartile and the median; one fourth had rates between the median and the third quartile; and one fourth had rates greater than the third quartile.

An alternative way of benchmarking is to compare the current incidence rates for an establishment to its own prior historical rates to determine if the rates are improving and if progress is satisfactory (using criteria set by the organization).

[a]Bureau of Labor Statistics. (1997). BLS Handbook of Methods. Washington, DC: U.S. Government Printing Office. (http://www.bls.gov/opub/hom/home.htm). (Note: In 2001, the National Safety Council substantially changed the nature of the award program through which rates were compiled in previous years. Such rates are no longer available from the Council.)
[b]Executive Office of the President, Office of Management and Budget. (1987). Standard Industrial Classification Manual. Springfield, VA: National Technical Information Service.

BENCHMARKING FLOW CHART

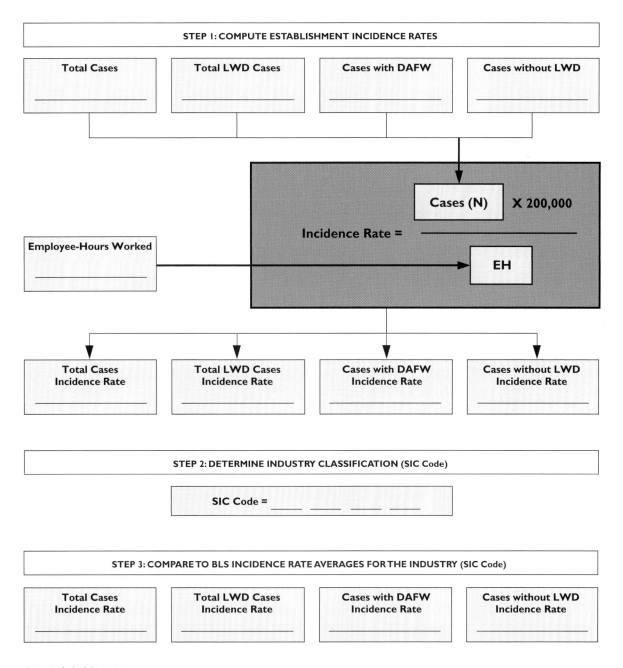

STEP 1: COMPUTE ESTABLISHMENT INCIDENCE RATES

Total Cases	Total LWD Cases	Cases with DAFW	Cases without LWD
_____	_____	_____	_____

$$\text{Incidence Rate} = \frac{\text{Cases (N)} \quad X\ 200,000}{\text{EH}}$$

Employee-Hours Worked

_____

Total Cases Incidence Rate	Total LWD Cases Incidence Rate	Cases with DAFW Incidence Rate	Cases without LWD Incidence Rate
_____	_____	_____	_____

STEP 2: DETERMINE INDUSTRY CLASSIFICATION (SIC Code)

SIC Code = _____ _____ _____ _____

STEP 3: COMPARE TO BLS INCIDENCE RATE AVERAGES FOR THE INDUSTRY (SIC Code)

Total Cases Incidence Rate	Total LWD Cases Incidence Rate	Cases with DAFW Incidence Rate	Cases without LWD Incidence Rate
_____	_____	_____	_____

See page 58 for detailed instructions.
LWD = Lost Workday
DAFW = Days Away From Work

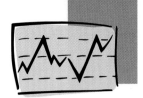

TRENDS IN OCCUPATIONAL INCIDENCE RATES

Three of the four occupational injury and illness incidence rates published by the Bureau of Labor Statistics for 2000 decreased from 1999, while the other remained unchanged. The incidence rate for total nonfatal cases was 6.1 per 100 full-time workers in 2000, down 3% from the 1999 rate of 6.3. The incidence rate for lost workday cases with days away from work was 1.8 in 2000, down 5% from 1.9 in 1999. The incidence rate in 2000 for nonfatal cases without lost workdays was 3.2, a decrease of 3% from the 1999 rate of 3.3. The 2000 incidence rate for total lost workday cases was 3.0, unchanged from 1999.

Beginning with 1992 data, the Bureau of Labor Statistics revised its annual survey to include only nonfatal cases and stopped publishing the incidence rate of lost workdays.

OCCUPATIONAL INJURY AND ILLNESS INCIDENCE RATES, BUREAU OF LABOR STATISTICS, UNITED STATES, 1973–2000

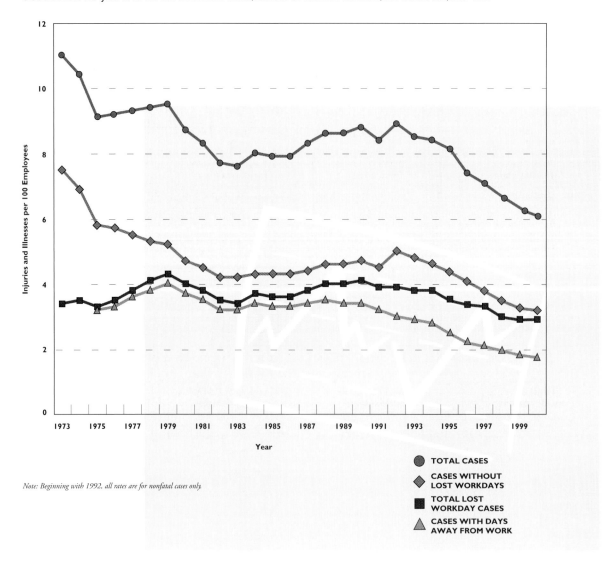

Note: Beginning with 1992, all rates are for nonfatal cases only.

OCCUPATIONAL INJURIES AND ILLNESSES

The tables below and on pages 62-64 present the results of the 2000 Survey of Occupational Injuries and Illnesses conducted by the Bureau of Labor Statistics (BLS), U.S. Department of Labor. The survey collects data on injuries and illnesses (from the OSHA 200 Log) and employee-hours worked from a nationwide sample of about 176,000 establishments representing the private sector of the economy. The survey excludes public employees, private households, the self-employed, and farms with fewer than 11 employees. The incidence rates give the number of cases per 100 full-time workers per year using 200,000 employee-hours as the equivalent. Definitions of the terms are given in the Glossary on page 173.

Beginning with 1992 data, the BLS revised its annual survey to include only nonfatal cases and stopped publishing incidence rates of lost workdays.

BLS ESTIMATES OF NONFATAL OCCUPATIONAL INJURY AND ILLNESS INCIDENCE RATES BY INDUSTRY DIVISION, 1999-2000

	Incidence Rates[c]							
		Lost Workday Cases						
	Total Cases		Total		With Days Away from Work		Cases Without Lost Workdays	
Industry Division	2000	1999	2000	1999	2000	1999	2000	1999
Private Sector[d]	**6.1**	**6.3**	**3.0**	**3.0**	**1.8**	**1.9**	**3.2**	**3.3**
Agriculture, forestry, and fishing[d]	7.1	7.3	3.6	3.4	2.5	2.4	3.5	3.9
Mining	4.7	4.4	3.0	2.7	2.4	2.0	1.7	1.7
Construction	8.3	8.6	4.1	4.2	3.2	3.3	4.2	4.4
Manufacturing	9.0	9.2	4.5	4.6	2.0	2.2	4.5	4.6
Transportation and public utilities	6.9	7.3	4.3	4.4	3.1	3.1	2.6	2.8
Wholesale and retail trade	5.9	6.1	2.7	2.7	1.7	1.8	3.3	3.4
Finance, insurance, and real estate	1.9	1.8	0.8	0.8	0.6	0.6	1.1	1.1
Services	4.9	4.9	2.2	2.2	1.4	1.5	2.6	2.6

Source: Bureau of Labor Statistics.

[a] *Industry Division and 2- and 3-digit SIC code totals on pages 62–64 include data for industries not shown separately.*

[b] Standard Industrial Classification Manual, 1987 Edition, *for industries shown on pages 62–64.*

[c] *Incidence Rate =* $\dfrac{\text{Number of injuries \& illnesses} \times 200{,}000}{\text{Total hours worked by all employees during period covered}}$

where 200,000 is the base for 100 full-time workers (working 40 hours per week, 50 weeks per year). The "Total Cases" rate is based on the number of cases with check marks in columns 2, 6, 9, and 13 of the OSHA 200 Log. The "Total Lost Workday Cases" rate is based on columns 2 and 9. The "Lost Workday Cases With Days Away From Work" rate is based on columns 3 and 10. The "Cases Without Lost Workdays" rate is based on columns 6 and 13.

[d] *Excludes farms with less than 11 employees.*

BLS ESTIMATES OF NONFATAL OCCUPATIONAL INJURY AND ILLNESS INCIDENCE RATES FOR SELECTED INDUSTRIES, 2000

| Industry[a] | SIC Code[b] | Incidence Rates[c] | | | |
| | | | Lost Workday Cases | | |
		Total Cases	Total	With Days Away from Work	Cases Without Lost Workdays
PRIVATE SECTOR[d]	—	**6.1**	**3.0**	**1.8**	**3.2**
Agriculture, Forestry, and Fishing[d]	—	**7.1**	**3.6**	**2.5**	**3.5**
Agricultural production	01-02	7.6	4.1	2.7	3.5
Agricultural services	07	6.8	3.3	2.3	3.5
Forestry	08	8.8	3.8	3.2	4.9
Mining	—	**4.7**	**3.0**	**2.4**	**1.7**
Metal mining	10	4.9	2.7	1.5	2.2
Coal mining	12	7.5	5.6	5.3	2.0
Oil and gas extraction	13	4.2	2.6	2.1	1.7
Crude petroleum and natural gas	131	1.7	0.7	0.6	1.0
Oil and gas field services	138	5.8	3.7	3.0	2.1
Nonmetallic minerals, except fuels	14	4.3	2.9	2.0	1.5
Construction	—	**8.3**	**4.1**	**3.2**	**4.2**
General building contractors	15	7.8	3.9	3.1	3.9
Residential building construction	152	7.1	3.7	3.2	3.4
Nonresidential building construction	154	8.8	4.1	3.0	4.6
Heavy construction, except building	16	7.6	3.7	2.7	3.9
Highway and street construction	161	8.2	3.9	2.9	4.3
Heavy construction, except highway	162	7.3	3.6	2.6	3.7
Special trade contractors	17	8.6	4.3	3.4	4.3
Plumbing, heating, air-conditioning	171	9.2	4.1	3.2	5.2
Painting and paper hanging	172	5.2	3.1	2.9	2.1
Electrical work	173	8.3	3.8	2.8	4.5
Masonry, stonework and plastering	174	9.1	4.8	3.9	4.3
Carpentry and floor work	175	9.7	5.2	4.0	4.5
Roofing, siding, and sheet metal work	176	11.0	5.8	4.8	5.2
Miscellaneous special trade contractors	179	7.7	4.0	3.2	3.7
Manufacturing	—	**9.0**	**4.5**	**2.0**	**4.5**
Durable goods	—	9.8	4.7	2.2	5.1
Lumber and wood products	24	12.1	6.1	3.3	6.0
Logging	241	9.3	4.6	3.1	4.7
Sawmills and planing mills	242	11.1	5.6	3.7	5.6
Millwork, plywood and structural members	243	12.1	6.2	3.1	5.9
Wood containers	244	13.3	6.7	4.7	6.7
Wood buildings and mobile homes	245	18.5	8.9	3.7	9.6
Furniture and fixtures	25	11.2	5.9	2.6	5.3
Household furniture	251	10.6	5.4	2.7	5.2
Office furniture	252	11.3	5.4	2.1	5.9
Public building and related furniture	253	15.8	9.5	3.0	6.3
Stone, clay, and glass products	32	10.4	5.5	2.9	4.9
Flat glass	321	15.2	6.2	2.4	9.0
Glass and glassware, pressed or blown	322	9.0	4.6	2.0	4.3
Products of purchased glass	323	10.4	5.0	2.1	5.3
Structural clay products	325	11.5	5.9	2.9	5.7
Concrete, gypsum, and plaster products	327	10.9	6.1	3.6	4.8
Miscellaneous nonmetallic mineral products	329	8.5	4.2	2.3	4.3
Primary metal industries	33	12.6	6.3	2.9	6.3
Blast furnace and basic steel products	331	9.2	4.5	2.2	4.7
Iron and steel foundries	332	21.0	9.2	4.0	11.8
Primary nonferrous metals	333	13.3	6.5	1.7	6.8
Nonferrous rolling and drawing	335	9.3	5.3	2.4	3.9
Nonferrous foundries (castings)	336	16.5	8.5	4.1	7.9
Fabricated metal products	34	11.9	5.5	2.8	6.4
Metal cans and shipping containers	341	8.9	3.4	1.3	5.6
Cutlery, hand tools, and hardware	342	10.1	5.0	2.6	5.1
Plumbing and heating, except electric	343	9.7	4.1	1.6	5.6
Fabricated structural metal products	344	13.3	5.9	3.3	7.4
Screw machine products, bolts, etc.	345	10.9	4.9	2.6	6.0
Metal forgings and stampings	346	14.0	6.8	2.9	7.2
Metal services, n.e.c.	347	11.2	5.8	2.6	5.4
Ordnance and accessories, n.e.c.	348	5.4	2.7	1.7	2.7
Miscellaneous fabricated metal products	349	10.8	5.0	2.4	5.7
Industrial machinery and equipment	35	8.2	3.6	1.8	4.6
Engines and turbines	351	7.5	3.3	1.7	4.2
Farm and garden machinery	352	9.4	4.3	2.3	5.1
Construction and related machinery	353	10.4	4.7	2.7	5.7
Metalworking machinery	354	9.0	3.9	1.8	5.1
Special industry machinery	355	7.8	3.3	1.8	4.5
General industrial machinery	356	9.2	4.0	2.1	5.2
Computer and office equipment	357	2.2	0.9	0.4	1.2
Refrigeration and service machinery	358	11.6	5.7	2.4	6.0

See source and footnotes on page 61.
n.e.c. = not elsewhere classified.

BLS ESTIMATES OF NONFATAL OCCUPATIONAL INJURY AND ILLNESS INCIDENCE RATES FOR SELECTED INDUSTRIES, 2000, Cont.

| Industry[a] | SIC Code[b] | Total Cases | Lost Workday Cases | | Cases Without Lost Workdays |
			Total	With Days Away from Work	
Industrial machinery, n.e.c.	359	8.9	3.6	2.2	5.4
Electronic and other electric equipment	36	5.7	2.9	1.2	2.7
Electric distribution equipment	361	9.1	5.0	2.0	4.2
Electrical industrial apparatus	362	6.5	3.0	1.2	3.5
Household appliances	363	10.9	5.2	1.8	5.7
Electric lighting and wiring equipment	364	7.7	4.0	1.6	3.8
Communications equipment	366	3.0	1.8	0.7	1.2
Electronic components and accessories	367	3.8	1.8	0.9	2.0
Misc. electrical equipment and supplies	369	8.6	4.5	1.4	4.1
Transportation equipment	37	13.7	6.3	2.5	7.5
Motor vehicles and equipment	371	16.8	7.4	2.8	9.4
Aircraft and parts	372	7.1	3.4	1.5	3.7
Ship and boat building and repairing	373	19.9	9.9	4.6	9.9
Railroad equipment	374	8.1	4.1	2.1	4.0
Motorcycles, bicycles, and parts	375	11.5	4.0	2.0	7.5
Guided missiles, space vehicles, parts	376	2.2	1.1	0.5	1.1
Instruments and related products	38	4.5	2.2	0.9	2.3
Search and navigation equipment	381	2.8	1.2	0.5	1.6
Measuring and controlling devices	382	4.4	2.1	1.0	2.3
Medical instruments and supplies	384	5.1	2.7	1.1	2.4
Ophthalmic goods	385	4.8	2.6	1.4	2.2
Miscellaneous manufacturing industries	39	7.2	3.6	1.8	3.6
Musical instruments	393	8.5	4.0	1.9	4.5
Toys and sporting goods	394	9.9	5.2	2.2	4.8
Pens, pencils, office, and art supplies	395	5.9	3.3	2.1	2.6
Costume jewelry and notions	396	4.1	2.5	1.5	1.6
Nondurable goods	—	7.8	4.2	1.8	3.5
Food and kindred products	20	12.4	7.3	2.7	5.0
Meat products	201	17.4	10.4	2.1	7.0
Dairy products	202	11.3	7.1	4.1	4.2
Preserved fruits and vegetables	203	8.8	5.1	2.4	3.7
Grain mill products	204	8.1	4.3	2.6	3.9
Bakery products	205	11.4	6.9	2.7	4.5
Sugar and confectionery products	206	10.0	4.7	1.8	5.4
Fats and oils	207	11.1	6.3	3.9	4.8
Beverages	208	11.0	6.7	3.1	4.3
Miscellaneous foods and kindred products	209	9.9	6.3	3.3	3.6
Tobacco products	21	6.2	3.1	1.8	3.1
Textile mill products	22	6.0	3.2	1.0	2.8
Broadwoven fabric mills, cotton	221	4.7	2.5	0.4	2.2
Broadwoven fabric mills, manmade	222	5.3	3.3	0.6	2.0
Narrow fabric mills	224	8.9	3.1	1.7	5.8
Knitting mills	225	5.3	3.1	1.0	2.2
Textile finishing, except wool	226	7.3	4.1	2.2	3.2
Carpets and rugs	227	4.8	2.4	0.5	2.4
Yarn and thread mills	228	5.9	2.7	0.6	3.2
Miscellaneous textile goods	229	8.5	4.3	2.0	4.2
Apparel and other textile products	23	6.1	3.0	1.3	3.1
Men's and boys' suits and coats	231	9.4	2.9	2.2	6.4
Men's and boys' furnishings	232	6.9	3.7	1.7	3.2
Women's and misses' outerwear	233	2.2	1.0	0.6	1.2
Women's and children's undergarments	234	5.5	2.8	0.9	2.8
Hats, caps, and millinery	235	6.7	3.6	2.5	3.1
Girls' and children's outerwear	236	6.5	1.8	1.3	4.7
Miscellaneous fabricated textile products	239	9.0	4.5	1.5	4.4
Paper and allied products	26	6.5	3.4	1.7	3.1
Paper mills	262	5.4	2.8	1.5	2.6
Paperboard mills	263	3.9	1.9	1.1	2.0
Paperboard containers and boxes	265	7.4	3.9	2.0	3.6
Printing and publishing	27	5.1	2.6	1.5	2.5
Newspapers	271	5.2	2.6	1.8	2.6
Periodicals	272	2.7	1.2	0.7	1.5
Books	273	5.0	2.7	1.2	2.3
Commercial printing	275	5.9	3.0	1.7	2.8
Manifold business forms	276	5.7	2.9	1.6	2.7
Blankbooks and bookbinding	278	6.7	4.0	2.3	2.7
Chemicals and allied products	28	4.2	2.2	1.0	2.0
Industrial inorganic chemicals	281	4.2	1.9	0.9	2.3
Plastics materials and synthetics	282	4.0	2.3	1.2	1.7
Drugs	283	4.0	2.1	1.0	2.0
Soap, cleaners, and toilet goods	284	5.0	2.6	1.3	2.4
Paints and allied products	285	6.3	3.3	1.2	3.0
Industrial organic chemicals	286	3.0	1.6	0.7	1.3
Agricultural chemicals	287	4.2	2.0	0.9	2.2

See source and footnotes on page 61.
n.e.c. = not elsewhere classified.

BLS ESTIMATES OF NONFATAL OCCUPATIONAL INJURY AND ILLNESS INCIDENCE RATES FOR SELECTED INDUSTRIES, 2000, Cont.

Industry[a]	SIC Code[b]	Total Cases	Incidence Rates[c]		Cases Without Lost Workdays
			Lost Workday Cases		
			Total	With Days Away from Work	
Miscellaneous chemical products	289	4.3	2.2	1.0	2.1
Petroleum and coal products	29	3.7	1.9	1.1	1.8
Asphalt paving and roofing materials	295	8.3	4.2	2.6	4.1
Miscellaneous petroleum and coal products	299	4.1	1.8	1.0	2.3
Rubber and miscellaneous plastics products	30	10.7	5.8	2.7	4.9
Tires and inner tubes	301	12.2	7.8	3.1	4.3
Hose and belting and gaskets and packing	305	8.4	4.7	2.3	3.7
Fabricated rubber products, n.e.c.	306	12.9	7.7	3.5	5.2
Miscellaneous plastic products, n.e.c.	308	10.5	5.4	2.5	5.1
Leather and leather products	31	9.0	4.3	2.1	4.7
Leather tanning and finishing	311	16.5	9.0	4.1	7.5
Footwear, except rubber	314	8.4	3.3	1.5	5.1
Transportation and Public Utilities	—	**6.9**	**4.3**	**3.1**	**2.6**
Railroad transportation	40	3.6	2.8	2.4	0.8
Local and interurban passenger transit	41	8.0	4.4	3.4	3.6
Local and suburban transportation	411	10.2	6.0	4.5	4.2
School buses	415	6.5	2.8	2.2	3.7
Trucking and warehousing	42	7.9	4.7	3.8	3.2
Trucking & courier services, except air	421	7.8	4.6	3.8	3.2
Public warehousing and storage	422	9.0	5.0	3.0	4.1
Water transportation	44	7.0	4.1	3.6	2.9
Transportation by air	45	13.9	9.4	6.7	4.5
Air transportation, scheduled	451	14.7	10.4	7.4	4.3
Transportation services	47	3.2	2.0	1.2	1.2
Communications	48	2.6	1.6	1.2	1.0
Telephone communications	481	2.4	1.6	1.2	0.8
Cable and other pay television services	484	4.7	2.7	1.6	2.0
Electric, gas, and sanitary services	49	6.3	3.4	1.9	2.8
Electric services	491	4.8	2.4	1.2	2.4
Gas production and distribution	492	6.1	3.1	1.6	3.0
Combination utility services	493	4.2	2.2	1.3	2.0
Sanitary services	495	10.5	6.3	3.6	4.2
Wholesale and Retail Trade	—	**5.9**	**2.7**	**1.7**	**3.3**
Wholesale trade	—	5.8	3.1	1.9	2.7
Wholesale trade-durable goods	50	5.1	2.5	1.5	2.6
Lumber and construction materials	503	9.1	4.9	2.8	4.3
Electrical goods	506	2.8	1.5	0.9	1.4
Machinery, equipment, and supplies	508	5.5	2.4	1.7	3.1
Wholesale trade-nondurable goods	51	6.9	4.0	2.4	3.0
Groceries and related products	514	9.6	6.0	3.4	3.6
Petroleum and petroleum products	517	3.6	2.0	1.5	1.6
Retail trade	—	5.9	2.5	1.6	3.4
Building materials and garden supplies	52	8.2	4.1	2.3	4.1
General merchandise stores	53	8.2	4.3	2.3	3.9
Food stores	54	8.0	3.7	2.3	4.4
Automotive dealers and service stations	55	5.6	2.1	1.6	3.5
Apparel and accessory stores	56	3.7	1.6	1.0	2.1
Home furniture, furnishings, and equipment	57	4.7	2.2	1.5	2.6
Eating and drinking places	58	5.3	1.7	1.3	3.6
Miscellaneous retail	59	3.9	1.7	1.1	2.1
Finance, Insurance, and Real Estate	—	**1.9**	**0.8**	**0.6**	**1.1**
Depository institutions	60	1.4	0.5	0.4	0.9
Insurance agents, brokers, and service	64	1.0	0.4	0.3	0.6
Real estate	65	4.1	2.0	1.4	2.1
Services	—	**4.9**	**2.2**	**1.4**	**2.6**
Hotels and other lodging places	70	6.9	3.3	1.9	3.6
Personal services	72	3.3	1.6	0.9	1.7
Business services	73	3.2	1.5	1.0	1.7
Services to buildings	734	7.0	3.2	2.1	3.8
Auto repair, services, and parking	75	5.0	2.2	1.7	2.9
Miscellaneous repair services	76	4.9	2.5	1.8	2.4
Amusement and recreation services	79	6.9	3.3	1.8	3.7
Health services	80	7.4	3.5	2.1	3.9
Nursing and personal care facilities	805	13.9	7.9	4.2	6.0
Hospitals	806	9.1	4.1	2.5	5.0
Legal services	81	0.7	0.3	0.2	0.5
Educational services	82	3.2	1.1	0.8	2.1
Social services	83	6.1	2.8	1.9	3.2
Child day care services	835	2.7	1.3	1.1	1.4
Engineering and management services	87	1.7	0.7	0.5	1.0

See source and footnotes on page 61.
n.e.c. = not elsewhere classified.

BLS ESTIMATES OF NONFATAL OCCUPATIONAL INJURY AND ILLNESS INCIDENCE RATES FOR SELECTED INDUSTRIES, 2000

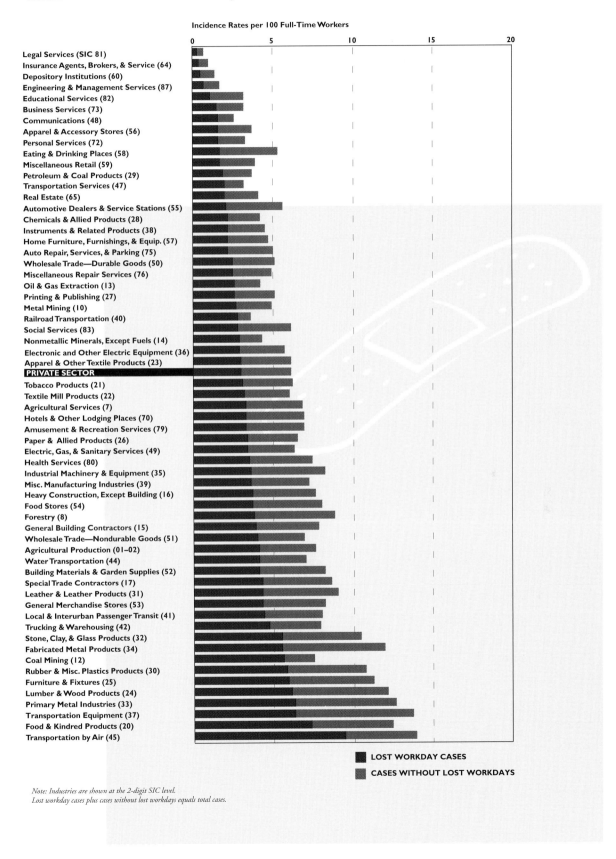

Incidence Rates per 100 Full-Time Workers

Legal Services (SIC 81)
Insurance Agents, Brokers, & Service (64)
Depository Institutions (60)
Engineering & Management Services (87)
Educational Services (82)
Business Services (73)
Communications (48)
Apparel & Accessory Stores (56)
Personal Services (72)
Eating & Drinking Places (58)
Miscellaneous Retail (59)
Petroleum & Coal Products (29)
Transportation Services (47)
Real Estate (65)
Automotive Dealers & Service Stations (55)
Chemicals & Allied Products (28)
Instruments & Related Products (38)
Home Furniture, Furnishings, & Equip. (57)
Auto Repair, Services, & Parking (75)
Wholesale Trade—Durable Goods (50)
Miscellaneous Repair Services (76)
Oil & Gas Extraction (13)
Printing & Publishing (27)
Metal Mining (10)
Railroad Transportation (40)
Social Services (83)
Nonmetallic Minerals, Except Fuels (14)
Electronic and Other Electric Equipment (36)
Apparel & Other Textile Products (23)
PRIVATE SECTOR
Tobacco Products (21)
Textile Mill Products (22)
Agricultural Services (7)
Hotels & Other Lodging Places (70)
Amusement & Recreation Services (79)
Paper & Allied Products (26)
Electric, Gas, & Sanitary Services (49)
Health Services (80)
Industrial Machinery & Equipment (35)
Misc. Manufacturing Industries (39)
Heavy Construction, Except Building (16)
Food Stores (54)
Forestry (8)
General Building Contractors (15)
Wholesale Trade—Nondurable Goods (51)
Agricultural Production (01–02)
Water Transportation (44)
Building Materials & Garden Supplies (52)
Special Trade Contractors (17)
Leather & Leather Products (31)
General Merchandise Stores (53)
Local & Interurban Passenger Transit (41)
Trucking & Warehousing (42)
Stone, Clay, & Glass Products (32)
Fabricated Metal Products (34)
Coal Mining (12)
Rubber & Misc. Plastics Products (30)
Furniture & Fixtures (25)
Lumber & Wood Products (24)
Primary Metal Industries (33)
Transportation Equipment (37)
Food & Kindred Products (20)
Transportation by Air (45)

■ LOST WORKDAY CASES
■ CASES WITHOUT LOST WORKDAYS

Note: Industries are shown at the 2-digit SIC level.
Lost workday cases plus cases without lost workdays equals total cases.

FATAL OCCUPATIONAL INJURIES AND NONFATAL INJURIES AND ILLNESSES BY INDUSTRY DIVISION

The tables on pages 67 through 77 present data on the characteristics of injured and ill workers and the injuries and illnesses that affected them. These data indicate how many workers are killed by on-the-job injuries and how many are affected by nonfatal injuries and illnesses. The data may be used to help set priorities for safety and health programs and for benchmarking.

The fatality information covers only deaths due to injuries and comes from the Bureau of Labor Statistics (BLS) Census of Fatal Occupational Injuries. The data are nine-year totals for the calendar years 1992–2000. The nine years were combined because counts for many of the items would be too small to publish if data for a single year were used.

The data on nonfatal cases cover both injuries and illnesses and come from the BLS Survey of Occupational Injuries and Illnesses for the 2000 reference year. The survey also is used to produce the incidence rates shown on the preceding pages. The estimates on the following pages are the number of cases involving days away from work (with or without days of restricted work activity).

Data are presented for the sex, age, occupation, and race or ethnic origin of the worker and for the nature of injury/illness, the part of body affected, the source of injury/illness, and the event or exposure that produced the injury/illness.

The text at the top of each page describes the kind of establishments that are included in the industry division, the number of workers in the industry division for 2000, and the annual average number of workers for the 1992–2000 period.

Page 67 shows nonfatal injury/illness data for the private sector of the economy (excluding government entities) and fatal injury data for all industries (including government). Pages 68 through 76 present the data for private sector industry divisions. Page 77 presents the fatal injury data for the Government industry division. (The BLS Survey does not cover government entities nationwide, so no nonfatal case data are available.)

PRIVATE SECTOR/ALL INDUSTRIES

The nonfatal occupational injury and illness data cover only the private sector of the economy and exclude employees in federal, state, and local government entities. The fatal injury data cover employees in both the private sector and government.

There were 136,402,000 people employed in 2000, of which 116,135,000 worked in the private sector and 20,267,000 in government. Over the nine years from 1992 through 2000, total employment averaged 128,148,000 per year with 108,366,000 in the private sector.

NUMBER OF NONFATAL OCCUPATIONAL INJURIES AND ILLNESSES INVOLVING DAYS AWAY FROM WORK[a] AND FATAL OCCUPATIONAL INJURIES BY SELECTED WORKER AND CASE CHARACTERISTICS, UNITED STATES

Characteristic	Private Industry[b,c] Nonfatal Cases, 2000	All Industries Fatalities, 1992–2000
Total	**1,664,018**	**55,919**
Sex		
Men	1,097,104	51,547
Women	555,722	4,366
Age		
Under 14	—	123
14 to 15	573	120
16 to 19	54,134	1,447
20 to 24	186,336	4,346
25 to 34	430,922	12,314
35 to 44	481,267	13,930
45 to 54	325,808	11,406
55 to 64	142,540	7,483
65 and over	25,335	4,647
Occupation		
Managerial and professional	99,086	6,162
Technical, sales, and administrative support	254,672	6,970
Service	278,121	4,563
Farming, forestry, and fishing	41,542	8,176
Precision production, craft, and repair	298,973	9,843
Operators, fabricators, and laborers	684,355	18,716
Military occupations	N/A	1,026
Race or ethnic origin[d]		
White, non-Hispanic	827,455	41,220
Black, non-Hispanic	139,280	5,695
Hispanic	186,029	5,958
Asian or Pacific Islander	25,857	1,732
American Indian or Alaskan Native	6,955	332
Not reported	478,442	981
Nature of injury, illness		
Sprains, strains	728,202	75
Fractures	116,713	317
Cuts, lacerations, punctures	141,649	8,725
Bruises, contusions	151,680	24
Heat burns	24,298	1,315
Chemical burns	9,395	59
Amputations	9,658	201
Carpal tunnel syndrome	27,697	—
Tendonitis	14,445	—
Multiple injuries	59,231	15,539
Soreness, Pain	118,040	10
Back pain	46,109	8
All other	263,011	29,654

Characteristic	Private Industry[b,c] Nonfatal Cases, 2000	All Industries Fatalities, 1992–2000
Part of body affected		
Head	110,251	13,744
Eye	53,816	6
Neck	28,615	1,148
Trunk	618,307	11,311
Back	411,143	716
Shoulder	96,118	20
Upper extremities	382,735	140
Finger	138,325	14
Hand, except finger	69,464	13
Wrist	85,192	7
Lower extremities	347,742	493
Knee	130,063	63
Foot, toe	76,343	26
Body systems	20,986	9,077
Multiple	145,558	19,569
All other	9,824	437
Source of injury, illness		
Chemicals, chemical products	25,411	1,383
Containers	240,068	755
Furniture, fixtures	56,441	156
Machinery	111,573	4,550
Parts and materials	182,525	3,790
Worker motion or position	258,504	25
Floor, ground surfaces	278,495	5,784
Handtools	74,830	970
Vehicles	138,788	23,758
Health care patient	74,610	14
All other	222,773	14,734
Event or exposure		
Contact with object, equipment	443,614	9,006
Struck by object	224,995	5,095
Struck against object	107,651	131
Caught in object, equipment, material	75,356	3,749
Fall to lower level	95,329	5,380
Fall on same level	198,861	500
Slips, trips	52,794	15
Overexertion	454,720	58
Overexertion in lifting	256,747	35
Repetitive motion	68,323	—
Exposed to harmful substance	69,059	5,123
Transportation accidents	73,014	23,372
Fires, explosions	3,656	1,760
Assault, violent act	23,506	10,287
by person	18,418	8,063
by other	5,087	2,224
All other	181,144	418

Source: National Safety Council tabulations of Bureau of Labor Statistics data.
Note: Because of rounding and data exclusion of nonclassifiable responses, data may not sum to the totals. Dashes (—) indicate data that do not meet publication guidelines. "N/A" means not applicable.
[a] *Days away from work include those that result in days away from work with or without restricted work activity.*
[b] *Excludes farms with fewer than 11 employees.*

[c] *Data conforming to OSHA definitions for mining operators in coal, metal, and nonmetal mining and for employees in railroad transportation are provided to BLS by the Mine Safety and Health Administration, U.S. Department of Labor; and the Federal Railroad Administration, U.S. Department of Transportation. Independent mining contractors are excluded from the coal, metal, and nonmetal mining industries.*
[d] *In the fatalities column, non-Hispanic categories include cases with Hispanic origin not reported.*

AGRICULTURE, FORESTRY, AND FISHING

The Agriculture, Forestry, and Fishing industry division includes production of crops and livestock, animal specialties, agricultural services, forestry (but excluding logging which is in the Manufacturing industry division), and commercial fishing, hunting, and trapping.

Employment in Agriculture, Forestry, and Fishing totaled 3,338,000 in 2000 and averaged 3,405,000 per year from 1992 through 2000. It is the second smallest industry division after Mining.

NUMBER OF NONFATAL OCCUPATIONAL INJURIES AND ILLNESSES INVOLVING DAYS AWAY FROM WORK[a] AND FATAL OCCUPATIONAL INJURIES BY SELECTED WORKER AND CASE CHARACTERISTICS, UNITED STATES, AGRICULTURE, FORESTRY, AND FISHING

Characteristic	Nonfatal Cases,[b] 2000	Fatalities, 1992–2000
Total	**37,256**	**7,337**
Sex		
Men	29,749	7,112
Women	7,480	224
Age		
Under 14	—	99
14 to 15	43	62
16 to 19	1,853	214
20 to 24	6,437	449
25 to 34	11,374	1,075
35 to 44	8,342	1,281
45 to 54	5,924	1,115
55 to 64	2,451	1,187
65 and over	473	1,842
Occupation		
Managerial and professional	761	93
Technical, sales, and administrative support	1,850	152
Service	830	23
Farming, forestry, and fishing	28,779	6,706
Precision production, craft, and repair	1,306	51
Operators, fabricators, and laborers	3,559	292
Race or ethnic origin[c]		
White, non-Hispanic	15,841	5,841
Black, non-Hispanic	1,321	311
Hispanic	14,754	891
Asian or Pacific Islander	380	121
American Indian or Alaskan Native	98	54
Not reported	4,862	119
Nature of injury, illness		
Sprains, strains	12,539	—
Fractures	3,722	26
Cuts, lacerations, punctures	3,932	321
Bruises, contusions	3,394	—
Heat burns	406	87
Chemical burns	102	—
Amputations	703	43
Carpal tunnel syndrome	228	—
Tendonitis	113	—
Multiple injuries	1,380	1,663
Soreness, Pain	1,775	—
Back pain	649	—
All other	8,962	5,190

Characteristic	Nonfatal Cases,[b] 2000	Fatalities, 1992–2000
Part of body affected		
Head	3,189	1,425
Eye	1,484	—
Neck	450	170
Trunk	10,917	1,916
Back	7,125	76
Shoulder	1,549	—
Upper extremities	10,299	31
Finger	4,211	—
Hand, except finger	2,228	—
Wrist	1,597	—
Lower extremities	8,790	72
Knee	2,758	—
Foot, toe	2,234	—
Body systems	488	1,814
Multiple	2,893	1,874
All other	231	35
Source of injury, illness		
Chemicals, chemical products	501	114
Containers	2,911	100
Furniture, fixtures	215	—
Machinery	3,445	1,073
Parts and materials	3,210	289
Worker motion or position	5,721	—
Floor, ground surfaces	6,140	474
Handtools	1,909	72
Vehicles	2,969	3,764
Health care patient	—	—
All other	10,231	1,449
Event or exposure		
Contact with object, equipment	11,621	1,713
Struck by object	5,802	911
Struck against object	2,540	15
Caught in object, equipment, material	2,375	782
Fall to lower level	2,923	481
Fall on same level	3,666	25
Slips, trips	1,342	—
Overexertion	6,018	—
Overexertion in lifting	3,509	—
Repetitive motion	510	—
Exposed to harmful substance	1,791	730
Transportation accidents	2,078	3,744
Fires, explosions	192	101
Assault, violent act	2,381	502
by person	—	142
by other	2,340	360
All other	4,736	40

Source: National Safety Council tabulations of Bureau of Labor Statistics data.

Note: Because of rounding and data exclusion of nonclassifiable responses, data may not sum to the totals. Dashes (—) indicate data that do not meet publication guidelines.

[a] Days away from work include those that result in days away from work with or without restricted work activity.

[b] Excludes farms with fewer than 11 employees.

[c] In the fatalities column, non-Hispanic categories include cases with Hispanic origin not reported.

The Mining industry division includes metal mining, coal mining, oil and gas extraction, and mining and quarrying of nonmetallic minerals such as stone, sand, and gravel.

Mining is the smallest industry division. Mining employment in 2000 amounted to 520,000 workers.

Over the nine years from 1992 through 2000, employment in Mining averaged 614,000 per year. Oil and gas extraction accounts for about three fifths of employment in this division.

NUMBER OF NONFATAL OCCUPATIONAL INJURIES AND ILLNESSES INVOLVING DAYS AWAY FROM WORK[a] AND FATAL OCCUPATIONAL INJURIES BY SELECTED WORKER AND CASE CHARACTERISTICS, UNITED STATES, MINING, QUARRYING, AND OIL AND GAS EXTRACTION

Characteristic	Nonfatal Cases,[b] 2000	Fatalities, 1992–2000
Total	14,084	1,427
Sex		
Men	13,850	1,410
Women	234	17
Age		
Under 14	—	—
14 to 15	—	—
16 to 19	395	27
20 to 24	1,604	128
25 to 34	3,496	366
35 to 44	3,507	417
45 to 54	3,547	313
55 to 64	1,263	122
65 and over	58	53
Occupation		
Managerial and professional	349	73
Technical, sales, and administrative support	184	32
Service	11	13
Farming, forestry, and fishing	—	—
Precision production, craft, and repair	7,603	771
Operators, fabricators, and laborers	5,614	533
Race or ethnic origin[c]		
White, non-Hispanic	4,878	1,173
Black, non-Hispanic	142	56
Hispanic	1,307	160
Asian or Pacific Islander	—	5
American Indian or Alaskan Native	21	20
Not reported	7,733	13
Nature of injury, illness		
Sprains, strains	5,544	—
Fractures	1,801	5
Cuts, lacerations, punctures	1,137	31
Bruises, contusions	1,598	—
Heat burns	188	50
Chemical burns	50	—
Amputations	127	7
Carpal tunnel syndrome	70	—
Tendonitis	20	—
Multiple injuries	864	476
Soreness, Pain	635	—
Back pain	299	—
All other	2,050	853

Characteristic	Nonfatal Cases,[b] 2000	Fatalities, 1992–2000
Part of body affected		
Head	1,168	298
Eye	266	—
Neck	259	26
Trunk	5,521	290
Back	3,240	12
Shoulder	528	—
Upper extremities	3,006	—
Finger	1,235	—
Hand, except finger	538	—
Wrist	477	—
Lower extremities	3,040	11
Knee	1,158	–
Foot, toe	640	–
Body systems	66	253
Multiple	998	540
All other	26	5
Source of injury, illness		
Chemicals, chemical products	808	83
Containers	878	27
Furniture, fixtures	129	6
Machinery	1,487	271
Parts and materials	3,319	177
Worker motion or position	668	—
Floor, ground surfaces	2,163	92
Handtools	961	8
Vehicles	774	407
Health care patient	—	—
All other	2,898	355
Event or exposure		
Contact with object, equipment	5,651	541
Struck by object	3,224	259
Struck against object	1,029	5
Caught in object, equipment, material	1,091	276
Fall to lower level	1,109	104
Fall on same level	1,017	8
Slips, trips	266	—
Overexertion	4,402	—
Overexertion in lifting	1,909	—
Repetitive motion	127	—
Exposed to harmful substance	497	151
Transportation accidents	231	429
Fires, explosions	73	154
Assault, violent act	--	28
by person	–	14
by other	–	14
All other	710	9

Source: National Safety Council tabulations of Bureau of Labor Statistics data.

Note: Because of rounding and data exclusion of nonclassifiable responses, data may not sum to the totals. Dashes (—) indicate data that do not meet publication guidelines.

[a] Days away from work include those that result in days away from work with or without restricted work activity.

[b] Data conforming to OSHA definitions for mining operators in coal, metal, and nonmetal mining are provided to BLS by the Mine Safety and Health Administration, U.S. Department of Labor. Independent mining contractors are excluded from the coal, metal, and nonmetal mining industries.

[c] In the fatalities column, non-Hispanic categories include cases with Hispanic origin not reported.

CONSTRUCTION

The Construction industry division includes establishments engaged in construction of buildings, heavy construction other than buildings, and special trade contractors such as plumbing, electrical, carpentry, etc.

In 2000, employment in the Construction industry division totaled 8,949,000 workers. Employment over the 1992–2000 period averaged 7,568,000 workers per year.

NUMBER OF NONFATAL OCCUPATIONAL INJURIES AND ILLNESSES INVOLVING DAYS AWAY FROM WORK[a] AND FATAL OCCUPATIONAL INJURIES BY SELECTED WORKER AND CASE CHARACTERISTICS, UNITED STATES, CONSTRUCTION

Characteristic	Nonfatal Cases, 2000	Fatalities, 1992–2000
Total	**194,410**	**9,607**
Sex		
Men	189,878	9,470
Women	4,382	137
Age		
Under 14	—	—
14 to 15	—	5
16 to 19	4,877	303
20 to 24	24,418	912
25 to 34	57,506	2,481
35 to 44	60,601	2,665
45 to 54	31,690	1,803
55 to 64	10,811	1,053
65 and over	1,292	367
Occupation		
Managerial and professional	2,528	592
Technical, sales, and administrative support	2,842	104
Service	442	20
Farming, forestry, and fishing	328	27
Precision production, craft, and repair	119,339	4,919
Operators, fabricators, and laborers	68,361	3,918
Race or ethnic origin[b]		
White, non-Hispanic	119,081	7,016
Black, non-Hispanic	9,112	771
Hispanic	26,583	1,470
Asian or Pacific Islander	1,425	96
American Indian or Alaskan Native	1,054	65
Not reported	37,155	189
Nature of injury, illness		
Sprains, strains	74,659	6
Fractures	21,536	37
Cuts, lacerations, punctures	23,231	253
Bruises, contusions	15,365	—
Heat burns	2,712	175
Chemical burns	972	5
Amputations	1,144	22
Carpal tunnel syndrome	1,036	—
Tendonitis	942	—
Multiple injuries	8,173	2,815
Soreness, Pain	11,326	—
Back pain	*4,989*	*—*
All other	33,315	6,289

Characteristic	Nonfatal Cases, 2000	Fatalities, 1992–2000
Part of body affected		
Head	15,090	2,614
Eye	*8,136*	*—*
Neck	2,401	141
Trunk	67,123	1,488
Back	*42,695*	*82*
Shoulder	*10,487*	*—*
Upper extremities	44,499	13
Finger	*16,253*	*5*
Hand, except finger	*10,325*	*—*
Wrist	*6,945*	*—*
Lower extremities	46,363	54
Knee	*17,937*	*5*
Foot, toe	*10,729*	*—*
Body systems	1,395	2,136
Multiple	15,805	3,118
All other	1,734	43
Source of injury, illness		
Chemicals, chemical products	1,928	181
Containers	10,264	122
Furniture, fixtures	3,176	42
Machinery	11,853	1,116
Parts and materials	45,032	1,370
Worker motion or position	27,516	—
Floor, ground surfaces	37,455	2,975
Handtools	16,488	111
Vehicles	11,404	2,230
Health care patient	—	—
All other	29,291	1,458
Event or exposure		
Contact with object, equipment	62,741	1,854
Struck by object	*34,463*	*915*
Struck against object	*13,374*	*19*
Caught in object, equipment, material	*7,830*	*914*
Fall to lower level	24,374	2,977
Fall on same level	14,635	43
Slips, trips	5,598	—
Overexertion	43,050	6
Overexertion in lifting	*23,536*	*6*
Repetitive motion	2,791	—
Exposed to harmful substance	6,505	1,645
Transportation accidents	8,014	2,461
Fires, explosions	952	270
Assault, violent act	488	286
by person	*330*	*144*
by other	*158*	*142*
All other	25,262	63

Source: National Safety Council tabulations of Bureau of Labor Statistics data.
Note: Because of rounding and data exclusion of nonclassifiable responses, data may not sum to the totals. Dashes (—) indicate data that do not meet publication guidelines.
[a] Days away from work include those that result in days away from work with or without restricted work activity.
[b] In the fatalities column, non-Hispanic categories include cases with Hispanic origin not reported.

MANUFACTURING

The Manufacturing industry division includes establishments engaged in the mechanical or chemical transformation of materials or substances into new products. It includes durable and nondurable goods such as food, textiles, apparel, lumber, wood products, paper and paper products, printing, chemicals and pharmaceuticals, petroleum and coal products, rubber and plastics products, metals and metal products, machinery, electrical equipment, transportation equipment, etc.

Manufacturing employment in 2000 was 19,868,000 workers. Average annual employment from 1992 through 2000 was 20,161,000 workers.

NUMBER OF NONFATAL OCCUPATIONAL INJURIES AND ILLNESSES INVOLVING DAYS AWAY FROM WORK[a] AND FATAL OCCUPATIONAL INJURIES BY SELECTED WORKER AND CASE CHARACTERISTICS, UNITED STATES, MANUFACTURING

Characteristic	Nonfatal Cases, 2000	Fatalities, 1992–2000	Characteristic	Nonfatal Cases, 2000	Fatalities, 1992–2000
Total	**376,574**	**6,587**	**Part of body affected**		
			Head	28,391	1,700
Sex			*Eye*	*18,020*	*—*
Men	280,977	6,207	Neck	5,643	119
Women	94,977	380	Trunk	131,069	1,434
			Back	*79,385*	*95*
Age			*Shoulder*	*23,906*	*—*
Under 14	—	6	Upper extremities	115,520	27
14 to 15	18	9	*Finger*	*48,184*	*—*
16 to 19	7,756	149	*Hand, except finger*	*19,668*	*—*
20 to 24	37,823	475	*Wrist*	*24,602*	*—*
25 to 34	96,976	1,409	Lower extremities	66,127	82
35 to 44	114,348	1,787	*Knee*	*23,909*	*16*
45 to 54	77,957	1,441	*Foot, toe*	*16,822*	*5*
55 to 64	34,912	992	Body systems	4,469	978
65 and over	3,928	308	Multiple	23,597	2,205
			All other	1,757	42
Occupation					
Managerial and professional	5,646	646	**Source of injury, illness**		
Technical, sales, and administrative support	20,835	468	Chemicals, chemical products	7,852	262
Service	6,713	112	Containers	51,153	203
Farming, forestry, and fishing	2,244	1,018	Furniture, fixtures	9,762	23
Precision production, craft, and repair	65,741	1,247	Machinery	44,809	1,082
			Parts and materials	67,661	663
Operators, fabricators, and laborers	273,544	3,059	Worker motion or position	70,369	6
			Floor, ground surfaces	40,486	484
Race or ethnic origin[b]			Handtools	20,307	77
White, non-Hispanic	200,319	4,926	Vehicles	19,811	1,973
Black, non-Hispanic	30,696	812	Health care patient	15	—
Hispanic	45,540	600	All other	44,351	1,814
Asian or Pacific Islander	6,333	120			
American Indian or Alaskan Native	1,506	34	**Event or exposure**		
Not reported	92,180	95	Contact with object, equipment	128,541	2,472
			Struck by object	*54,119*	*1,537*
Nature of injury, illness			*Struck against object*	*28,420*	*28*
Sprains, strains	145,106	19	*Caught in object, equipment, material*	*34,244*	*904*
Fractures	26,165	38	Fall to lower level	12,720	437
Cuts, lacerations, punctures	38,907	483	Fall on same level	31,313	81
Bruises, contusions	32,369	—	Slips, trips	9,990	7
Heat burns	6,048	264	Overexertion	97,384	16
Chemical burns	2,821	31	*Overexertion in lifting*	*51,232*	*11*
Amputations	4,516	39	Repetitive motion	30,584	—
Carpal tunnel syndrome	10,910	—	Exposed to harmful substance	18,289	626
Tendonitis	5,780	—	Transportation accidents	7,575	1,938
Multiple injuries	11,835	1,706	Fires, explosions	795	409
Soreness, Pain	22,873	—	Assault, violent act	698	546
Back pain	*8,433*	*—*	*by person*	*430*	*327*
All other	69,244	4,000	*by other*	*268*	*219*
			All other	38,686	55

Source: National Safety Council tabulations of Bureau of Labor Statistics data.
Note: Because of rounding and data exclusion of nonclassifiable responses, data may not sum to the totals. Dashes (—) indicate data that do not meet publication guidelines.
[a] Days away from work include those that result in days away from work with or without restricted work activity.
[b] In the fatalities column, non-Hispanic categories include cases with Hispanic origin not reported.

TRANSPORTATION AND PUBLIC UTILITIES

This industry division includes transportation by rail, highway, air, water, or pipeline and associated transportation services; communications by telephone, radio, television, cable, or satellite; and electric, gas, and sanitary services.

Employment in the Transportation and Public Utilities industry division totaled 8,084,000 in 2000 and averaged 7,372,000 workers per year from 1992 through 2000.

NUMBER OF NONFATAL OCCUPATIONAL INJURIES AND ILLNESSES INVOLVING DAYS AWAY FROM WORK[a] AND FATAL OCCUPATIONAL INJURIES BY SELECTED WORKER AND CASE CHARACTERISTICS, UNITED STATES, TRANSPORTATION AND PUBLIC UTILITIES[b]

Characteristic	Nonfatal Cases, 2000	Fatalities, 1992–2000	Characteristic	Nonfatal Cases, 2000	Fatalities, 1992–2000
Total	**207,037**	**8,493**	**Part of body affected**		
			Head	12,453	1,783
Sex			*Eye*	*4,501*	*—*
Men	160,910	8,104	Neck	5,555	148
Women	40,040	389	Trunk	82,264	1,529
			Back	*54,417*	*97*
Age			*Shoulder*	*13,793*	*—*
Under 14	—	—	Upper extremities	33,213	9
14 to 15	—	—	*Finger*	*9,265*	*—*
16 to 19	3,583	79	*Hand, except finger*	*5,440*	*—*
20 to 24	18,244	420	*Wrist*	*8,351*	*—*
25 to 34	54,055	1,839	Lower extremities	49,587	49
35 to 44	66,104	2,395	*Knee*	*19,129*	*8*
45 to 54	44,038	2,184	*Foot, toe*	*9,223*	*—*
55 to 64	17,369	1,179	Body systems	2,721	1,124
65 and over	2,257	382	Multiple	19,897	3,774
			All other	1,348	77
Occupation					
Managerial and professional	3,477	311	**Source of injury, illness**		
Technical, sales, and			Chemicals, chemical products	2,155	137
administrative support	29,666	828	Containers	45,609	87
Service	12,779	122	Furniture, fixtures	4,378	7
Farming, forestry, and fishing	429	20	Machinery	5,096	221
Precision production, craft,			Parts and materials	17,718	398
and repair	28,067	701	Worker motion or position	29,675	—
Operators, fabricators,			Floor, ground surfaces	34,057	272
and laborers	131,890	6,496	Handtools	3,713	66
			Vehicles	37,561	6,090
Race or ethnic origin[c]			Health care patient	1,507	—
White, non-Hispanic	76,397	6,185	All other	25,569	1,213
Black, non-Hispanic	16,521	1,198			
Hispanic	12,288	707	**Event or exposure**		
Asian or Pacific Islander	1,787	224	Contact with object,		
American Indian or			equipment	46,234	693
Alaskan Native	474	27	*Struck by object*	*24,947*	*439*
Not reported	99,570	151	*Struck against object*	*11,643*	*10*
			Caught in object, equipment,		
Nature of injury, illness			*material*	*6,092*	*240*
Sprains, strains	104,734	6	Fall to lower level	13,663	251
Fractures	11,575	27	Fall on same level	20,685	27
Cuts, lacerations, punctures	9,948	887	Slips, trips	7,645	—
Bruises, contusions	21,563	—	Overexertion	62,304	—
Heat burns	833	293	*Overexertion in lifting*	*35,186*	*—*
Chemical burns	796	6	Repetitive motion	4,494	—
Amputations	364	43	Exposed to harmful substance	6,716	494
Carpal tunnel syndrome	2,023	—	Transportation accidents	18,540	5,866
Tendonitis	1,060	—	Fires, explosions	178	132
Multiple injuries	6,761	3,167	Assault, violent act	1,314	985
Soreness, Pain	18,357	—	*by person*	*766*	*849*
Back pain	*6,955*	*—*	*by other*	*548*	*136*
All other	29,024	4,062	All other	25,265	43

Source: National Safety Council tabulations of Bureau of Labor Statistics data.

Note: Because of rounding and data exclusion of nonclassifiable responses, data may not sum to the totals. Dashes (—) indicate data that do not meet publication guidelines.

[a] Days away from work include those that result in days away from work with or without restricted work activity.

[b] Data conforming to OSHA definitions for employees in railroad transportation are provided to BLS by the Federal Railroad Administration, U.S. Department of Transportation.

[c] In the fatalities column, non-Hispanic categories include cases with Hispanic origin not reported.

WHOLESALE TRADE

Establishments in Wholesale Trade generally sell merchandise to retailers; to industrial, commercial, institutional, farm construction contractors, or professional business users; to other wholesalers; or to agents or brokers.

Wholesale Trade employed 5,407,000 people in 2000 and an average of 4,946,000 people annually from 1992 through 2000.

NUMBER OF NONFATAL OCCUPATIONAL INJURIES AND ILLNESSES INVOLVING DAYS AWAY FROM WORK[a] AND FATAL OCCUPATIONAL INJURIES BY SELECTED WORKER AND CASE CHARACTERISTICS, UNITED STATES, WHOLESALE TRADE

Characteristic	Nonfatal Cases, 2000	Fatalities, 1992–2000
Total	**136,110**	**2,240**
Sex		
Men	115,992	2,135
Women	19,308	104
Age		
Under 14	—	—
14 to 15	—	—
16 to 19	2,830	44
20 to 24	15,497	177
25 to 34	39,379	473
35 to 44	41,736	555
45 to 54	23,084	458
55 to 64	9,252	335
65 and over	1,305	190
Occupation		
Managerial and professional	4,904	187
Technical, sales, and administrative support	20,580	586
Service	1,424	27
Farming, forestry, and fishing	1,674	44
Precision production, craft, and repair	16,316	227
Operators, fabricators, and laborers	90,228	1,155
Race or ethnic origin[b]		
White, non-Hispanic	78,033	1,714
Black, non-Hispanic	11,615	185
Hispanic	16,445	233
Asian or Pacific Islander	1,883	56
American Indian or Alaskan Native	778	6
Not reported	27,356	46
Nature of injury, illness		
Sprains, strains	65,272	8
Fractures	9,342	16
Cuts, lacerations, punctures	9,837	241
Bruises, contusions	11,705	—
Heat burns	800	77
Chemical burns	922	—
Amputations	508	9
Carpal tunnel syndrome	1,287	—
Tendonitis	802	—
Multiple injuries	4,907	685
Soreness, Pain	9,299	—
Back pain	*3,502*	—
All other	21,429	1,202

Characteristic	Nonfatal Cases, 2000	Fatalities, 1992–2000
Part of body affected		
Head	7,698	534
Eye	*3,576*	—
Neck	2,901	39
Trunk	57,262	458
Back	*37,784*	*19*
Shoulder	*8,166*	—
Upper extremities	24,245	6
Finger	*9,247*	—
Hand, except finger	*4,380*	—
Wrist	*4,618*	—
Lower extremities	29,717	29
Knee	*9,815*	*5*
Foot, toe	*7,042*	—
Body systems	1,335	290
Multiple	12,013	864
All other	938	20
Source of injury, illness		
Chemicals, chemical products	1,673	52
Containers	32,279	65
Furniture, fixtures	3,172	—
Machinery	9,118	163
Parts and materials	15,227	119
Worker motion or position	20,010	—
Floor, ground surfaces	19,760	159
Handtools	3,735	27
Vehicles	17,442	1,270
Health care patient	—	—
All other	13,661	383
Event or exposure		
Contact with object, equipment	35,349	389
Struck by object	*18,089*	*213*
Struck against object	*8,653*	*6*
Caught in object, equipment, material	*6,308*	*169*
Fall to lower level	8,521	143
Fall on same level	12,160	23
Slips, trips	4,287	—
Overexertion	42,014	—
Overexertion in lifting	*26,032*	—
Repetitive motion	4,330	—
Exposed to harmful substance	3,931	124
Transportation accidents	8,974	1,171
Fires, explosions	242	88
Assault, violent act	593	288
by person	*135*	*203*
by other	*459*	*85*
All other	15,708	11

Source: National Safety Council tabulations of Bureau of Labor Statistics data.
Note: Because of rounding and data exclusion of nonclassifiable responses, data may not sum to the totals. Dashes (—) indicate data that do not meet publication guidelines.
[a] Days away from work include those that result in days away from work with or without restricted work activity.
[b] In the fatalities column, non-Hispanic categories include cases with Hispanic origin not reported.

RETAIL TRADE

Establishments in Retail Trade generally sell merchandise for personal or household consumption. Retail Trade is the second largest industry division after Services.

Retail Trade employed 22,316,000 people in 2000 and an average of 21,256,000 people annually from 1992 through 2000.

NUMBER OF NONFATAL OCCUPATIONAL INJURIES AND ILLNESS INVOLVING DAYS AWAY FROM WORK[a] AND FATAL OCCUPATIONAL INJURIES BY SELECTED WORKER AND CASE CHARACTERISTICS, UNITED STATES, RETAIL TRADE

Characteristic	Nonfatal Cases, 2000	Fatalities, 1992–2000
Total	**291,648**	**6,052**
Sex		
Men	161,146	5,019
Women	128,801	1,032
Age		
Under 14	—	7
14 to 15	340	14
16 to 19	26,103	296
20 to 24	47,409	601
25 to 34	73,854	1,344
35 to 44	67,394	1,364
45 to 54	42,023	1,173
55 to 64	21,566	762
65 and over	6,268	481
Occupation		
Managerial and professional	10,761	820
Technical, sales, and administrative support	91,586	3,054
Service	79,582	707
Farming, forestry, and fishing	1,009	17
Precision production, craft, and repair	30,721	305
Operators, fabricators, and laborers	76,842	1,103
Race or ethnic origin[b]		
White, non-Hispanic	149,350	3,765
Black, non-Hispanic	22,171	722
Hispanic	26,880	717
Asian or Pacific Islander	5,956	723
American Indian or Alaskan Native	732	32
Not reported	86,559	93
Nature of injury, illness		
Sprains, strains	122,337	—
Fractures	17,397	34
Cuts, lacerations, punctures	36,893	3,587
Bruises, contusions	29,218	—
Heat burns	9,420	85
Chemical burns	1,593	—
Amputations	941	—
Carpal tunnel syndrome	3,360	—
Tendonitis	2,169	—
Multiple injuries	9,961	767
Soreness, Pain	18,864	—
Back pain	7,553	
All other	39,495	1,568

Characteristic	Nonfatal Cases, 2000	Fatalities, 1992–2000
Part of body affected		
Head	15,528	1,922
Eye	6,533	—
Neck	4,580	193
Trunk	104,033	1,685
Back	71,414	133
Shoulder	15,082	6
Upper extremities	76,296	10
Finger	30,388	—
Hand, except finger	15,871	—
Wrist	13,827	—
Lower extremities	60,041	47
Knee	22,414	6
Foot, toe	14,667	—
Body systems	2,776	390
Multiple	25,162	1,753
All other	3,232	52
Source of injury, illness		
Chemicals, chemical products	3,373	97
Containers	63,186	37
Furniture, fixtures	15,358	16
Machinery	21,256	77
Parts and materials	17,372	189
Worker motion or position	38,239	
Floor, ground surfaces	57,011	239
Handtools	17,481	335
Vehicles	19,170	1,361
Health care patient	—	
All other	39,188	3,697
Event or exposure		
Contact with object, equipment	83,430	238
Struck by object	47,091	143
Struck against object	22,410	6
Caught in object, equipment, material	8,878	86
Fall to lower level	12,453	146
Fall on same level	47,343	73
Slips, trips	10,788	—
Overexertion	74,571	—
Overexertion in lifting	50,741	—
Repetitive motion	7,364	—
Exposed to harmful substance	14,264	185
Transportation accidents	9,109	1,283
Fires, explosions	778	102
Assault, violent act	3,479	3,979
by person	2,789	3,673
by other	690	306
All other	28,070	41

Source: National Safety Council tabulations of Bureau of Labor Statistics data.
Note: Because of rounding and data exclusion of nonclassifiable responses, data may not sum to the totals. Dashes (—) indicate data that do not meet publication guidelines.
[a]Days away from work include those that result in days away from work with or without restricted work activity.
[b]In the fatalities column, non-Hispanic categories include cases with Hispanic origin not reported.

FINANCE, INSURANCE, AND REAL ESTATE

Establishments in the Finance, Insurance, and Real Estate industry division include banks and other savings institutions; securities and commodities brokers, dealers, exchanges, and services; insurance carriers, brokers, and agents; real estate operators, developers, agents, and brokers; and holding and other investment offices.

Finance, Insurance, and Real Estate had 8,538,000 workers in 2000 and an annual average of 8,048,000 from 1992 through 2000.

NUMBER OF NONFATAL OCCUPATIONAL INJURIES AND ILLNESSES INVOLVING DAYS AWAY FROM WORK[a] AND FATAL OCCUPATIONAL INJURIES BY SELECTED WORKER AND CASE CHARACTERISTICS, UNITED STATES, FINANCE, INSURANCE, AND REAL ESTATE

Characteristic	Nonfatal Cases, 2000	Fatalities, 1992–2000
Total	**39,472**	**969**
Sex		
Men	18,124	747
Women	21,275	221
Age		
Under 14	—	—
14 to 15	—	—
16 to 19	563	—
20 to 24	3,548	38
25 to 34	8,947	160
35 to 44	10,816	221
45 to 54	8,746	253
55 to 64	4,363	163
65 and over	957	129
Occupation		
Managerial and professional	5,509	355
Technical, sales, and administrative support	15,994	357
Service	7,529	122
Farming, forestry, and fishing	2,916	39
Precision production, craft, and repair	5,024	46
Operators, fabricators, and laborers	2,107	42
Race or ethnic origin[b]		
White, non-Hispanic	19,214	752
Black, non-Hispanic	3,852	77
Hispanic	3,820	86
Asian or Pacific Islander	1,084	29
American Indian or Alaskan Native	347	—
Not reported	11,155	21
Nature of injury, illness		
Sprains, strains	15,224	—
Fractures	2,961	8
Cuts, lacerations, punctures	3,101	305
Bruises, contusions	2,445	—
Heat burns	230	11
Chemical burns	108	—
Amputations	161	—
Carpal tunnel syndrome	2,182	—
Tendonitis	595	—
Multiple injuries	1,640	248
Soreness, Pain	2,307	—
Back pain	*753*	—
All other	8,516	392

Characteristic	Nonfatal Cases, 2000	Fatalities, 1992–2000
Part of body affected		
Head	1,939	252
Eye	*599*	—
Neck	605	21
Trunk	12,010	199
Back	*8,333*	*18*
Shoulder	*1,344*	—
Upper extremities	8,868	—
Finger	*2,552*	—
Hand, except finger	*1,170*	—
Wrist	*3,301*	—
Lower extremities	8,059	10
Knee	*2,386*	—
Foot, toe	*1,539*	—
Body systems	1,211	131
Multiple	5,840	340
All other	940	14
Source of injury, illness		
Chemicals, chemical products	520	29
Containers	4,294	—
Furniture, fixtures	2,405	—
Machinery	2,421	28
Parts and materials	1,204	39
Worker motion or position	8,489	--
Floor, ground surfaces	8,814	103
Handtools	2,003	28
Vehicles	3,103	347
Health care patient	262	--
All other	5,958	391
Event or exposure		
Contact with object, equipment	7,541	47
Struck by object	*4,269*	*27*
Struck against object	*2,118*	—
Caught in object, equipment, material	*649*	*17*
Fall to lower level	2,611	90
Fall on same level	6,590	16
Slips, trips	1,134	—
Overexertion	7,754	—
Overexertion in lifting	*4,925*	—
Repetitive motion	3,906	—
Exposed to harmful substance	1,439	74
Transportation accidents	2,513	341
Fires, explosions	34	10
Assault, violent act	436	386
by person	*326*	*302*
by other	*110*	*84*
All other	5,515	—

Source: National Safety Council tabulations of Bureau of Labor Statistics data.
Note: Because of rounding and data exclusion of nonclassifiable responses, data may not sum to the totals. Dashes (—) indicate data that do not meet publication guidelines.
[a] Days away from work include those that result in days away from work with or without restricted work activity.
[b] In the fatalities column, non-Hispanic categories include cases with Hispanic origin not reported.

SERVICES

Establishments in the Services industry division provide services, rather than merchandise, for individuals, businesses, government agencies, and other organizations. Broad categories in this industry division include lodging places, personal and business services, automobile services, repair services, motion pictures, amusement and recreation services, health, legal, education, and social services, etc.

Services is the largest industry division with 39,170,000 workers in 2000 and an annual average of 35,007,000 from 1992 through 2000.

NUMBER OF NONFATAL OCCUPATIONAL INJURIES AND ILLNESSES INVOLVING DAYS AWAY FROM WORK[a] AND FATAL OCCUPATIONAL INJURIES BY SELECTED WORKER AND CASE CHARACTERISTICS, UNITED STATES, SERVICES

Characteristic	Nonfatal Cases, 2000	Fatalities, 1992–2000
Total	**394,922**	**6,903**
Sex		
Men	154,347	5,753
Women	237,707	1,149
Age		
Under 14	—	5
14 to 15	469	16
16 to 19	10,861	166
20 to 24	39,791	579
25 to 34	100,649	1,580
35 to 44	111,033	1,722
45 to 54	78,636	1,351
55 to 64	38,129	897
65 and over	7,625	579
Occupation		
Managerial and professional	61,765	2,145
Technical, sales, and administrative support	66,669	837
Service	180,430	1,447
Farming, forestry, and fishing	6,517	154
Precision production, craft, and repair	25,798	1,048
Operators, fabricators, and laborers	51,804	1,216
Race or ethnic origin[b]		
White, non-Hispanic	187,117	5,004
Black, non-Hispanic	55,533	789
Hispanic	35,972	702
Asian or Pacific Islander	7,170	243
American Indian or Alaskan Native	1,829	43
Not reported	107,302	122
Nature of injury, illness		
Sprains, strains	195,554	9
Fractures	19,988	71
Cuts, lacerations, punctures	21,457	1,478
Bruises, contusions	39,174	5
Heat burns	6,319	141
Chemical burns	2,455	—
Amputations	824	17
Carpal tunnel syndrome	5,474	—
Tendonitis	3,918	—
Multiple injuries	13,307	1,936
Soreness, Pain	28,536	—
Back pain	11,127	—
All other	57,917	3,240

Characteristic	Nonfatal Cases, 2000	Fatalities, 1992–2000
Part of body affected		
Head	21,577	1,707
Eye	8,130	—
Neck	9,230	156
Trunk	160,166	1,266
Back	115,549	81
Shoulder	21,089	—
Upper extremities	72,186	23
Finger	20,901	—
Hand, except finger	12,761	—
Wrist	19,476	—
Lower extremities	78,975	68
Knee	31,105	8
Foot, toe	13,889	5
Body systems	6,783	1,102
Multiple	42,960	2,515
All other	3,045	66
Source of injury, illness		
Chemicals, chemical products	7,154	315
Containers	37,535	66
Furniture, fixtures	19,784	36
Machinery	14,376	279
Parts and materials	17,850	328
Worker motion or position	58,960	5
Floor, ground surfaces	71,690	634
Handtools	9,778	180
Vehicles	29,483	2,968
Health care patient	70,211	7
All other	58,100	2,085
Event or exposure		
Contact with object, equipment	72,554	624
Struck by object	38,831	388
Struck against object	21,175	29
Caught in object, equipment, material	7,879	202
Fall to lower level	17,510	494
Fall on same level	56,412	120
Slips, trips	13,841	—
Overexertion	128,149	11
Overexertion in lifting	69,688	7
Repetitive motion	13,529	—
Exposed to harmful substance	19,343	666
Transportation accidents	17,925	2,774
Fires, explosions	495	237
Assault, violent act	13,483	1,895
by person	11,896	1,381
by other	1,588	510
All other	41,681	82

Source: National Safety Council tabulations of Bureau of Labor Statistics data.
Note: Because of rounding and data exclusion of nonclassifiable responses, data may not sum to the totals. Dashes (—) indicate data that do not meet publication guidelines.
[a]Days away from work include those that result in days away from work with or without restricted work activity.
[b]In the fatalities column, non-Hispanic categories include cases with Hispanic origin not reported.

Government includes workers at all levels from federal civilian and military to state, county, and municipal.

Government employment totaled 20,267,000 in 2000. From 1992 through 2000, Government employment averaged 19,782,000 per year.

NUMBER OF NONFATAL OCCUPATIONAL INJURIES AND ILLNESSES INVOLVING DAYS AWAY FROM WORK[a] AND FATAL OCCUPATIONAL INJURIES BY SELECTED WORKER AND CASE CHARACTERISTICS, UNITED STATES, GOVERNMENT

Characteristic	Nonfatal Cases,[b] 2000	Fatalities, 1992–2000	Characteristic	Nonfatal Cases,[b] 2000	Fatalities, 1992–2000
Total	(b)	5,825	**Part of body affected**		
			Head		1,385
Sex			Eye		—
Men		5,139	Neck		123
Women		685	Trunk		954
			Back		89
Age			Shoulder		—
Under 14		—	Upper extremities		13
14 to 15		8	Finger		—
16 to 19		144	Hand, except finger		—
20 to 24		542	Wrist		—
25 to 34		1,499	Lower extremities		64
35 to 44		1,409	Knee		10
45 to 54		1,234	Foot, toe		5
55 to 64		725	Body systems		780
65 and over		241	Multiple		2,434
			All other		72
Occupation					
Managerial and professional		894	**Source of injury, illness**		
Technical, sales, and administrative support		514	Chemicals, chemical products		93
			Containers		43
Service		1,955	Furniture, fixtures		18
Farming, forestry, and fishing		122	Machinery		215
Precision production, craft, and repair		500	Parts and materials		196
			Worker motion or position		5
Operators, fabricators, and laborers		776	Floor, ground surfaces		308
			Handtools		61
Military occupations		1,025	Vehicles		3,124
			Health care patient		7
Race or ethnic origin[c]			All other		1,755
White, non-Hispanic		4,509			
Black, non-Hispanic		711	**Event or exposure**		
Hispanic		345	Contact with object, equipment		379
Asian or Pacific Islander		97	Struck by object		223
American Indian or Alaskan Native		43	Struck against object		9
			Caught in object, equipment, material		145
Not reported		120	Fall to lower level		216
			Fall on same level		79
Nature of injury, illness			Slips, trips		—
Sprains, strains		19	Overexertion		12
Fractures		47	Overexertion in lifting		7
Cuts, lacerations, punctures		1,065	Repetitive motion		—
Bruises, contusions			Exposed to harmful substance		385
Heat burns		119	Transportation accidents		3,148
Chemical burns		—	Fires, explosions		248
Amputations		14	Assault, violent act		1,300
Carpal tunnel syndrome		—	by person		971
Tendonitis		—	by other		329
Multiple injuries		1,961	All other		55
Soreness, Pain		—			
Back pain		—			
All other		2,591			

Source: National Safety Council tabulations of Bureau of Labor Statistics data.
Note: Because of rounding and data exclusion of nonclassifiable responses, data may not sum to the totals. Dashes (—) indicate data that do not meet publication guidelines.
[a] Days away from work include those that result in days away from work with or without restricted work activity.
[b] Data for government entities not collected in the BLS national Survey of Occupational Injuries and Illnesses.
[c] In the fatalities column, non-Hispanic categories include cases with Hispanic origin not reported.

OCCUPATIONAL
HEALTH

OCCUPATIONAL HEALTH

Approximately 362,500 occupational illnesses were recognized or diagnosed by employers in 2000, according to the Bureau of Labor Statistics (BLS). Disorders associated with repeated trauma were the most common illness with 241,800 new cases, followed by skin diseases and disorders (nearly 42,000), and respiratory conditions due to toxic agents (14,700).

The overall incidence rate of occupational illness for all workers was 39.4 per 10,000 full-time workers. Of the major industry divisions, manufacturing had the highest rate in 2000, 114.1 per 10,000 full-time workers. Workers in manufacturing also had the highest rates for disorders associated with repeated trauma, respiratory conditions due to toxic agents, and disorders due to physical agents. Agriculture had the second highest incidence rate, 29.2, although agricultural workers had the highest rate of all the industry divisions for skin diseases and disorders and for poisoning. Mining had the highest incidence rate for dust diseases of the lungs.

The table below shows the number of occupational illnesses and the incidence rate per 10,000 full-time workers as measured by the 2000 BLS survey. To convert these to incidence rates per 100 full-time workers, which are comparable to other published BLS rates, divide the rates in the table by 100. The BLS survey records illnesses only for the year in which they are recognized or diagnosed as work-related. Since only recognized cases are included, the figures underestimate the incidence of occupational illness.

NUMBER OF OCCUPATIONAL ILLNESSES AND INCIDENCE RATES BY INDUSTRY AND TYPE OF ILLNESS, UNITED STATES, 2000

Occupational Illness	Private Sector[a]	Agricul-ture[a,b]	Mining[b]	Con-struction	Manu-facturing	Trans. & Pub. Util.	Trade[b]	Finance[b]	Services
Number of Illnesses (in thousands)									
All Illnesses	**362.5**	**4.4**	**0.9**	**6.3**	**209.7**	**16.7**	**37.2**	**18.6**	**68.7**
Disorders associated with repeated trauma	241.8	1.0	0.6	2.2	163.9	9.6	20.4	14.9	29.1
Skin diseases, disorders	41.8	2.1	(c)	1.3	18.6	2.1	3.2	0.6	14.0
Respiratory conditions due to toxic agents	14.7	0.1	(c)	0.5	5.5	1.0	1.7	0.6	5.4
Disorders due to physical agents	13.9	0.4	(c)	0.5	8.4	0.6	1.4	0.4	2.1
Poisoning	3.3	0.1	(c)	0.3	1.4	0.3	0.3	(c)	0.9
Dust diseases of the lungs	1.7	(c)	0.1	0.1	0.5	0.2	0.3	0.1	0.4
All other occupational diseases	45.1	0.6	0.1	1.4	11.3	2.9	9.9	2.0	16.9
Incidence Rate per 10,000 Full-Time Workers									
All Illnesses	**39.4**	**29.2**	**15.5**	**10.4**	**114.1**	**25.2**	**15.4**	**27.4**	**24.7**
Disorders associated with repeated trauma	26.3	6.7	10.6	3.7	89.2	14.5	8.5	21.9	10.4
Skin diseases, disorders	4.6	13.7	0.5	2.1	10.1	3.2	1.3	0.8	5.0
Respiratory conditions due to toxic agents	1.6	0.8	0.4	0.9	3.0	1.5	0.7	0.9	1.9
Disorders due to physical agents	1.5	2.8	0.7	0.9	4.6	0.9	0.6	0.6	0.7
Poisoning	0.4	0.9	0.2	0.4	0.8	0.4	0.1	(c)	0.3
Dust diseases of the lungs	0.2	0.2	1.7	0.1	0.3	0.3	0.1	0.1	0.2
All other occupational diseases	4.9	4.0	1.5	2.3	6.2	4.4	4.1	2.9	6.1

Source: Bureau of Labor Statistics, U.S. Department of Labor. Components may not add to totals due to rounding.
[a] Private sector includes all industries except government, but excludes farms with less than 11 employees.
[b] Agriculture includes forestry and fishing; mining includes quarrying and oil and gas extraction; trade includes wholesale and retail; finance includes insurance and real estate.
[c] Fewer than 50 cases.

NONFATAL OCCUPATIONAL ILLNESS INCIDENCE RATES, U.S. PRIVATE INDUSTRY, 1994–2000

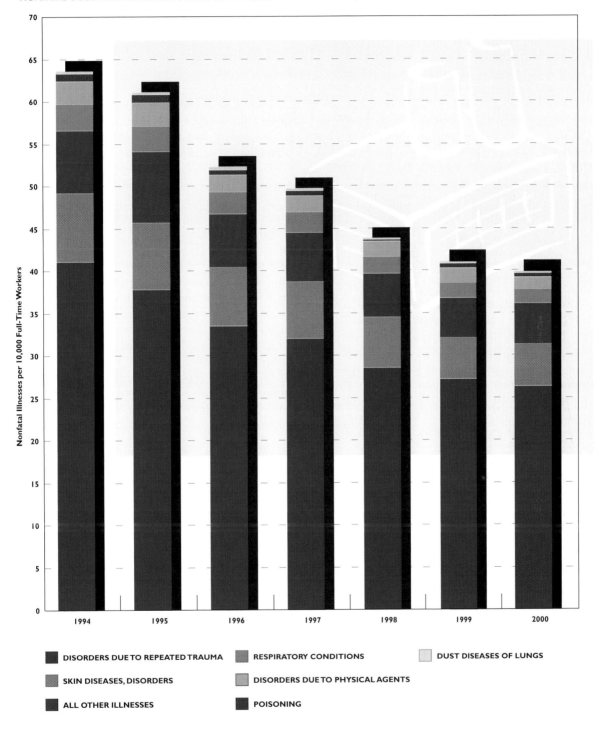

DISORDERS DUE TO REPEATED TRAUMA   RESPIRATORY CONDITIONS   DUST DISEASES OF LUNGS

SKIN DISEASES, DISORDERS   DISORDERS DUE TO PHYSICAL AGENTS

ALL OTHER ILLNESSES   POISONING

DISEASE PREVENTION, HEALTH PROMOTION, AND WORKPLACE PRODUCTIVITY

Disease prevention and health promotion (DP/HP) programs have become commonplace in the North American workplace, with over 80% of worksites with 50 or more employees and virtually all those with 750 or more employees offering programs and resources aimed at improving worker health. Evaluations of DP/HP programs have found positive effects of such interventions on health risk and less definitive, but generally positive outcomes regarding their affect on reducing medical costs. In addition to their effect on health care costs, DP/HP programs may also affect overall corporate performance via the influence of positive worker health on workplace productivity.

Health care issues are a major contributing factor to corporate productivity. Health care is expensive and costs continue to grow at rates above the Consumer Price Index. Managed care is just beginning to respond to employers with large numbers of employees who are requesting that health care services not only contain costs and improve the quality and appropriateness of care, but also start to show value in terms of linking the human resource potential of good health with corporate success. The perception of the value of workplace health investment has thus moved along a continuum from simply cost containment, to DP/HP initiatives that are fully integrated with other health benefits to manage the total health of the workforce, to the final stage of investing in worker health as an integral component of overall corporate success.

Once the decision has been made to focus on productivity as an important outcome metric, the challenge becomes how to best measure it. The history of productivity measurement reveals different approaches for different jobs and industries with little overlap. Unfortunately, most jobs do not actually produce objective counts of tasks performed, while white-collar workers may only receive performance evaluations once per year. In addition, the most commonly shared measure—absences—is often only valid for hourly-paid workforces and overlooks gradations of impairment of workers who are present. There is a critical need to better quantify the value produced by employees. The true impact of poor health can only be evaluated through an accurate assessment of work production.

The results of an extensive search of DP/HP interventions published between 1993 and 1998 resulted in three categories of results based on the type of DP/HP intervention used. The overall results indicated that it was possible for DP/HP programs to have long-term payback for direct medical costs but short-term payback for performance improvements (or vice versa). Methods available for measuring the relationship between health status and worker performance/on-the-job capacity are scarce and the evidence for a performance-based cost-benefit is very limited. Two major and universal challenges to the success of DP/HP programs are getting high participation rates and maintaining behavior change over time. There is strong and convincing evidence that (a) personal health risk factors (e.g., smoking, weight, sedentary behavior, dietary patterns) are related to increased incidence of related illnesses, (b) health status influences health-related costs, and (c) DP/HP interventions improve personal health status. Also, the evidence showing the medical cost-benefit of DP/HP interventions is moderate and increasing.

The three types of interventions included in the review were those focused on early detection, behavior change, and care seeking. The intervention of greatest value for early detection involved that for depression; interventions associated with behavior change included exercise for back pain-related symptoms, smoking cessation, adult influenza vaccinations, and stress management; while care-seeking interventions involved minor illnesses and the use of the emergency room. The table on page 83 provides a summary of those conditions that may have the highest value to the worksite based on the magnitude of the condition, evidence that intervention can influence the condition, and evidence that a return on investment is achievable within a reasonable time frame. A decision framework was developed to make use of this summary data to quantify productivity, organizational cost, and performance loss outcomes for corporate decision makers.

Riedel, J.E., Lynch, W., Baase, C., Hymel, P., & Peterson, K.W. (2001). *The effect of disease prevention and health promotion on workplace productivity: A literature review.* American Journal of Health Promotion, 15(3), 167-191.

INTERVENTIONS OF GREATEST VALUE TO THE WORKSITE BASED ON MAGNITUDE OF DIRECT MEDICAL COST/PERFORMANCE LOSS (DMC/PL), DOCUMENTED EVIDENCE OF BENEFIT, AND RETURN ON INVESTMENT (ROI) TIMEFRAME

Intervention	Magnitude of DMC/PL	Evidence of Benefit	ROI Timeframe
Early Detection			
Depression	Moderate prevalence		
	Moderate DMC	Cost effect for DMC	Short-term
	High PL	Cost effect for PL	Short-term
Behavior Change			
Exercise—back pain-related	Very high prevalence		
	Moderate DMC	Unknown for DMC	Unknown
	High lost work days	Small reduction in absenteeism	Short-term
Smoking cessation	High prevalence		
	High DMC	Cost impact for DMC	Long-term
	High PL	Cost impact for PL	Short-term
Adult vaccinations—influenza	Very high prevalence		
	Low to moderate DMC	Cost impact for DMC	Short-term
	High PL	Cost impact for PL	Short-term
Stress management	High prevalence		
	Very high DMC	Unknown for DMC	Unknown
	Very high PL	Unknown for PL	Unknown
Care Seeking			
Minor illnesses	Very high prevalence		
	Very high DMC	Cost impact for DMC	Short-term
	Unknown PL	Unknown for PL	Unknown
Use of ER	Very high prevalence		
	Very high DMC	Cost impact for DMC	Short-term
	Unknown PL	Unknown for PL	Unknown

See Source on page 82.

MOTOR VEHICLE

MOTOR VEHICLE, 2001

Between 1912 and 2001, motor-vehicle deaths per 10,000 registered vehicles were reduced 94%, from 33 to less than 2. In 1912, there were 3,100 fatalities when the number of registered vehicles totaled only 950,000. In 2001, there were 42,900 fatalities, but registrations soared to 231 million.

While mileage data were not available in 1912, the 2001 mileage death rate of 1.54 per 100,000,000 vehicle miles was down 1% from 2000 and the lowest rate on record. Disabling injuries in motor-vehicle accidents totaled 2,300,000 in 2001, and total motor-vehicle costs were estimated at $199.6 billion. Costs include wage and productivity losses, medical expenses, administrative expenses, motor-vehicle property damage, and employer costs.

Motor-vehicle deaths increased 1% from 2000 to 2001 and also increased 1% from 1999. Miles traveled was

up about 1%, the number of registered vehicles increased 2%, and the population increased 1%. As a result, the mileage death rate was down slightly, the registration death rate was down 1%, and the population death rate was unchanged from 2000 to 2001.

Compared with 1991, 2001 motor-vehicle deaths decreased by about 1%. However, mileage, registration, and population death rates were all sharply lower in 2001 compared to 1991 (see chart on opposite page).

The word "accident" may be used in this section as well as the word "crash." When used, "accident" has a specific meaning as defined in the *Manual on Classification of Motor Vehicle Traffic Accidents, ANSI D16.2-1996*. "Crash" is generally used by the National Highway Traffic Safety Administration to mean the same as accident, but it is not formally defined.

Deaths	**42,900**
Disabling injuries	**2,300,000**
Cost	**$199.6 billion**
Motor-vehicle mileage	**2,778 billion**
Registered vehicles in the United States	**230,800,000**
Licensed drivers in the United States	**193,300,000**
Death rate per 100,000,000 vehicle miles	**1.54**
Death rate per 10,000 registered vehicles	**1.86**
Death rate per 100,000 population	**15.4**

ACCIDENT AND VEHICLE TOTALS, 2001

Severity of Accident	Number of Accidents	Drivers (Vehicles) Involved
Fatal	38,700	55,700
Disabling injury	1,500,000	2,700,000
Property damage and nondisabling injury[a]	11,000,000	18,500,000
Total (rounded)	12,500,000	21,300,000

[a] *Estimating procedures for these figures were revised beginning with the 1990 edition.*

TRAVEL, DEATHS, AND DEATH RATES, UNITED STATES, 1925–2001

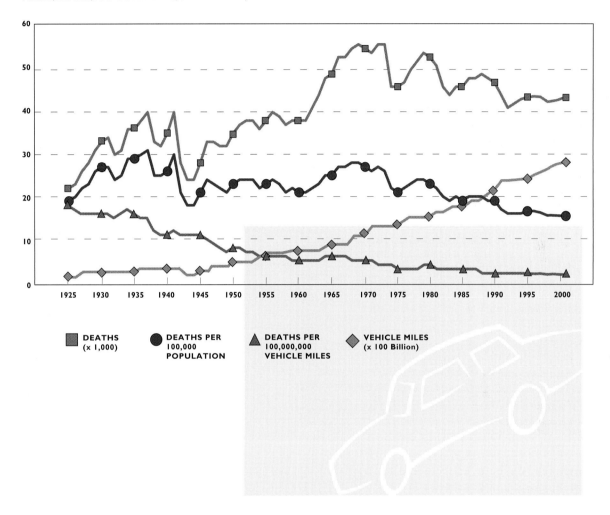

DEATHS
(x 1,000)

DEATHS PER
100,000
POPULATION

DEATHS PER
100,000,000
VEHICLE MILES

VEHICLE MILES
(x 100 Billion)

DEATHS DUE TO MOTOR-VEHICLE ACCIDENTS, 2001

TYPE OF ACCIDENT AND AGE OF VICTIM

All Motor-Vehicle Accidents

Includes deaths involving mechanically or electrically powered highway-transport vehicles in motion (except those on rails), both on and off the highway or street.

	Total	Change from 2000	Death Rate[a]
Deaths	42,900	+1%	15.4
Nonfatal injuries	2,300,000		

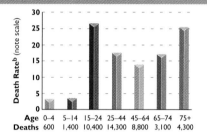

Age	0–4	5–14	15–24	25–44	45–64	65–74	75+
Deaths	600	1,400	10,400	14,300	8,800	3,100	4,300

Collision Between Motor Vehicles

Includes deaths from collisions of two or more motor vehicles. Motorized bicycles and scooters, trolley buses, and farm tractors or road machinery traveling on highways are motor vehicles.

	Total	Change from 2000	Death Rate[a]
Deaths	18,400	–4%	6.6
Nonfatal injuries	1,730,000		

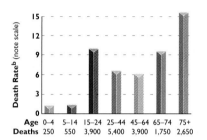

Age	0–4	5–14	15–24	25–44	45–64	65–74	75+
Deaths	250	550	3,900	5,400	3,900	1,750	2,650

Collision with Fixed Object

Includes deaths from collisions in which the first harmful event is the striking of a fixed object such as a guardrail, abutment, impact attenuator, etc.

	Total	Change from 2000	Death Rate[a]
Deaths	12,300	+4%	4.4
Nonfatal injuries	320,000		

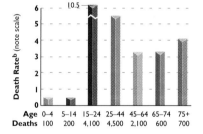

Age	0–4	5–14	15–24	25–44	45–64	65–74	75+
Deaths	100	200	4,100	4,500	2,100	600	700

Pedestrian Accidents

Includes all deaths of persons struck by motor vehicles, either on or off a street or highway, regardless of the circumstances of the accident.

	Total	Change from 2000	Death Rate[a]
Deaths	5,800	+4%	2.1
Nonfatal injuries	90,000		

See footnotes on page 89.

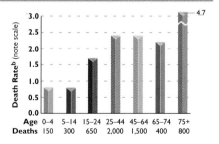

Age	0–4	5–14	15–24	25–44	45–64	65–74	75+
Deaths	150	300	650	2,000	1,500	400	800

Noncollision Accidents

Includes deaths from accidents in which the first injury or damage-producing event was an overturn, jackknife, or other type of noncollision.

	Total	Change from 2000	Death Rate[a]
Deaths	5,100	+9%	1.8
Nonfatal injuries	100,000		

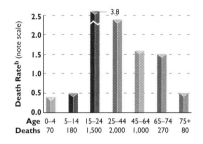

Age	0–4	5–14	15–24	25–44	45–64	65–74	75+
Deaths	70	180	1,500	2,000	1,000	270	80

Collision with Pedalcycle

Includes deaths of pedalcyclists and motor-vehicle occupants from collisions between pedalcycles and motor vehicles on streets, highways, private driveways, parking lots, etc.

	Total	Change from 2000	Death Rate[a]
Deaths	800	0%	0.3
Nonfatal injuries	54,000		

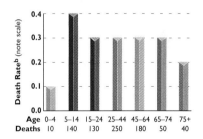

Age	0–4	5–14	15–24	25–44	45–64	65–74	75+
Deaths	10	140	130	250	180	50	40

Collision with Railroad Train

Includes deaths from collisions of motor vehicles (moving or stalled) and railroad vehicles at public or private grade crossings. In other types of accidents, classification requires motor vehicle to be in motion.

	Total	Change from 2000	Death Rate[a]
Deaths	400	+0%	0.1
Nonfatal injuries	2,000		

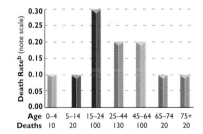

Age	0–4	5–14	15–24	25–44	45–64	65–74	75+
Deaths	10	20	100	130	100	20	20

Other Collision

Includes deaths from motor-vehicle collisions not specified in other categories above. Most of the deaths arose out of accidents involving animals or animal-drawn vehicles.

	Total	Change from 2000	Death Rate[a]
Deaths	100	0%	(c)
Nonfatal Injuries	4,000		

Note: Procedures and benchmarks for estimating deaths by type of accident and age were changed in 1990. Estimates for 1987 and later years are not comparable to earlier years. The noncollision and fixed object categories were most affected by the changes.
[a] Deaths per 100,000 population.
[b] Deaths per 100,000 population in each age group.
[c] Death rate was less than 0.05.

TYPE OF MOTOR-VEHICLE ACCIDENT

Although motor-vehicle deaths occur more often in collisions between motor vehicles than any other type of accident, this type represents only about 43% of the total. Collisions between a motor vehicle and a fixed object were the next most common type, with about 29% of the deaths, followed by pedestrian accidents and noncollisions (rollovers, etc.).

While collisions between motor vehicles accounted for less than half of motor-vehicle fatalities, this accident type represented 75% of injuries, 70% of injury accidents, and 69% of all accidents. Single-vehicle accidents involving collisions with fixed objects, pedestrians, and noncollisions, on the other hand,

accounted for a greater proportion of fatalities and fatal accidents compared to less serious accidents. These three accident types made up 54% of fatalities and 57% of fatal accidents, but 27% or less of injuries, injury accidents, or all accidents.

Of collisions between motor vehicles, angle collisions cause the greatest number of deaths, about 8,900 in 2001, and the greatest number of nonfatal injuries as well as fatal and injury accidents. The table below shows the estimated number of motor-vehicle deaths, injuries, fatal accidents, injury accidents, and all accidents, for various types of accidents.

MOTOR-VEHICLE DEATHS AND INJURIES AND NUMBER OF ACCIDENTS BY TYPE OF ACCIDENT, 2001

Type of Accident	Deaths	Nonfatal Injuries	Fatal Accidents	Injury Accidents	All Accidents
Total	**42,900**	**2,300,000**	**38,700**	**1,500,000**	**12,500,000**
Collision with—					
Pedestrian	5,800	90,000	4,800	50,000	150,000
Other motor vehicle	18,400	1,730,000	15,500	1,050,000	8,630,000
Angle collision	*8,900*	*843,000*	*7,700*	*495,000*	*3,710,000*
Head-on collision	*7,000*	*100,000*	*5,400*	*53,000*	*270,000*
Rear-end collision	*1,800*	*710,000*	*1,700*	*452,000*	*3,760,000*
Sideswipe and other two-vehicle collisions	*700*	*77,000*	*700*	*50,000*	*890,000*
Railroad train	400	2,000	300	1,000	5,000
Pedalcycle	800	54,000	800	35,000	100,000
Animal, animal-drawn vehicle	100	4,000	100	4,000	520,000
Fixed object	12,300	320,000	12,300	290,000	2,695,000
Noncollision	**5,100**	**100,000**	**4,900**	**70,000**	**400,000**

Source: National Safety Council estimates, based on reports from state traffic authorities. Procedures for estimating the number of accidents by type were changed for the 1998 edition and are not comparable to estimates in previous editions (see Technical Appendix).

ESTIMATING MOTOR-VEHICLE CRASH COSTS

There are two methods commonly used to measure the costs of motor-vehicle crashes. One is the *economic cost* framework and the other is the *comprehensive cost* framework.

Economic costs may be used by a community or state to estimate the economic impact of motor-vehicle crashes that occurred within its jurisdiction in a given time period. It is a measure of the productivity lost and expenses incurred because of the crashes. Economic costs, however, should not be used for cost-benefit analysis because they do not reflect what society pays to prevent a statistical fatality or injury.

There are five economic cost components: (a) wage and productivity losses, which include wages, fringe benefits, household production, and travel delay; (b) medical expenses, including emergency service costs; (c) administrative expenses, which include the administrative cost of private and public insurance plus police and legal costs; (d) motor-vehicle damage, including the value of damage to property; and (e) employer costs for crashes involving workers.

The information below shows the average economic costs in 2001 per death (*not* per fatal crash), per injury (*not* per injury crash), and per property-damage crash.

ECONOMIC COSTS, 2001

Death	**$1,040,000**
Nonfatal disabling injury	**$36,500**
Incapacitating injury[a]	$49,500
Nonincapacitating evident injury[a]	$16,500
Possible injury[a]	$9,400
Property-damage crash (including minor injuries)	**$6,500**

Comprehensive costs include not only the economic cost components, but also a measure of the value of lost quality of life associated with the deaths and injuries, that is, what society is willing to pay to prevent them. The values of lost quality of life were obtained through empirical studies of what people actually pay to reduce their safety and health risks, such as through the purchase of air bags or smoke detectors. Comprehensive costs should be used for cost-benefit analysis, but because the lost quality of life represents only a dollar equivalence of intangible qualities, they do not represent real economic losses and should not be used to determine the economic impact of past crashes.

The information below shows the average comprehensive costs in 2001 on a per-person basis.

COMPREHENSIVE COSTS, 2001

Death	**$3,340,000**
Incapacitating injury[a]	$165,000
Nonincapacitating evident injury[a]	$42,500
Possible injury[a]	$20,200
No injury	**$1,900**

Source: National Safety Council estimates (see the Technical Appendix) and Children's Safety Network Economics and Insurance Resource Center, Pacific Institute for Research and Evaluation.
[a]*Committee on Motor Vehicle Traffic Accident Classification. (1997). Manual on Classification of Motor Vehicle Traffic Accidents, ANSI D16.1-1996 (6th ed.). Itasca, IL: National Safety Council.*
Note: The National Safety Council's cost estimating procedures were extensively revised for the 1993 edition. New components were added, new benchmarks adopted, and a new discount rate assumed. The costs are not comparable to those of prior years.

STATE LAWS

Currently all states and the District of Columbia have 21-year-old drinking age and child safety seat laws. Breath-alcohol ignition interlock device laws are currently in effect in 40 states. Mandatory belt use laws are in effect in 49 states plus the District of Columbia. Graduated licensing is in effect in some form in 43 states and the District of Columbia.

STATE LAWS

State	Alcohol Laws					Mandatory Belt Use Law		Graduated Licensing Laws				
	Administrative License Revocation^a	BAC Limit^b	Zero Tolerance Limit^c for Minors	Alcohol Ignition Interlock Device^d	Enforcement	Seating Positions Covered by Law	Minimum Instructional Permit Period^e	Minimum Hours of Supervised Driving^f	Passenger Restrictions	Nighttime Driving Restrictions	Unrestricted License Minimum Age^g
Alabama	1996	0.08	0.02	no	standard	front	6 mo.	30/–	none	yes	17 yrs. & 6 mo.
Alaska	1983	0.10	0.00	yes	secondary	all	6 mo.	none	none	no	16 yrs.
Arizona	1992	0.10	0.00	yes	secondary	front	5 mo.	25/5	none	no	16 yrs.
Arkansas	1995	0.08	0.02	yes	secondary	front	6 mo.	none	none	no	16 yrs.
California	1989	0.08	0.01	yes^h	standard	all	6 mo.	50/10	yes	yes	17 yrs.
Colorado	1983	0.10	0.02	yes^h	secondary	front	6 mo.	50/10	none	yes	17 yrs.
Connecticut	1990	0.10	0.02	no	standard	front^i	6 mo.	none	none	no	16 yrs. & 4 mo.
Delaware	yes	0.10	0.02	yes^h	standard	front	6 mo.	none^j	yes	yes	16 yrs. & 10 mo.
District of Columbia	yes	0.08	0.00	no	standard	all	6 mo.	40+10^k	yes	yes	18 yrs.
Florida	1990	0.08	0.02	yes	secondary	front	12 mo.	50/10	none	yes	18 yrs.
Georgia	1995	0.08	0.02	yes^h	standard	front^i	12 mo.	40/6	yes	yes	18 yrs.
Hawaii	1990	0.08	0.02	no	standard	front^l	3 mo.	none	none	no	16 yrs.
Idaho	1994	0.08	0.02	yes	secondary	front	4 mo.	50/10	none	yes	16 yrs.
Illinois	1986	0.08	0.00	yes^h	secondary	front	3 mo.	25/–	none	yes	17 yrs.
Indiana	yes	0.10	0.02	yes	standard	front	2 mo.	none	yes	yes	18 yrs.
Iowa	1982	0.10	0.02	yes	standard	front	6 mo.	20/2	none	yes	17 yrs.
Kansas	1988	0.08	0.02	yes	secondary	front	none	50/10	none	no	16 yrs.
Kentucky	no	0.08	0.02	yes^h	standard	all	6 mo.	none	none	yes^o	16 yrs. & 6 mo.
Louisiana	1984	0.10	0.02	yes	standard	front^l	3 mo.	none	none	yes	17 yrs.
Maine	1984	0.08	0.00	yes^h	secondary	all	3 mo.	35/5	yes	no	16 yrs. & 3 mo.
Maryland	1989	0.08^m	0.00	yes	standard	front^n	4 mo.	40/–	none	yes	17 yrs. & 7 mo.
Massachusetts	1994	0.08	0.02	no	secondary	all	6 mo.	12/–	yes	yes	18 yrs.
Michigan	no	0.10	0.02	yes^h	standard	front^i	6 mo.	50/10	none	yes	17 yrs.
Minnesota	1976	0.10	0.01	no	secondary	front^i	6 mo.	30/10	none	no	17 yrs.
Mississippi	1983	0.10	0.02	yes^h	secondary	front	6 mo.	none	none	yes	16 yrs.
Missouri	1987	0.10	0.02	yes^h	secondary	front^i	6 mo.	20/–	none	yes	18 yrs.
Montana	no	0.10	0.02	yes	secondary	all	none	none	none	no	15 yrs.
Nebraska	1993	0.08	0.02	yes	secondary	front^i	none	50/–^k	none	yes	17 yrs.
Nevada	1983	0.10	0.02	yes^h	secondary	all	none	50/–	none	no	16 yrs.
New Hampshire	1993	0.08	0.02	no	no law	—	3 mo.	20/–	none	yes	18 yrs.
New Jersey	no	0.10	0.01	yes^h	standard	front	6 mo.	none	none	yes	17 yrs. & 6 mo.
New Mexico	1984	0.08	0.02	yes^h	standard	all	6 mo.	50/10	yes	yes	16 yrs. & 6 mo.
New York	1994^p	0.10^m	0.02	yes^h	standard	front^i	none	none	none	yes	17 yrs.
North Carolina	1983	0.08	0.00	yes^h	standard	front^i	12 mo.	none	none	yes	16 yrs. & 6 mo.
North Dakota	1983	0.10	0.02	yes^h	secondary	front	6 mo.	none	none	no	16 yrs.
Ohio	1993	0.10	0.02	yes	secondary	front	6 mo.	50/10	none	yes	17 yrs.
Oklahoma	1983	0.10	0.00	yes	standard	front	none	none	none	no	16 yrs.
Oregon	1983	0.08	0.00	yes	secondary	all	6 mo.	50/–	yes	yes	17 yrs.
Pennsylvania	no	0.10	0.02	yes^h	secondary	front	6 mo.	50/–	none	yes	17 yrs.
Rhode Island	no	0.08	0.02	yes^h	secondary	all	6 mo.	none	none	yes	17 yrs. & 6 mo.
South Carolina	1998	0.10	0.02	no	standard	front^q	6 mo.	40/10	yes	yes	16 yrs. & 6 mo.
South Dakota	no	0.08	0.02	no	secondary	front	6 mo.^r	none	none	yes	16 yrs.
Tennessee	no	0.10	0.02	yes	secondary	front^i	6 mo.	50/10	yes	yes	17 yrs.
Texas	1995	0.08	0.00	yes^h	standard	front	6 mo.	none	none	yes	16 yrs. & 6 mo.
Utah	1983	0.08	0.00	yes	secondary^s	all	none	30/10	yes	yes	17 yrs.
Vermont	1969^p	0.08	.02 (<18)	no	secondary	all	12 mo.	40/10	yes	no	16 yrs. & 6 mo.
Virginia	1995	0.08	0.02	yes	secondary	front	9 mo.	40/10	yes	yes	18 yrs.
Washington	1998	0.08	0.02	yes^h	standard	all	6 mo.	50/10	yes	yes	17 yrs.
West Virginia	1981	0.10	0.02	yes	secondary	front^i	6 mo.	30/–^k	yes	yes	17 yrs.
Wisconsin	1988	0.10^t	.00 (<19)	yes^h	secondary	front^q	6 mo.	30/10	yes	yes	16 yrs. & 9 mo.
Wyoming	1973	0.08	0.02	no	secondary	all	10 days	none	none	no	16 yrs.

Source: Offices of State Governor's Highway Safety Representatives (survey of state laws as of May 2002). Graduated licensing data adapted from Insurance Institute for Highway Safety: U.S. Licensing Systems for Young Drivers, © 2002, used by permission.

a Year original law became effective, not when grandfather clauses expired.
b Blood alcohol concentration that constitutes the threshold of legal intoxication.
c Blood alcohol concentration that constitutes "zero tolerance" threshold for minors (<21 years of age unless otherwise noted).
d Legislation for instruments designed to prevent drivers from starting their cars when breath alcohol content is at or above a set point.
e Minimum instructional periods often include time spent in driver's education classes.
f Figures shown as follows: Total hours/Nighttime hours. For example, 25/5 means 25 hours of supervised driving, 5 of which must be at night.
g Minimum age to obtain unrestricted license, provided driver is crash and violation free. Alcohol restrictions still apply at least until 21.
h Primarily for repeat offenders (CA, CO, DE, GA, IL, KY, ME, MI, MS, MO, NV, NJ, NM, NY, NC, ND, PA, RI, TX, WA, WI). Under certain circumstances, a judge may order interlock installation.

i Required for certain ages at all seating positions.
j No minimum amount of supervised driving, but with level 1 permit driving has to be supervised at all times for the first 6 months.
k DC: 40 hours of supervised driving during learner's stage; 10 hours at night during intermediate stage. NE, WV: none if driver's education course completed.
l Front for all occupants and back seat occupants 17 and under in HI, and through age 12 in LA.
m BAC of 0.07 is prima facie evidence of DUI (MD). BAC of 0.05—0.10 constitutes driving while ability impaired (NY).
n Excluding front center seat. Required for all seats for occupants under 16.
o During permit period only.
p Revocation by judicial action (NY) or Department of Motor Vehicles (VT).
q Belt use required in rear seat if lap/shoulder belt is available.
r Three-month instructional period with driver's education.
s Secondary for 19 and older, standard for under 19.
t 0.08 after second DUI conviction.

TEENAGE SEAT BELT USE

Teenage drivers in the U.S. have a higher crash risk than any other age group, whether measured in terms of miles driven or population. In 2000, 4,698 teenagers ages 16-19 died as the result of a motor-vehicle crash, with teenagers representing 11% of all driver fatalities, 11% of all pedestrian and cyclist fatalities, and 16% of all passenger fatalities. Teenagers are also known to have lower seat belt use than older age groups. Therefore, the consequences of teenagers' higher crash risks are compounded by their failure to wear seat belts. A recent paper examined teenage belt use rates in the U.S. using data for drivers who were fatally injured in traffic crashes during the period 1995–2000.

Belt use during the study period was 36% among fatally injured teenage drivers and 23% among fatally injured teenage passengers. Significant predictors of states' belt use included the states' mean observed belt use rate, 2000 population, existence of a primary belt use law, and 2000 median household income. For teenagers, the existence of a primary belt use law was the factor with the highest predictive value; a primary law was associated with a 6.6 percentage point increase in belt use among fatally injured teenage drivers.

Belt use among teenage drivers declined with age. Lower belt use also was associated with male drivers;

drivers of SUVs, vans, or pickup trucks rather than cars; older vehicles; crashes occurring from midnight to 5:59 A.M. rather than from 6 A.M. to 11:59 P.M.; and crashes occurring on rural roadways. Driver belt use declined as the number of teenage passengers increased, but increased in the presence of at least one passenger 30 years of age or older.

State belt use rates exhibited a wide degree of variability, with rates for the period 1995–2000 for fatally injured teenage drivers ranging from 20% or less in six states to more than 60% in two states. When comparing states' driver belt use rates, states with strong primary belt use laws and high rates of observed belt use for all ages had the highest teen belt use rates. States seeking to increase teenage belt use are encouraged to enact strong primary belt use laws accompanied by highly publicized efforts to enforce those laws. It is estimated that if belt use rates for teenagers involved in potentially fatal crashes had been 60% instead of the 52% observed in potentially fatal crashes during the study period 1995–2000, an additional 804 drivers would have survived. At use rates of 70% and 80%, the estimated number of additional drivers saved increases to 1,655 and 2,507, respectively.

Source: McCartt, A. T., & Shabanova, V. I. (July, 2002). Teenage seat belt use: White paper. Trumbull, CT: Pruesser Research Group, Inc.

PERCENT BELT USE AMONG FATALLY INJURED 16- TO 19-YEAR-OLD DRIVERS, UNITED STATES 1995–2000

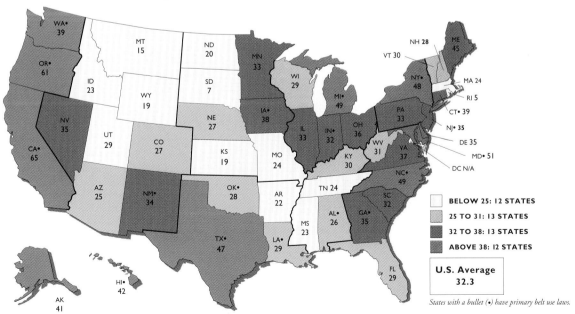

ALCOHOL

According to studies conducted by the National Highway Traffic Safety Administration (NHTSA), about 40% of all traffic fatalities in 2000 involved an intoxicated or alcohol-impaired driver or nonmotorist. In 2000, 31% of all traffic fatalities occurred in crashes where at least one driver or nonoccupant was intoxicated (blood alcohol concentration [BAC] of 0.10 or greater). Of the 12,892 people killed in such crashes, 69% were themselves intoxicated. The other 31% were passengers, nonintoxicated drivers, or nonintoxicated nonoccupants. The following data summarizes the extent of alcohol involvement in motor-vehicle crashes:

• Traffic fatalities in alcohol-related crashes rose by 4% from 1999 to 2000 and declined by 25% from 1990 to 2000. (See corresponding chart.) In 1990, alcohol-related fatalities accounted for 50% of all traffic deaths.

• According to NHTSA, alcohol was involved in 40% of fatal crashes and 8% of all crashes, both fatal and nonfatal, in 2000.

• Approximately 1.5 million drivers were arrested in 1999 for driving under the influence of alcohol or narcotics.

• About 3 in every 10 Americans will be involved in an alcohol-related crash at some time in their lives.

• There were 16,653 alcohol-related traffic fatalities in 2000, an average of one alcohol-related fatality every 32 minutes. An average of one person every 2 minutes is injured in a crash where alcohol is present.

• In 2000, alcohol was present in 30% of all fatal crashes on weekdays, compared to 53% on weekends. The rate of alcohol involvement in fatal crashes during the day is 18%, compared to 61% at night.

PERCENT OF TOTAL TRAFFIC FATALITIES WITH ALCOHOL PRESENT, BY STATE, 2000

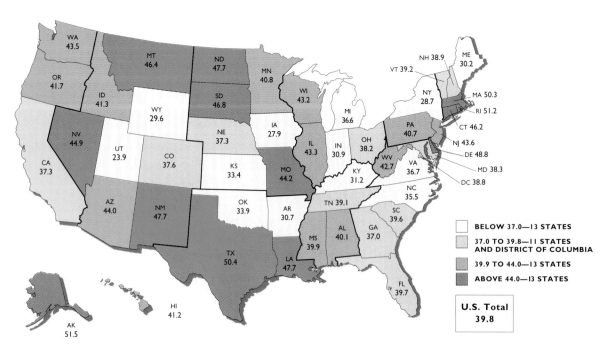

- From 1990 to 2000, intoxication rates decreased for drivers of all age groups. The greatest decrease was for 16-to-20-year-old drivers (29%). NHTSA estimates that 20,043 lives have been saved by 21-year-old minimum drinking age laws since 1975. All states and the District of Columbia now have such laws.

- Safety belts were used by about 22% of fatally injured intoxicated drivers, compared to 32% of fatally injured alcohol-impaired drivers and 51% of fatally injured sober drivers.

- The driver, pedestrian, or both were intoxicated in 38% of all fatal pedestrian crashes in 2000. In these crashes, the intoxication rate for pedestrians was more than double the rate for drivers.

- The cost of alcohol-related motor-vehicle crashes is estimated by the National Safety Council at $31.2 billion in 2001.

Source: National Center for Statistics and Analysis. (2001). Traffic Safety Facts 2000—Alcohol. Washington, DC: National Highway Traffic Safety Administration.

PERCENT OF ALL TRAFFIC FATALITIES THAT OCCURRED IN ALCOHOL-RELATED CRASHES, 1990–2000

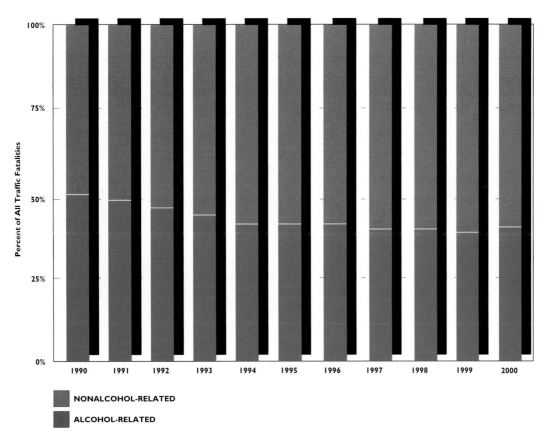

NONALCOHOL-RELATED

ALCOHOL-RELATED

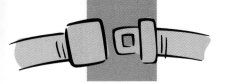

OCCUPANT PROTECTION

Safety Belts
- When used, lap/shoulder safety belts reduce the risk of fatal injury to front seat passenger car occupants by 45% and reduce the risk of moderate-to-critical injury by 50%.

- For light truck occupants, safety belts reduce the risk of fatal injury by 60% and moderate-to-critical injury by 65%.

- Forty-nine states and the District of Columbia have mandatory belt use laws in effect, the only exception being New Hampshire. Thirty-two of the states with belt use laws in effect in 2000 specified secondary enforcement (i.e., police officers are permitted to write a citation only after a vehicle is stopped for some other traffic infraction). Seventeen states and the District of Columbia had laws that allowed primary enforcement, enabling officers to stop vehicles and write citations whenever they observe violations of the belt law.

- Safety belts saved an estimated 11,889 lives in 2000 among passenger vehicle occupants over 4 years old. An *additional* 9,238 lives could have been saved in 2000 if all passenger vehicle occupants over age 4 wore safety belts. From 1975 through 2000, an estimated 135,102 lives were saved by safety belts.

- Safety belts provide the greatest protection against occupant ejection. Among crashes in which a fatality occurred in 2000, only 1% of restrained passenger car occupants were ejected, compared to 22% of unrestrained occupants.

- The results of a 1995 study by the National Highway Traffic Safety Administration suggest that belt use among fatally injured occupants was at least 15% higher in states with primary enforcement laws.

Air Bags
- Air bags, combined with lap/shoulder belts, offer the best available protection for passenger vehicle occupants. The overall fatality-reducing effectiveness for air bags is estimated at 12% over and above the benefits from using safety belts alone.

- Lap/shoulder belts should always be used, even in a vehicle with an air bag. Air bags are a supplemental form of protection and are not designed to deploy in crashes that are not severe.

- Children in rear-facing child seats should not be placed in the front seat of vehicles equipped with passenger-side air bags. The impact of the deploying air bag could result in injury to the child.

- An estimated 1,584 lives were saved by air bags in 2000 and a total of 6,553 lives were saved from 1987 through 2000.

- Beginning September 1997, all new passenger cars were required to have driver and passenger side air bags. In 1998, the same requirement went into effect for light trucks.

ESTIMATED LIVES SAVED BY SAFETY BELT USE, 1975–2000

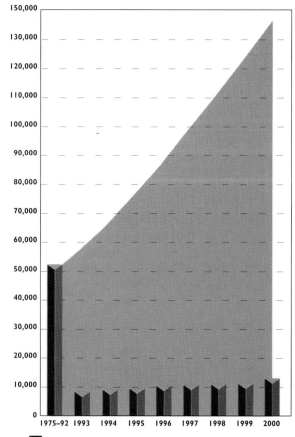

■ LIVES SAVED—SAFETY BELTS

▨ CUMULATIVE LIVES SAVED—SAFETY BELTS

Child restraints

- Child restraints saved an estimated 316 lives in 2000 among children under the age of 5. Of the 316 lives saved, 282 were attributed to the use of child safety seats while 33 lives were spared with the use of adult belts.

- At 100% child safety seat use for children under the age of 5, an estimated additional 143 lives could have been saved in 2000.

- All states and the District of Columbia have had child restraint use laws in effect since 1985.

- Research has shown that child safety seats reduce fatal injury in passenger cars by 71% for infants (less than 1 year old), and by 54% for toddlers (1–4 years old). For infants and toddlers in light trucks, the corresponding reductions are 58% and 59%, respectively.

- In 2000, there were 529 occupant fatalities among children less than 5 years of age. Of these, an estimated 47% were totally unrestrained.

- An estimated 4,816 lives have been saved by child restraints from 1975 through 2000.

Motorcycle Helmets

- Motorcycle helmets are estimated to be 29% effective in preventing fatal injuries to motorcyclists.

- Helmets saved the lives of 631 motorcyclists in 2000. An additional 382 lives could have been saved if all motorcyclists had worn helmets.

- According to the latest observational survey by the National Highway Traffic Safety Administration (NHTSA), helmet use was at 67% in 1998. Previous NHTSA surveys have reported helmet use to be essentially 100% in areas with helmet use laws governing all riders, compared to 34% to 54% at sites with no helmet use laws or laws limited to minors. Reported helmet use rates for fatally injured motorcyclists in 2000 were 55% for operators and 48% for passengers, the same as in 1999.

- In 2000, 20 states, the District of Columbia, and Puerto Rico required helmet use by all motorcycle operators and passengers. In another 27 states, only persons under 18 were required to wear helmets. Three states had no laws requiring helmet use.

Source: National Center for Statistics and Analysis. (2001). Traffic Safety Facts 2000—Occupant Protection; Traffic Safety Facts 2000—Motorcycles. Washington, DC: National Highway Traffic Safety Administration.

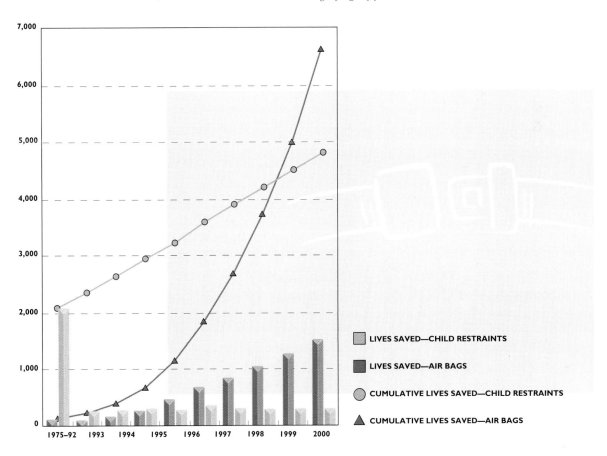

LIVES SAVED—CHILD RESTRAINTS

LIVES SAVED—AIR BAGS

CUMULATIVE LIVES SAVED—CHILD RESTRAINTS

CUMULATIVE LIVES SAVED—AIR BAGS

DEATHS AND DEATH RATES BY DAY AND NIGHT

About 58% of all motor-vehicle deaths in 2001 occurred during the day, while the remainder occurred at night. Death rates based on mileage, however, were over two times higher at night than during the day with vehicle miles traveled by night representing only 25% of the total.

Source: State traffic authorities and the Federal Highway Administration.

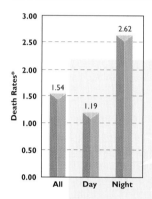

DEATH RATES BY DAY AND NIGHT, 2001

*Per 100,000,000 vehicle miles

DEATHS AND MILEAGE DEATH RATES BY MONTH

Motor-vehicle deaths in 2001 were at their lowest level in February and increased to their highest level in December. In 2001, the highest monthly mileage death rate of 1.86 deaths per 100,000,000 vehicle miles occurred in December. The overall rate for the year was 1.54.

Source: Deaths—National Safety Council estimates. Mileage—Federal Highway Administration, Traffic Volume Trends.

MOTOR-VEHICLE DEATHS AND MILEAGE DEATH RATES BY MONTH, 2001

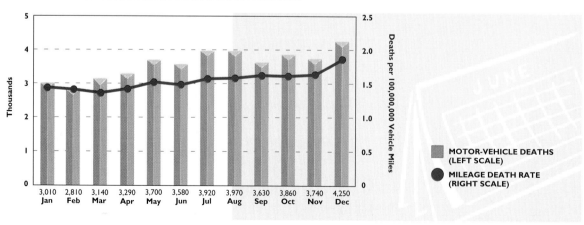

MOTOR-VEHICLE ACCIDENTS
BY TIME OF DAY AND DAY OF WEEK

More fatal accidents occurred on Saturday than any other day of the week in 2001, according to reports from state traffic authorities. Nearly 18% of fatal accidents occurred on Saturday, compared to about 16% on Fridays and over 15% on Sundays. For all accidents, Friday had the highest percentage with about 17%.

Patterns by hour of day for fatal accidents show peaks during afternoon rush hour for weekdays and, especially, late night for weekends. For all accidents, peaks occur during both morning and afternoon rush hours.

PERCENT OF WEEKLY ACCIDENTS BY HOUR OF DAY AND DAY OF WEEK, UNITED STATES, 2001

Time of Day	Fatal Accidents								All Accidents							
	Total	Mon.	Tues.	Wed.	Thurs.	Fri.	Sat.	Sun.	Total	Mon.	Tues.	Wed.	Thurs.	Fri.	Sat.	Sun.
All Hours	100.0%	12.9%	12.6%	12.1%	13.3%	15.9%	17.7%	15.5%	100.0%	14.5%	14.3%	14.6%	14.6%	17.2%	13.9%	10.9%
Midnight–3:59 A.M.	14.6%	1.5%	1.1%	1.2%	1.7%	1.7%	3.8%	3.6%	6.2%	0.6%	0.5%	0.5%	0.6%	0.7%	1.6%	1.6%
4:00–7:59 A.M.	11.8%	1.6%	1.9%	1.4%	1.5%	1.6%	1.9%	1.9%	10.3%	1.7%	1.8%	1.7%	1.7%	1.6%	1.0%	0.8%
8:00–11:59 A.M.	13.4%	1.8%	2.0%	1.8%	1.9%	1.8%	2.2%	1.9%	18.0%	2.8%	2.8%	2.8%	2.8%	2.9%	2.4%	1.5%
Noon–3:59 P.M.	18.8%	2.8%	2.7%	2.3%	2.7%	3.0%	2.7%	2.6%	26.3%	4.0%	3.8%	3.8%	3.8%	4.7%	3.6%	2.7%
4:00–7:59 P.M.	22.7%	2.9%	2.9%	3.0%	2.9%	3.9%	3.7%	3.3%	26.8%	3.9%	4.0%	4.1%	4.1%	4.8%	3.2%	2.7%
8:00–11:59 P.M.	18.7%	2.3%	2.0%	2.3%	2.6%	3.9%	3.4%	2.2%	12.3%	1.4%	1.4%	1.6%	1.6%	2.4%	2.3%	1.6%

Source: Based on reports from 13 state traffic authorities.
Note: Column and row totals may not equal sums of parts due to rounding.

PERCENT OF ACCIDENTS BY TIME OF DAY AND DAY OF WEEK, 2001

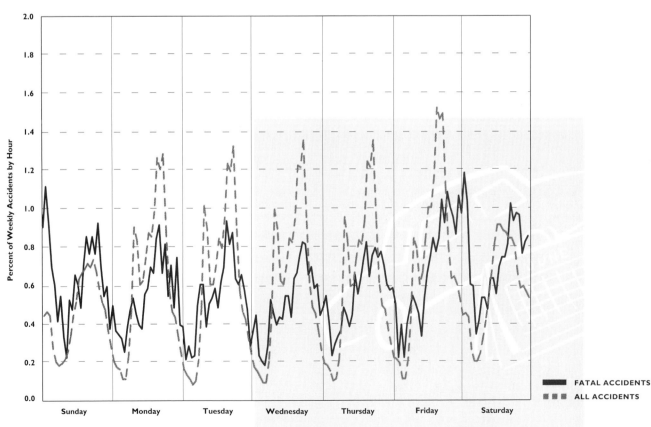

TYPE OF MOTOR VEHICLE

The types of vehicles listed in the table below are classified by body style, not by vehicle use. The light truck category includes both commercial and noncommercial trucks under 10,000 pounds gross vehicle weight. It also includes minivans and sport-utility vehicles. The medium/heavy truck category includes truck tractors with or without semi-trailers.

Passenger Cars

In 2001, passenger cars comprised about 60% of the registered vehicles and were involved in more than their share of motor-vehicle accidents (63.7%). Approximately three-fifths of all motor-vehicle occupant fatalities are passenger car occupants. (See corresponding chart.)

Trucks

Light trucks represent about 35% of all motor-vehicle registrations and about 37% of vehicles involved in fatal accidents. Medium and heavy trucks account for over 4% of registered vehicles and about 8% of vehicles involved in fatal accidents. Medium and heavy truck occupants as well as light truck occupants are slightly under-represented in motor-vehicle occupant fatalities compared to their proportion of registrations. Medium and heavy truck occupants account for only about

2% of all motor-vehicle occupant fatalities, and light truck occupants account for 33%.

There were 887,000 light truck occupants and 31,000 large truck occupants injured in 2000, according to the National Highway Traffic Safety Administration.

Motorcycles

The number of registered motorcycles in the United States totaled about 4,346,000 in 2001, compared to approximately 4,177,000 a decade earlier. Although motorcycles accounted for less than 2% of the total 226,000,000 vehicle registrations in 2001, they were over-represented in the distribution of fatalities by type of vehicle. Of the 36,200 occupant deaths in motor-vehicle accidents in 2001, about 2,600 (7%) were motorcycle riders. Approximately 58,000 riders and passengers were injured in 2000 according to the National Highway Traffic Safety Administration.

Motorcycles traveled an estimated 10.5 billion miles in 2001. The 2001 mileage death rate for motorcycle riders is estimated to be about 25 occupant deaths per 100,000,000 miles of motorcycle travel, about 21 times the mileage death rate for occupants of other types of vehicles (passenger autos, trucks, buses, etc.).

TYPES OF MOTOR VEHICLES INVOLVED IN ACCIDENTS, 2001

Type of Vehicle	In Fatal Accidents		In All Accidents		Percent of Total Vehicle Registrations[a]	No. of Occupant Fatalities
	Number	Percent	Number	Percent		
All Types	**55,700**	**100.0%**	**21,300,000**	**100.0%**	**100.0%**	**36,200[b]**
Passenger cars	26,500	47.6	13,570,000	63.7	59.2	20,100
Trucks	25,300	45.4	7,440,000	34.9	38.6	12,520
Light trucks	20,600	37.0	6,690,000	31.4	34.5	11,800
Medium/heavy trucks	4,700	8.4	750,000	3.5	4.1	720
Farm tractor, equipment	100	0.2	7,000	(c)	(d)	50
Buses, commercial	100	0.2	65,000	0.3	0.1	(e)
Buses, school	200	0.3	56,000	0.3	0.3	30
Motorcycles	2,600	4.7	119,000	0.6	} 1.9	2,600
Motor scooters, motor bikes	100	0.2	2,000	(c)		100
Other	800	1.4	41,000	0.2	(d)	800

Source: Based on reports from 15 state traffic authorities. Vehicle registrations based on data from Federal Highway Administration. Estimating procedures were changed for the 1998 edition and are not comparable to estimates in previous editions.

[a] Percentage figures are based on numbers of vehicles and do not reflect miles traveled or place of travel, both of which affect accident experience. Percents may not add due to rounding.
[b] In addition to these occupant fatalities, there were 5,800 pedestrian, 800 pedalcyclist, and 100 other deaths.
[c] Less than 0.05%.
[d] Data not available.
[e] Less than 5.

REGISTRATIONS, INVOLVEMENTS, AND OCCUPANT FATALITIES BY TYPE OF VEHICLE, 2001

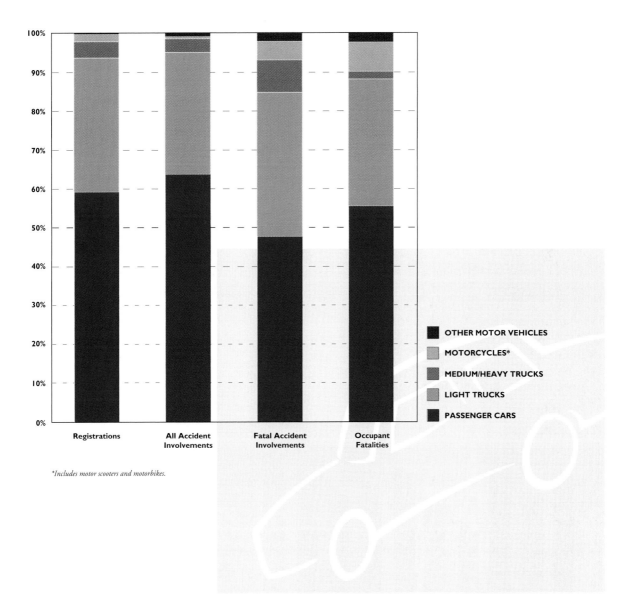

OTHER MOTOR VEHICLES
MOTORCYCLES*
MEDIUM/HEAVY TRUCKS
LIGHT TRUCKS
PASSENGER CARS

*Includes motor scooters and motorbikes.

SCHOOL BUS TRANSPORTATION, 2000

School bus-related crashes killed 144 persons and injured an estimated 20,000 persons nationwide in 2000, according to data from the National Highway Traffic Safety Administration's (NHTSA) Fatality Analysis Reporting System (FARS) and General Estimates System (GES).

A school bus-related crash is defined by NHTSA to be any crash in which a vehicle, regardless of body design, used as a school bus is directly or indirectly involved, such as a crash involving school children alighting from a vehicle.

Over the period from 1995–2000, about 71% of the deaths in fatal school bus-related crashes were occupants of vehicles other than the school bus and 18% were pedestrians. About 6% were school bus passengers and 3% were school bus drivers.

Of the pedestrians killed in school bus-related crashes over this period, approximately 75% were struck by the school bus.

Out of the people injured in school bus-related crashes from 1995 through 2000, about 43% were school bus passengers, 9% were school bus drivers, and another 44% were occupants of other vehicles. The remainder were pedestrians, pedalcyclists, and other or unknown type persons.

Characteristics of school bus transportation
School Bus Fleet (www.schoolbusfleet.com/stats.cfm) found that in the 1999–2000 school year, 49 states reported about 23.0 million public school pupils were transported at public expense and 31 states reported another 0.8 million private school pupils were transported at public expense. This compares to estimates from the U.S. Department of Education of enrollments in fall 1999 in grades K–12 of about 46.8 million public school pupils and 5.9 million private school pupils nationwide. About 458,000 school buses were reported in use in 50 states, and the buses in 43 states traveled about 4.1 billion route miles.

FATALITIES IN SCHOOL BUS-RELATED CRASHES, UNITED STATES, 1991–2000

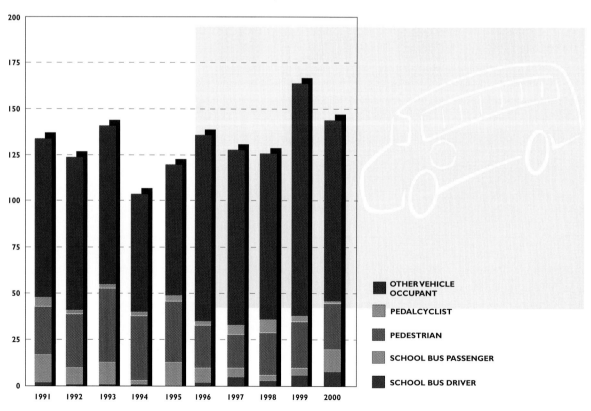

DEATHS AND INJURIES IN SCHOOL BUS-RELATED CRASHES, UNITED STATES, 1995–2000

	1995	1996	1997	1998	1999	2000
Deaths						
Total	121	136	128	126	164	144
School bus driver	0	2	5	3	6	8
School bus passenger	13	8	5	3	4	12
Pedestrian	33	23	18	23	25	25
Pedalcyclist	3	2	5	7	3	1
Occupant of other vehicle	71	101	95	90	126	98
Other or Unknown	1	0	0	0	0	0
Injuries						
Total	18,000	15,000	19,000	17,000	18,000	20,000
School bus driver	2,000	1,000	2,000	2,000	1,000	2,000
School bus passenger	7,000	7,000	10,000	6,000	8,000	8,000
Pedestrian	(a)	(a)	(a)	(a)	(a)	1,000
Pedalcyclist	(a)	(a)	(a)	(a)	(a)	(a)
Occupant of other vehicle	8,000	6,000	7,000	9,000	8,000	9,000
Other or Unknown	(a)	(a)	(a)	(a)	(a)	(a)

Source: National Highway Traffic Safety Administration. Traffic Safety Facts, *1995–2000 editions. Washington, DC: Author.*
[a]*Less than 500.*

PEDESTRIAN DEATHS IN SCHOOL BUS-RELATED CRASHES, UNITED STATES, 1995–2000

	Age Group				
	All Ages	**Under 5**	**5–9**	**10–15**	**16 and older**
1995	33	3	12	7	11
Struck by bus	*23*	*3*	*7*	*2*	*11*
1996	23	1	11	3	8
Struck by bus	*16*	*0*	*7*	*1*	*8*
1997	18	0	8	3	7
Struck by bus	*16*	*0*	*6*	*3*	*7*
1998	23	3	9	1	10
Struck by bus	*20*	*3*	*6*	*1*	*10*
1999	25	0	13	4	8
Struck by bus	*19*	*0*	*10*	*2*	*7*
2000	25	5	10	2	8
Struck by bus	*16*	*2*	*8*	*0*	*6*

Source: National Highway Traffic Safety Administration. Traffic Safety Facts, *1995–2000 editions. Washington, DC: Author.*

AGE OF DRIVER

The table below shows the total number of licensed drivers and drivers involved in accidents by selected ages and age groups. The figures in the last two columns indicate the frequency of accident involvement on the basis of the number of drivers in each age group. The fatal accident involvement rates per 100,000 drivers in each age group ranged from a low of 18 for drivers 65 to 74 years of age to a high of 65 for drivers aged 19. The all accident involvement rates per 100 drivers in each age group ranged from 6 for drivers in the 65-to-74 and 75-and-over age groups to 34 for drivers aged 16.

On the basis of miles driven by each age group, however, involvement rates (not shown in the table) are highest for young and for old drivers. For drivers aged 16 to 19, the fatal involvement rate per 100 million vehicle miles traveled was 9.2 in 1990, about three times the overall rate for all drivers in passenger vehicles, 3.0. The rate for drivers aged 75 and over was 11.5, the highest of all age groups. The same basic U-shaped curve is found for injury accident involvement rates.[a]

[a] Massie, D., Campbell, K., & Williams, A. (1995). *Traffic accident involvement rates by driver age and gender.* Accident Analysis and Prevention, 27 (1), 73–87.

AGE OF DRIVER—TOTAL NUMBER AND NUMBER IN ACCIDENTS, 2001

| Age Group | Licensed Drivers | | Drivers in Accidents | | | | | |
| | Number | Percent | Fatal | | All | | Per No. of Drivers | |
			Number	Percent	Number	Percent	Fatal[a]	All[b]
Total	193,300,000	100.0%	55,700	100.0%	21,300,000	100.0%	29	11
Under 16	57,000	(c)	300	0.5	90,000	0.4	(d)	(d)
16	1,506,000	0.8	900	1.6	510,000	2.4	60	34
17	2,331,000	1.2	1,300	2.3	660,000	3.1	56	28
18	2,850,000	1.5	1,800	3.2	810,000	3.8	63	28
19	3,212,000	1.7	2,100	3.8	780,000	3.7	65	24
19 and under	9,956,000	5.2	6,400	11.5	2,850,000	13.4	64	29
20	3,253,000	1.7	1.700	3.1	720,000	3.4	52	22
21	3,396,000	1.8	1,900	3.4	670,000	3.1	56	20
22	3,227,000	1.7	1,600	2.9	610,000	2.9	50	19
23	3,235,000	1.7	1,500	2.7	570,000	2.7	46	18
24	3,275,000	1.7	1,300	2.3	530,000	2.5	40	16
20–24	16,386,000	8.5	8,000	14.4	3,100,000	14.6	49	19
25–34	34,967,000	18.1	11,500	20.6	4,670,000	21.9	33	13
35–44	42,732,000	22.1	10,900	19.6	4,350,000	20.4	26	10
45–54	37,823,000	19.6	8,500	15.3	3,160,000	14.8	22	8
55–64	23,481,000	12.1	4,600	8.3	1,620,000	7.6	20	7
65–74	16,030,000	8.3	2,900	5.2	890,000	4.2	18	6
75 and over	11,925,000	6.2	2,900	5.2	660,000	3.1	24	6

Source: National Safety Council estimates. Drivers in accidents based on reports from 11 state traffic authorities. Total licensed drivers from the Federal Highway Administration; age distribution by National Safety Council.
Note: Percents may not add to total due to rounding.
[a] Drivers in fatal accidents per 100,000 licensed drivers in each age group.
[b] Drivers in all accidents per 100 licensed drivers in each age group.
[c] Less than 0.05.
[d] Rates for drivers under age 16 are substantially overstated due to the high proportion of unlicensed drivers involved.

Of the estimated 193,300,000 licensed drivers in 2001, about 97,100,000 (50.2%) were males and 96,200,000 (49.8%) were females. Males account for about 62% of the miles driven each year, according to the latest estimates, and females for 38%. At least part of the difference in involvement rates, cited below, may be due to differences in the time, place, and circumstances of driving.

For fatal accidents, males have higher involvement rates than females. About 40,800 male drivers and 14,900 female drivers were involved in fatal accidents in 2001. The involvement rate per one billion miles driven was 24 for males and 14 for females. For all accidents, females have higher involvement rates than males. About 12,700,000 male drivers and 8,600,000 female drivers were involved in all accidents in 2001. Their involvement rates per 10 million miles driven were 74 and 82, respectively.

IMPROPER DRIVING

In most motor-vehicle accidents, factors are present relating to the driver, the vehicle, and the road, and it is the interaction of these factors that often sets up the series of events that results in an accident. The table below relates only to the driver, and shows the principal kinds of improper driving in accidents in 2001 as reported by police.

Exceeding the posted speed limit or driving at an unsafe speed was the most common error in fatal accidents. Right-of-way violations predominated in the injury and all accidents categories.

While some drivers were under the influence of alcohol or other drugs, this represents the driver's physical condition—not a driving error. See page 94 for a discussion of alcohol involvement in traffic accidents.

Correcting the improper practices listed below could reduce the number of accidents. This does not mean, however, that road and vehicle conditions can be disregarded.

IMPROPER DRIVING REPORTED IN ACCIDENTS, 2001

Kind of Improper Driving	Fatal Accidents	Injury Accidents	All Accidents
Total	**100.0%**	**100.0%**	**100.0%**
Improper driving	**59.5**	**57.1**	**54.1**
Speed too fast or unsafe	23.0	14.6	11.7
Right of way	17.9	18.5	18.3
Failed to yield	*9.4*	*13.8*	*11.7*
Disregarded signal	*4.9*	*3.4*	*4.7*
Passed stop sign	*3.6*	*1.3*	*1.9*
Drove left of center	6.3	0.9	0.9
Made improper turn	0.8	1.8	2.3
Improper overtaking	0.9	0.6	0.8
Followed too closely	0.4	4.2	5.4
Other improper driving	10.2	16.5	14.7
No improper driving stated	**40.5**	**42.9**	**45.9**

Source: Based on reports from 9 state traffic authorities.

PEDESTRIANS

In 2001, there were an estimated 5,800 pedestrian deaths and 90,000 injuries in motor-vehicle accidents. About half of these deaths and injuries occur when pedestrians cross or enter streets. Walking in the roadway accounted for about 9% of pedestrian deaths and injuries, with more cases occurring while walking with traffic than against traffic.

The distribution of pedestrian deaths and injuries by action varies for persons of different ages. Crossing or entering at or between intersections was the leading type for each age group. However, this type varied from a low of 49.1% of the total for those aged 0 to 4 years, to a high of 61.7% for those aged 65 and over (see corresponding chart).

DEATHS AND INJURIES OF PEDESTRIANS BY AGE AND ACTION, 2001

Actions	Total[a]	Age of Persons Killed or Injured							
		0–4	5–9	10–14	15–19	20–24	25–44	45–64	65 & Over
All Actions	*100.0%*	*3.6%*	*9.7%*	*12.0%*	*10.9%*	*8.2%*	*27.1%*	*16.9%*	*8.8%*
Totals	**100.0%**	**100.0%**	**100.0%**	**100.0%**	**100.0%**	**100.0%**	**100.0%**	**100.0%**	**100.0%**
Crossing or entering at or between intersections	53.0%	49.1%	56.6%	55.1%	49.4%	49.5%	49.4%	55.3%	61.7%
Walking in the roadway	9.1%	6.9%	6.7%	11.2%	11.6%	9.0%	8.6%	9.9%	7.3%
with traffic	*4.6%*	*2.2%*	*2.4%*	*4.3%*	*5.3%*	*5.3%*	*4.8%*	*5.7%*	*4.5%*
against traffic	*4.5%*	*4.7%*	*4.4%*	*6.9%*	*6.2%*	*3.7%*	*3.8%*	*4.2%*	*2.8%*
Standing (or playing) in roadway	6.3%	10.7%	9.5%	5.6%	6.0%	7.7%	6.9%	4.2%	3.9%
Pushing/working on a vehicle in the roadway	1.2%	0.3%	0.2%	0.4%	1.4%	1.8%	1.6%	1.4%	1.3%
Other working in the roadway	1.1%	0.0%	0.0%	0.2%	0.3%	1.5%	2.0%	1.8%	0.1%
Not in the roadway	8.9%	8.4%	6.5%	7.5%	9.3%	10.3%	10.8%	9.7%	6.3%
Other	8.4%	12.7%	10.4%	8.7%	8.1%	9.3%	7.9%	7.0%	8.8%
Not stated	12.0%	11.8%	10.1%	11.3%	14.0%	10.9%	12.7%	10.7%	10.5%

Source: Based on reports from 13 state traffic authorities.
[a] Total includes "Age Unknown."

PEDESTRIAN DEATHS AND INJURIES BY AGE AND ACTION, 2001

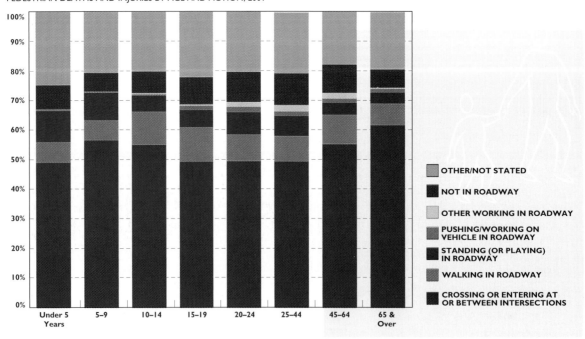

The estimated number of deaths from pedalcycle–motor-vehicle collisions increased from about 750 in 1940 to 1,200 in 1980, then declined to about 800 in 2001. Nonfatal disabling injuries were estimated to number 54,000 in 2001.

In 1999, 652 pedalcyclists died in motor-vehicle crashes and 148 in other accidents according to National Center for Health Statistics mortality data. Males accounted for more than 87% of all pedalcycle deaths, seven times the female fatalities.

Emergency-room–treated injuries associated with bicycles and bicycle accessories were estimated to total

608,608 in 2000, according to the U.S. Consumer Product Safety Commission (see also page 124). The CPSC reported that bike helmet use was 50% in 1998. About 38% of adults and 69% of children under 16 reported wearing bike helmets regularly. The Bicycle Helmet Safety Institute estimates that helmets reduce the risk of all head injuries by up to 85% and reduce the risk of severe head injuries by about one-third. In 2001, 19 states, the District of Columbia, and at least 86 localities had bicycle helmet laws according to the Bicycle Helmet Safety Institute.

Source: National Safety Council estimates and tabulations of National Center for Health Statistics mortality data. Rodgers, G.B., & Tinsworth, D. (1999). Bike Helmets. Consumer Product Safety Review, 4 (1), 1-4.

PEDALCYCLE FATALITIES BY SEX AND AGE GROUP, UNITED STATES, 1999

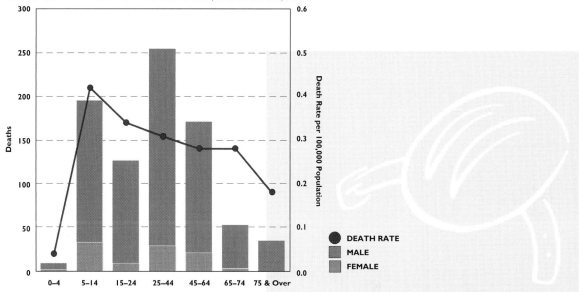

PEDALCYCLE FATALITIES BY MONTH, UNITED STATES, 1999

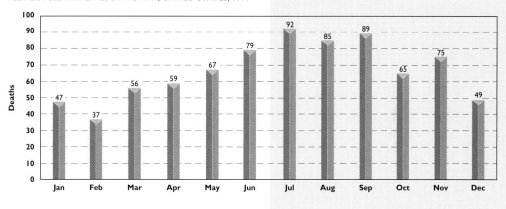

WORK ZONE DEATHS AND INJURIES

In 2000 there were 1,093 people killed and 50,001 people injured in work zone crashes (see table below). Compared to 1999, work zone fatalities and injuries increased 26% and 9%, respectively. Of the 1,093 people killed in work zones, 931 were in construction zones, 100 were in maintenance zones, 12 were in utility zones, and 50 were in an unknown type of work zone.

Over the nine years from 1992 through 2000, work zone deaths have ranged from 638 to 1,093 and averaged 792 per year.

Based on a National Safety Council survey in May 2002 of state governor's highway safety representatives, at least 45 states reported having either work zone speed laws in effect or special penalties for traffic violations in work zones, such as increased or doubled fines.

PERSONS KILLED AND INJURED IN WORK ZONES, UNITED STATES, 2000

	Total	Vehicle Occupants	Pedestrians	Pedalcyclists	Other Nonmotorists
Killed	1,093	916	157	11	9
Injured	50,001	48,784	944	249	24

Source: National Safety Council tabulations of data from National Highway Traffic Safety Administration—2000 Fatality Analysis Reporting System (FARS) and 2000 General Estimates System (GES).

EMERGENCY VEHICLES

CRASHES INVOLVING EMERGENCY VEHICLES, UNITED STATES, 2000

	Ambulance		Fire Truck/Car		Police Car	
	Total	Emergency Use[a]	Total	Emergency Use[a]	Total	Emergency Use[a]
Emergency vehicles in fatal crashes	29	15	21	16	119	44
Emergency vehicles in injury crashes	1,973	1,063	867	604	10,283	4,471
Emergency vehicles in all crashes	**6,516**	**3,809**	**4,123**	**2,288**	**32,328**	**11,011**
Emergency vehicle drivers killed	1	0	4	2	28	8
Emergency vehicle passengers killed	5	1	2	2	5	1
Other vehicle occupants killed	24	16	12	11	88	43
Nonmotorists killed	3	2	3	1	26	8
Total killed in crashes	**33**	**19**	**21**	**16**	**147**	**60**
Total injured in crashes	**3,686**	**1,746**	**1,731**	**1,433**	**16,409**	**8,199**

Source: National Safety Council tabulations of data from National Highway Traffic Safety Administration—2000 Fatality Analysis Reporting System (FARS) and 2000 General Estimates System (GES).
[a]Emergency lights and/or sirens in use.

FLEET ACCIDENT RATES
BY TYPE OF VEHICLE

FLEET ACCIDENT RATES BY TYPE OF VEHICLE, 1999–2001, SUMMARIZED FROM THE NATIONAL FLEET SAFETY CONTEST

Type of Vehicle/Industry	2001			Accidents per 1,000,000 Vehicle Miles	
	No. of Fleets Reporting	No. of Vehicles	Vehicle Miles (Thousands)	2001	1999–2001
Trucks	75	22,454	248,337	5.93	3.96
Government	3	709	9,149	8.20	8.27
Mail Contractors	6	138	13,614	0.44	0.88
Tractor-Trailers	2	64	8,889	0.45	0.87
Straight Truck	4	74	4,725	0.42	1.23
Postal Service	23	1,187	8,227	12.76	12.87
Intercity	4	160	2,369	5.06	6.79
City	2	37	1,073	3.73	8.33
Light Delivery Vehicles (LLV)	17	990	4,783	18.61	15.41
Trucks—Other Industries	18	641	24,220	2.52	3.56
Intercity	12	554	22,661	2.56	2.73
City	6	87	1,559	1.92	4.04
Utilities	25	19,779	193,124	5.75	5.16
Electric Utilities	12	14,311	130,394	5.43	4.77
Water Distribution Utilities	5	581	5,027	12.53	10.74
Communication Utilities	1	18	257	0.00	1.63
Gas Distribution Utilities	6	4,820	56,893	5.96	5.77
Gas Transmission Utilities	1	49	551	1.81	3.09
Buses	28	2,013	65,011	11.77	9.60
Intercity Bus	6	346	20,907	3.63	3.67
Scheduled Route Service	5	340	20,762	3.66	3.70
Charter Group	1	6	145	0.00	0.00
School Bus	13	899	13,323	18.24	12.35
Transit Bus	9	768	30,780	13.45	23.27
Cars	6	175	1,494	21.71	14.05
Emergency & Medical Response	3	85	637	32.92	27.51
Passenger Car—Other Industries	3	90	857	10.50	6.53

Source: Based upon reports of National Safety Council members participating in the National Fleet Safety Contest. The data should not be interpreted as representative of the industries listed or of Council members.

Definitions
Reportable Accident—Any incident involving death, injury, or property damage, regardless of preventability of the incident or the cost of the property damage, except when the vehicle was properly parked.
Intercity Operation—Includes fleets that travel more than 50 miles from their terminal.
City Operation—Includes fleets that travel less than 50 miles from their terminal.

Note: The totals for Trucks, Buses, and Cars may include some other industries/types of operation that are not listed separately.

MOTOR-VEHICLE DEATHS AND RATES

MOTOR-VEHICLE DEATHS AND RATES, UNITED STATES, 1913–2001

Year	No. of Deaths	Estimated No. of Vehicles (Millions)	Estimated Vehicle Miles (Billions)	Estimated No. of Drivers (Millions)	Death Rates		
					Per 10,000 Motor Vehicles	Per 100,000,000 Vehicle Miles	Per 100,000 Population
1913	4,200	1.3	(a)	2.0	33.38	(a)	4.4
1914	4,700	1.8	(a)	3.0	26.65	(a)	4.8
1915	6,600	2.5	(a)	3.0	26.49	(a)	6.6
1916	8,200	3.6	(a)	5.0	22.66	(a)	8.1
1917	10,200	5.1	(a)	7.0	19.93	(a)	10.0
1918	10,700	6.2	(a)	9.0	17.37	(a)	10.3
1919	11,200	7.6	(a)	12.0	14.78	(a)	10.7
1920	12,500	9.2	(a)	14.0	13.53	(a)	11.7
1921	13,900	10.5	(a)	16.0	13.25	(a)	12.9
1922	15,300	12.3	(a)	19.0	12.47	(a)	13.9
1923	18,400	15.1	85	22.0	12.18	21.65	16.5
1924	19,400	17.6	104	26.0	11.02	18.65	17.1
1925	21,900	20.1	122	30.0	10.89	17.95	19.1
1926	23,400	22.2	141	33.0	10.54	16.59	20.1
1927	25,800	23.3	158	34.0	11.07	16.33	21.8
1928	28,000	24.7	173	37.0	11.34	16.18	23.4
1929	31,200	26.7	197	40.0	11.69	15.84	25.7
1930	32,900	26.7	206	40.0	12.32	15.97	26.7
1931	33,700	26.1	216	39.0	12.91	15.60	27.2
1932	29,500	24.4	200	36.0	12.09	14.75	23.6
1933	31,363	24.2	201	35.0	12.96	15.60	25.0
1934	36,101	25.3	216	37.0	14.27	16.71	28.6
1935	36,369	26.5	229	39.0	13.72	15.88	28.6
1936	38,089	28.5	252	42.0	13.36	15.11	29.7
1937	39,643	30.1	270	44.0	13.19	14.68	30.8
1938	32,582	29.8	271	44.0	10.93	12.02	25.1
1939	32,386	31.0	285	46.0	10.44	11.35	24.7
1940	34,501	32.5	302	48.0	10.63	11.42	26.1
1941	39,969	34.9	334	52.0	11.45	11.98	30.0
1942	28,309	33.0	268	49.0	8.58	10.55	21.1
1943	23,823	30.9	208	46.0	7.71	11.44	17.8
1944	24,282	30.5	213	45.0	7.97	11.42	18.3
1945	28,076	31.0	250	46.0	9.05	11.22	21.2
1946	33,411	34.4	341	50.0	9.72	9.80	23.9
1947	32,697	37.8	371	53.0	8.64	8.82	22.8
1948	32,259	41.1	398	55.0	7.85	8.11	22.1
1949	31,701	44.7	424	59.3	7.09	7.47	21.3
1950	34,763	49.2	458	62.2	7.07	7.59	23.0
1951	36,996	51.9	491	64.4	7.13	7.53	24.1
1952	37,794	53.3	514	66.8	7.10	7.36	24.3
1953	37,956	56.3	544	69.9	6.74	6.97	24.0
1954	35,586	58.6	562	72.2	6.07	6.33	22.1
1955	38,426	62.8	606	74.7	6.12	6.34	23.4
1956	39,628	65.2	631	77.9	6.07	6.28	23.7
1957	38,702	67.6	647	79.6	5.73	5.98	22.7
1958	36,981	68.8	665	81.5	5.37	5.56	21.3
1959	37,910	72.1	700	84.5	5.26	5.41	21.5
1960	38,137	74.5	719	87.4	5.12	5.31	21.2
1961	38,091	76.4	738	88.9	4.98	5.16	20.8
1962	40,804	79.7	767	92.0	5.12	5.32	22.0
1963	43,564	83.5	805	93.7	5.22	5.41	23.1
1964	47,700	87.3	847	95.6	5.46	5.63	25.0
1965	49,163	91.8	888	99.0	5.36	5.54	25.4
1966	53,041	95.9	930	101.0	5.53	5.70	27.1
1967	52,924	98.9	962	103.2	5.35	5.50	26.8
1968	54,862	103.1	1,016	105.4	5.32	5.40	27.5
1969	55,791	107.4	1,071	108.3	5.19	5.21	27.7
1970	54,633	111.2	1,120	111.5	4.92	4.88	26.8
1971	54,381	116.3	1,186	114.4	4.68	4.57	26.3
1972	56,278	122.3	1,268	118.4	4.60	4.43	26.9
1973	55,511	129.8	1,309	121.6	4.28	4.24	26.3
1974	46,402	134.9	1,290	125.6	3.44	3.59	21.8
1975	45,853	137.9	1,330	129.8	3.33	3.45	21.3
1976	47,038	143.5	1,412	133.9	3.28	3.33	21.6

See source and footnotes on page 111.

MOTOR-VEHICLE DEATHS AND RATES, UNITED STATES, 1913–2001, Cont.

| Year | No. of Deaths | Estimated No. of Vehicles (Millions) | Estimated Vehicle Miles (Billions) | Estimated No. of Drivers (Millions) | Death Rates | | |
					Per 10,000 Motor Vehicles	Per 100,000,000 Vehicle Miles	Per 100,000 Population
1977	49,510	148.8	1,477	138.1	3.33	3.35	22.5
1978	52,411	153.6	1,548	140.8	3.41	3.39	23.6
1979	53,524	159.6	1,529	143.3	3.35	3.50	23.8
1980	53,172	161.6	1,521	145.3	3.29	3.50	23.4
1981	51,385	164.1	1,556	147.1	3.13	3.30	22.4
1982	45,779	165.2	1,592	150.3	2.77	2.88	19.8
1983	44,452	169.4	1,657	154.2	2.62	2.68	19.0
1984	46,263	171.8	1,718	155.4	2.69	2.69	19.6
1985	45,901	177.1	1,774	156.9	2.59	2.59	19.3
1986	47,865	181.4	1,835	159.5	2.63	2.60	19.9
1987	48,290	183.9	1,924	161.8	2.63	2.51	19.9
1988	49,078	189.0	2,026	162.9	2.60	2.42	20.1
1989	47,575	191.7	2,107	165.6	2.48	2.26	19.3
1990	46,814	192.9	2,148	167.0	2.43	2.18	18.8
1991	43,536	192.5	2,172	169.0	2.26	2.00	17.3
1992	40,982	194.4	2,240	173.1	2.11	1.83	16.1
1993	41,893	198.0	2,297	173.1	2.12	1.82	16.3
1994	42,524	201.8	2,360	175.4	2.11	1.80	16.3
1995	43,363	205.3	2,423	176.6	2.11	1.79	16.5
1996	43,649	210.4	2,486	179.5	2.07	1.76	16.5
1997	43,458	211.5	2,562	182.7	2.05	1.70	16.2
1998	43,501	215.0	2,632	185.2	2.02	1.65	16.1
1999[b]	42,401	220.5	2,691	187.2	1.92	1.58	15.5
2000[b]	42,500	225.8	2,750	190.6	1.88	1.55	15.4
2001[c]	42,900	230.8	2,778	193.3	1.86	1.54	15.4
Changes							
1991 to 2001	−1%	+20%	+28%	+14%	−18%	−23%	−11%
2000 to 2001	+1%	+2%	+1%	+1%	−1%	−1%	0%

Source: Deaths from National Center for Health Statistics except 1964, 2000, and 2001, which are National Safety Council estimates based on data from state traffic authorities. See Technical Appendix for comparability. Motor-vehicle registrations, mileage, and drivers estimated by Federal Highway Administration except 2001 registrations and drivers, which are National Safety Council estimates.
[a] *Mileage data inadequate prior to 1923.*
[b] *Revised.*
[c] *Preliminary.*

MOTOR-VEHICLE
DEATHS BY TYPE OF ACCIDENT

MOTOR-VEHICLE DEATHS BY TYPE OF ACCIDENT, UNITED STATES, 1913–2001

Year	Total Deaths	Deaths from Collision with—							Deaths from Noncollision Accidents	Nontraffic Deaths[a]
		Pedestrians	Other Motor Vehicles	Railroad Trains	Streetcars	Pedal-cycles	Animal-Drawn Vehicle or Animal	Fixed Objects		
1913	4,200	(b)	(b)	(b)	(b)	(b)	(b)	(b)	(b)	(c)
1914	4,700	(b)	(b)	(b)	(b)	(b)	(b)	(b)	(b)	(c)
1915	6,600	(b)	(b)	(b)	(b)	(b)	(b)	(b)	(b)	(c)
1916	8,200	(b)	(b)	(b)	(b)	(b)	(b)	(b)	(b)	(c)
1917	10,200	(b)	(b)	(b)	(b)	(b)	(b)	(b)	(b)	(c)
1918	10,700	(b)	(b)	(b)	(b)	(b)	(b)	(b)	(b)	(c)
1919	11,200	(b)	(b)	(b)	(b)	(b)	(b)	(b)	(b)	(c)
1920	12,500	(b)	(b)	(b)	(b)	(b)	(b)	(b)	(b)	(c)
1921	13,900	(b)	(b)	(b)	(b)	(b)	(b)	(b)	(b)	(c)
1922	15,300	(b)	(b)	(b)	(b)	(b)	(b)	(b)	(b)	(c)
1923	18,400	(b)	(b)	(b)	(b)	(b)	(b)	(b)	(b)	(c)
1924	19,400	(b)	(b)	1,130	410	(b)	(b)	(b)	(b)	(c)
1925	21,900	(b)	(b)	1,410	560	(b)	(b)	(b)	(b)	(c)
1926	23,400	(b)	(b)	1,730	520	(b)	(b)	(b)	(b)	(c)
1927	25,800	10,820	3,430	1,830	520	(b)	(b)	(b)	(b)	(c)
1928	28,000	11,420	4,310	2,140	570	(b)	(b)	540	8,070	(c)
1929	31,200	12,250	5,400	2,050	530	(b)	(b)	620	9,380	(c)
1930	32,900	12,900	5,880	1,830	480	(b)	(b)	720	9,970	(c)
1931	33,700	13,370	6,820	1,710	440	(b)	(b)	870	9,570	(c)
1932	29,500	11,490	6,070	1,520	320	350	400	800	8,500	(c)
1933	31,363	12,840	6,470	1,437	318	400	310	900	8,680	(c)
1934	36,101	14,480	8,110	1,457	332	500	360	1,040	9,820	(c)
1935	36,369	14,350	8,750	1,587	253	450	250	1,010	9,720	(c)
1936	38,089	15,250	9,500	1,697	269	650	250	1,060	9,410	(c)
1937	39,643	15,500	10,320	1,810	264	700	200	1,160	9,690	(c)
1938	32,582	12,850	8,900	1,490	165	720	170	940	7,350	(c)
1939	32,386	12,400	8,700	1,330	150	710	200	1,000	7,900	(c)
1940	34,501	12,700	10,100	1,707	132	750	210	1,100	7,800	(c)
1941	39,969	13,550	12,500	1,840	118	910	250	1,350	9,450	(c)
1942	28,309	10,650	7,300	1,754	124	650	240	850	6,740	(c)
1943	23,823	9,900	5,300	1,448	171	450	160	700	5,690	(c)
1944	24,282	9,900	5,700	1,663	175	400	140	700	5,600	(c)
1945	28,076	11,000	7,150	1,703	163	500	130	800	6,600	(c)
1946	33,411	11,600	9,400	1,703	174	450	130	950	8,900	(c)
1947	32,697	10,450	9,900	1,736	102	550	150	1,000	8,800	(c)
1948	32,259	9,950	10,200	1,474	83	500	100	1,000	8,950	(c)
1949	31,701	8,800	10,500	1,452	56	550	140	1,100	9,100	838
1950	34,763	9,000	11,650	1,541	89	440	120	1,300	10,600	900
1951	36,996	9,150	13,100	1,573	46	390	100	1,400	11,200	966
1952	37,794	8,900	13,500	1,429	32	430	130	1,450	11,900	970
1953	37,956	8,750	13,400	1,506	26	420	120	1,500	12,200	1,026
1954	35,586	8,000	12,800	1,289	28	380	90	1,500	11,500	1,004
1955	38,426	8,200	14,500	1,490	15	410	90	1,600	12,100	989
1956	39,628	7,900	15,200	1,377	11	440	100	1,600	13,000	888
1957	38,702	7,850	15,400	1,376	13	460	80	1,700	11,800	1,016
1958	36,981	7,650	14,200	1,316	9	450	80	1,650	11,600	929
1959	37,910	7,850	14,900	1,202	6	480	70	1,600	11,800	948
1960	38,137	7,850	14,800	1,368	5	460	80	1,700	11,900	995
1961	38,091	7,650	14,700	1,267	5	490	80	1,700	12,200	1,065
1962	40,804	7,900	16,400	1,245	3	500	90	1,750	12,900	1,029
1963	43,564	8,200	17,600	1,385	10	580	80	1,900	13,800	990
1964	47,700	9,000	19,600	1,580	5	710	100	2,100	14,600	1,123
1965	49,163	8,900	20,800	1,556	5	680	120	2,200	14,900	1,113
1966	53,041	9,400	22,200	1,800	2	740	100	2,500	16,300	1,108
1967	52,924	9,400	22,000	1,620	3	750	100	2,350	16,700	1,165
1968	54,862	9,900	22,400	1,570	4	790	100	2,700	17,400	1,061
1969	55,791	10,100	23,700	1,495	2	800	100	3,900[d]	15,700[d]	1,155
1970	54,633	9,900	23,200	1,459	3	780	100	3,800	15,400	1,140
1971	54,381	9,900	23,100	1,378	2	800	100	3,800	15,300	1,015
1972	56,278	10,300	23,900	1,260	2	1,000	100	3,900	15,800	1,064
1973	55,511	10,200	23,600	1,194	2	1,000	100	3,800	15,600	1,164
1974	46,402	8,500	19,700	1,209	1	1,000	100	3,100	12,800	1,088
1975	45,853	8,400	19,550	979	1	1,000	100	3,130	12,700	1,033
1976	47,038	8,600	20,100	1,033	2	1,000	100	3,200	13,000	1,026

See source and footnotes on page 113.

MOTOR-VEHICLE DEATHS BY TYPE OF ACCIDENT, UNITED STATES, 1913–2001, Cont.

Year	Total Deaths	Deaths from Collision with—							Deaths from Noncollision Accidents	Nontraffic Deaths[a]
		Pedestrians	Other Motor Vehicles	Railroad Trains	Streetcars	Pedal-cycles	Animal-Drawn Vehicle or Animal	Fixed Objects		
1977	49,510	9,100	21,200	902	3	1,100	100	3,400	13,700	1,053
1978	52,411	9,600	22,400	986	1	1,200	100	3,600	14,500	1,074
1979	53,524	9,800	23,100	826	1	1,200	100	3,700	14,800	1,271
1980	53,172	9,700	23,000	739	1	1,200	100	3,700	14,700	1,242
1981	51,385	9,400	22,200	668	1	1,200	100	3,600	14,200	1,189
1982	45,779	8,400	19,800	554	1	1,100	100	3,200	12,600	1,066
1983	44,452	8,200	19,200	520	1	1,100	100	3,100	12,200	1,024
1984	46,263	8,500	20,000	630	0	1,100	100	3,200	12,700	1,055
1985	45,901	8,500	19,900	538	2	1,100	100	3,200	12,600	1,079
1986	47,865	8,900	20,800	574	2	1,100	100	3,300	13,100	998
1987	48,290	7,500[e]	20,700	554	1	1,000[e]	100	13,200[e]	5,200[e]	993
1988	49,078	7,700	20,900	638	2	1,000	100	13,400	5,300	1,054
1989	47,575	7,800	20,300	720	2	900	100	12,900	4,900	989
1990	46,814	7,300	19,900	623	2	900	100	13,100	4,900	987
1991	43,536	6,600	18,200	541	1	800	100	12,600	4,700	915
1992	40,982	6,300	17,600	521	2	700	100	11,700	4,100	997
1993	41,893	6,400	18,300	553	3	800	100	11,500	4,200	994
1994	42,524	6,300	18,900	549	1	800	100	11,500	4,400	1,017
1995	43,363	6,400	19,000	514	(c)	800	100	12,100	4,400	1,032
1996	43,649	6,100	19,600	373	(c)	800	100	12,100	4,600	1,127
1997	43,458	5,900	19,900	371	(c)	800	100	12,000	4,400	1,118
1998	43,501	5,900	19,700	309	(c)	700	100	12,200	4,600	1,310
1999[f]	42,401	6,100	18,600	314	1	800	100	11,800	4,700	1,436
2000[f]	42,500	5,600	19,100	400	(c)	800	100	11,800	4,700	1,400
2001[g]	42,900	5,800	18,400	400	(c)	800	100	12,300	5,100	1,400
Changes in Deaths										
1991 to 2001	−1%	−12%	+1%	−26%	—	0%	0%	−2%	+9%	+53%
2000 to 2001	+1%	+4%	−4%	0%	—	0%	0%	+4%	+9%	0%

Source: Total deaths from National Center for Health Statistics except 1964 and 2000-2001, which are National Safety Council estimates based on data from state traffic authorities. Most totals by type are estimated and may not add to the total deaths. See Technical Appendix for comparability.
[a] See definition, page 175. Nontraffic deaths are included in appropriate accident type totals in table; in 1999, 46% of the specified nontraffic deaths were pedestrians.
[b] Insufficient data for approximations.
[c] Data not available.
[d] 1969 through 1986 totals are not comparable to previous years.
[e] Procedures and benchmarks for estimating deaths for certain types of accidents were changed for the 1990 edition. Estimates for 1987 and later years are not comparable to earlier years.
[f] Revised.
[g] Preliminary.

MOTOR-VEHICLE DEATHS BY TYPE OF ACCIDENT, UNITED STATES, 2001

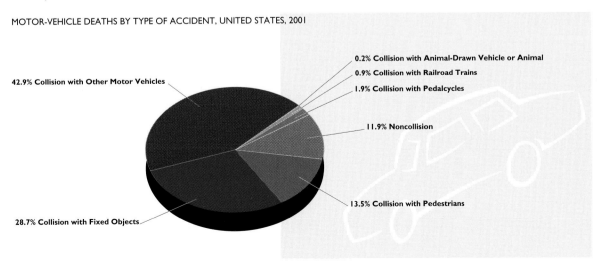

0.2% Collision with Animal-Drawn Vehicle or Animal
0.9% Collision with Railroad Trains
1.9% Collision with Pedalcycles
42.9% Collision with Other Motor Vehicles
11.9% Noncollision
13.5% Collision with Pedestrians
28.7% Collision with Fixed Objects

MOTOR-VEHICLE DEATHS BY AGE

MOTOR-VEHICLE DEATHS BY AGE, UNITED STATES, 1913–2001

Year	All Ages	Under 5 Years	5–14 Years	15–24 Years	25–44 Years	45–64 Years	65–74 Years	75 & Over[a]
1913	4,200	300	1,100	600	1,100	800	300	
1914	4,700	300	1,200	700	1,200	900	400	
1915	6,600	400	1,500	1,000	1,700	1,400	600	
1916	8,200	600	1,800	1,300	2,100	1,700	700	
1917	10,200	700	2,400	1,400	2,700	2,100	900	
1918	10,700	800	2,700	1,400	2,500	2,300	1,000	
1919	11,200	900	3,000	1,400	2,500	2,100	1,300	
1920	12,500	1,000	3,300	1,700	2,800	2,300	1,400	
1921	13,900	1,100	3,400	1,800	3,300	2,700	1,600	
1922	15,300	1,100	3,500	2,100	3,700	3,100	1,800	
1923	18,400	1,200	3,700	2,800	4,600	3,900	2,200	
1924	19,400	1,400	3,800	2,900	4,700	4,100	2,500	
1925	21,900	1,400	3,900	3,600	5,400	4,800	2,800	
1926	23,400	1,400	3,900	3,900	5,900	5,200	3,100	
1927	25,800	1,600	4,000	4,300	6,600	5,800	3,500	
1928	28,000	1,600	3,800	4,900	7,200	6,600	3,900	
1929	31,200	1,600	3,900	5,700	8,000	7,500	4,500	
1930	32,900	1,500	3,600	6,200	8,700	8,000	4,900	
1931	33,700	1,500	3,600	6,300	9,100	8,200	5,000	
1932	29,500	1,200	2,900	5,100	8,100	7,400	4,800	
1933	31,363	1,274	3,121	5,649	8,730	7,947	4,642	
1934	36,101	1,210	3,182	6,561	10,232	9,530	5,386	
1935	36,369	1,253	2,951	6,755	10,474	9,562	5,374	
1936	38,089	1,324	3,026	7,184	10,807	10,089	5,659	
1937	39,643	1,303	2,991	7,800	10,877	10,475	6,197	
1938	32,582	1,122	2,511	6,016	8,772	8,711	5,450	
1939	32,386	1,192	2,339	6,318	8,917	8,292	5,328	
1940	34,501	1,176	2,584	6,846	9,362	8,882	5,651	
1941	39,969	1,378	2,838	8,414	11,069	9,829	6,441	
1942	28,309	1,069	1,991	5,932	7,747	7,254	4,316	
1943	23,823	1,132	1,959	4,522	6,454	5,996	3,760	
1944	24,282	1,203	2,093	4,561	6,514	5,982	3,929	
1945	28,076	1,290	2,386	5,358	7,578	6,794	4,670	
1946	33,411	1,568	2,508	7,445	8,955	7,532	5,403	
1947	32,697	1,502	2,275	7,251	8,775	7,468	5,426	
1948	32,259	1,635	2,337	7,218	8,702	7,190	3,173	2,004
1949	31,701	1,667	2,158	6,772	8,892	7,073	3,116	2,023
1950	34,763	1,767	2,152	7,600	10,214	7,728	3,264	2,038
1951	36,996	1,875	2,300	7,713	11,253	8,276	3,444	2,135
1952	37,794	1,951	2,295	8,115	11,380	8,463	3,472	2,118
1953	37,956	2,019	2,368	8,169	11,302	8,318	3,508	2,271
1954	35,586	1,864	2,332	7,571	10,521	7,848	3,247	2,203
1955	38,426	1,875	2,406	8,656	11,448	8,372	3,455	2,214
1956	39,628	1,770	2,640	9,169	11,551	8,573	3,657	2,268
1957	38,702	1,785	2,604	8,667	11,230	8,545	3,560	2,311
1958	36,981	1,791	2,710	8,388	10,414	7,922	3,535	2,221
1959	37,910	1,842	2,719	8,969	10,358	8,263	3,487	2,272
1960	38,137	1,953	2,814	9,117	10,189	8,294	3,457	2,313
1961	38,091	1,891	2,802	9,088	10,212	8,267	3,467	2,364
1962	40,804	1,903	3,028	10,157	10,701	8,812	3,696	2,507
1963	43,564	1,991	3,063	11,123	11,356	9,506	3,786	2,739
1964	47,700	2,120	3,430	12,400	12,500	10,200	4,150	2,900
1965	49,163	2,059	3,526	13,395	12,595	10,509	4,077	3,002
1966	53,041	2,182	3,869	15,298	13,282	11,051	4,217	3,142
1967	52,924	2,067	3,845	15,646	12,987	10,902	4,285	3,192
1968	54,862	1,987	4,105	16,543	13,602	11,031	4,261	3,333
1969	55,791	2,077	4,045	17,443	13,868	11,012	4,210	3,136
1970	54,633	1,915	4,159	16,720	13,446	11,099	4,084	3,210
1971	54,381	1,885	4,256	17,103	13,307	10,471	4,108	3,251
1972	56,278	1,896	4,258	17,942	13,758	10,836	4,138	3,450
1973	55,511	1,998	4,124	18,032	14,013	10,216	3,892	3,236
1974	46,402	1,546	3,332	15,905	11,834	8,159	3,071	2,555
1975	45,853	1,576	3,286	15,672	11,969	7,663	3,047	2,640
1976	47,038	1,532	3,175	16,650	12,112	7,770	3,082	2,717

See source and footnotes on page 115.

MOTOR-VEHICLE DEATHS BY AGE, UNITED STATES, 1913–2001, Cont.

Year	All Ages	Under 5 Years	5–14 Years	15–24 Years	25–44 Years	45–64 Years	65–74 Years	75 & Over[a]
1977	49,510	1,472	3,142	18,092	13,031	8,000	3,060	2,713
1978	52,411	1,551	3,130	19,164	14,574	8,048	3,217	2,727
1979	53,524	1,461	2,952	19,369	15,658	8,162	3,171	2,751
1980	53,172	1,426	2,747	19,040	16,133	8,022	2,991	2,813
1981	51,385	1,256	2,575	17,363	16,447	7,818	3,090	2,836
1982	45,779	1,300	2,301	15,324	14,469	6,879	2,825	2,681
1983	44,452	1,233	2,241	14,289	14,323	6,690	2,827	2,849
1984	46,263	1,138	2,263	14,738	15,036	6,954	3,020	3,114
1985	45,901	1,195	2,319	14,277	15,034	6,885	3,014	3,177
1986	47,865	1,188	2,350	15,227	15,844	6,799	3,096	3,361
1987	48,290	1,190	2,397	14,447	16,405	7,021	3,277	3,553
1988	49,078	1,220	2,423	14,406	16,580	7,245	3,429	3,775
1989	47,575	1,221	2,266	12,941	16,571	7,287	3,465	3,824
1990	46,814	1,123	2,059	12,607	16,488	7,282	3,350	3,905
1991	43,536	1,076	2,011	11,664	15,082	6,616	3,193	3,894
1992	40,982	1,020	1,904	10,305	14,071	6,597	3,247	3,838
1993	41,893	1,081	1,963	10,500	14,283	6,711	3,116	4,239
1994	42,524	1,139	2,026	10,660	13,966	7,097	3,385	4,251
1995	43,363	1,004	2,055	10,600	14,618	7,428	3,300	4,358
1996	43,649	1,035	1,980	10,576	14,482	7,749	3,419	4,408
1997	43,458	933	1,967	10,208	14,167	8,134	3,370	4,679
1998	43,501	921	1,868	10,026	14,095	8,416	3,410	4,765
1999[b]	42,401	834	1,771	10,128	13,516	8,342	3,276	4,534
2000[b]	42,500	800	1,500	10,400	13,900	8,800	2,700	4,400
2001[c]	42,900	600	1,400	10,400	14,300	8,800	3,100	4,300
Changes in Deaths								
1991 to 2001	–1%	–44%	–30%	–11%	–5%	+33%	–3%	+10%
2000 to 2001	+1%	–25%	–7%	0%	+3%	0%	+15%	–2%

Source: 1913 to 1932 calculated from National Center for Health Statistics data for registration states; 1933 to 1963, 1965 to 1999 are NCHS totals. All other figures are National Safety Council estimates. See Technical Appendix for comparability.
[a] Includes "age unknown." In 1999 these deaths numbered 30.
[b] Revised.
[c] Preliminary.

MOTOR-VEHICLE DEATHS BY AGE, UNITED STATES, 2001

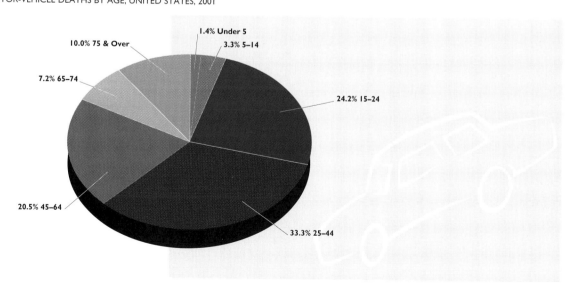

10.0% 75 & Over
1.4% Under 5
3.3% 5–14
7.2% 65–74
24.2% 15–24
20.5% 45–64
33.3% 25–44

MOTOR-VEHICLE DEATH RATES

Year	All Ages	Under 5 Years	5–14 Years	15–24 Years	25–44 Years	45–64 Years	65–74 Years	75 & Over
1913	4.4	2.3	5.5	3.1	3.8	5.3	8.5	
1914	4.8	2.5	5.7	3.5	4.1	6.2	9.3	
1915	6.6	3.5	7.3	5.0	5.6	8.8	13.5	
1916	8.1	4.7	8.6	6.0	7.0	10.7	15.8	
1917	10.0	5.6	10.6	7.4	8.6	12.6	18.6	
1918	10.3	6.9	12.3	7.7	8.3	13.7	21.2	
1919	10.7	7.5	13.9	7.5	8.1	12.4	24.1	
1920	11.7	8.6	14.6	8.7	8.8	13.5	27.0	
1921	12.9	9.0	14.5	9.2	10.2	15.4	31.0	
1922	13.9	9.2	15.0	10.8	11.1	17.2	34.9	
1923	16.5	9.7	15.6	13.4	13.6	21.0	40.5	
1924	17.1	11.1	16.1	14.3	13.7	21.8	43.7	
1925	19.1	11.0	15.6	17.2	15.8	25.0	48.9	
1926	20.1	11.0	15.9	18.6	17.1	26.3	51.4	
1927	21.8	12.8	16.0	20.0	18.8	28.9	56.9	
1928	23.4	12.7	15.5	21.9	20.2	32.4	62.2	
1929	25.7	13.4	15.6	25.6	22.3	35.6	68.6	
1930	26.7	13.0	14.7	27.4	23.9	37.0	72.5	
1931	27.2	13.3	14.5	27.9	24.8	37.4	70.6	
1932	23.6	11.3	12.0	22.6	22.0	32.9	63.6	
1933	25.0	12.0	12.7	24.8	23.4	34.7	63.1	
1934	28.6	11.7	13.0	28.6	27.2	40.7	71.0	
1935	28.6	12.3	12.2	29.2	27.6	39.9	68.9	
1936	29.7	13.2	12.6	30.8	28.2	41.3	70.5	
1937	30.8	13.0	12.7	33.2	28.2	42.0	75.1	
1938	25.1	11.0	10.8	25.4	22.5	34.3	64.1	
1939	24.7	11.2	10.4	26.5	22.6	32.2	60.2	
1940	26.1	11.1	11.5	28.7	23.5	33.9	62.1	
1941	30.0	12.7	12.6	35.7	27.5	37.0	68.6	
1942	21.1	9.5	8.8	25.8	19.2	26.9	44.5	
1943	17.8	9.4	8.6	20.6	16.1	21.9	37.6	
1944	18.3	9.6	9.1	22.5	16.6	21.6	38.2	
1945	21.2	10.0	10.3	27.8	19.7	24.2	44.1	
1946	23.9	11.9	10.8	34.4	21.1	26.4	49.6	
1947	22.8	10.5	9.7	32.8	20.3	25.7	48.2	
1948	22.1	11.0	9.8	32.5	19.8	24.3	39.6	55.4
1949	21.3	10.7	9.0	30.7	19.9	23.4	37.8	53.9
1950	23.0	10.8	8.8	34.5	22.5	25.1	38.8	52.4
1951	24.1	10.9	9.2	36.0	24.7	26.5	39.5	53.0
1952	24.3	11.3	8.7	38.6	24.7	26.7	38.5	50.8
1953	24.0	11.5	8.5	39.1	24.5	25.8	37.7	52.6
1954	22.1	10.4	8.1	36.2	22.6	24.0	33.9	49.0
1955	23.4	10.2	8.0	40.9	24.5	25.2	35.1	47.1
1956	23.7	9.4	8.4	42.9	24.6	25.3	36.2	46.4
1957	22.7	9.2	8.0	39.7	23.9	24.8	34.4	45.5
1958	21.3	9.1	8.1	37.0	22.3	22.6	33.5	42.3
1959	21.5	9.1	7.9	38.2	22.2	23.2	32.3	41.8
1960	21.2	9.6	7.9	37.7	21.7	22.9	31.3	41.1
1961	20.8	9.2	7.6	36.5	21.8	22.5	30.7	40.5
1962	22.0	9.3	8.1	38.4	22.9	23.7	32.2	41.7
1963	23.1	9.8	8.0	40.0	24.3	25.2	32.6	44.3
1964	25.0	10.5	8.8	42.6	26.8	26.6	35.5	45.2
1965	25.4	10.4	8.9	44.2	27.0	27.0	34.6	45.4
1966	27.1	11.4	9.7	48.7	28.5	27.9	35.4	46.2
1967	26.8	11.2	9.5	48.4	27.8	27.1	35.6	45.4
1968	27.5	11.1	10.1	49.8	28.8	27.0	35.1	46.0
1969	27.7	12.0	9.9	50.7	29.1	26.6	34.3	42.0
1970	26.8	11.2	10.2	46.7	27.9	26.4	32.7	42.2
1971	26.3	10.9	10.5	45.7	27.4	24.7	32.4	41.3
1972	26.9	11.1	10.7	47.1	27.4	25.3	32.0	42.6
1973	26.3	11.9	10.5	46.3	27.2	23.6	29.4	39.1
1974	21.8	9.4	8.6	40.0	22.4	18.8	22.6	30.1
1975	21.3	9.8	8.6	38.7	22.1	17.5	21.9	30.1
1976	21.6	9.8	8.4	40.3	21.8	17.6	21.6	30.1

See source and footnotes on page 117.

MOTOR-VEHICLE DEATH RATES^a BY AGE, UNITED STATES, 1913–2000, Cont.

Year	All Ages	Under 5 Years	5–14 Years	15–24 Years	25–44 Years	45–64 Years	65–74 Years	75 & Over
1977	22.5	9.5	8.5	43.3	22.7	18.1	20.9	29.3
1978	23.6	9.9	8.6	45.4	24.6	18.2	21.5	28.7
1979	23.8	9.1	8.3	45.6	25.6	18.4	20.7	28.1
1980	23.4	8.7	7.9	44.8	25.5	18.0	19.1	28.0
1981	22.4	7.4	7.5	41.1	25.2	17.6	19.4	27.5
1982	19.8	7.5	6.7	36.8	21.5	15.5	17.5	25.2
1983	19.0	7.0	6.6	34.8	20.6	15.0	17.2	26.0
1984	19.6	6.4	6.7	36.4	21.0	15.6	18.2	27.7
1985	19.3	6.7	6.9	35.7	20.5	15.4	17.9	27.5
1986	19.9	6.6	7.0	38.5	21.0	15.2	18.1	28.3
1987	19.9	6.6	7.1	37.1	21.3	15.7	18.8	29.1
1988	20.1	6.7	7.1	37.8	21.2	15.9	19.5	30.2
1989	19.3	6.6	6.5	34.6	20.8	15.9	19.4	29.8
1990	18.8	6.0	5.8	34.2	20.4	15.7	18.5	29.7
1991	17.3	5.6	5.6	32.1	18.3	14.2	17.5	28.9
1992	16.1	5.2	5.2	28.5	17.1	13.6	17.6	27.8
1993	16.3	5.5	5.3	29.1	17.3	13.5	16.7	30.0
1994	16.3	5.8	5.4	29.5	16.8	13.9	18.1	29.4
1995	16.5	5.1	5.4	29.3	17.5	14.2	17.6	29.4
1996	16.5	5.4	5.2	29.2	17.3	14.4	18.3	29.0
1997	16.2	4.9	5.1	27.9	17.0	14.7	18.2	29.9
1998^b	16.1	4.9	4.8	26.9	16.9	14.7	18.5	29.8
1999^b	15.8	4.8	4.6	27.0	15.6	14.9	17.9	31.2
2000^c	15.6	4.8	3.8	27.3	16.2	15.0	14.8	29.4
Changes in Rates								
1990 to 2000	–17%	–20%	–34%	–20%	–21%	–4%	–20%	–1%
1999 to 2000	–1%	0%	–17%	+1%	+4%	+1%	–17%	–6%

Source: 1913 to 1932 calculated from National Center for Health Statistics data for registration states; 1933 to 1963, 1965 to 1998 are NCHS totals. All other figures are National Safety Council estimates. See Technical Appendix for comparability.
^a *Death rates are deaths per 100,000 population in each age group.*
^b *Revised.*
^c *Preliminary.*

HOME AND
COMMUNITY

PUBLIC, 2001

Between 1912 and 2001, public unintentional-injury deaths per 100,000 population were reduced 77% from 30 to 7. In 1912, an estimated 28,000 to 30,000 persons died from public non-motor-vehicle injuries. In 2001, with a population nearly tripled, and travel and recreational activity greatly increased, only 19,000 persons died of public unintentional injuries and 6,300,000 suffered disabling injuries. The public class excludes deaths involving motor vehicles and persons at work or at home.

The number of public unintentional-injury deaths decreased by 900, or 5%, from the revised 2000 figure of 19,900. The death rate per 100,000 population decreased from 7.2 to 6.8, or 6%.

With an estimated 6,300,000 disabling unintentional injuries occurring in public places and a population of nearly 278 million people, on average about 1 person in 44 experienced such an injury.

The Council adopted the Bureau of Labor Statistics' Census of Fatal Occupational Injuries count for

work-related unintentional injuries retroactive to 1992 data. Because of the lower Work class total resulting from this change, several thousand unintentional-injury deaths that had been classified by the Council as work-related had to be reassigned to the Home and Public classes. For this reason, long-term historical comparisons for these three classes should be made with caution. See the Technical Appendix for an explanation of the methodological changes.

Beginning with 1999 data, which became available in September 2001, deaths are now classified according to the 10th revision of the *International Classification of Diseases*. Overall, about 3% more deaths are classified as due to "unintentional injuries" under the new classification system than under the 9th revision. The difference varies across causes of death. See the Technical Appendix for more information on comparability. Caution should be used in comparing data classified under the two systems.

Deaths 19,000
Disabling injuries 6,300,000
Death rate per 100,000 population 6.8
Costs . . . . $82.1 billion

PUBLIC DEATHS AND DEATH RATES, UNITED STATES, 1992–2001

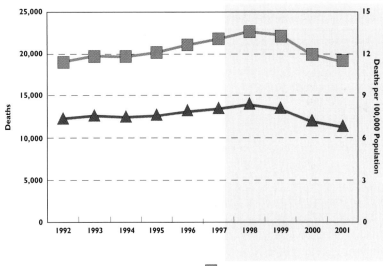

■ DEATHS (LEFT SCALE)
▲ DEATH RATES (RIGHT SCALE)

PRINCIPAL TYPES OF PUBLIC UNINTENTIONAL-INJURY DEATHS, UNITED STATES, 1981–2001

Year	Total Public[a]	Falls	Drowning	Poisoning	Suffocation by Ingestion	Fires, Burns	Firearms	Mechnical Suffocation	Air Transport	Water Transport	Rail Transport[b]
1981	19,800	4,300	4,100	(c)	(c)	600	700	(c)	1,100	1,000	400
1982	19,500	4,100	4,000	(c)	(c)	500	700	(c)	1,200	1,100	400
1983	19,400	4,100	4,000	(c)	(c)	500	700	(c)	1,000	1,100	400
1984	18,300	4,100	3,300	(c)	(c)	500	700	(c)	900	900	400
1985	18,800	4,100	3,300	(c)	(c)	500	600	(c)	1,000	900	400
1986	18,700	3,900	3,600	(c)	(c)	500	600	(c)	800	900	400
1987	18,400	4,000	3,200	(c)	(c)	500	600	(c)	900	800	400
1988	18,400	4,100	3,100	(c)	(c)	500	600	(c)	700	800	400
1989	18,200	4,200	3,000	(c)	(c)	500	600	(c)	800	700	400
1990	17,400	4,300	2,800	(c)	(c)	400	500	(c)	700	800	400
1991	17,600	4,500	2,800	(c)	(c)	400	600	(c)	700	700	500
1992	19,000	4,400	2,500	(c)	(c)	200	400	(c)	700	700	600
1993	19,700	4,600	2,800	(c)	(c)	200	400	(c)	600	700	600
1994	19,600	4,700	2,400	(c)	(c)	200	400	(c)	600	600	600
1995	20,100	5,000	2,800	(c)	(c)	200	300	(c)	600	700	500
1996	21,000	5,300	2,500	(c)	(c)	200	300	(c)	700	600	500
1997	21,700	5,600	2,600	(c)	(c)	200	300	(c)	500	600	400
1998	22,600	6,000	2,900	(c)	(c)	200	300	(c)	500	600	500
1999[d,e]	22,200	4,800	2,600	2,800	2,000	200	300	500	500	600	400
2000[e]	19,900	4,200	2,200	2,700	2,100	(c)	(c)	400	400	400	500
2001[f]	19,000	4,500	2,300	2,900	2,000	(c)	(c)	300	500	400	500

Source: National Safety Council estimates based on data from the National Center for Health Statistics and state vital statistics departments. The Council adopted the Bureau of Labor Statistics' Census of Fatal Occupational Injuries count for work-related unintentional injuries retroactive to 1992 data. Because of the lower Work class total resulting from this change, several thousand unintentional-injury deaths that had been classified by the Council as work-related, had to be reassigned to the Home and Public classes. For this reason long-term historical comparisons for these three classes should be made with caution. See the Technical Appendix for an explanation of the methodological changes.
[a] *Includes some deaths not shown separately.*
[b] *Includes subways and elevateds.*
[c] *Estimates not available.*
[d] *In 1999, a revision was made in the International Classification of Diseases. See the Technical Appendix for more information on comparability with earlier years.*
[e] *Revised.*
[f] *Preliminary.*

PRINCIPAL TYPES OF PUBLIC UNINTENTIONAL-INJURY DEATHS, UNITED STATES, 2001

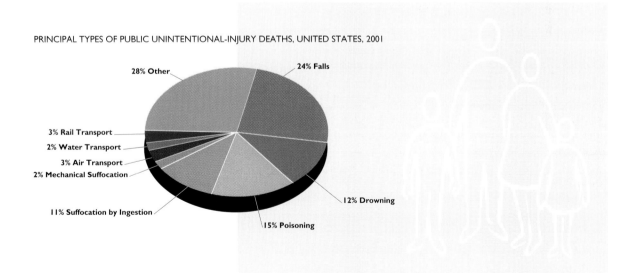

28% Other
24% Falls
3% Rail Transport
2% Water Transport
3% Air Transport
2% Mechanical Suffocation
11% Suffocation by Ingestion
15% Poisoning
12% Drowning

DEATHS DUE TO UNINTENTIONAL PUBLIC INJURIES, 2001

TYPE OF EVENT AND AGE OF VICTIM

All Public

Includes deaths in public places or places used in a public way and not involving motor vehicles. Most sports, recreation, and transportation deaths are included. Excludes deaths in the course of employment.

	Total	Change from 2000	Death Rate[a]
Deaths	19,000	−5%	6.8

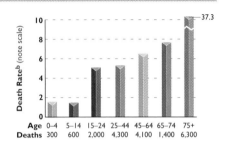

Falls

Includes deaths from falls from one level to another or on the same level in public places. Excludes deaths from falls in moving vehicles.

	Total	Change from 2000	Death Rate[a]
Deaths	4,500	+7%	1.6

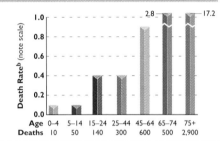

Poisoning

Includes deaths from drugs, medicines, other solid and liquid substances, and gases and vapors. Excludes poisonings from spoiled foods, salmonella, etc., which are classified as disease deaths.

	Total	Change from 2000	Death Rate[a]
Deaths	2,900	+7%	1.0

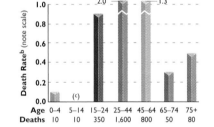

Drowning

Includes drownings of person swimming or playing in water, or falling into water, except on home premises or at work. Excludes drownings involving boats, which are in water transportation.

	Total	Change from 2000	Death Rate[a]
Deaths	2,300	+5%	0.8

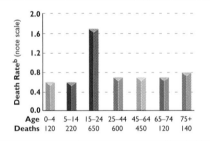

Suffocation by Ingestion

Includes deaths from unintentional ingestion or inhalation of food or other objects resulting in the obstruction of respiratory passages.

	Total	Change from 2000	Death Rate[a]
Deaths	2,000	−5%	0.7

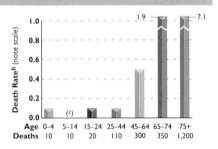

See footnotes on page 123.

Air Transport

Includes deaths in private flying, passengers in commercial aviation, and deaths of military personnel in the U.S. Excludes crews and persons traveling in the course of employment.

	Total	Change from 2000	Death Rate[a]
Deaths	500	+25%	0.2

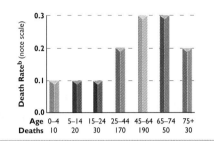

Age	0–4	5–14	15–24	25–44	45–64	65–74	75+
Deaths	10	20	30	170	190	50	30

Railroad

Includes deaths arising from railroad vehicles in motion (except involving motor vehicles), subway and elevated trains, and persons boarding or alighting from standing trains. Excludes crews and persons traveling in the course of employment.

	Total	Change from 2000	Death Rate[a]
Deaths	500	0%	0.2

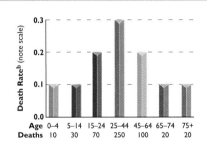

Age	0–4	5–14	15–24	25–44	45–64	65–74	75+
Deaths	10	30	70	250	100	20	20

Water Transport

Includes deaths in water transport accidents from falls, burns, etc., as well as drownings. Excludes crews and persons traveling in the course of employment.

	Total	Change from 2000	Death Rate[a]
Deaths	400	0%	0.1

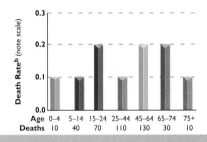

Age	0–4	5–14	15–24	25–44	45–64	65–74	75+
Deaths	10	40	70	110	130	30	10

Mechanical Suffocation

Includes deaths from hanging and strangulation, and suffocation in enclosed or confined spaces, cave-ins, or by bed clothes, plastic bags, or similar materials.

	Total	Change from 2000	Death Rate[a]
Deaths	300	–25%	0.1

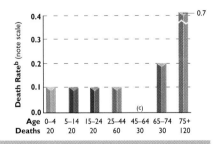

Age	0–4	5–14	15–24	25–44	45–64	65–74	75+
Deaths	20	20	20	60	30	30	120

All Other Public

Most important types included are: excessive natural heat or cold, firearms, fires and flames, and machinery.

	Total	Change from 2000	Death Rate[a]
Deaths	5,600	–20%	2.0

[a] Deaths per 100,000 population.
[b] Deaths per 100,000 population in each age group.
[c] Rate less than 0.05.

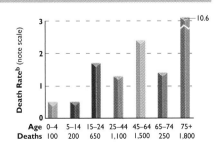

Age	0–4	5–14	15–24	25–44	45–64	65–74	75+
Deaths	100	200	650	1,100	1,500	250	1,800

SPORTS AND RECREATION INJURIES

The table below shows estimates of injuries treated in hospital emergency departments and participants associated with various sports and recreational activities. Differences between the two sources in methods, coverage, classification systems, and definitions can affect comparisons among sports. Because this list of sports is not complete, because the frequency and duration of participation is not known, and because the number of participants varies greatly, no inference should be made concerning the relative hazard of these sports or rank with respect to risk of injury. In particular, it is *not* appropriate to calculate injury rates from these data.

SPORTS PARTICIPATION AND INJURIES, UNITED STATES, 2000

Sport or Activity	Participants	Injuries	Percent of Injuries by Age				
			0–4	5–14	15–24	25–64	65 & Over
Archery	4,500,000	4,326	7.3	21.7	21.9	47.5	1.6
Baseball & softball	29,600,000	308,931	2.5	38.0	28.6	30.4	0.5
Basketball	27,100,000	600,256	0.4	32.2	46.1	21.0	0.1
Bicycle riding[a]	43,100,000	608,608	6.1	54.7	15.1	22.1	2.1
Billiards, pool	32,500,000	6,036	11.8	19.4	21.8	45.8	1.3
Bowling	43,100,000	22,890	8.5	15.6	14.7	50.4	10.3
Boxing	(b)	13,704	1.1	11.7	51.6	35.7	0.0
Exercise	(b)	185,031[c]	3.5	17.1	22.7	49.2	7.5
Fishing	49,300,000	72,751	3.5	23.5	13.0	51.0	9.0
Football[d]	17,300,000	399,501	0.4	46.5	42.9	10.2	0.1
Golf	26,400,000	45,064[e]	5.3	21.5	10.4	45.5	17.1
Gymnastics	(b)	37,583[f]	3.5	71.7	21.5	3.3	0.0
Hockey: street, roller, & field	(b)	7,239[g,h]	1.3	34.8	33.3	30.5	0.0
Horseback riding	9,500,000	79,095	1.2	19.8	17.2	59.2	2.7
Horseshoe pitching	(b)	2,349	14.7	29.3	20.9	31.5	3.6
Ice hockey	1,900,000	17,691[h]	0.0	33.0	40.1	25.5	0.5
Ice skating	6,700,000	25,813[i]	2.2	54.0	15.3	27.5	0.7
Martial arts	5,400,000	24,277	0.2	22.7	34.8	42.1	0.2
Mountain climbing	(b)	4,010	2.1	9.3	42.2	46.3	0.0
Racquetball, squash, & paddleball	3,200,000	9,169	0.0	8.5	28.6	62.3	0.6
Roller skating	29,000,000	134,641[i,j]	1.5	62.9	14.0	21.4	0.3
Rugby	(b)	9,870	0.0	3.9	74.8	21.3	0.0
Scuba diving	1,600,000	1,435	0.0	6.6	9.6	83.8	0.0
Skateboarding	9,100,000	86,781	1.4	57.5	31.6	9.1	0.3
Snowmobiling	(b)	17,696	1.6	11.9	23.2	62.9	0.4
Soccer	12,900,000	185,064	0.3	46.2	37.2	16.2	0.1
Swimming	60,700,000	164,255[k]	10.0	41.6	17.6	28.1	2.6
Tennis	10,000,000	24,231	1.8	17.4	20.1	49.3	11.4
Track & field	(b)	17,552	0.5	46.9	47.3	3.6	1.3
Volleyball	12,300,000	64,527	0.2	24.4	42.7	31.9	0.7
Water skiing	5,900,000	11,461	0.0	7.8	28.7	62.8	0.6
Weight lifting	24,800,000	68,054	5.9	10.6	37.2	45.3	1.0
Wrestling	(b)	52,797	1.1	39.2	49.8	9.8	0.1

Source: Participants—National Sporting Goods Association (NSGA); figures include those 7 years of age or older who participated more than once per year except for bicycle riding and swimming, which include those who participated six or more times per year. Injuries—Consumer Product Safety Commission (CPSC); figures include only injuries treated in hospital emergency departments.
a Excludes mountain biking.
b Data not available.
c Includes exercise equipment (33,806 injuries) and exercise activity (151,225 injuries).
d Includes touch and tackle football.
e Excludes golf carts (9,073 injuries).
f Excludes trampolines (100,303 injuries).
g There were 3,259 injuries in street hockey, 3,980 in roller hockey, and no estimate for field hockey.
h Excludes 42,665 injuries in hockey, unspecified.
i Excludes 21,532 injuries in skating, unspecified.
j Includes 2x2 (44,477 injuries) and in-line (90,164 injuries).
k Includes injuries associated with swimming, swimming pools, pool slides, diving or diving boards, and swimming pool equipment.

Football

There were eight fatalities directly related to football during the 2001 season compared to three in 2000. Seven were associated with high school football and one with sandlot. In 2001, there were 15 indirect fatalities caused by systemic failure as a result of exertion while participating in football activities or by a complication, compared to 12 in 2000. In 2001, 10 were associated with high school, 3 with college, and 2 with professional football.

Source: Mueller, F.O., & Diehl, J.L. (2002). Annual Survey of Football Injury Research, 1931–2001. Indianapolis, IN: National Collegiate Athletic Association.

Recreational Boating

In 2000, deaths associated with recreational boating numbered 701 in the United States and its territories, according to the United States Coast Guard. Drowning accounted for 519 of the deaths. The Coast Guard estimates that about 445 boaters who drowned could have been saved by wearing a life jacket. Alcohol was reported to be involved in 215 (31%) of the deaths.

Snowboarding and Alpine Skiing

According to the National Ski Areas Association, there were 45 skiing/snowboarding fatalities and about 50 serious injuries (e.g., paraplegics and head injuries) nationwide during the 2000-2001 season. Of the fatalities, 36 were skiers (23 male and 13 female) and 9 were snowboarders (7 males and 2 female). There were 54.4 million skier/snowboarder visits to ski areas nationwide during the 2000-2001 season.

An in-depth study of skier/snowboarder injuries based on reports from 13 resorts found that the overall rate of reported injury for skiing was 2.63 per 1,000 skier visits in 2000–2001, virtually unchanged from 2.66 in 1988–1990. For snowboarding, the injury rate increased from 3.37 to 6.97 per 1,000 visits. In the 2000–2001 season, about 31% of visits were due to snowboarders and 69% to other than snowboarding. (Snowboarding accounted for only 5% of visits in 1990.) Based on these rates, the authors estimate about 124,000 reported snowboarding injuries and 104,000 reported skiing injuries nationally for the 2000–2001 season for a total of 228,000.

About 30% of injuries to snowboarders are fractures compared to 15% for skiers. The wrist is the most commonly injured body part for snowboarders (25% vs. 5% for skiers). The knee is the most commonly injured body part for skiers (30% vs. 10% for snowboarders). About 20% of snowboarding incidents take place while jumping compared to about 5% for skiing. Over 70% of snowboarder incidents result from impact with the snow surface compared to 50% for skiers.

Collisions with fixed objects and other persons on the slope have not increased over time. In 1978–1981, such incidents accounted for 13% of injuries. In 1988–1990, it was 15%, and it was 13% in the current study.

Source: Shealy, J.E., & Ettlinger, C.F. (2002). 2000/2001 NSAA 10 Year Interval Injury Study. Lakewood, CO: National Ski Areas Association.

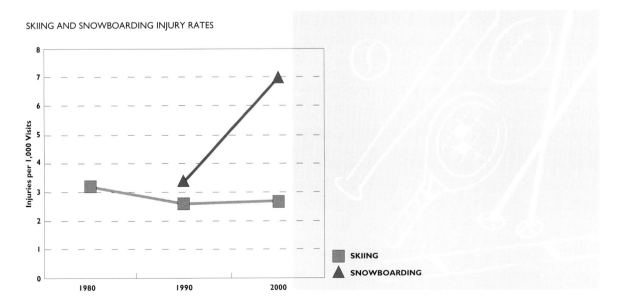

SKIING AND SNOWBOARDING INJURY RATES

Injuries per 1,000 Visits

■ SKIING
▲ SNOWBOARDING

WEATHER

The National Weather Service collects data on fatalities, injuries, and damage caused by severe weather events. In 2000, the NWS reported 476 fatalities, 2,796 injuries, $5.6 billion in property damage, and $3.3 billion in crop damage in the 50 states, Puerto Rico, Guam, and the Virgin Islands. The table and map below summarize the fatalities by region for the 50 United States.

The 2000 weather-related fatality total of 476 was about half the 1999 total of 908 and also less than the 1991–2000 average of 603 per year. Extreme heat was the leading cause of fatalities in 2000. The 30-year average (1971–2000) for floods is 127 deaths per year; for lightning, 73; for tornadoes, 69; and for hurricanes, 16. The 10-year average for extreme cold is 28, and for heat, 206.

HAZARDOUS WEATHER FATALITIES BY REGION, UNITED STATES, 2000

Region	Total[a]	Lightning	Tornado	Tropical Cyclone	Heat	Flood	Cold	Winter Weather	Wind
Total U.S.	471	50	41	0	158	38	26	41	51
Pacific	63	0	0	0	13	3	2	11	7
Mountain	31	6	0	0	0	2	0	10	2
West North Central	43	1	2	0	19	7	3	5	3
West South Central	130	8	4	0	87	10	2	9	7
East North Central	30	4	1	0	1	9	2	2	6
East South Central	55	5	14	0	20	1	3	0	12
Middle Atlantic	34	3	0	0	17	1	5	1	4
South Atlantic	78	20	20	0	1	5	9	2	7
New England	7	3	0	0	0	0	0	1	3

Source: National Weather Service. Summary of Natural Hazard Statistics for 2000 in the United States. Retrieved August 2002 from *www.nws.noaa.gov/om/hazstats.shtml.*
[a] Includes other hazardous weather conditions not shown separately (e.g., coastal storms, avalanches, fog, etc.).

HAZARDOUS WEATHER FATALITIES, 2000

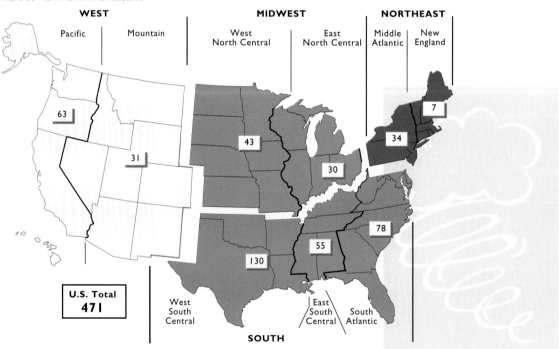

Unintentional firearms-related deaths down 46% from the 1993 high.

FIREARMS

Firearm-related deaths from unintentional, intentional, and undetermined causes totaled 28,874 in 1999, a decrease of 6.0% from 1998. Suicides accounted for 57% of firearms deaths, about 38% were homicides, and almost 3% were unintentional deaths. Males dominate all categories of firearms deaths and accounted for more than 85% of the total.

The numbers of homicide, suicide, and unintentional deaths by firearms have decreased each of the last five years. Compared to 1993, homicides were down

41%, suicides were down 12%, and unintentional deaths decreased 46%.

Hospital emergency department surveillance data indicate an estimated 23,237 nonfatal unintentional firearm-related injuries in 2000. For assault and legal intervention there were an estimated 49,432 nonfatal injuries and 3,016 intentionally self-inflicted nonfatal injuries.

Sources: Hoyert, D.L.; Arias, E.; Smith, B.L.; Murphy, S.L.; & Kochanek, K.D. (2001). Deaths: Final data for 1999. National Vital Statistics Report, 49(8), 68–69; Centers for Disease Control and Prevention, National Center for Injury Prevention and Control, WISQARS™ (http://www.cdc.gov/ncipc/wisqars/).

DEATHS INVOLVING FIREARMS, BY AGE AND SEX, UNITED STATES, 1999

Type & Sex	All Ages	Under 5 Years	5–14 Years	15–19 Years	20–24 Years	25–44 Years	45–64 Years	65–74 Years	75 & Over
Total Firearms Deaths	**28,874**	**73**	**416**	**2,896**	**3,899**	**11,209**	**6,028**	**2,034**	**2,319**
Male	24,700	41	308	2,560	3,496	9,385	5,008	1,786	2,116
Female	4,174	32	108	336	403	1,824	1,020	248	203
Unintentional	**824**	**12**	**76**	**126**	**125**	**279**	**140**	**33**	**33**
Male	707	7	60	115	114	234	119	31	27
Female	117	5	16	11	11	45	21	2	6
Suicide	**16,599**	**—**	**103**	**975**	**1,340**	**5,718**	**4,537**	**1,791**	**2,135**
Male	14,479	—	80	867	1,216	4,856	3,845	1,615	2,000
Female	2,120	—	23	108	124	862	692	176	135
Homicide	**10,828**	**58**	**224**	**1,708**	**2,330**	**4,916**	**1,266**	**193**	**133**
Male	8,944	31	155	1,498	2,071	4,023	970	124	72
Female	1,884	27	69	210	259	893	296	69	61
Legal Intervention	**299**	**0**	**1**	**19**	**45**	**188**	**43**	**2**	**1**
Male	293	0	1	19	45	183	42	2	1
Female	6	0	0	0	0	5	1	0	0
Undetermined[a]	**324**	**3**	**12**	**68**	**59**	**108**	**42**	**15**	**17**
Male	277	3	12	61	50	89	32	14	16
Female	47	0	0	7	9	19	10	1	1

[a] Undetermined means the intentionality of the deaths (unintentional, homicide, suicide) was not determined.

FIREARMS DEATHS BY INTENTIONALITY AND YEAR, UNITED STATES, 1990–1999

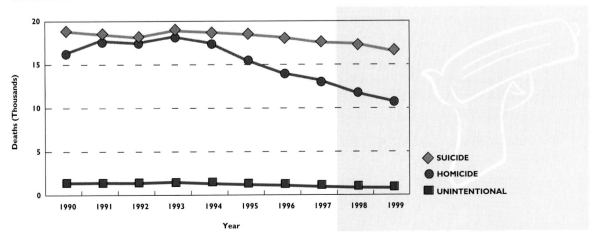

TRANSPORTATION ACCIDENT COMPARISONS

Passenger transportation incidents account for over one-fifth of all unintentional-injury deaths. But the risk of death to the passenger, expressed on a per mile basis, varies greatly by transportation mode. Automobile travel presents the greatest risk; air, rail, and bus travel have much lower death rates. The tables below show the latest information on passenger transportation deaths and death rates.

The automobile statistics shown in the tables below represent all passenger car usage, both intercity and local, and exclude vans, sport utility vehicles, and light trucks. The bus data also include intercity and local (transit) bus travel. Railroad includes both intercity

(Amtrak) and local commuting travel. Scheduled airlines includes both large airlines and commuter airlines but excludes on-demand air taxis and charter operations.

In comparing the four modes, automobile drivers (except taxi drivers) are considered passengers. Bus drivers and airline or railroad crews are not considered passengers.

Other comparisons are possible based on passenger-trips, vehicle-miles, or vehicle-trips, but passenger-miles is the most commonly used basis for comparing the safety of various modes of travel.

TRANSPORTATION ACCIDENT DEATH RATES, 1998–2000

Mode of Transportation	2000			1998–2000 Average Death Rate
	Passenger Deaths	Passenger Miles (Billions)	Deaths per 100,000,000 Passenger Miles	
Passenger automobiles[a]	20,444	2,547.0	0.80	0.83
Buses[b]	3[c]	56.2	0.005	0.04
Transit buses	1	21.4	0.005	0.01
Intercity buses	1	34.8	0.003	0.04
Railroad passenger trains[d]	4	13.9	0.03	0.05
Scheduled airlines[e]	87	498.6	0.02	0.01

Sources: Automobile and bus passenger deaths—Fatality Analysis Reporting System data. Railroad passenger deaths—Federal Railroad Administration. Airline passenger deaths—National Transportation Safety Board. Passenger miles for intercity buses, railroad, and airlines —National Safety Council estimates based on historical data from Wilson, R. A. (2001). Transportation in America, 18th edition. Washington, DC: Eno Transportation Foundation, Inc. Passenger miles for transit buses—American Public Transit Association. All other figures—National Safety Council estimates.

[a] Includes taxi passengers. Drivers of passenger automobiles are considered passengers.
[b] Figures exclude school buses.
[c] Deaths include "other" and "unknown" bus types.
[d] Includes commutation.
[e] Includes large airlines and scheduled commuter airlines; excludes cargo service and suicide/sabotage.

PASSENGER DEATHS AND DEATH RATES, UNITED STATES, 1991–2000

Year	Passenger Automobiles		Buses		Railroad Passenger Trains		Scheduled Airlines	
	Deaths	Rate[a]	Deaths	Rate[a]	Deaths	Rate[a]	Deaths	Rate[a]
1991	22,215	0.91	16	0.04	8	0.06	100	0.03
1992	21,257	0.83	17	0.04	3	0.02	38	0.01
1993	21,414	0.86	9	0.02	58	0.45	19	0.01
1994	21,813	0.91	13	0.03	5	0.04	245	0.06
1995	22,288	0.97	16	0.03	0	0.00	159	0.04
1996	22,359	0.96	10	0.02	12	0.09	329	0.08
1997	21,920	0.92	4	0.01	6	0.05	42	0.01
1998	21,099	0.86	26	0.05	4	0.03	0	0.00
1999	20,763	0.83	39	0.07	14	0.10	17	0.003
2000	20,444	0.80	3	0.01	4	0.03	87	0.02
10-year average	21,557	0.88	15	0.03	11	0.08	104	0.02

Sources: See table above.
[a] Deaths per 100,000,000 passenger miles.

PASSENGER[a] DEATH RATES, UNITED STATES, 1998–2000

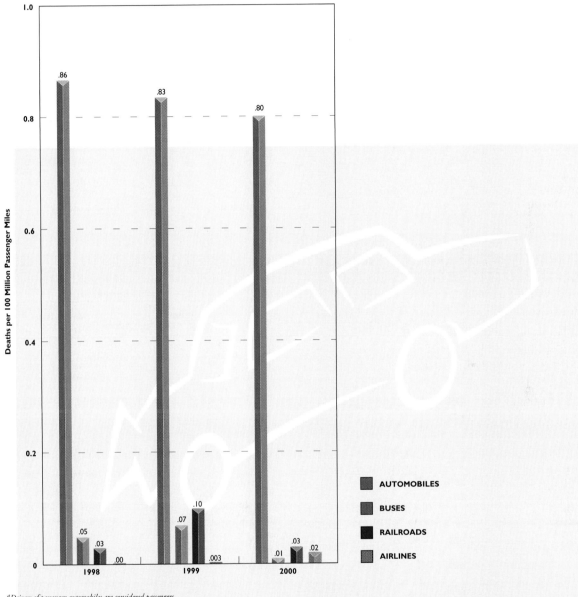

<small>Deaths per 100 Million Passenger Miles</small>

.86
.83
.80

.05 .03 .00
.07 .10 .003
.01 .03 .02

1998   1999   2000

■ AUTOMOBILES

■ BUSES

■ RAILROADS

■ AIRLINES

[a] *Drivers of passenger automobiles are considered passengers.*

AVIATION

Worldwide passenger deaths in scheduled air service totaled 577 in 2001, according to preliminary data from the International Civil Aviation Organization, a specialized United Nations agency with 188 member states. The death rate per 100 million passenger miles in 2001 was 0.02, down from 0.03 in 2000. Aircraft accidents involving a passenger fatality totaled 13. Passenger deaths per year averaged 862 for the last 10 years.

WORLDWIDE SCHEDULED AIR SERVICE ACCIDENTS, DEATHS, AND DEATH RATES, 1986–2001

Year	Aircraft Accidents[a]	Passenger Deaths	Death Rate[b]	Year	Aircraft Accidents[a]	Passenger Deaths	Death Rate[b]
1986	24	641	0.04	1994	27	1,170	0.05
1987	25	900	0.06	1995	25	711	0.03
1988	29	742	0.04	1996	24	1,146	0.05
1989	29	879	0.05	1997	25	921	0.04
1990	27	544	0.03	1998	20	904	0.03
1991	29	638	0.03	1999	21	499	0.02
1992	28	1,070	0.06	2000	18	757	0.03
1993	33	864	0.04	2001[c]	13	577	0.02

Source: International Civil Aviation Organization. Figures include the USSR up to 1992 and the Commonwealth of Independent States thereafter. (USSR/CIS excluded in earlier editions.)
[a] Involving a passenger fatality.
[b] Passenger deaths per 100 million passenger miles.
[c] Preliminary.

U.S. CIVIL AVIATION ACCIDENTS, DEATHS, AND DEATH RATES, 1997–2001

| | Accidents | | Deaths[a] | Accident Rates | | | |
| | | | | Per 100,000 Flight-Hours | | Per Million Aircraft-Miles | |
Year	Total	Fatal		Total	Fatal	Total	Fatal
Large Airlines[b]							
1997	44	3	3	0.292	0.020	0.0069	0.0005
1998	43	1	1	0.270	0.006	0.0068	0.0002
1999	47	2	12	0.282	0.012	0.0070	0.0003
2000	51	3	92	0.292	0.017	0.0071	0.0004
2001[b]	36	6	531	0.200	0.013	0.0050	0.0003
Commuter Airlines[b]							
1997	16	5	46	1.628	0.509	0.0650	0.0203
1998	8	0	0	2.262	—	0.1576	—
1999	13	5	12	3.793	1.459	0.2481	0.0954
2000	12	1	5	3.212	0.268	0.2636	0.0220
2001	7	2	13	2.118	0.605	0.1797	0.0513
On-Demand Air Taxis[b]							
1997	82	15	39	2.65	0.48	—	—
1998	77	17	45	2.03	0.45	—	—
1999	73	12	38	2.21	0.36	—	—
2000	81	22	71	2.28	0.62	—	—
2001	72	18	60	2.12	0.53	—	—
General Aviation[b]							
1997[c]	1,845	350	631	7.21	1.36	—	—
1998[c]	1,904	364	624	7.45	1.42	—	—
1999	1,906	340	619	6.41	1.14	—	—
2000	1,838	343	594	6.33	1.18	—	—
2001	1,721	321	553	6.56	1.22	—	—

Source: National Transportation Safety Board: 2001 preliminary, 1997–2000 revised; exposure data for rates from Federal Aviation Administration.
[a] Includes passengers, crew members, and others.
[b] Civil aviation accident statistics collected by the National Transportation Safety Board are classified according to the Federal air regulations under which the flights were made. The classifications are (1) large airlines operating scheduled service under Title 14, Code of Federal Regulations, part 121 (14 CFR 121); (2) commuter carriers operating scheduled service under 14 CFR 135; (3) unscheduled, "on-demand" air taxis under 14 CFR 135; and (4) "general aviation," which includes accidents involving aircraft flown under rules other than 14 CFR 121 and 14 CFR 135. Not shown in the table are nonscheduled air carrier operations under 14 CFR 121, which experienced four accidents and no fatalities in 2001. Since 1997, Large Airlines includes aircraft with 10 or more seats, formerly operated as commuter carriers under 14 CFR 135.
[c] Suicide/sabotage is included in "accident" and fatality totals but excluded from rates—Large Airlines, 2001 (4 crashes/265 deaths), General Aviation, 1997 (1/1), 1998 (2/2).

Highway-rail grade-crossing incidents and trespassing accounted for approximately 94% of all rail-related deaths over the 1992-2001 period. Injuries to on-duty railroad employees accounted for approximately 76% of all nonfatal conditions. About 48% of deaths not associated with highway-rail incidents or trespassing were to employees on duty. Passengers on trains and persons lawfully on railroad property accounted for the remainder.

DEATHS AND NONFATAL CASES RAILROAD ACCIDENTS AND INCIDENTS, UNITED STATES, 1992–2001

	Total	Highway-Rail Crossing Incident?		Occuring in Other Than Highway-Rail Crossing		Employees On Duty At Highway-Rail Crossing?		Passengers on Trains[a] At Highway-Rail Crossing?	
		Yes	No	Trespassers	Others	Yes	No	Yes	No
Death									
1992	1,170	579	591	533	58	2	32	0	3
1993	1,279	626	653	523	130	3	44	0	58
1994	1,226	615	611	529	82	1	30	0	5
1995	1,146	579	567	494	73	2	32	0	0
1996	1,039	488	551	471	80	1	32	0	12
1997	1,063	461	602	533	69	0	37	0	6
1998	1,008	431	577	536	41	4	23	2	2
1999	932	402	530	479	51	2	29	11	3
2000	937	425	512	463	49	2	22	0	4
2001	967	419	548	509	39	1	21	0	3
Nonfatal conditions									
1992	21,383	1,975	19,408	540	18,868	157	17,598	82	329
1993	19,121	1,837	17,284	509	16,775	143	15,220	44	515
1994	16,812	1,961	14,851	452	14,399	125	12,955	84	413
1995	14,440	1,894	12,546	461	12,085	123	10,654	30	543
1996	12,558	1,610	10,948	474	10,474	79	9,120	24	489
1997	11,767	1,540	10,227	516	9,711	111	8,184	43	558
1998	11,459	1,303	10,156	513	9,643	122	8,276	19	516
1999	11,700	1,396	10,304	445	9,859	140	8,482	43	438
2000	11,643	1,219	10,424	414	10,010	100	8,323	10	648
2001	10,886	1,155	9,731	405	9,326	95	7,674	19	689

Source: Federal Railroad Administration.
[a] *Passengers on trains are persons on, boarding, or alighting, other than railroad employees.*

HIGHWAY-RAIL GRADE-CROSSING CASUALTIES, UNITED STATES, 1991–2001

Year	Deaths				Nonfatal Injuries			
	Total	Motor-Vehicle	Pedestrian	Other	Total	Motor-Vehicle	Pedestrian	Other
1992	579	506	49	24	1,975	1,891	31	53
1993	626	554	48	24	1,837	1,760	28	49
1994	615	542	50	23	1,961	1,885	30	46
1995	579	508	47	24	1,894	1,825	28	41
1996	488	415	60	13	1,610	1,545	31	34
1997	461	419	38	4	1,540	1,494	33	13
1998	431	369	50	12	1,303	1,257	33	13
1999	402	345	45	12	1,396	1,338	35	23
2000	425	361	51	13	1,219	1,169	34	16
2001	419	343	67	9	1,155	1,108	31	16

Source: Federal Railroad Administration. Includes both public and private grade crossings.

HOME, 2001

Between 1912 and 2001, unintentional-home-injury deaths per 100,000 population were reduced 57% from 28 to 12. In 1912, when there were 21 million households, an estimated 26,000 to 28,000 persons were killed by unintentional home injuries. In 2001, with more than 104 million households and the population nearly tripled, home deaths numbered 33,200.

The injury total of 8,000,000 means that 1 person in 35 in the United States was disabled one full day or more by unintentional injuries received in the home in 2001. Disabling injuries are more numerous in the home than in the workplace and in motor-vehicle crashes combined.

The National Health Interview Survey indicates that about 13,592,000 episodes of home injuries occurred in 1997 (the latest year available). This means that about 1 person in 20 incurred a home injury requiring medical attention. About 42% of all medically attended injuries occurred at home. See page 23 for definitions and numerical differences between National Health Interview Survey and National Safety Council figures.

The Council adopted the Bureau of Labor Statistics' Census of Fatal Occupational Injuries count for work-related unintentional injuries retroactive to 1992 data. Because of the lower Work class total resulting from this change, several thousand unintentional-injury deaths that had been classified by the Council as work-related had to be reassigned to the Home and Public classes. For this reason long-term historical comparisons for these three classes should be made with caution. See the Technical Appendix for an explanation of the methodological changes.

Beginning with 1999 data, which became available in September 2001, deaths are now classified according to the 10th revision of the International Classification of Diseases. Overall, about 3% more deaths are classified as due to "unintentional injuries" under the new classification system than under the 9th revision. The difference varies across causes of death. See the Technical Appendix for more information on comparability. Caution should be used in comparing data classified under the two systems.

Deaths **33,200**
Disabling injuries **8,000,000**
Death rate per 100,000 population **12.0**
Costs . . . . **$118.1 billion**

HOME DEATHS AND DEATH RATES, UNITED STATES, 1992–2001

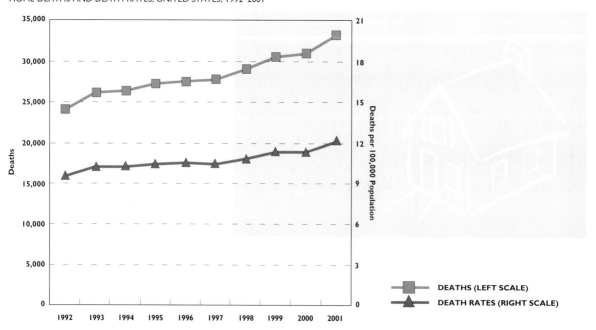

PRINCIPAL TYPES OF HOME UNINTENTIONAL-INJURY DEATHS, UNITED STATES, 1981–2001

Year	Total Home	Falls	Fires, Burns[a]	Suffocation, Ing. Obj.	Suffocation, Mechanical	Drowning	Poisoning	Natural Heat/Cold	Firearms	Other
1981	21,700	6,800	4,700	2,000	500	(b)	3,400	(b)	1,000	3,300
1982	21,200	6,500	4,300	2,100	600	(b)	3,500	(b)	1,000	3,200
1983	21,200	6,500	4,100	2,200	600	(b)	3,500	(b)	900	3,400
1984	21,200	6,400	4,100	2,300	600	(b)	3,700	(b)	900	3,200
1985	21,600	6,500	4,000	2,400	600	(b)	3,900	(b)	900	3,300
1986	21,700	6,100	4,000	2,500	600	(b)	4,300	(b)	800	3,400
1987	21,400	6,300	3,900	2,500	600	(b)	4,100	(b)	800	3,200
1988	22,700	6,600	4,100	2,600	600	(b)	4,800	(b)	800	3,200
1989	22,500	6,600	3,900	2,500	600	(b)	5,000	(b)	800	3,100
1990	21,500	6,700	3,400	2,300	600	(b)	4,500	(b)	800	3,200
1991	22,100	6,900	3,400	2,200	700	(b)	5,000	(b)	800	3,100
1992	24,000	7,700	3,700	1,500	700	900	5,200	(b)	1,000	3,300
1993	26,100	7,900	3,700	1,700	700	900	6,500	(b)	1,100	3,600
1994	26,300	8,100	3,700	1,600	800	900	6,800	(b)	900	3,500
1995	27,200	8,400	3,500	1,500	800	900	7,000	(b)	900	4,200
1996	27,500	9,000	3,500	1,500	800	900	7,300	(b)	800	3,700
1997	27,700	9,100	3,200	1,500	800	900	7,800	(b)	700	3,500
1998	29,000	9,500	2,900	1,800	800	1,000	8,400	(b)	600	4,000
1999[c,d]	30,500	7,600	3,000	1,900	1,100	900	9,300	700	600	5,400
2000[d]	30,900	8,000	3,500	2,200	1,100	1,000	9,900	500	500	4,200
2001[e]	33,200	9,000	3,500	2,200	1,000	900	11,500	600	600	3,900

Source: National Safety Council estimates based on data from National Center for Health Statistics and state vital statistics departments. The Council adopted the Bureau of Labor Statistics' Census of Fatal Occupational Injuries count for work-related unintentional injuries retroactive to 1992 data. Because of the lower Work class total resulting from this change, several thousand unintentional-injury deaths that had been classified by the Council as work-related, had to be reassigned to the Home and Public classes. For this reason long-term historical comparisons for these three classes should be made with caution. See the Technical Appendix for an explanation of the methodological changes.
[a] Includes deaths resulting from conflagration, regardless of nature of injury.
[b] Included in Other.
[c] In 1999, a revision was made in the International Classification of Diseases. See the Technical Appendix for comparability with earlier years.
[d] Revised.
[e] Preliminary.

PRINCIPAL TYPES OF HOME UNINTENTIONAL-INJURY DEATHS, UNITED STATES, 2001

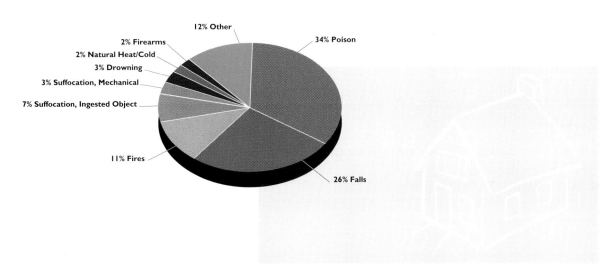

12% Other
2% Firearms
2% Natural Heat/Cold
3% Drowning
3% Suffocation, Mechanical
7% Suffocation, Ingested Object
11% Fires
34% Poison
26% Falls

DEATHS DUE TO UNINTENTIONAL HOME INJURIES, 2001

TYPE OF EVENT AND AGE OF VICTIM

All Home

Includes deaths in the home and on home premises to occupants, guests, and trespassers. Also includes hired household workers but excludes other persons working on home premises.

	Total	Change from 2000	Death Rate[a]
Deaths	33,200	+7%	12.0

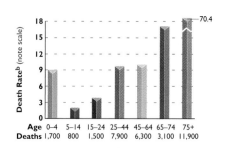

Age	0–4	5–14	15–24	25–44	45–64	65–74	75+
Deaths	1,700	800	1,500	7,900	6,300	3,100	11,900

Poisoning

Includes deaths from drugs, medicines, other solid and liquid substances, and gases and vapors. Excludes poisonings from spoiled foods, salmonella, etc., which are classified as disease deaths.

	Total	Change from 2000	Death Rate[a]
Deaths	11,500	+16%	4.1

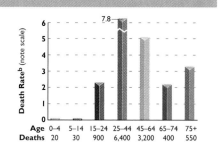

Age	0–4	5–14	15–24	25–44	45–64	65–74	75+
Deaths	20	30	900	6,400	3,200	400	550

Falls

Includes deaths from falls from one level to another or on the same level in the home or on home premises.

	Total	Change from 2000	Death Rate[a]
Deaths	9,000	+13%	3.2

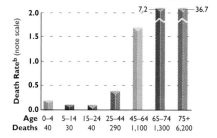

Age	0–4	5–14	15–24	25–44	45–64	65–74	75+
Deaths	40	30	40	290	1,100	1,300	6,200

Fires, Burns, and Deaths Associated with Fires

Includes deaths from fires, burns, and injuries in conflagrations in the home—such as asphyxiation, falls, and struck by falling objects. Excludes burns from hot objects or liquids.

	Total	Change from 2000	Death Rate[a]
Deaths	3,500	0%	1.3

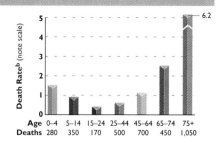

Age	0–4	5–14	15–24	25–44	45–64	65–74	75+
Deaths	280	350	170	500	700	450	1,050

Suffocation by Ingested Object

Includes deaths from unintentional ingestion or inhalation of objects or food resulting in the obstruction of respiratory passages.

	Total	Change from 2000	Death Rate[a]
Deaths	2,200	0%	0.8

See footnotes on page 135.

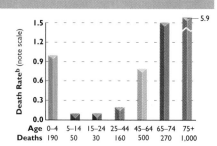

Age	0–4	5–14	15–24	25–44	45–64	65–74	75+
Deaths	190	50	30	160	500	270	1,000

Mechanical Suffocation

Includes deaths from smothering by bed clothes, thin plastic materials, etc.; suffocation by cave-ins or confinement in closed spaces; and mechanical strangulation and hanging.

	Total	Change from 2000	Death Rate[a]
Deaths	1,000	–9%	0.4

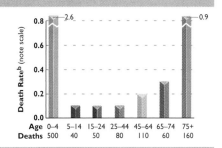

Age	0–4	5–14	15–24	25–44	45–64	65–74	75+
Deaths	500	40	50	80	110	60	160

Drowning

Includes drownings of persons in or on home premises—such as in swimming pools and bathtubs. Excludes drowning in floods and other cataclysms.

	Total	Change from 2000	Death Rate[a]
Deaths	900	–10%	0.3

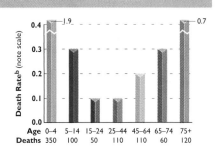

Age	0–4	5–14	15–24	25–44	45–64	65–74	75+
Deaths	350	100	50	110	110	60	120

Firearms

Includes firearms injuries in or on home premises—such as while cleaning or playing with guns. Excludes deaths from explosive materials.

	Total	Change from 2000	Death Rate[a]
Deaths	600	+20%	0.2

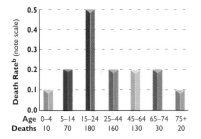

Age	0–4	5–14	15–24	25–44	45–64	65–74	75+
Deaths	10	70	180	160	130	30	20

Natural Heat or Cold

Includes deaths resulting from exposure to excessive natural heat and cold (e.g., extreme weather conditions).

	Total	Change from 2000	Death Rate[a]
Deaths	600	+20%	0.2

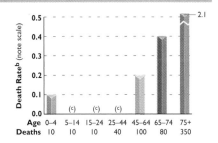

Age	0–4	5–14	15–24	25–44	45–64	65–74	75+
Deaths	10	10	10	40	100	80	350

All Other Home

Most important types included are: struck by or against objects, machinery, and electric current.

	Total	Change from 2000	Death Rate[a]
Deaths	3,900	–7%	1.4

[a] Deaths per 100,000 population.
[b] Deaths per 100,000 population in each age group.
[c] Death rate less than 0.05.

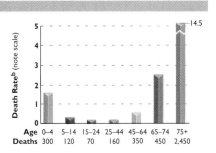

Age	0–4	5–14	15–24	25–44	45–64	65–74	75+
Deaths	300	120	70	160	350	450	2,450

Approximately 2.3 million human poisoning exposure cases were reported in 1999.

UNINTENTIONAL POISONINGS

Deaths from unintentional poisoning numbered 12,186 in 1999, the latest year for which detailed tabulations are available. The death rate per 100,000 population was 4.5–6.7 for males and 2.4 for females.

Beginning with 1999 data, the mortality classification scheme changed from the 9th revision to the 10th revision of the International Classification of Diseases (see the Technical Appendix for more information). The change in poisoning deaths from 1998 to 1999 may be affected by the classification change as well as changes in the level of poisoning safety. Keeping this in mind, note that total poisoning deaths increased approximately 13% from 10,801 in 1998 to 12,186 in 1999.

Almost half of the poisoning deaths (49%) were classified in the "narcotics and psychodysleptics (hallucinogens), not elsewhere classified," category, which includes many illegal drugs such as cocaine, heroin, cannabinol, and LSD.

Carbon monoxide poisoning is included in the category of "other gases and vapors." Deaths due to alcohol poisoning numbered 320 in 1999, but alcohol may also be present in combination with other drugs.

Total human poisoning exposure cases, both fatal and nonfatal, reported to poison control centers were estimated to number 2.3 million in 1999, or about 8.4 reported exposures per 1,000 population, according to the American Association of Poison Control Centers.

UNINTENTIONAL POISONING DEATHS BY TYPE, AGE, AND SEX, UNITED STATES, 1999

Type of Poison	All Ages	0–4 Years	5–14 Years	15–19 Years	20–24 Years	25–44 Years	45–64 Years	65 Years & Over
Both Sexes								
Total Poisoning Deaths	12,186	46	40	260	704	6,904	3,512	720
Deaths per 100,000 population	*4.5*	*0.2*	*0.1*	*1.3*	*3.9*	*8.3*	*5.9*	*2.1*
Nonopioid analgesics, antipyretics, and antirheumatics (X40)	168	4	2	4	7	60	65	26
Antiepileptic, sedative-hypnotic, antiparkinsonism, and psychotropic drugs, n.e.c. (X41)	671	4	3	19	37	347	226	35
Narcotics and psychodysleptics (hallucinogens), n.e.c. (X42)	6,009	3	4	117	356	3,708	1,740	81
Other drugs acting on the autonomic nervous system (X43)	21	1	1	0	0	11	6	2
Other and unspecified drugs, medicaments, and biological substances (X44)	4,286	12	6	68	241	2,399	1,167	393
Alcohol (X45)	320	0	1	7	17	158	121	16
Organic solvents and halogenated hydrocarbons and their vapors (X46)	63	1	3	12	4	26	8	9
Other gases and vapors (X47)	534	17	12	29	36	174	150	116
Pesticides (X48)	12	0	1	1	1	2	4	3
Other and unspecified chemical and noxious substances (X49)	102	4	7	3	5	19	25	39
Males								
Total Poisoning Deaths	8,887	28	25	195	559	5,177	2,554	349
Deaths per 100,000 population	*6.7*	*0.3*	*0.1*	*1.9*	*6.1*	*12.6*	*8.9*	*2.4*
Nonopioid analgesics, antipyretics, and antirheumatics (X40)	82	2	1	2	5	25	33	14
Antiepileptic, sedative-hypnotic, antiparkinsonism, and psychotropic drugs, n.e.c. (X41)	412	1	2	11	23	226	139	10
Narcotics and psychodysleptics (hallucinogens), n.e.c. (X42)	4,808	2	2	90	296	2,962	1,406	50
Other drugs acting on the autonomic nervous system (X43)	13	1	1	0	0	6	3	2
Other and unspecified drugs, medicaments, and biological substances (X44)	2,796	9	3	52	184	1,648	740	160
Alcohol (X45)	254	0	1	6	14	128	93	12
Organic solvents and halogenated hydrocarbons and their vapors (X46)	53	1	3	9	3	22	6	9
Other gases and vapors (X47)	410	9	9	21	29	149	118	75
Pesticides (X48)	10	0	1	1	1	2	3	2
Other and unspecified chemical and noxious substances (X49)	49	3	2	3	4	9	13	15
Females								
Total Poisoning Deaths	3,299	18	15	65	145	1,727	958	371
Deaths per 100,000 population	*2.4*	*0.2*	*0.1*	*0.7*	*1.6*	*4.1*	*3.1*	*1.8*
Nonopioid analgesics, antipyretics, and antirheumatics (X40)	86	2	1	2	2	35	32	12
Antiepileptic, sedative-hypnotic, antiparkinsonism, and psychotropic drugs, n.e.c. (X41)	259	3	1	8	14	121	87	25
Narcotics and psychodysleptics (hallucinogens), n.e.c. (X42)	1,201	1	2	27	60	746	334	31
Other drugs acting on the autonomic nervous system (X43)	8	0	0	0	0	5	3	0
Other and unspecified drugs, medicaments, and biological substances (X44)	1,490	3	3	16	57	751	427	233
Alcohol (X45)	66	0	0	1	3	30	28	4
Organic solvents and halogenated hydrocarbons and their vapors (X46)	10	0	0	3	1	4	2	0
Other gases and vapors (X47)	124	8	3	8	7	25	32	41
Pesticides (X48)	2	0	0	0	0	0	1	1
Other and unspecified chemical and noxious substances (X49)	53	1	5	0	1	10	12	24

Source: National Safety Council tabulations of National Center for Health Statistics mortality data.
Note: n.e.c. = not elsewhere classified.

UNINTENTIONAL POISONINGS, 1990–1999

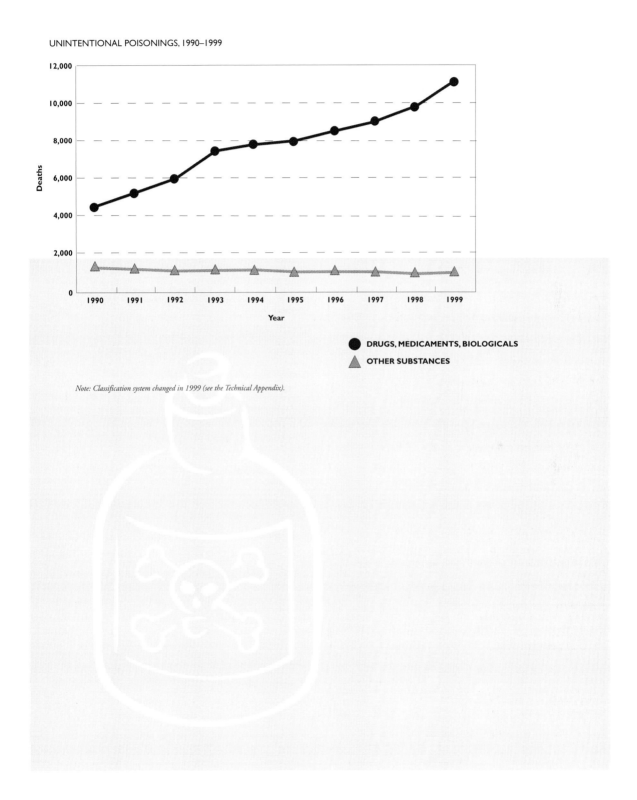

Note: Classification system changed in 1999 (see the Technical Appendix).

Floors and stairs were each associated with more than 1,000,000 emergency department visits in 2002.

INJURIES ASSOCIATED WITH CONSUMER PRODUCTS

The following list of items found in and around the home was selected from the U.S. Consumer Product Safety Commission's National Electronic Injury Surveillance System (NEISS) for 2000. The NEISS estimates are calculated from a statistically representative sample of hospitals in the United States. Injury totals represent estimates of the number of hospital emergency department-treated cases nationwide associated with various products. However, product involvement may or may not be the cause of the injury.

ESTIMATED HOSPITAL EMERGENCY DEPARTMENT VISITS RELATED TO SELECTED CONSUMER PRODUCTS, UNITED STATES, 2000
(excluding most sports or sports equipment; see also page 124)

Description	Injuries[a]
Home Workshop Equipment	
Saws (hand or power)	95,875
Hammers	40,707
Household Packaging and Containers	
Household containers and packaging	204,422
Bottles and jars	80,186
Bags	32,921
Paper products	20,015
Housewares	
Knives	459,898
Tableware and flatware (excl. knives)	109,146
Drinking glasses	98,924
Scissors	31,512
Waste containers, trash baskets, etc.	31,381
Cookware, bowls and canisters	28,690
Home Furnishings, Fixtures, and Accessories	
Beds	466,464
Tables, n.e.c.[b]	311,208
Chairs	298,894
Bathtubs and showers	201,465
Ladders	161,627
Sofas, couches, davenports, divans, etc.	130,540
Rugs and carpets	122,249
Other furniture[c]	89,548
Toilets	55,806
Misc. decorating items	40,835
Stools	35,682
Benches	27,420
Mirrors or mirror glass	24,497
Electric lighting equipment	22,739
Sinks	22,047
Home Structures and Construction Materials	
Stairs or steps	1,048,257
Floors or flooring materials	1,033,938
Other doors[d]	346,288
Ceilings and walls	290,830
Household cabinets, racks, and shelves	253,186
Nails, screws, tacks, or bolts	158,982
Windows	141,031
Porches, balconies, open-side floors	136,950
House repair and construction materials	125,805
Fences or fence posts	118,603
Poles	59,358
Door sills or frames	45,268
Handrails, railings, or banisters	40,927
Counters or countertops	40,349

Description	Injuries[a]
Glass doors	35,437
Cabinet or door hardware	21,758
General Household Appliances	
Refrigerators	29,980
Ranges	25,322
Heating, Cooling, and Ventilating Equipment	
Pipes (excluding smoking pipes)	35,226
Home Communication and Entertainment Equipment	
Televisions	41,462
Personal Use Items	
Footwear	109,681
Wheelchairs	95,877
Jewelry	72,300
Crutches, canes, walkers	69,349
First aid equipment	50,880
Coins	34,852
Razors and shavers	34,279
Daywear	33,174
Desk supplies	30,018
Hair grooming equipment and accessories	22,459
Other clothing[e]	21,569
Yard and Garden Equipment	
Lawn mowers	81,888
Pruning, trimming, and edging equipment	45,253
Chainsaws	26,711
Other unpowered garden tools[f]	26,635
Sports and Recreation Equipment	
Trampolines	100,303
Skateboards	86,781
All-terrain vehicles	84,900
Monkey bars or other playground climbing equipment	81,060
Swimming pools	80,110
Toys, n.e.c.	78,370
Swings or swing sets	76,181
Minibikes or trail bikes	54,674
Slides or sliding boards	50,086
Scooters (unpowered)	42,505
Sleds	38,546
Other playground equipment[g]	29,652
Miscellaneous Products	
Carts	45,708
Hot water	42,712

Source: U.S. Consumer Product Safety Commission, National Electronic Injury Surveillance System, Product Summary Report, All Products, CY2000. Products are listed above if the estimate was greater than 20,000 cases.
[a] *Estimated number of product-related injuries in the United States and territories that were treated in hospital emergency departments.*
[b] *Excludes baby changing and television tables or stands.*

[c] *Includes cabinets, racks, shelves, desks, bureaus, chests, buffets, etc.*
[d] *Excludes glass doors and garage doors.*
[e] *Excludes costumes, masks, daywear, footwear, nightwear, and outerwear.*
[f] *Includes cultivators, hoes, pitchforks, rakes, shovels, spades, and trowels.*
[g] *Excludes monkey bars, seesaws, slides, and swings.*
n.e.c. = not elsewhere classified.

Preschool children (age 5 and under) and older adults (age 65 and over) were at greatest risk of fire deaths in homes during the 1994–1998 period analyzed by the National Fire Protection Association. Home fire death rates were more than twice the national average for adults age 65 and older, nearly three times the national average for adults age 75 and older, and four-and-a-half times the national average for adults age 85 and older. Preschool children died at a rate roughly twice the national average.

Smoking materials were the leading cause of fire deaths for all age groups combined—24% of all deaths and a rate of 3.1 deaths per million population per year. The rate among adults increased with age from 1.6 for ages 20–29 to 12.7 for ages 85 and over. Child-playing fires accounted for the largest share (35%) of preschooler home fire deaths. The leading cause of fatal fires was also child playing for ages 6–9; incendiary or suspicious for ages 10–19 and 20–29; and smoking for ages 30–49, 50–64, 65–74, 75–84, and 85 and over.

Half of all victims (52%) were asleep with no special limitations or impairments noted when the fire occurred. The majority of victims overall (58%) were outside the room of fire origin when fire began. Adults ages 65 and older were different, as 48% were in the room of fire origin and 21% were intimate with ignition, compared to 16% of victims of all age groups. One-third of preschool victims had the physical and developmental limitations captured by the phrase "too young to act." One-third of adults 65 and older had

either specific physical or mental disabilities or the more general limitations captured by the phrase "too old to act."

In addition to differences in risk by age group, there were gender differences. The fire death rate for males during 1994–98 was 43% higher than for females. This pattern of higher risk for males was reflected to varying degrees across all age groups. The risk index difference was least pronounced for children ages 6–9, where it was only 1%.

For nonfatal civilian (nonfirefighter) injuries in home fires, the 85-and-over age group was the only high-risk age group that was also high-risk for home fire deaths. Their injury rate was 90% higher than the all-ages average. Adults age 20–29 were the second highest risk group for fire injuries, with an injury rate 33% higher than the national average.

Smoke inhalation alone (without burns or other injuries) accounted for the largest share (44%) of civilian home fire injuries and more than half of the injuries to children ages 0–5 and 6–9 and to older adults ages 75–84, and 85 and older. A higher percentage of children 0–5 and adults 75 and older were deemed "unable to act" at the time of injury compared with other age groups. Males were more at risk from injury in home fires than females for all age groups. The largest difference was in the 85-and-older group.

Source: Hall, Jr., J.R. (2001). Patterns of Fire Casualties in Home Fires by Age and Sex. *Quincy, MA: National Fire Protection Association.*

CIVILIAN FIRE DEATHS AND RATES IN HOMES BY AGE AND SEX, UNITED STATES, 1994–1998 ANNUAL AVERAGE

Age Group	Both Sexes			Males			Females		
	Deaths	Rate[a]	Risk Index[b]	Deaths	Rate[a]	Risk Index[b]	Deaths	Rate[a]	Risk Index[b]
All ages	**3,509**	**13.2**	**1.00**	**2,029**	**15.6**	**1.18**	**1,479**	**10.9**	**0.83**
0–5	612	26.2	1.98	352	29.5	2.23	260	22.8	1.72
6–9	167	10.9	0.82	86	10.9	0.83	81	10.8	0.82
10–19	213	5.6	0.43	123	6.3	0.48	90	4.9	0.37
20–29	277	7.6	0.57	164	8.9	0.67	113	6.3	0.47
30–49	814	9.8	0.74	539	13.0	0.99	275	6.6	0.50
59–64	466	13.2	1.00	292	17.2	1.30	174	9.5	0.72
65–74	362	19.4	1.47	197	23.6	1.79	165	16.0	1.21
75–84	370	32.4	2.45	178	39.7	3.00	192	27.6	2.09
85 & older	227	60.4	4.56	99	92.2	6.97	128	47.7	3.61
65 & older	**959**	**28.3**	**2.14**	**474**	**34.1**	**2.56**	**485**	**24.3**	**1.84**

Source: Hall, J.R., Jr. (2001). Patterns of Fire Casualties in Home Fires by Age and Sex. *Quincy, MA: National Fire Protection Association.*
[a] *Deaths per 1,000,000 population.*
[b] *Age/sex-specific death rate divided by the all-ages-both-sexes death rate.*

ELECTROCUTIONS ASSOCIATED WITH CONSUMER PRODUCTS

A current strategic goal of the U.S. Consumer Product Safety Commission (CPSC) involves reducing the death rate from consumer product–related electrocutions by 20% from 1994 to the year 2004. A recent report provides fatality estimates and death rates associated with the use of consumer products in order to evaluate progress toward reaching the strategic goal.

Total electrocutions in the United States have decreased 23% from 710 deaths in 1988 to 550 in 1998, according to data from the National Center for Health Statistics (NCHS). During this same period, the estimated number of electrocutions related to consumer products decreased from 290 in 1988 to 200 in 1998, a reduction of 31%. Both of these downward trends were significant, as was the 40% decline in the age-adjusted death rates from consumer product–related electrocutions from 1.18 per million population to 0.74 over the same time period. Since 1994, the death rate from consumer product–related fatalities has declined about 17%; in order to reduce the electrocution death rate by 20% and meet the CPSC goal, the death rate needs to consistently fall to 0.71 or below.

Small appliances including extension cords, microwaves, and battery chargers were the most frequently reported group of products (24%) involved in consumer product–related electrocutions in 1998. Large appliances such as air conditioners, pumps, and generators were the next most frequently reported group of products (19%), followed by power tools such as saws, drills, and pressure washers, which were involved in 14% of the consumer product–related electrocutions. Installed household wiring accounted for 13% of the electrocution deaths, and lighting equipment, mostly lamps and light fixtures, was responsible for 9% of the deaths.

Antennas and ladders that came in contact with overhead power lines were responsible for 6% and 5% of the electrocution deaths, respectively. Farm and lawn and garden equipment accounted for 2% of the electrocutions. Other products, including pipes, poles, fences, and amusement rides, accounted for the remaining 11% of the fatalities.

Source: Hiser, S. (July, 2001). 1998 Electrocutions Associated with Consumer Products. Washington, DC: U.S. Consumer Product Safety Commission.

ELECTROCUTIONS RELATED TO CONSUMER PRODUCTS, UNITED STATES, 1988–1998

Year	Total Electrocutions	Consumer Product–Related Electrocutions		
		Number	Percent of Total	Death Rate[a]
1988	710	290	41%	1.18
1989	710	300	42%	1.21
1990	670	270	40%	1.09
1991	630	250	40%	0.99
1992	530	200	38%	0.78
1993	550	210	38%	0.82
1994	560	230	41%	0.89
1995	560	230	41%	0.88
1996	480	190	40%	0.72
1997	490	190	39%	0.71
1998	550	200	36%	0.74

[a] *Death rate per million U.S. population for consumer product–related electrocutions.*

CHILDREN AND IN-HOME DROWNINGS

For the four-year period 1996 through 1999, 459 children under the age of five died from complications of drowning or near-drowning in products located in and around the home, according to a study by the U.S. Consumer Product Safety Commission. The products studied included products holding water except for swimming pools and wading pools. (About 350 children under age 5 drown in swimming pools each year.)

Bathtubs accounted for 292 or 64% of the deaths. About half of these deaths involved children under the age of one and in over 61% of the cases the children were reported to have been in the bathtub without a bathing aid. The child was reported to have been left unsupervised in 222 of the 231 cases where supervision status was known.

Falling into a 5-gallon bucket accounted for 58 (13%) of the deaths. All of the children were 18 months old or younger when the incident occurred and most involved buckets that contained dirty water and that were located most frequently in the kitchen. About the same number of children, 55 (12%), died as a result of drowning in residential spas or hot tubs. About 56% of

these children were under age 2. Children reportedly accessed the spas and hot tubs through open or broken gates and sliding glass doors, under soft covers on the spa, or while a cover was left open.

Household toilets were involved in 16 of the drowning deaths, with all of the incidents involving children under age 3. In addition, 38 children drowned in other products around the home, including such items as buckets other than 5-gallon buckets, home landscape ponds, sinks, water coolers, and garbage cans, among others.

PRODUCT-RELATED IN-HOME DROWNING DEATHS OF CHILDREN UNDER 5, UNITED STATES, 1996-1999

Product	Deaths
Bathtubs	292
5-Gallon buckets	58
Spas and hot tubs	55
Toilets	16
Other products	38
Total	**459**

Source: Sweet, Debra. (2002). Children and in-home drownings. Consumer Product Safety Review, 6(4), 1-3.

CHILDREN LEFT UNATTENDED IN OR AROUND MOTOR VEHICLES

Although national attention is focused on the dangers to children as occupants of motor vehicles (MVs) in traffic on public roads, children who are unattended in or around MVs that are not in traffic are also at risk for injury or death. During the period July 2000 through June 2001 there were an estimated 9,160 nonfatal injuries and 78 fatal injuries among children aged 14 or younger who were left unattended in or around motor vehicles that were not in traffic. About 42% of the injured children were 4 years of age or less and 62% were male. About 57% of the injuries were minor contusions and abrasions and 26% were more serious fractures or internal injuries. Most of the injuries occurred near the home (48%) or on public property (31%). The most common type of nonfatal incident was being struck by a

motor vehicle, followed by being run over or backed over and falling out or off of a vehicle.

Of the 78 fatalities to children during the period July 2000 to June 2001, 64 (82%) were less than 4 years old and 42 (54%) were male. The most common type of fatal accident was exposure to excessive heat inside an MV (35%), followed by being backed over (27%) and being hurt when a child put an MV in motion (13%). In 73% of the cases, the MV was located near a home and in half of the cases, the child lived at that home. The driver was the parent in 12 of the 21 cases in which a child was backed over.

Source: Centers for Disease Control and Prevention. (2002). Injuries and deaths among children left unattended in or around motor vehicles—United States, July 2000-June 2001. MMWR, 51(26), 570-572.

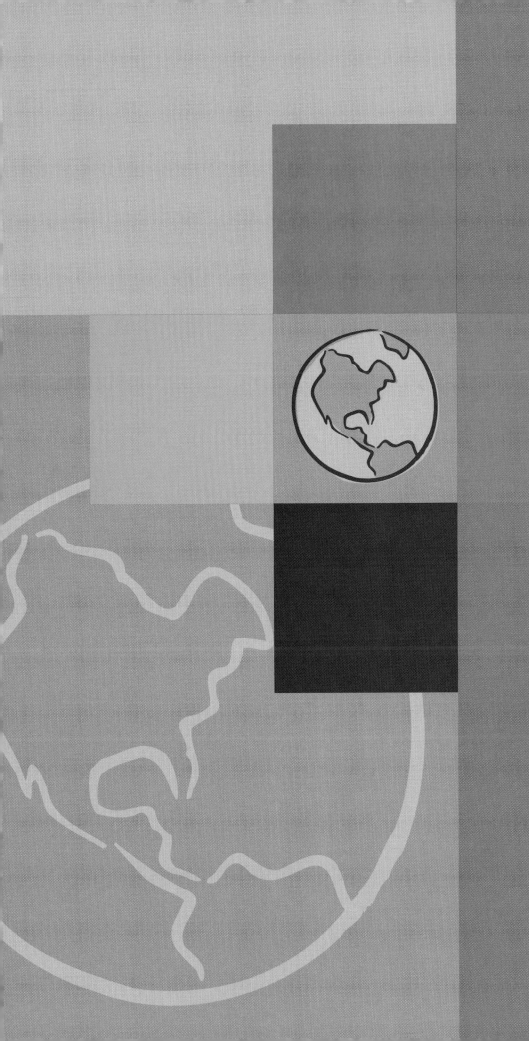

ENVIRONMENTAL
HEALTH

AIR QUALITY

The U.S. Environmental Protection Agency monitors air quality by tracking six principal pollutants two ways: first, by measuring emissions from all sources and, second, by measuring levels of the pollutants in ambient air at monitoring stations around the country. The six key pollutants are described here, and the current monitoring results are presented.

NO$_x$

Nitrogen oxides (NO$_x$) include nitrogen dioxide (NO$_2$), nitric oxide (NO), and other oxides of nitrogen. These gases play a major role in the formation of ozone, particulate matter, haze, and acid rain. The major cause is high-temperature combustion from such sources as automobiles and power plants, home heaters, and gas stoves.

O$_3$

Ground-level ozone is the principal component of smog and is formed by the reaction of volatile organic compounds (VOC) and nitrogen oxides in the presence of heat and sunlight. Short-term and prolonged exposure to ozone has been linked to respiratory problems.

SO$_2$

Sulfur dioxide is formed when fuel containing sulfur (mainly coal and oil) is burned and during metal smelting and other industrial processes. High concentrations of sulfur dioxide can aggravate asthma, chronic lung disease, and cardiovascular disease.

PM$_{10}$

Particulate matter is the general term for a mixture of solid particles and liquid droplets found in the air. PM$_{10}$ refers to all particles less than or equal to 10 micrometers in diameter. Particulate matter is associated with heart and lung disease.

CO

Carbon monoxide is formed by incomplete combustion of fuel. The main source is motor-vehicle exhaust. Carbon monoxide reduces the ability of the blood to deliver oxygen to the body's organs and tissues.

Pb

Lead is an element that is released into the air during industrial processes such as smelting and battery manufacturing. Exposure to lead can adversely affect the kidneys, liver, nervous system, and other organs.

Source: Office of Air Quality Planning and Standards. (2001). Latest Findings on National Air Quality: 2000 Status and Trends. Research Triangle Park, NC: U.S. Environmental Protection Agency.

PERCENT CHANGE IN AIR QUALITY AND EMISSIONS, UNITED STATES, 1992–2000

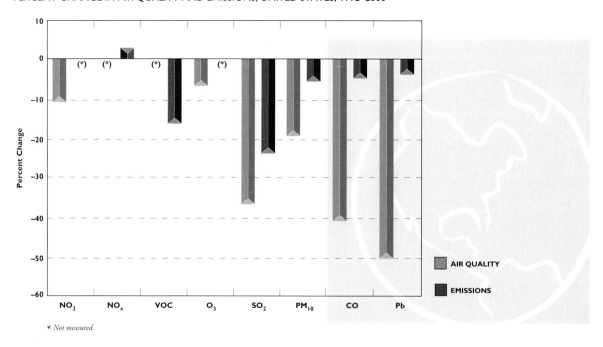

* Not measured.

There are more than 54,000 community water systems in the United States—systems that provide drinking water to at least 25 people or 15 service connections and serve the same population year-round. About 263 million people get their water from such systems.

One of the U.S. Environmental Protection Agency's goals under the Government Performance and Results Act is that, by 2005, the population served by community water systems providing drinking water that meets all existing health-based standards will increase to 95% from a baseline of 83% in 1994. The graph and map below show the progress toward that goal.

Source: Office of Water. (2001). Factoids: Drinking Water and Ground Water Statistics for 2000. *EPA816–K–01–004. Washington, DC: U.S. Environmental Protection Agency.*

PERCENT OF POPULATION SERVED BY COMMUNITY WATER SYSTEMS PROVIDING
DRINKING WATER THAT MEETS ALL EXISTING HEALTH-BASED STANDARDS, UNITED STATES, 1993–2000

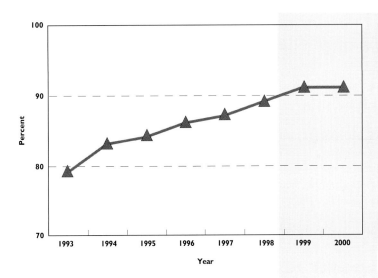

PERCENT OF POPULATION SERVED BY COMMUNITY WATER SYSTEMS PROVIDING DRINKING
WATER THAT MEETS ALL EXISTING HEALTH-BASED STANDARDS BY REGION, UNITED STATES, 2000

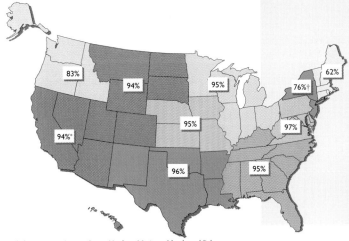

*Includes: American Samoa, Guam, Northern Marianas Islands, and Palau.
†Includes: Puerto Rico and Virgin Islands.

ASTHMA

Asthma is a chronic, episodic, inflammatory condition of the lungs. Asthma attacks can be triggered by environmental pollutants such as sulfur dioxide, dust mites, cockroaches, animal dander, tobacco smoke, and mold. For this reason, asthma is considered by some to be an environmental health problem.

A recent report from the Centers for Disease Control and Prevention summarized the surveillance activities for asthma from 1980 through 1999. It drew on data from the National Health Interview Survey, the National Ambulatory Medical Care Survey, the National Hospital Ambulatory Medical Care Survey, the National Hospital Discharge Survey, and the mortality component of the National Vital Statistics System.

From 1980 through 1996, self-reported 12-month asthma prevalence increased 73.9% to 14.6 million persons or 54.6 per 1,000 population. Beginning in 1997 the measures of asthma prevalence are based on a medical diagnosis. In 1997, 26.7 million people (96.6 per 1,000 population) reported a physician diagnosis of asthma during their lifetime. The number of persons with an asthma diagnosis who experienced an attack or episode during the preceding 12 months was 11.1 million (40.7 per 1,000 population).

The number of office visits for asthma increased from 5.9 million in 1980 to 10.8 million in 1999. The number of emergency department visits increased 36% and the rate of emergency department visits increased 29% from 1992 to 1999. Hospitalizations for asthma peaked in the mid-1980s and has gradually declined since then.

Deaths and death rates due to asthma increased from 1980 to 1995 and have remained steady or declined slightly since then.

The report indicates that the prevalence of asthma and office visit rates for asthma do not vary significantly by region[a] of the country. Rates for emergency department visits are higher than average in the Northeast and Midwest and lower in the South and West. Hospitalization rates are much higher in the Northeast than in other regions. Death rates in the West and Midwest due to asthma are higher than the total U.S. rate; death rate in the South and Northeast are lower than the national average.

Source: Mannino, D.M., Homa, D.M., Akinbami, L.J., Moorman, J.E., Gwynn, C., & Redd, S.C. (2002). Surveillance for asthma—United States, 1980-1999. Morbidity and Mortality Weekly Report, 51(SS-1).
[a] *Regions: Northeast—CT, MA, ME, NH, NJ, NY, PA, RI, VT. Midwest—IA, IL, IN, KS, MI, MO, MN, ND, NE, OH, SD, WI. South—AL, AR, DC, DE, FL, GA, KY, LA, MD, MS, NC, OK, SC, TN, TX, VA, WV. West—AK, AZ, CA, CO, HI, ID, MT, NM, NV, OR, UT, WA, WY.*

ASTHMA SURVEILLANCE, UNITED STATES, 1999

Demographic Group	Persons with Asthma Episode or Attack During Previous 12 Months		Physician Office and Hospital Outpatient Department Visits for Asthma		Emergency Department Visits for Asthma		Hospitalizations for Asthma		Deaths with Asthma as the Underlying Cause	
	Number	Rate[a]	Number	Rate[a]	Number	Rate[b]	Number	Rate[b]	Number	Rate[c]
Total	10,488,000	38.4	10,808,000	39.8	1,997,000	73.3	478,000	17.6	4,657	17.2
Race										
White	8,226,000	37.6	8,810,000	39.6	1,313,000	59.4	236,000	10.6	3,328	14.2
Black	1,535,000	42.7	1,478,000	41.9	63,000	174.3	128,000	35.6	1,145	38.7
Other	727,000	38.9	520,000	36.8	54,000	38.4	42,000	31.5	184	20.4
Missing[d]							72,000			
Sex										
Male	4,310,000	31.6	4,827,000	36.6	932,000	68.6	190,000	14.1	1,620	13.1
Female	6,178,000	44.5	5,981,000	43.4	1,065,000	77.2	288,000	20.6	3,037	20.4
Age Group										
0-4	825,000	42.1	1,150,000	60.6	269,000	141.8	105,000	55.4	32	1.7
5-14	2,288,000	56.4	2,387,000	60.4	389,000	98.5	85,000	21.5	144	3.6
15-34	3,208,000	42.2	1,960,000	25.9	616,000	81.3	77,000	10.1	444	5.9
35-64	3,451,000	33.4	4,069,000	39.3	601,000	58.1	138,000	13.4	1,637	15.8
65+	717,000	22.1	1,243,000	36.2	122,000	35.5	73,000	21.1	2,400	69.9

Source: Mannino, D.M., Homa, D.M., Akinbami, L.J., Moorman, J.E., Gwynn, C., & Redd, S.C. (2002). Surveillance for asthma—United States, 1980–1999. Morbidity and Mortality Weekly Report, 51(SS-1).
[a] *Per 1,000 population. Race, sex, and total rates age-adjusted to the 2000 standard U.S. population.*
[b] *Per 10,000 population. Race, sex, and total rates age-adjusted to the 2000 standard U.S. population.*
[c] *Per 1,000,000 population. Race, sex, and total rates age-adjusted to the 2000 standard U.S. population.*
[d] *Race data were not collected by certain hospitals in the hospital discharge survey.*

Research on the health effects of exposure to electromagnetic fields (EMF) is continuing. Some of the more recent research is summarized here.

The relationship between power-frequency (50/60hz) EMF and childhood leukemia has been studied for more than 20 years with mixed results. McBride et al. (1999), conducted a case-control study of 399 children under 15 years old living in five Canadian provinces who were diagnosed with leukemia between 1990 and 1994 along with 399 controls. Exposure was assessed by 48-hour personal EMF measurement, measurements at the subjects' residences from conception to diagnosis date, and 24-hour magnetic field bedroom measurements. Personal magnetic fields were not related to risk of leukemia or acute lymphatic leukemia. No clear association was established with predicted magnetic field exposure either two years before diagnosis or over the subject's lifetime, or with personal electric fields. A statistically nonsignificant association was observed between very high wiring configurations compared to underground wiring among residences of subjects two years before diagnosis. Overall, the findings did not support a relation between power-frequency EMF exposure and risk of childhood leukemia.

Another case-control study (408 pairs) conducted by the National Cancer Institute (Kleinerman et al., 2000) analyzed distance to transmission and three-phase primary distribution lines within 40 m of homes and created an exposure index of distance and strength of multiple power lines. Neither distance nor exposure index was related to risk of childhood acute lymphoblastic leukemia. Residence near high-voltage lines did not increase risk.

A case-control study in the United Kingdom of 2,226 matched pairs investigated the relationship between all childhood cancers and exposure to power-frequency EMF (UK, 1999). Household and school EMF measurements were used to estimate average exposure in the year before the date of diagnosis or an equivalent date for controls. Comparing children with mean exposures >0.2 µT to those with exposures <0.1 µT, found no increased risk of acute lymphoblastic leukemia, all leukemia, central nervous system tumors, other malignant disease, or all malignant disease combined.

A case-control study from Chinese Taipei investigated the association between elevated exposure to power-frequency EMF and cognitive impairment (Li, Sung, & Wu, 2002). Elderly individuals with cognitive impairment were matched with controls. Former electrical workers or persons living within 100 m of high-voltage transmission lines were considered to have higher exposure to EMF. Compared with background exposure, the risk was equal to or close to unity for persons with occupational exposure to EMF, higher residential exposure, or both occupational and residential exposure. The authors conclude that their findings provide little support for a link between power frequency EMF and cognitive impairment, but do not preclude a possible association with any specific neurodegenerative disease previously investigated.

A Swedish study examined the prevalence of self-reported hypersensitivity to EMF (Hillert et al., 2002). A survey of 15,000 men and women from 19 to 80 years old was conducted in 1997 with a response rate of 73%. Overall, 1.5% of respondents reported hypersensitivity to EMF. Prevalence was higher among women than men, increased with age, and was greater among single- and low-income people. The EMF-hypersensitive group also reported, to a significantly greater extent, other symptoms, allergies, and hypersensitivities than did the rest of the respondents. The authors conclude that there is widespread concern among the general population about risks to health posed by EMF and that more research is warranted to explore ill health among people reporting hypersensitivity to EMF.

Hillert, L., Berglind, N., Arnetz, B.B., & Bellander, T. (2002). Prevalence of self-reported hypersensitivity to electric or magnetic fields in a population-based questionnaire survey. Scandinavian Journal of Work Environment and Health, 28(1), 33–41.
Kleinerman, R.A., Kaune, W.T., Hatch, E.E., Wacholder, S., Linet, M.S., Robison, L.L., et al. (2000). Are children living near high-voltage power lines at increased risk of acute lymphoblastic leukemia? American Journal of Epidemiology, 151(5), 512–515.
Li, C.-Y., Sung, F-C., & Wu, S.C. (2002). Risk of cognitive impairment in relation to elevated exposure to electromagnetic fields. Journal of Occupational and Environmental Medicine, 44(1), 66–72.
McBride, M.L., Gallagher, R.P., Theriault, G., Armstrong, B.G., Tamaro, S., Spinelli, J.J., et al. (1999). Power-frequency electric and magnetic fields and risk of childhood leukemia in Canada. American Journal of Epidemiology, 149(9), 831–842.
UK Childhood Cancer Study Investigators. (1999). Exposure to power-frequency magnetic fields and the risk of childhood cancer. Lancet, 354, 1925–1931.

STATE DATA

STATE DATA

This section on state-level data has been expanded to include data for occupational and motor-vehicle injuries as well as general mortality.

Death rates for unintentional injuries (U-I) can vary greatly from one type of injury to the next and from state to state. The graph on the next page shows for each state the death rates (per 100,000 population) for total unintentional-injury deaths and the four leading types of unintentional-injury deaths nationally—motor-vehicle crashes, falls, poisonings, and choking (inhalation or ingestion of food or other object that obstructs breathing).

The map on page 152 shows graphically the overall unintentional-injury death rates by state.

The charts on pages 153 through 155 show (a) total unintentional-injury deaths and where U-I rank as a cause of death in each state and (b) the five leading causes of U-I deaths in each state.

Unintentional injuries as a whole are the fifth leading cause of death in the United States and in 33 states. U-I are the third leading cause of death in Alaska and New Mexico and the fourth leading cause in 9 states. U-I rank sixth in 5 states (Maryland, New Jersey, New York, Ohio, and Rhode Island), seventh in Massachusetts, and eighth in the District of Columbia.

Motor-vehicle crashes were the leading cause of U-I deaths in every state, but poisoning was the leading cause in the District of Columbia. The second leading cause of U-I deaths was falls in 32 states, poisoning in 18 states, and motor-vehicle crashes in the District of Columbia. The most common third leading causes of U-I deaths were poisoning in 24 states, falls in 15 states and the District of Columbia, drowning and choking in 4 states each, and fires in 3 states. Choking was the fourth leading cause of U-I deaths in 21 states and the District of Columbia, while the fourth ranking cause was drowning in 17 states, fires and flames in 7 states, poisoning or mechanical suffocation in 2 states each, and air transport in 1 state (Alaska).

The table on pages 156 and 157 shows the number of U-I deaths by state for the 17 most common types of injury events. State populations are also shown to facilitate computation of detailed death rates.

The table on page 158 consists of a 3-year state-by-state comparison of unintentional-injury deaths and death rates for 1999, 1998, and 1997. Because of the change in mortality classification schemes from ICD-9 to ICD-10 in 1999, caution must be exercised in making comparisons of 1999 data with earlier years. A comparability study conducted by the National Center for Health Statistics indicates that if the 1998 mortality data had been coded according to ICD-10, then the U-I death total would have been about 3% greater. See the Technical Appendix for more information.

Page 159 shows fatal occupational injuries by state and counts of deaths for some of the principal types of events—transportation accidents, assaults and violent acts, contacts with objects and equipment, falls, exposure to harmful substances or environments, and fires and explosions.

Nonfatal occupational injury and illness incidence rates for most states are shown in the table on page 160 and graphically in the map on page 161.

Pages 162 and 163 show motor-vehicle–related deaths and death rates by state both in tables and maps.

UNINTENTIONAL-INJURY DEATH RATES BY STATE, UNITED STATES, 1999

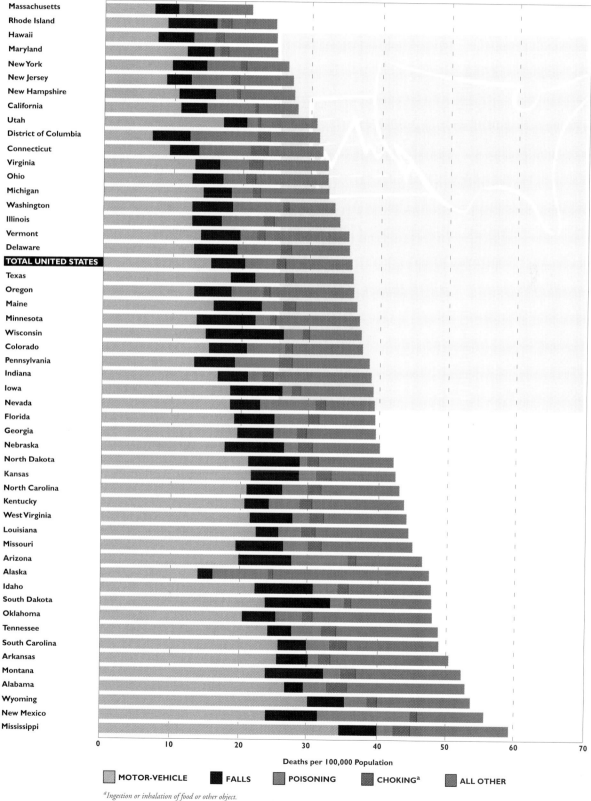

Deaths per 100,000 Population

■ MOTOR-VEHICLE   ■ FALLS   ■ POISONING   ■ CHOKING^a   ■ ALL OTHER

^a*Ingestion or inhalation of food or other object.*

UNINTENTIONAL-INJURY DEATH RATES BY STATE

DEATH RATES PER 100,000 POPULATION BY STATE, 1999

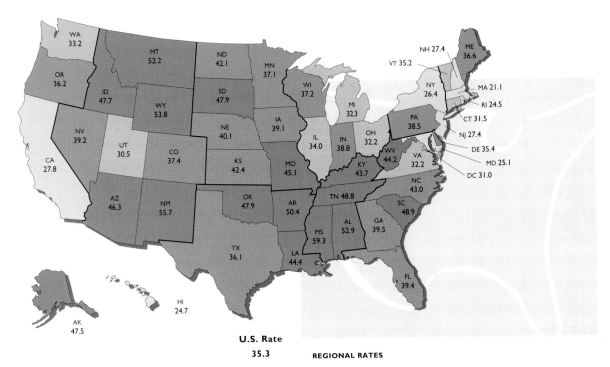

WA 33.2
MT 52.2
ND 42.1
MN 37.1
NH 27.4
ME 36.6
VT 35.2
OR 36.2
ID 47.7
SD 47.9
WI 37.2
NY 26.4
MA 21.1
RI 24.5
WY 53.8
MI 32.3
PA 38.5
CT 31.5
NV 39.2
NE 40.1
IA 39.1
NJ 27.4
UT 30.5
IL 34.0
IN 38.8
OH 32.2
DE 35.4
CA 27.8
CO 37.4
KS 42.4
MO 45.1
WV 44.2
VA 32.2
MD 25.1
DC 31.0
AZ 46.3
NM 55.7
OK 47.9
AR 50.4
KY 43.7
NC 43.0
TN 48.8
SC 48.9
MS 59.3
AL 52.9
GA 39.5
TX 36.1
LA 44.4
FL 39.4
HI 24.7
AK 47.5

U.S. Rate
35.3

BELOW 30.5: 8 STATES
30.5 TO 35.3: 8 STATES STATES AND DISTRICT OF COLUMBIA
35.4 TO 43.0: 17 STATES
ABOVE 43.0: 17 STATES

REGIONAL RATES

New England (CT, ME, MA, NH, RI, VT)	26.5
Middle Atlantic (NJ, NY, PA)	30.4
East N. Central (IL, IN, MI, OH, WI)	34.2
West N. Central (IA, KS, MN, MO, NE, ND, SD)	41.3
South Atlantic (DE, DC, FL, GA, MD, NC, SC, VA, WV)	38.3
East S. Central (AL, KY, MS, TN)	50.4
West S. Central (AR, LA, OK, TX)	39.8
Mountain (AZ, CO, ID, MT, NV, NM, UT, WY)	43.1
Pacific (AK, CA, HI, OR, WA)	29.3

Source: National Center for Health Statistics, and U.S. Census Bureau.

UNINTENTIONAL-INJURY DEATHS BY STATE

The following series of charts is a state-by-state ranking of the five leading causes of deaths due to unintentional injuries (U-I) based on 1999 data. The first line of each section gives the rank of unintentional-injury deaths among all causes of death, the total number of U-I deaths, and the rate of U-I deaths per 100,000 population. The following lines list the five leading types of unintentional-injury deaths along with the number and rate for each type.

TOTAL UNITED STATES

Rank	Cause	Deaths	Rate
5	All U-I	97,860	35.9
1	Motor-vehicle	42,401	15.5
2	Falls	13,162	4.8
3	Poisoning[a]	12,186	4.5
4	Choking[b]	3,885	1.4
5	Drowning[c]	3,529	1.3

ALABAMA

Rank	Cause	Deaths	Rate
4	All U-I	2,313	52.9
1	Motor-vehicle	1,162	26.6
2	Poisoning[a]	145	3.3
3	Choking[b]	130	3.0
4	Fires and flames	127	2.9
5	Falls	120	2.7

ALASKA

Rank	Cause	Deaths	Rate
3	All U-I	294	47.5
1	Motor-vehicle	87	14.0
2	Poisoning[a]	49	7.9
3	Drowning[c]	27	4.4
4	Air transport	24	3.9
5	Water transport	17	2.7

ARIZONA

Rank	Cause	Deaths	Rate
5	All U-I	2,214	46.3
1	Motor-vehicle	945	19.8
2	Poisoning[a]	387	8.1
3	Falls	361	7.6
4	Drowning[c]	76	1.6
5	Choking[b]	64	1.3

ARKANSAS

Rank	Cause	Deaths	Rate
5	All U-I	1,287	50.4
1	Motor-vehicle	649	25.4
2	Falls	117	4.6
3	Drowning[c]	52	2.0
4	Choking[b]	47	1.8
5	Fires and flames	38	1.5

CALIFORNIA

Rank	Cause	Deaths	Rate
5	All U-I	9,198	27.8
1	Motor-vehicle	3,641	11.0
2	Poisoning[a]	2,248	6.8
3	Falls	1,213	3.7
4	Drowning[c]	417	1.3
5	Fires and flames	219	0.7

COLORADO

Rank	Cause	Deaths	Rate
5	All U-I	1,519	37.4
1	Motor-vehicle	620	15.3
2	Poisoning[a]	222	5.5
3	Falls	219	5.4
4	Choking[b]	46	1.1
5	Drowning[c]	45	1.1

CONNECTICUT

Rank	Cause	Deaths	Rate
5	All U-I	1,034	31.5
1	Motor-vehicle	308	9.4
2	Poisoning[a]	239	7.3
3	Falls	138	4.2
4	Choking[b]	84	2.6
5	Fires and flames	30	0.9

DELAWARE

Rank	Cause	Deaths	Rate
5	All U-I	267	35.4
1	Motor-vehicle	98	13.0
2	Poisoning[a]	47	6.2
2	Falls	47	6.2
4	Choking[b]	12	1.6
4	Fires and flames	12	1.6

DISTRICT OF COLUMBIA

Rank	Cause	Deaths	Rate
8	All U-I	161	31.0
1	Poisoning[a]	50	9.6
2	Motor-vehicle	36	6.9
3	Falls	28	5.4
4	Choking[b]	10	1.9
5	Natural heat/cold	5	1.0

FLORIDA

Rank	Cause	Deaths	Rate
5	All U-I	5,961	39.4
1	Motor-vehicle	2,872	19.0
2	Falls	873	5.8
3	Poisoning[a]	728	4.8
4	Drowning[c]	315	2.1
5	Choking[b]	250	1.7

GEORGIA

Rank	Cause	Deaths	Rate
4	All U-I	3,078	39.5
1	Motor-vehicle	1,521	19.5
2	Falls	402	5.2
3	Poisoning[a]	256	3.3
4	Drowning[c]	144	1.8
5	Fires and flames	121	1.6

HAWAII

Rank	Cause	Deaths	Rate
4	All U-I	293	24.7
1	Motor-vehicle	90	7.6
2	Falls	60	5.1
3	Poisoning[a]	36	3.0
4	Drowning[c]	33	2.8
5	Choking[b]	16	1.3

IDAHO

Rank	Cause	Deaths	Rate
4	All U-I	597	47.7
1	Motor-vehicle	278	22.2
2	Falls	105	8.4
3	Poisoning[a]	44	3.5
4	Drowning[c]	21	1.7
5	Choking[b]	20	1.6

ILLINOIS

Rank	Cause	Deaths	Rate
5	All U-I	4,125	34.0
1	Motor-vehicle	1,537	12.7
2	Poisoning[a]	733	6.0
3	Falls	509	4.2
4	Choking[b]	189	1.6
5	Fires and flames	157	1.3

INDIANA

Rank	Cause	Deaths	Rate
5	All U-I	2,309	38.9
1	Motor-vehicle	988	16.6
2	Falls	257	4.3
3	Poisoning[a]	124	2.1
4	Mechanical suffocation	104	1.7
5	Choking[b]	94	1.6

IOWA

Rank	Cause	Deaths	Rate
5	All U-I	1,123	39.1
1	Motor-vehicle	529	18.4
2	Falls	214	7.5
3	Fires and flames	43	1.5
4	Choking[b]	40	1.4
5	Poisoning[a]	38	1.3

KANSAS

Rank	Cause	Deaths	Rate
5	All U-I	1,126	42.4
1	Motor-vehicle	570	21.5
2	Falls	184	6.9
3	Poisoning[a]	67	2.5
4	Choking[b]	59	2.2
5	Fires and flames	28	1.1

See footnotes on page 155.

KENTUCKY

Rank	Cause	Deaths	Rate
5	All U-I	1,730	43.7
1	Motor-vehicle	814	20.6
2	Poisoning[a]	174	4.4
3	Falls	139	3.5
4	Choking[b]	74	1.9
5	Fires and flames	68	1.7

LOUISIANA

Rank	Cause	Deaths	Rate
4	All U-I	1,940	44.4
1	Motor-vehicle	976	22.3
2	Poisoning[a]	146	3.3
3	Falls	138	3.2
4	Drowning[c]	95	2.2
5	Choking[b]	93	2.1

MAINE

Rank	Cause	Deaths	Rate
5	All U-I	458	36.6
1	Motor-vehicle	199	15.9
2	Falls	87	6.9
3	Poisoning[a]	37	3.0
4	Choking[b]	24	1.9
5	Drowning[c]	23	1.8

MARYLAND

Rank	Cause	Deaths	Rate
6	All U-I	1,296	25.1
1	Motor-vehicle	609	11.8
2	Falls	195	3.8
3	Fires and flames	70	1.4
4	Choking[b]	68	1.3
5	Poisoning[a]	43	0.8

MASSACHUSETTS

Rank	Cause	Deaths	Rate
7	All U-I	1,303	21.1
1	Motor-vehicle	441	7.1
2	Falls	207	3.4
3	Choking[b]	70	1.1
4	Mechanical suffocation	60	1.0
5	Poisoning[a]	53	0.9

MICHIGAN

Rank	Cause	Deaths	Rate
5	All U-I	3,188	32.3
1	Motor-vehicle	1,411	14.3
2	Falls	390	4.0
3	Poisoning[a]	293	3.0
4	Fires and flames	181	1.8
5	Choking[b]	119	1.2

MINNESOTA

Rank	Cause	Deaths	Rate
5	All U-I	1,772	37.1
1	Motor-vehicle	646	13.5
2	Falls	402	8.4
3	Poisoning[a]	102	2.1
4	Drowning[c]	67	1.4
5	Fires and flames	47	1.0
5	Mechanical suffocation	47	1.0

MISSISSIPPI

Rank	Cause	Deaths	Rate
4	All U-I	1,642	59.3
1	Motor-vehicle	956	34.5
2	Falls	151	5.5
3	Fires and flames	84	3.0
4	Choking[b]	72	2.6
5	Poisoning[a]	64	2.3

MISSOURI

Rank	Cause	Deaths	Rate
5	All U-I	2,465	45.1
1	Motor-vehicle	1,061	19.4
2	Falls	374	6.8
3	Poisoning[a]	198	3.6
4	Choking[b]	107	2.0
5	Fires and flames	76	1.4

MONTANA

Rank	Cause	Deaths	Rate
5	All U-I	461	52.2
1	Motor-vehicle	210	23.8
2	Falls	74	8.4
3	Poisoning[a]	21	2.4
4	Choking[b]	20	2.3
5	Drowning[c]	18	2.0

NEBRASKA

Rank	Cause	Deaths	Rate
5	All U-I	668	40.1
1	Motor-vehicle	295	17.7
2	Falls	141	8.5
3	Choking[b]	36	2.2
4	Poisoning[a]	33	2.0
5	Drowning[c]	23	1.4

NEVADA

Rank	Cause	Deaths	Rate
5	All U-I	710	39.2
1	Motor-vehicle	333	18.4
2	Poisoning[a]	145	8.0
3	Falls	77	4.3
4	Drowning[c]	32	1.8
5	Choking[b]	27	1.5

NEW HAMPSHIRE

Rank	Cause	Deaths	Rate
5	All U-I	329	27.4
1	Motor-vehicle	129	10.7
2	Falls	63	5.2
3	Poisoning[a]	35	2.9
4	Fires and flames	8	0.7
5	Choking[b]	7	0.6
5	Drowning[c]	7	0.6
5	Mechanical suffocation	7	0.6
5	Natural heat/cold	7	0.6

NEW JERSEY

Rank	Cause	Deaths	Rate
6	All U-I	2,227	27.3
1	Motor-vehicle	727	8.9
2	Poisoning[a]	453	5.6
3	Falls	283	3.5
4	Choking[b]	104	1.3
5	Fires and flames	74	0.9

NEW MEXICO

Rank	Cause	Deaths	Rate
3	All U-I	969	55.7
1	Motor-vehicle	415	23.9
2	Poisoning[a]	233	13.4
3	Falls	131	74
4	Drowning[c]	30	1.7
5	Choking[b]	19	1.1

NEW YORK

Rank	Cause	Deaths	Rate
6	All U-I	4,797	26.4
1	Motor-vehicle	1,759	9.7
2	Falls	890	4.9
3	Poisoning[a]	850	4.7
4	Fires and flames	203	1.1
5	Choking[b]	186	1.0

NORTH CAROLINA

Rank	Cause	Deaths	Rate
5	All U-I	3,290	43.0
1	Motor-vehicle	1,597	20.9
2	Falls	389	5.1
3	Poisoning[a]	283	3.7
4	Choking[b]	154	2.0
5	Fires and flames	143	1.9

NORTH DAKOTA

Rank	Cause	Deaths	Rate
5	All U-I	297	42.1
1	Motor-vehicle	134	21.1
2	Falls	47	7.4
3	Drowning[c]	12	1.9
4	Choking[b]	11	1.7
5	Fires and flames	7	1.1
5	Poisoning[a]	7	1.1

See footnotes on page 155.

OHIO

Rank	Cause	Deaths	Rate
6	All U-I	3,630	32.2
1	Motor-vehicle	1,427	12.7
2	Falls	493	4.4
3	Poisoning[a]	360	3.2
4	Choking[b]	174	1.5
5	Fires and flames	147	1.3

OKLAHOMA

Rank	Cause	Deaths	Rate
5	All U-I	1,609	47.9
1	Motor-vehicle	686	20.4
2	Falls	161	4.8
3	Poisoning[a]	127	3.8
4	Fires and flames	64	1.9
5	Choking[b]	54	1.6

OREGON

Rank	Cause	Deaths	Rate
5	All U-I	1,199	36.2
1	Motor-vehicle	433	13.1
2	Falls	177	5.3
3	Poisoning[a]	153	4.6
4	Drowning[c]	49	1.5
5	Choking[b]	32	1.0

PENNSYLVANIA

Rank	Cause	Deaths	Rate
5	All U-I	4,614	38.5
1	Motor-vehicle	1,580	13.2
2	Poisoning[a]	755	6.3
3	Falls	701	5.8
4	Choking[b]	245	2.0
5	Fires and flames	162	1.4

RHODE ISLAND

Rank	Cause	Deaths	Rate
6	All U-I	243	24.5
1	Motor-vehicle	89	9.0
2	Falls	69	7.0
3	Choking[b]	16	1.6
4	Drowing[c]	12	1.2
5	Fires and flames	6	0.6

SOUTH CAROLINA

Rank	Cause	Deaths	Rate
4	All U-I	1,901	48.9
1	Motor-vehicle	996	25.6
2	Falls	159	4.1
3	Poisoning[a]	129	3.3
4	Choking[b]	98	2.5
5	Fires and flames	92	2.4

SOUTH DAKOTA

Rank	Cause	Deaths	Rate
4	All U-I	351	47.9
1	Motor-vehicle	174	23.7
2	Falls	69	9.4
3	Drowning[c]	16	2.2
4	Poisoning[a]	14	1.9
5	Fires and flames	9	1.2

TENNESSEE

Rank	Cause	Deaths	Rate
5	All U-I	2,677	48.8
1	Motor-vehicle	1,322	24.1
2	Poisoning[a]	235	4.3
3	Falls	186	3.4
4	Fires and flames	147	2.7
5	Choking[b]	118	2.2

TEXAS

Rank	Cause	Deaths	Rate
5	All U-I	7,227	36.1
1	Motor-vehicle	3,669	18.3
2	Poisoning[a]	849	4.2
3	Falls	710	3.5
4	Drowning[c]	313	1.6
5	Choking[b]	252	1.3

UTAH

Rank	Cause	Deaths	Rate
4	All U-I	650	30.5
1	Motor-vehicle	364	17.1
2	Falls	70	3.3
3	Poisoning[a]	31	1.5
4	Drowning[c]	23	1.1
5	Mechanical suffocation	12	0.6

VERMONT

Rank	Cause	Deaths	Rate
5	All U-I	209	35.2
1	Motor-vehicle	83	14.0
2	Falls	33	5.6
3	Poisoning[a]	14	2.4
4	Drowning[c]	8	1.3
5	Choking[b]	7	1.2

VIRGINIA

Rank	Cause	Deaths	Rate
5	All U-I	2,214	32.2
1	Motor-vehicle	897	13.1
2	Poisoning[a]	280	4.1
3	Falls	240	3.5
4	Choking[b]	142	2.1
5	Fires and flames	81	1.2

WASHINGTON

Rank	Cause	Deaths	Rate
5	All U-I	1,914	33.3
1	Motor-vehicle	732	12.7
2	Poisoning[a]	413	7.2
3	Falls	333	5.8
4	Drowning[c]	85	1.5
5	Fires and flames	51	0.9

WEST VIRGINIA

Rank	Cause	Deaths	Rate
5	All U-I	798	44.2
1	Motor-vehicle	387	21.4
2	Falls	111	6.1
3	Poisoning[a]	46	2.5
4	Choking[b]	38	2.1
5	Fires and flames	37	2.0

WISCONSIN

Rank	Cause	Deaths	Rate
5	All U-I	1,955	37.2
1	Motor-vehicle	775	14.8
2	Falls	587	11.2
3	Poisoning[a]	141	2.7
4	Drowning[c]	66	1.3
5	Choking[b]	58	1.1

WYOMING

Rank	Cause	Deaths	Rate
5	All U-I	258	53.8
1	Motor-vehicle	144	30.0
2	Falls	25	5.2
3	Poisoning[a]	16	3.3
4	Drowning[c]	7	1.5
4	Choking[b]	7	1.5

Source: National Safety Council tabulations of National Center for Health Statistics mortality data for 1999.
[a]*Solid, liquid, gas, or vapor poisoning.*
[b]*Inhalation or ingestion of food or other object.*
[c]*Excludes transport drownings.*

UNINTENTIONAL-INJURY DEATHS BY STATE AND TYPE OF EVENT, UNITED STATES, 1999

State	Population (000)	Total[a]	Motor-vehicle[b]	Falls	Poisoning			Choking[c]	Drowing[d]	Fires, Flames, and Smoke
					Total	Solid, Liquid	Gases, Vapors			
Total U.S.	272,691	97,860	42,401	13,162	12,186	11,589	597	3,885	3,529	3,348
Alabama	4,370	2,313	1,162	120	145	122	23	130	73	127
Alaska	620	294	87	13	49	43	6	5	27	7
Arizona	4,778	2,214	945	361	387	376	11	64	76	43
Arkansas	2,551	1,287	649	117	35	31	4	47	52	38
California	33,145	9,198	3,641	1,213	2,248	2,208	40	155	417	219
Colorado	4,056	1,519	620	219	222	214	8	46	45	26
Connecticut	3,282	1,034	308	138	239	238	1	84	27	30
Delaware	754	267	98	47	47	43	4	12	9	12
Dist. of Columbia	519	161	36	28	50	49	1	10	2	4
Florida	15,111	5,961	2,872	873	728	703	25	250	315	117
Georgia	7,788	3,078	1,521	402	256	232	24	119	144	121
Hawaii	1,185	293	90	60	36	36	0	16	33	2
Idaho	1,252	597	278	105	44	39	5	20	21	12
Illinois	12,128	4,125	1,537	509	733	699	34	189	100	157
Indiana	5,943	2,309	988	257	124	108	16	94	65	89
Iowa	2,869	1,123	529	214	38	28	10	40	23	43
Kansas	2,654	1,126	570	184	67	61	6	59	27	28
Kentucky	3,961	1,730	814	139	174	155	19	74	49	68
Louisiana	4,372	1,940	976	138	146	131	15	93	95	82
Maine	1,253	458	199	87	37	35	2	24	23	22
Maryland	5,172	1,296	609	195	43	40	3	68	38	70
Massachusetts	6,175	1,303	441	207	53	46	7	70	43	48
Michigan	9,864	3,188	1,411	390	293	257	36	119	115	181
Minnesota	4,776	1,772	646	402	102	94	8	45	67	47
Mississippi	2,769	1,642	956	151	64	61	3	72	57	84
Missouri	5,468	2,465	1,061	374	198	177	21	107	65	76
Montana	883	461	210	74	21	17	4	20	18	12
Nebraska	1,666	668	295	141	33	25	8	36	23	14
Nevada	1,809	710	333	77	145	141	4	27	32	14
New Hampshire	1,201	329	129	63	35	34	1	7	7	8
New Jersey	8,143	2,227	727	283	453	447	6	104	71	74
New Mexico	1,740	969	415	131	233	221	12	19	30	11
New York	18,197	4,797	1,759	890	850	821	29	186	134	203
North Carolina	7,651	3,290	1,597	389	283	266	17	154	115	143
North Dakota	634	267	134	47	7	7	0	11	12	7
Ohio	11,257	3,630	1,427	493	360	334	26	174	97	147
Oklahoma	3,358	1,609	686	161	127	111	16	54	52	64
Oregon	3,316	1,199	433	177	153	142	11	32	49	31
Pennsylvania	11,994	4,614	1,580	701	755	721	34	245	102	162
Rhode Island	991	243	89	69	5	4	1	16	12	6
South Carolina	3,886	1,901	996	159	129	124	5	98	62	92
South Dakota	733	351	174	69	14	14	0	8	16	9
Tennessee	5,484	2,677	1,322	186	235	218	17	118	85	147
Texas	20,044	7,227	3,669	710	849	822	27	252	313	218
Utah	2,130	650	364	70	31	26	5	10	23	4
Vermont	594	209	83	33	14	13	1	7	8	5
Virginia	6,873	2,214	897	240	280	267	13	142	79	81
Washington	5,756	1,914	732	333	413	409	4	50	85	51
West Virginia	1,807	798	387	111	46	40	6	38	23	37
Wisconsin	5,250	1,955	775	587	141	126	15	58	66	51
Wyoming	480	258	144	25	16	13	3	7	7	4

See footnotes on page 157.

UNINTENTIONAL-INJURY DEATHS BY STATE AND TYPE OF EVENT, UNITED STATES, 1999, Cont.

State	Mechanical Suffocation	Natural Heat or Cold	Firearms	Machinery	Struck By/Against Object	Electric Current	Rail Transport	Water Transport	Air Transport	All Other Accidents
Total U.S.	1,618	1,192	824	622	842	437	493	679	715	11,927
Alabama	21	27	51	9	22	13	8	12	15	378
Alaska	3	13	3	1	2	2	0	17	24	41
Arizona	32	34	17	2	14	5	8	8	15	203
Arkansas	23	23	24	21	12	16	11	21	24	174
California	132	51	47	57	72	30	74	49	73	720
Colorado	21	8	9	11	10	1	3	12	21	245
Connecticut	12	11	2	2	6	3	10	3	7	152
Delaware	3	7	1	0	3	0	1	1	0	26
Dist. of Columbia	1	5	1	0	2	0	2	0	0	20
Florida	79	20	14	25	39	38	25	63	58	445
Georgia	73	37	18	17	41	16	14	18	19	262
Hawaii	6	1	0	0	0	0	0	5	2	42
Idaho	6	3	9	4	10	1	3	7	13	61
Illinois	74	105	22	30	35	17	32	22	24	539
Indiana	104	33	23	17	21	16	7	11	14	446
Iowa	12	10	6	10	15	6	11	5	7	154
Kansas	17	10	10	3	17	5	4	6	14	105
Kentucky	32	16	35	18	11	9	0	15	15	261
Louisiana	14	28	28	21	24	14	8	40	13	220
Maine	4	3	4	4	4	2	0	8	2	35
Maryland	24	27	1	8	7	4	10	7	10	175
Massachusetts	60	22	0	5	8	5	12	5	7	317
Michigan	44	34	14	23	19	16	11	23	28	467
Minnesota	47	19	8	13	9	6	7	10	8	336
Mississippi	16	18	41	11	30	8	9	25	3	97
Missouri	49	50	25	16	28	13	10	14	22	357
Montana	9	8	9	6	4	1	4	6	3	56
Nebraska	15	8	5	1	12	5	7	3	3	67
Nevada	7	10	2	1	5	3	3	0	8	43
New Hampshire	7	7	0	5	5	1	0	3	3	49
New Jersey	26	45	8	9	11	0	12	11	11	382
New Mexico	10	15	11	7	10	1	3	2	2	69
New York	56	68	23	30	26	15	28	18	21	490
North Carolina	68	20	25	12	23	16	21	17	16	391
North Dakota	3	5	1	3	3	1	2	1	4	26
Ohio	64	49	34	28	31	15	17	13	18	663
Oklahoma	13	28	28	16	9	16	7	9	11	328
Oregon	14	13	13	13	16	5	8	11	19	212
Pennsylvania	108	64	36	17	35	9	18	9	17	756
Rhode Island	3	3	0	1	1	3	1	0	1	33
South Carolina	55	36	30	10	13	10	11	15	2	183
South Dakota	6	5	4	7	6	4	0	2	6	21
Tennessee	28	26	47	26	23	11	10	20	11	382
Texas	93	63	66	34	63	49	32	46	54	716
Utah	12	7	1	5	5	3	1	5	10	99
Vermont	5	5	2	2	0	0	0	0	1	44
Virginia	21	33	24	16	21	9	6	17	23	325
Washington	28	12	12	7	21	2	12	40	19	97
West Virginia	12	6	11	9	20	4	3	3	3	85
Wisconsin	44	36	15	24	17	8	6	17	7	103
Wyoming	2	5	4	5	1	0	1	4	4	29

Source: National Safety Council tabulations of National Center for Health Statistics mortality data.
[a]Deaths are by place of occurrence and exclude nonresident aliens. See also page 152.
[b]See page 162 for motor-vehicle deaths by place of residence.
[c]Inhalation or ingestion of food or other object.
[d]Excludes water transport drownings.

UNINTENTIONAL-INJURY DEATHS BY STATE, UNITED STATES, 1997–1999

State	Deaths[a]			Death Rate[c]		
	1999[b]	1998	1997	1999	1998	1997
Total U.S.	97,860	97,835	95,644	35.9	35.9	35.7
Alabama	2,313	2,181	2,255	52.9	49.9	52.2
Alaska	294	267	286	47.5	43.1	47.0
Arizona	2,214	2,314	2,192	46.3	48.4	48.2
Arkansas	1,287	1,197	1,262	50.4	46.9	50.0
California	9,198	9,132	8,897	27.8	27.6	27.6
Colorado	1,519	1,542	1,476	37.4	38.0	37.9
Connecticut	1,034	1,063	980	31.5	32.4	30.0
Delaware	267	292	286	35.4	38.8	38.9
Dist. of Columbia	161	309	260	31.0	59.5	49.2
Florida	5,961[b]	5,976	5,640	39.4	39.5	38.4
Georgia	3,078	3,140	3,091	39.5	40.3	41.3
Hawaii	293	319	365	24.7	26.9	30.7
Idaho	597	585	575	47.7	46.7	47.5
Illinois	4,125	3,668	3,176	34.0	30.2	26.4
Indiana	2,309	2,165	2,077	38.9	36.4	35.4
Iowa	1,123	1,068	1,060	39.1	37.2	37.1
Kansas	1,126	1,086	959	42.4	40.9	36.7
Kentucky	1,730	1,728	1,757	43.7	43.6	45.0
Louisiana	1,940	1,955	1,957	44.4	44.7	45.0
Maine	458	452	444	36.6	36.1	35.7
Maryland	1,296	1,334	1,326	25.1	25.8	26.0
Massachusetts	1,303	1,311	1,269	21.1	21.2	20.8
Michigan	3,188	3,059	3,081	32.3	31.0	31.5
Minnesota	1,772	1,747	1,681	37.1	36.6	35.9
Mississippi	1,642	1,697	1,570	59.3	61.3	57.5
Missouri	2,465	2,645	2,562	45.1	48.4	47.4
Montana	461	495	487	52.2	56.1	55.5
Nebraska	668	679	669	40.1	40.8	40.4
Nevada	710	777	722	39.2	42.9	43.1
New Hampshire	329	349	334	27.4	29.1	28.5
New Jersey	2,227	2,133	2,268	27.3	26.2	28.2
New Mexico	969	1,065	1,076	55.7	61.2	62.5
New York	4,797	4,520	4,803	26.4	24.8	26.5
North Carolina	3,290	3,332	3,128	43.0	43.6	42.1
North Dakota	267	303	274	42.1	47.8	42.8
Ohio	3,630	3,463	3,388	32.2	30.8	30.2
Oklahoma	1,609	1,565	1,600	47.9	46.6	48.3
Oregon	1,199	1,411	1,342	36.2	42.5	41.4
Pennsylvania	4,614	4,563	4,819	38.5	38.0	40.1
Rhode Island	243	252	227	24.5	25.4	23.0
South Carolina	1,901	1,841	1,708	48.9	47.4	45.1
South Dakota	351	369	311	47.9	50.3	42.6
Tennessee	2,677	2,914	2,847	48.8	53.1	52.9
Texas	7,227	7,426	7,148	36.1	37.0	36.9
Utah	650	720	734	30.5	33.8	35.5
Vermont	209	223	220	35.2	37.6	37.4
Virginia	2,214	2,295	2,279	32.2	33.4	33.9
Washington	1,914	1,893	1,865	33.3	32.9	33.3
West Virginia	798	842	797	44.2	46.6	43.9
Wisconsin	1,955	1,914	1,855	37.2	36.5	35.7
Wyoming	258[b]	259	259	53.8	54.0	54.0

Source: National Safety Council estimates based on data from National Center for Health Statistics and U.S. Bureau of the Census. See Technical Appendix for comparability.
[a]Deaths for each state are by place of occurrence. All death totals exclude nonresident aliens.
[b]Latest official figures.
[c]Rates are deaths per 100,000 population.

FATAL OCCUPATIONAL INJURIES BY STATE

In general, the states with the largest number of persons employed have the largest number of work-related fatalities. The four largest states—California, Florida, New York, and Texas—accounted for more than one fourth of the total fatalities in the United States. Each state's industry mix, geographical features, age of population, and other characteristics of the workforce must be considered when evaluating state fatality profiles.

FATAL OCCUPATIONAL INJURIES BY STATE AND EVENT OR EXPOSURE, UNITED STATES, 2000

State	Deaths per 100,000 workers	Total[a]	Transpor-tation[b]	Assaults & Violent Acts[c]	Contact with Objects & Equipment	Falls	Exposure to Harmful Substances or Environments	Fires & Explosions
Total	**4.3**	**5,915**	**2,571**	**929**	**1,005**	**734**	**480**	**177**
Alabama	5.0	103	58	11	13	12	8	—
Alaska	17.5	53	39	—	8	—	—	—
Arizona	5.2	118	69	12	15	14	7	—
Arkansas	8.9	106	56	15	21	8	—	—
California	3.4	553	230	112	69	72	60	9
Colorado	5.2	117	58	25	15	12	7	—
Connecticut	3.2	55	18	9	16	7	—	—
Delaware	3.3	13	—	—	—	—	—	—
District of Columbia	4.9	13	—	8	—	—	—	—
Florida	4.5	329	135	65	43	51	27	7
Georgia	4.8	195	88	30	28	25	17	6
Hawaii	3.5	20	6	8	—	—	—	—
Idaho	5.5	35	23	—	6	—	—	—
Illinois	3.3	205	85	29	44	25	11	9
Indiana	5.3	159	66	29	27	15	18	—
Iowa	4.6	71	30	—	13	14	10	—
Kansas	6.2	85	50	5	10	15	—	—
Kentucky	6.9	132	65	13	27	13	10	—
Louisiana	7.4	143	68	11	25	17	16	6
Maine	3.9	26	17	—	—	—	—	—
Maryland	3.1	84	28	16	14	18	7	—
Massachusetts	2.1	67	21	16	11	12	—	6
Michigan	3.1	156	50	26	37	20	16	6
Minnesota	2.5	68	25	5	18	13	—	—
Mississippi	9.9	125	63	18	24	5	11	—
Missouri	5.2	148	68	30	19	15	8	8
Montana	9.1	42	22	6	10	—	—	—
Nebraska	6.5	59	39	—	11	—	—	—
Nevada	5.3	51	33	7	—	—	—	—
New Hampshire	1.9	13	5	—	—	—	—	—
New Jersey	2.8	115	49	15	19	23	6	—
New Mexico	4.4	35	20	—	6	—	—	—
New York	2.7	233	66	68	38	41	11	8
North Carolina	6.1	234	101	39	40	30	18	5
North Dakota	10.3	34	9	—	12	5	—	—
Ohio	3.7	207	82	35	40	32	14	—
Oklahoma	5.1	82	41	9	12	—	9	6
Oregon	3.0	52	24	—	14	—	—	—
Pennsylvania	3.4	199	88	26	35	30	17	—
Rhode Island	1.4	7	—	—	—	—	—	—
South Carolina	5.9	114	54	16	21	8	9	5
South Dakota	8.9	35	19	---	6	---	—	—
Tennessee	5.9	160	71	24	31	17	16	—
Texas	5.7	572	216	101	91	76	64	21
Utah	5.7	61	32	—	9	5	7	6
Vermont	4.6	15	—	—	8	—	—	—
Virginia	4.2	148	48	26	22	22	18	12
Washington	2.6	75	33	10	19	8	—	—
West Virginia	5.9	46	23	5	9	—	—	—
Wisconsin	3.7	107	49	14	25	9	8	—
Wyoming	13.9	36	17	—	7	—	—	—

Source: U.S. Department of Labor, Bureau of Labor Statistics, except rates that are National Safety Council estimates.
Note: Dashes (—) indicate no data or data that do not meet publication criteria.
[a] Includes event or exposure categories not shown separately. U.S. total includes 4 deaths for which the state could not be determined.
[b] Includes highway, nonhighway, air, water, and rail fatalities, and fatalities resulting from being struck by a vehicle.
[c] Includes violence by persons, self-inflicted injury, and attacks by animals.

NONFATAL OCCUPATIONAL INJURY AND ILLNESS INCIDENCE RATES[a] BY STATE, PRIVATE INDUSTRY, 2000

State	Total Cases	Lost Workday Cases		Cases Without Lost Workdays
		Total[b]	With Days away from Work[c]	
Private Industry[d]	**6.1**	**3.0**	**1.8**	**3.2**
Alabama	6.2	3.0	1.6	3.2
Alaska	7.6	3.7	3.2	3.9
Arizona	5.8	2.6	1.5	3.2
Arkansas	6.5	3.0	1.7	3.5
California	6.1	3.2	1.9	2.9
Colorado	—	—	—	
Connecticut	6.7	3.5	2.1	3.2
Delaware	5.3	2.7	1.8	2.6
District of Columbia	—	—	—	—
Florida	5.8	2.8	1.6	3.0
Georgia	5.1	2.4	1.2	2.7
Hawaii	6.0	3.5	3.1	2.5
Idaho	—	—	—	—
Illinois	6.1	2.9	1.7	3.2
Indiana	7.6	3.5	1.8	4.0
Iowa	8.2	3.8	1.8	4.4
Kansas	7.8	3.3	1.7	4.4
Kentucky	8.3	4.4	2.5	3.9
Louisiana	4.3	2.1	1.4	2.2
Maine	9.0	5.4	2.7	3.6
Maryland	4.6	2.3	1.8	2.3
Massachusetts	5.5	3.0	2.2	2.5
Michigan	8.1	4.0	1.8	4.1
Minnesota	7.0	3.5	1.9	3.4
Mississippi	—	—	—	—
Missouri	6.8	3.1	1.7	3.7
Montana	8.2	3.1	2.5	5.1
Nebraska	6.6	3.4	2.1	3.2
Nevada	7.2	3.1	1.7	4.0
New Hampshire	—	—	—	—
New Jersey	4.9	2.4	1.8	2.4
New Mexico	4.4	2.1	1.6	2.3
New York	3.9	2.1	1.9	1.8
North Carolina	5.3	2.6	1.4	2.8
North Dakota	—	—	—	—
Ohio	—	—	—	—
Oklahoma	6.6	3.0	1.8	3.6
Oregon	6.3	3.1	1.9	3.2
Pennsylvania	—	—	—	—
Rhode Island	7.1	3.8	2.9	3.3
South Carolina	5.5	2.4	1.4	3.0
South Dakota	—	—	—	—
Tennessee	6.6	3.2	1.8	3.4
Texas	4.7	2.6	1.6	2.1
Utah	6.7	2.8	1.5	3.9
Vermont	6.9	3.2	2.2	3.7
Virginia	5.3	2.6	1.7	2.6
Washington	8.5	3.5	2.6	4.9
West Virginia	7.0	3.9	3.4	3.1
Wisconsin	—	—	—	—
Wyoming	8.9	4.2	2.5	4.7

Source: Bureau of Labor Statistics, U.S. Department of Labor.
Note: Because of rounding, components may not add to totals. Dashes (—) indicate data not available.
[a] Incidence rates represent the number of injuries and illnesses per 100 full-time workers using 200,000 hours as the equivalent.
[b] Total lost workday cases involve days away from work, days of restricted work activity, or both.
[c] Days-away-from-work cases include those that result in days away from work with or without restricted work activity.
[d] Data cover all 50 states.

NONFATAL OCCUPATIONAL AND ILLNESS INCIDENCE RATES BY STATE, PRIVATE INDUSTRY, 2000

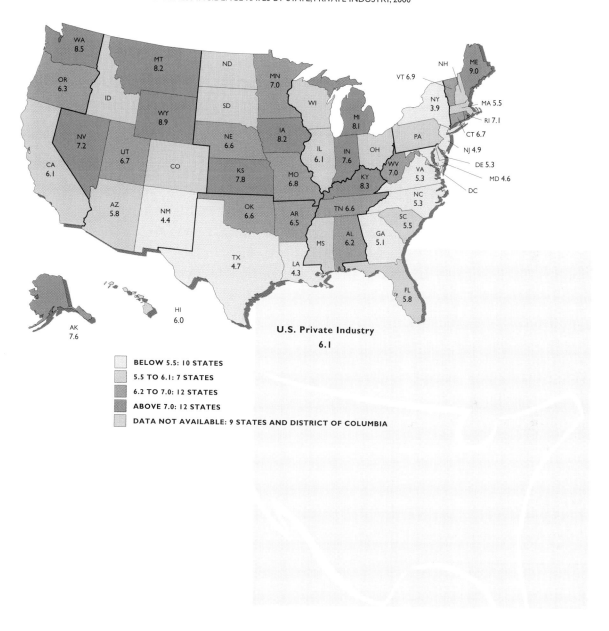

WA 8.5
MT 8.2
ND
MN 7.0
NH
ME 9.0
VT 6.9
OR 6.3
ID
WY 8.9
SD
WI
NY 3.9
MA 5.5
RI 7.1
CT 6.7
NV 7.2
UT 6.7
CO
NE 6.6
IA 8.2
IL 6.1
IN 7.6
MI 8.1
OH
PA
NJ 4.9
DE 5.3
MD 4.6
DC
CA 6.1
KS 7.8
MO 6.8
KY 8.3
WV 7.0
VA 5.3
AZ 5.8
NM 4.4
OK 6.6
AR 6.5
TN 6.6
NC 5.3
SC 5.5
MS
AL 6.2
GA 5.1
TX 4.7
LA 4.3
FL 5.8
AK 7.6
HI 6.0

U.S. Private Industry
6.1

BELOW 5.5: 10 STATES
5.5 TO 6.1: 7 STATES
6.2 TO 7.0: 12 STATES
ABOVE 7.0: 12 STATES
DATA NOT AVAILABLE: 9 STATES AND DISTRICT OF COLUMBIA

MOTOR-VEHICLE DEATHS BY STATE, UNITED STATES, 1998–2001

State	Motor-Vehicle Traffic Deaths (Place of Accident)				Total Motor-Vehicle Deaths[a] (Place of Residence)			
	Number		Mileage Rate[b]		Number		Population Rate[b]	
	2001	2000	2001	2000	1999[c]	1998	1999	1998
Total U.S.[a]	42,900	42,500	1.5	1.6	42,401	43,501	15.5	16.1
Alabama	997	990	1.7	1.7	1,162	1,103	26.6	25.4
Alaska	85	103	1.8	2.2	87	72	14.0	11.7
Arizona	1,047	1,036	2.1	2.1	945	941	19.8	20.2
Arkansas	611	652	2.1	2.2	649	680	25.4	26.8
California	3,926	3,730	1.3	1.2	3,641	3,779	11.0	11.6
Colorado	736	679	1.7	1.6	620	663	15.3	16.7
Connecticut	317	342	1.0	1.1	308	341	9.4	10.4
Delaware	136	128	1.6	1.5	98	116	13.0	15.6
Dist. of Columbia	72	52	2.0	1.5	36	56	6.9	10.7
Florida	3,013	2,998	2.0	2.0	2,872	2,941	19.0	19.7
Georgia	1,506	1,548	1.4	1.5	1,521	1,657	19.5	21.7
Hawaii	141	133	1.6	1.5	90	124	7.6	10.4
Idaho	259	275	1.9	2.0	278	269	22.2	21.9
Illinois	1,414	1,414	1.4	1.4	1,537	1,521	12.7	12.6
Indiana	909	892	1.3	1.2	988	1,046	16.6	17.7
Iowa	447	445	1.5	1.5	529	462	18.4	16.1
Kansas	494	461	1.7	1.6	570	550	21.5	20.8
Kentucky	850	824	1.8	1.7	814	823	20.6	20.9
Louisiana	957	937	2.3	2.3	976	983	22.3	22.5
Maine	191	167	1.3	1.2	199	180	15.9	14.4
Maryland	662	617	1.3	1.2	609	647	11.8	12.6
Massachusetts	477	433	0.9	0.8	441	485	7.1	7.9
Michigan	1,328	1,382	1.3	1.4	1,411	1,472	14.3	15.0
Minnesota	568	625	1.1	1.2	646	674	13.5	14.3
Mississippi	784	949	2.2	2.6	956	963	34.5	35.0
Missouri	1,098	1,157	1.6	1.7	1,061	1,147	19.4	21.1
Montana	230	237	2.3	2.4	210	219	23.8	24.9
Nebraska	246	276	1.3	1.5	295	346	17.7	20.8
Nevada	311	325	1.7	1.8	333	349	18.4	20.0
New Hampshire	142	126	1.2	1.0	129	140	10.7	11.8
New Jersey	745	732	1.1	1.1	727	783	8.9	9.7
New Mexico	464	437	2.0	1.9	415	385	23.9	22.2
New York	1,490	1,353	1.1	1.0	1,759	1,686	9.7	9.3
North Carolina	1,523	1,563	1.7	1.7	1,597	1,672	20.9	22.2
North Dakota	105	86	1.4	1.2	134	118	21.1	18.5
Ohio	1,379	1,249	1.3	1.2	1,427	1,451	12.7	12.9
Oklahoma	670	658	1.5	1.5	686	777	20.4	23.3
Oregon	487	451	1.4	1.3	433	550	13.1	16.8
Pennsylvania	—	—	—	—	1,580	1,661	13.2	13.8
Rhode Island	81	81	1.0	1.0	89	86	9.0	8.7
South Carolina	1,061	1,061	2.3	2.3	996	992	25.6	25.8
South Dakota	171	173	2.0	2.0	174	165	23.7	22.6
Tennessee	1,188	1,235	1.8	1.9	1,322	1,223	24.1	22.5
Texas	3,727	3,519	1.7	1.6	3,669	3,769	18.3	19.1
Utah	291	376	1.3	1.6	364	395	17.1	18.8
Vermont	—	79	—	1.1	83	82	14.0	13.9
Virginia	935	930	1.2	1.2	897	942	13.1	13.9
Washington	649	630	1.2	1.2	732	750	12.7	13.2
West Virginia	376	410	1.9	2.1	387	375	21.4	20.7
Wisconsin	764	801	1.3	1.4	775	755	14.8	14.5
Wyoming	186	152	2.3	1.9	144	135	30.0	28.1

Source: Motor-Vehicle Traffic Deaths are provisional counts from state traffic authorities; Total Motor-Vehicle Deaths are from the National Center for Health Statistics (see also page 156).
[a] Includes both traffic and nontraffic motor-vehicle deaths. See definitions of motor-vehicle traffic and nontraffic accidents on page 175.
[b] The mileage death rate is deaths per 100,000,000 vehicle miles; the population death rate is deaths per 100,000 population. Death rates are National Safety Council estimates.
[c] Latest year available. See Technical Appendix for comparability.
Note: Dash (—) indicates data not reported.

MILEAGE DEATH RATES, 2001
MOTOR-VEHICLE TRAFFIC DEATHS PER 100,000,000 VEHICLE MILES

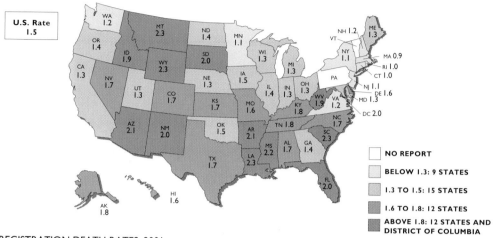

U.S. Rate
1.5

NO REPORT

BELOW 1.3: 9 STATES

1.3 TO 1.5: 15 STATES

1.6 TO 1.8: 12 STATES

ABOVE 1.8: 12 STATES AND
DISTRICT OF COLUMBIA

REGISTRATION DEATH RATES, 2001
MOTOR-VEHICLE TRAFFIC DEATHS PER 10,000 MOTOR VEHICLES

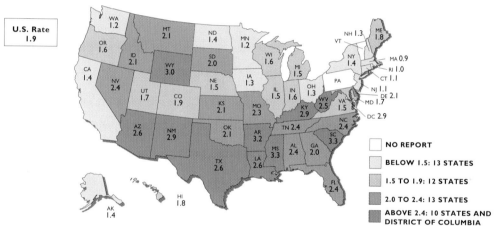

U.S. Rate
1.9

NO REPORT

BELOW 1.5: 13 STATES

1.5 TO 1.9: 12 STATES

2.0 TO 2.4: 13 STATES

ABOVE 2.4: 10 STATES AND
DISTRICT OF COLUMBIA

POPULATION DEATH RATES, 2001
MOTOR-VEHICLE TRAFFIC DEATHS PER 100,000 POPULATION

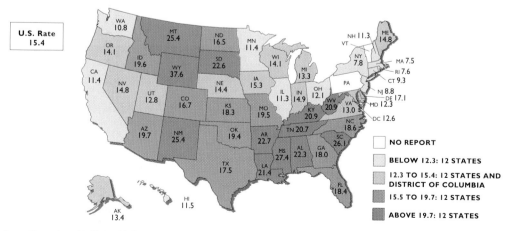

U.S. Rate
15.4

NO REPORT

BELOW 12.3: 12 STATES

12.3 TO 15.4: 12 STATES AND
DISTRICT OF COLUMBIA

15.5 TO 19.7: 12 STATES

ABOVE 19.7: 12 STATES

Source: Rates estimated by National Safety Council based on data from state traffic authorities, National Center for Health Statistics, Federal Highway Administration, and the U.S. Census Bureau.

TECHNICAL APPENDIX

This appendix gives a brief explanation of some of the sources and methods used by the National Safety Council (NSC) Statistics Department in preparing the estimates of deaths, injuries, and costs presented in this book. Because many of the estimates depend on death certificate data provided by the states or the National Center for Health Statistics (NCHS), it begins with a brief introduction to the certification and classification of deaths.

Certification and classification. The medical certification of death involves entering information on the death certificate about the disease or condition directly leading to death, antecedent causes, and other significant conditions. The death certificate is then registered with the appropriate authority and a code is assigned for the underlying cause of death. The underlying cause is defined as "(a) the disease or injury which initiated the train of morbid events leading directly to death, or (b) the circumstances of the accident or violence which produced the fatal injury" (World Health Organization [WHO], 1992). Deaths are classified and coded on the basis of a WHO standard, the International Statistical Classification of Diseases and Related Health Problems, commonly known as the International Classification of Diseases or ICD (WHO, 1992). For deaths due to injury and poisoning, the ICD provides a system of "external cause" codes to which the underlying cause of death is assigned. (See pages 18–19 of *Injury Facts*® for a condensed list of external cause codes.)

Comparability across ICD revisions. The ICD is revised periodically and these revisions can affect comparability from year to year. The sixth revision (1948) substantially expanded the list of external causes and provided for classifying the place of occurrence. Changes in the classification procedures for the sixth revision as well as the seventh (1958) and eighth (1968) revisions classified as diseases some deaths that were previously classified as injuries. The eighth revision also expanded and reorganized some external cause sections. The ninth revision (1979) provided more detail on the agency involved, the victim's activity, and the place of occurrence. The tenth revision, which was adopted in the United States effective with 1999 data, completely revised the transportation-related categories. Specific external cause categories affected by the revisions are noted in the historical tables.

The table at the end of this appendix (page 171) shows the ICD-9 codes, the ICD-10 codes, and a comparability ratio for each of the principal causes of unintentional-injury death. The comparability ratio represents the net effect of the new revision on statistics for the cause of death. The comparability ratio was obtained by classifying a sample of death certificates under both ICD-9 and ICD-10 and then dividing the number of deaths for a selected cause classified under ICD-10 by the number classified to the most nearly comparable ICD-9 cause. A comparability ratio of 1.00 indicates no net change due to the new classification scheme. A ratio less than 1.00 indicates fewer deaths assigned to a cause under ICD-10 than under ICD-9. A ratio greater than 1.00 indicates an increase in assignment of deaths to a cause under ICD-10 compared to ICD-9.

The broad category of "accidents" or "unintentional injuries" under ICD-9 included complications and misadventures of surgical and medical care (E870–E879) and adverse effects of drugs in therapeutic use (E930–E949). These categories are not included in "accidents" or "unintentional injuries" under ICD-10. In 1998, deaths in these two categories numbered 3,228 and 276, respectively.

Under ICD-9, the code range for falls (E880–E888) included a code for "fracture, cause unspecified" (E887). A similar code does not appear in ICD-10 (W00–W19, which probably accounts for the low comparability ratio (0.8409). In 1998, deaths in code E887 numbered 3,679.

Fatality estimates. The Council uses four classes to categorize unintentional injuries: Motor Vehicle, Work, Home, and Public. Each class represents an environment and an intervention route for injury prevention through a responsible authority such as a police department, an employer, a home owner, or a public health department.

Motor vehicle. The Motor-Vehicle class can be identified by the underlying cause of death (see the table on page 171).

Work. Beginning with the 1992 data year, the National Safety Council adopted the Bureau of Labor Statistics' Census of Fatal Occupational Injuries (CFOI) figure as the authoritative count of unintentional work-related deaths. The CFOI system is described in detail in Toscano and Windau (1994).

The 2-Way Split. After subtracting the Motor-Vehicle and Work figures from the unintentional-injury total (ICD-10 codes V01–X59, Y85–Y86), the remainder belong to the Home and Public classes. The Home class can be identified by the "place of occurrence" subclassification (code .0) used with most nontransport deaths; the Public class is the remainder. Missing "place of occurrence" information, however, prevents the direct determination of the Home and Public class totals. Because of this, the Council allocates nonmotor-vehicle, nonwork deaths into the Home and Public classes based on the external cause, age group, and cases with specified "place of occurrence." This procedure, known as the 2-Way Split, uses the most recent death certificate data available from the NCHS and the CFOI data for the same calendar year. For each cause-code group and age group combination, the Motor-Vehicle and Work deaths are subtracted and the remainder, including those with "place of occurrence" unspecified, are allocated to Home and Public in the same proportion as those with "place of occurrence" specified.

The table on page 171 shows the ICD-10 cause-codes and CFOI event codes for the most common causes of unintentional-injury death. The CFOI event codes (BLS, 1992) do not match exactly with ICD cause codes, so there is some error in the allocation of deaths among the classes.

State reporting system. The Council operates a reporting system through which participating states send monthly tabulations of unintentional-injury death data by age group, class, and type of event or industry. This is known as the Injury Mortality Tabulation reporting system. These data are used to make current year estimates based on the most recent 2-Way Split and CFOI data.

Linking up to current year. The benchmark data published by NCHS are usually two years old and the CFOI data are usually one year old. The link-relative technique is used to make current year estimates from these data using the state vital statistics data. This method assumes that the change in deaths from one year to the next in states reporting for both years reflects the change in deaths for the entire nation. The ratio is calculated and multiplied times the benchmark figure, resulting in an estimate for the next year. It may be necessary to repeat the process, depending on the reference year of the benchmark. For example, the 1999 NCHS and CFOI data were used this year for a 2-Way Split and state data were used to make estimates for 2000 and 2001 Home and Public classes using the link-relative technique. CFOI data for 2000 were also available, so it was necessary only to make 2001 Work estimates.

Revisions of prior years. When the figures for a given year are published by NCHS, the 2-Way Split based on those figures and the CFOI become the final estimate of unintentional-injury deaths by class, age group, and type of event or industry. Subsequent years are revised by repeating the link-relative process described above. For example, in the 2002 edition of *Injury Facts®*, the 1999 NCHS and CFOI data were used to produce final estimates using the 2-Way Split, the 2000 estimates were revised using more complete state data and 2000 CFOI figures, and the new 2001 estimates were made with the state data available in the spring of 2002.

Nonfatal injury estimates. The Council uses the concept of "disabling injury" to define the kinds of injuries included in its estimates. See page 23 for the definition of disabling injury and the National Health Interview Survey (NHIS) injury definitions.

Injury to death ratios. There is no national injury surveillance system that provides disabling injury estimates on a current basis. The National Health Interview Survey, a household survey conducted by the NCHS (see page 23), produces national estimates using its own definition of injury, but the data are not published until well after the reference year (Adams, Hendershot, & Marano, 1999). For this reason, the

Council uses injury-to-death ratios to estimate nonfatal disabling injuries for the current year. Complete documentation of the background and new procedure, effective with the 1993 edition, may be found in Landes, Ginsburg, Hoskin, and Miller (1990).

The ratios, one for each class, are a 3-year moving average of the NHIS injury data and the corresponding Council estimates of deaths. Because the NHIS does not use the Council's definition of disabling injury, the NHIS data are adjusted to approximate the disabling concept. The adjustment involves counting only injuries that result in two or more days of restricted activity. (The NHIS counts only whole days of restricted activity even though the definition is stated in terms of half days. One day counted includes from one-half day up to one and one-half days of actual restriction. Two days counted includes from one and one-half up to two and one-half.)

Comparability over time. Even though the injury-to-death ratios are updated each time a new NHIS is released, the resulting estimates are not direct measures of nonfatal injuries and should not be compared with prior years.

Population sources. All population figures used in computing rates are taken from various reports published by the Bureau of the Census, U.S. Department of Commerce, on their Internet web site (www.census.gov). Resident population is used for computing rates.

Costs (pp. 4–7). The procedures for estimating the economic losses due to fatal and nonfatal unintentional injuries were extensively revised for the 1993 edition of *Accident Facts*®. New components were added, new benchmarks adopted, and a new discount rate assumed. All of these changes resulted in significantly higher cost estimates. For this reason, it must be re-emphasized that the cost estimates should not be compared to those in earlier editions of the book.

The Council's general philosophy underlying its cost estimates is that the figures represent income not received or expenses incurred because of fatal and nonfatal unintentional injuries. Stated this way, the

Council's cost estimates are a measure of the economic impact of unintentional injuries and may be compared to other economic measures such as gross domestic product, per capita income, or personal consumption expenditures. (See page 91 and "lost quality of life" [p. 169] for a discussion of injury costs for cost-benefit analysis.)

The general approach followed was to identify a benchmark unit cost for each component, adjust the benchmark to the current year using an appropriate inflator, estimate the number of cases to which the component applied, and compute the product. Where possible, benchmarks were obtained for each class: Motor Vehicle, Work, Home, and Public.

Wage and productivity losses include the value of wages, fringe benefits, and household production for all classes, and travel delay for the Motor Vehicle class.

For fatalities, the present value of after-tax wages, fringe benefits, and household production was computed using the human capital method. The procedure incorporates data on life expectancy from the NCHS life tables, employment likelihood from the Bureau of Labor Statistics household survey, and mean earnings from the Bureau of the Census money income survey. The discount rate used was 4%, reduced from 6% used in earlier years. The present value obtained is highly sensitive to the discount rate; the lower the rate, the greater the present value.

For permanent partial disabilities, an average of 17% of earning power is lost (Berkowitz & Burton, 1987). The incidence of permanent disabilities, adjusted to remove intentional injuries, was computed from data on hospitalized cases from the National Hospital Discharge Survey (NHDS) and nonhospitalized cases from the National Health Interview Survey and National Council on Compensation Insurance data on probabilities of disability by nature of injury and part of body injured.

For temporary disabilities, an average daily wage, fringe benefit, and household production loss was calculated, and this was multiplied by the number of days of restricted activity from the NHIS.

Travel delay costs were obtained from the Council's estimates of the number of fatal, injury, and property damage crashes and an average delay cost per crash from Miller et al. (1991).

Medical expenses, including ambulance and helicopter transport costs, were estimated for fatalities, hospitalized cases, and nonhospitalized cases in each class.

The incidence of hospitalized cases was derived from the NHDS data adjusted to eliminate intentional injuries. Average length of stay was benchmarked from Miller, Pindus, Douglass, and Rossman (1993b) and adjusted to estimate lifetime length of stay. The cost per hospital day was benchmarked to the National Medical Expenditure Survey (NMES).

Nonhospitalized cases were estimated by taking the difference between total NHIS injuries and hospitalized cases. Average cost per case was based on NMES data adjusted for inflation and lifetime costs.

Medical cost of fatalities was benchmarked to data from the National Council on Compensation Insurance (1989) to which was added the cost of a premature funeral and coroner costs (Miller et al., 1991).

Cost per ambulance transport was benchmarked to NMES data and cost per helicopter transport was benchmarked to data in Miller et al. (1993a). The number of cases transported was based on data from Rice and MacKenzie (1989) and the National Electronic Injury Surveillance System.

Administrative expenses include the administrative cost of private and public insurance, which represents the cost of having insurance, and police and legal costs.

The administrative cost of motor-vehicle insurance was the difference between premiums earned (adjusted to remove fire, theft, and casualty premiums) and pure losses incurred, based on data from A. M. Best. Workers' compensation insurance administration was based on A. M. Best data for private carriers and regression estimates using Social Security Administration data for state funds and the self-insured. Administrative costs of public insurance (mainly

Medicaid and Medicare) amount to about 4% of the medical expenses paid by public insurance, which were determined from Rice and MacKenzie (1989) and Hensler et al. (1991).

Average police costs for motor-vehicle crashes were taken from Miller et al. (1991) and multiplied by the Council's estimates of the number of fatal, injury, and property-damage crashes.

Legal expenses include court costs, and plaintiff's and defendant's time and expenses. Hensler et al. (1991) provided data on the proportion of injured persons who hire a lawyer, file a claim, and get compensation. Kakalik and Pace (1986) provided data on costs per case.

Fire losses were based on data published by the National Fire Protection Association in the *NFPA Journal.* The allocation into the classes was based on the property use for structure fires and other NFPA data for non-structure fires.

Motor-vehicle damage costs were benchmarked to Blincoe and Faigin (1992) and multiplied by the Council's estimates of crash incidence.

Employer costs for work injuries is an estimate of the productivity costs incurred by employers. It assumes each fatality or permanent injury resulted in 4 person-months of disruption; each serious injury, 1 person-month; and each minor to moderate injury, 2 person-days. Each injury to a nonworker was assumed to involve 2 days of worker productivity loss. Average hourly earnings for supervisors and nonsupervisory workers were computed and then multiplied by the incidence and hours lost per case. Property damage and production delays (except motor-vehicle related) are not included in the estimates but can be substantial.

Lost quality of life is the difference between the value of a statistical fatality or statistical injury and the value of after-tax wages, fringe benefits, and household production. Because this does not represent real income not received or expenses incurred, it is not included in the total economic cost figure. If included, the resulting *comprehensive costs* can be used in cost-benefit analysis because the total costs then represent the maximum amount society should spend to prevent a statistical death or injury.

Work deaths and injuries (p. 48). The method for estimating total work-related deaths and injuries is discussed above. The breakdown of deaths by industry division for the current year is obtained from the CFOI and state Injury Mortality Tabulation figures using the link-relative technique (also discussed above).

The estimate of nonfatal disabling injuries by industry division is made by multiplying the estimate of employment for each industry division by the BLS estimate of the incidence rate of cases involving days away from work for each division (e.g., BLS, 2001) and then adjusting the results so that they add to the work-injury total previously established. The "private sector" average incidence rate is used for the government division, which is not covered in the BLS survey.

Employment. The employment estimates for 1992 to the present were changed for the 1998 edition. Estimates for these years in prior editions are not comparable. The total employment figure used by the Council represents the number of persons in the civilian labor force, aged 16 and older, who were wage or salary workers, self-employed, or unpaid family workers, plus active duty military personnel resident in the U.S. The total employment estimate is a combination of three figures — total civilian employment from the Current Population Survey (CPS) as published in *Employment and Earnings,* plus the difference between total resident population and total civilian population, which represents active duty military personnel.

Employment by industry division is obtained from an unpublished Bureau of Labor Statistics table titled "Employed and experienced unemployed persons by detailed industry and class of worker, Annual Average [year] (based on CPS)."

Time lost (p. 51) is the product of the number of cases and the average time lost per case. Deaths average 150 workdays lost in the current year and 5,850 in future years; permanent disabilities involve 75 and 565 days lost in current and future years, respectively; temporary

disabilities involve 17 days lost in the current year only. Off-the-job injuries to workers are assumed to result in similar lost time.

Off-the-job (p. 52) deaths and injuries are estimated by assuming that employed persons incur injuries at the same rate as the entire population.

Motor-Vehicle section (pp. 86–117). Estimates of miles traveled, registered vehicles and licensed drivers are published by the Federal Highway Administration in *Highway Statistics* and *Traffic Volume Trends.*

In addition to the death certificate data from NCHS and state registrars, the Council receives annual summary reports of traffic crash characteristics from about 15 states. Most national estimates are made using various ratios and percent distributions from the state crash data.

Beginning with the 1998 edition of *Accident Facts®*, national estimates of crashes by manner of collision (p. 90) and motor-vehicles involved in crashes by type of vehicle (p. 100) are made using the percent changes from the previous year to the current year as reported by the states. This percent change is then applied to benchmark figures obtained from the National Highway Traffic Safety Administration (NHTSA), Fatality Analysis Reporting System (FARS), and General Estimates System (GES) data for the previous year, which yields the current year estimates. These current year estimates are then adjusted to add to the Councils overall number of deaths, injuries, and fatal, injury, and property damage-only crashes that are listed on page 86. Because of these changes, comparisons to previous years should not be made.

Fleet accident rates (p. 109) represents the experience of motor fleets that participated in the Council's National Fleet Safety Contest. For the purposes of the contest, all death and injury accidents were included as well as *all* accidents (preventable or not preventable) resulting in property damage except when the vehicle was properly parked. Because of the nature of the reporting system, these accident rates cannot be considered representative of the national experience of motor fleets.

REFERENCES

Adams, P.F., Hendershot, G.E., & Marano, M.A. (1999). Current estimates from the National Health Interview Survey, 1996. *Vital and Health Statistics* 10(200). Hyattsville, MD: National Center for Health Statistics.

Berkowitz, M., & Burton, J.F., Jr. (1987). *Permanent Disability Benefits in Workers' Compensation.* Kalamazoo, MI: W.E. Upjohn Institute for Employment Research.

Blincoe, L.J., & Faigin, B.M. (1992). *Economic Cost of Motor Vehicle Crashes, 1990.* Springfield, VA: National Technical Information Service.

Bureau of Labor Statistics [BLS]. (1992). *Occupational Injury & Illness Classification Manual.* Itasca, IL: National Safety Council.

Bureau of Labor Statistics [BLS]. (2001, December 18). *Workplace Injuries and Illnesses in 2000.* Press release USDL-01-472.

Hensler, D.R., Marquis, M.S., Abrahamse, A.F., Berry, S.H., Ebener, P.A., Lewis, E.D., Lind, E.A., MacCoun, R.J., Manning, W.G., Rogowski, J.A., & Vaiana, M.E. (1991). *Compensation for Accidental Injuries in the United States.* Santa Monica, CA: The RAND Corporation.

Hoyert, D.L., Arias, E., Smith, B.L., Murphy, S.L., & Kochanek, K.D. (2001). Deaths: final data for 1999. *National Vital Statistics Reports, 49*(8).

Kakalik, J.S., & Pace, N. (1986). *Costs and Compensation Paid in Tort Litigation.* R-3391-ICJ. Santa Monica, CA: The RAND Corporation.

Landes, S.R., Ginsburg, K.M., Hoskin, A.F., & Miller, T.A. (1990). *Estimating Nonfatal Injuries.* Itasca, IL: Statistics Department, National Safety Council.

Miller, T., Viner, J., Rossman, S., Pindus, N., Gellert, W., Douglass, J., Dillingham, A., & Blomquist, G. (1991). *The Costs of Highway Crashes.* Springfield, VA: National Technical Information Service.

Miller, T.R., Brigham, P.A., Cohen, M.A., Douglass, J.B., Galbraith, M.S., Lestina, D.C., Nelkin, V.S., Pindus, N.M., & Smith-Regojo, P. (1993a). Estimating the costs to society of cigarette fire injuries. *Report to Congress in Response to the Fire Safe Cigarette Act of 1990.* Washington, DC: U.S. Consumer Product Safety Commission.

Miller, T.R., Pindus, N.M., Douglass, J.B., & Rossman, S.B. (1993b). *Nonfatal Injury Incidence, Costs, and Consequences: A Data Book.* Washington, DC: The Urban Institute Press.

Rice, D.P., & MacKenzie, E.J. (1989). *Cost of Injury in the United States: A Report to Congress.* Atlanta, GA: Centers for Disease Control and Prevention.

Toscano, G., & Windau, J. (1994). The changing character of fatal work injuries. *Monthly Labor Review, 117*(10), 17-28.

World Health Organization. (1977). *Manual of the International Statistical Classification of Diseases, Injuries, and Causes of Death.* Geneva, Switzerland: Author.

World Health Organization. (1992). *International Statistical Classification of Diseases and Related Health Problems—Tenth Revision.* Geneva, Switzerland: Author.

SELECTED UNINTENTIONAL-INJURY CODE GROUPINGS

Manner of Injury	ICD-9 Codes[a]	ICD-10 Codes[b]	Comparability Ratio[c]	OI&ICM[d] Event Codes
Unintentional Injuries	E800–E869, E880–E929[e]	V01–X59, Y85–Y86	1.0305 (1.0278–1.0333)[f]	00–60, 63–9999
Railway accident	E800–E807	V05, V15, V80.6, V81(.2–.9)	n/a	44
Motor-vehicle accident	E810–E825	V02–V04, V09.0, V09.2, V12–V14, V19.0–V19.2, V19.4–V19.6, V20–V79, V80.3–V80.5, V81.0–V81.1, V82.0–V82.1, V83–V86, V87.0–V87.8, V88.0–V88.8, V89.0, V89.2	0.9754 (0.9742–0.9766)	41, 42, 43
Water transport accident	E830–E838	V90–V94	n/a	45
Air transport accident	E840–E845	V95–V97	n/a	46
Poisoning by solids & liquids	E850–58, E860–66	X40–X49	n/a	344
Poisoning by gases and vapors	E867–E869			341
Falls	E880–E888	W00–W19	0.8409 (0.8313–0.8505)	1
Fires and burns	E890–E899	X00–X09	0.9743 (0.9568–0.9918)	51
Drowning	E910 W65	W74	0.9965 (0.9716–1.0213)	381
Suffocation by ingestion or inhalation	E911–E912	W78–W80	n/a	382
Mechanical suffocation	E913	W75–W77, W81–W84	n/a	383, 384, 389
Firearms	E922	W32–W34	1.0579 (1.0331-1.0828)	0220, 0222, 0229 with source = 911[g]

Source: National Safety Council.
Note: n/a means comparability ratio not calculated or does not meet standards of reliability or precision.
[a] *WHO (1977).*
[b] *WHO (1992).*
[c] *Hoyert, Arias, Smith, et al. (2001). Table III.*
[d] *BLS (1992).*
[e] *The National Safety Council has used E800–E949 for unintentional injuries. The code group in the table omits complications and misadventures of surgical and medical care (E870–E879) and adverse effects of drugs in therapeutic use (E930–E949).*
[f] *Figures in parentheses are the 95% confidence interval for the comparability ratio.*
[g] *Struck by flying object where the source of injury was a bullet.*

OTHER SOURCES

The following organizations may be useful for obtaining more current data or more detailed information on various subjects in *Injury Facts®*.

American Association of Poison Control Centers
3201 New Mexico Avenue, Suite 310
Washington, DC 20016
(202) 362-7217
www.aapcc.org
aapcc@poison.org

Bureau of Labor Statistics
U.S. Department of Labor
2 Massachusetts Avenue, NE
Washington, DC 20212
(202) 691-7828
www.bls.gov
blsdata_staff@bls.gov

Bureau of the Census
U.S. Department of Commerce
Public Information Office
Washington, DC 20233-8200
(301) 457-2794
www.census.gov

Bureau of Justice Statistics
810 7th Street, NW
Washington DC 20531
(202) 307-5933
www.ojp.usdoj.gov

Bureau of Transportation Statistics
U.S. Department of Transportation
400 7th Street, SW, Room 3103
Washington, DC 20590
(800) 853-1352
www.bts.gov
answers@bts.gov

Centers for Disease Control and Prevention
1600 Clifton Road
Atlanta, GA 30333
(404) 639-3534 or (800) 311-3435
www.cdc.gov

Chemical Safety Board
2175 K Street, NW, Suite 400
Washington, DC 20037
(202) 261-7600
www.chemsafety.gov
info@csb.gov

Eno Transportation Foundation
1634 I Street, NW, Suite 500
Washington, DC 20006
(202) 879-4700
www.enotrans.com

Environmental Protection Agency, U.S.
1200 Pennsylvania Avenue, NW
Washington, DC 20460
(202) 260-2090
www.epa.gov
public-access@epa.gov

European Agency for Safety and Health at Work
Gran Via, 33
E-48009 Bilbao, Spain
Phone: +34 944-794-360
Fax: +34 944-794-383
http://europe.osha.eu.int
information@osha.eu.int

Federal Aviation Administration
U.S. Department of Transportation
National Aviation Safety Data Analysis Center
800 Independence Avenue, SW
Washington, DC 20591
(202) 366-4000
www.faa.gov

Federal Bureau of Investigation
935 Pennsylvania Avenue, NW
Washington, DC 20535-0001
(202) 324-3000
www.fbi.gov

Federal Highway Administration
U.S. Department of Transportation
400 7th Street, SW
Washington, DC 20590
(202) 366-0660
www.fhwa.dot.gov
execsecretariat.fhwa@fhwa.dot.gov

Federal Motor Carrier Safety Administration
U.S. Department of Transportation
400 7th Street, SW
Washington, DC 20590
(800) 832-5660
www.fmcsa.dot.gov

Federal Railroad Administration
U.S. Department of Transportation
1120 Vermont Avenue, NW
Washington, DC 20590
(202) 366-2760
www.fra.dot.gov

Federal Transit Administration
400 7th Street, SW
Washington, DC 20590
www.fta.dot.gov

FedStats
Gateway to official statistical information available to the public from more than 100 federal agencies.
www.fedstats.gov

FirstGov
Gateway to federal, state, local, tribal, and international government web sites.
www.firstgov.gov

Insurance Information Institute
110 William Street
New York, NY 10038
(212) 346-5500
www.iii.org

Insurance Institute for Highway Safety
1005 N. Glebe Road, Suite 800
Arlington, VA 22201
(703) 247-1500
www.highwaysafety.org

International Hunter Education Association
P.O. Box 490
Wellington, CO 80549-0490
(970) 568-7954
www.ihea.com
ihea@frii.com

International Labour Office
4, rue des Morillons
CH-1211 Geneva 22
Switzerland
Phone: +41-22-799-6111
Fax: +41-22-798-8685
www.ilo.org
ilo@ilo.org

Mine Safety and Health Administration
1100 Wilson Boulevard, 21st Floor
Arlington, VA 22209-3939
(202) 693-9400
www.msha.gov

Motorcycle Safety Foundation
2 Jenner Street, Suite 150
Irvine, CA 92718-3812
(714) 727-3227
www.msf-usa.org

National Academy of Social Insurance
1776 Massachusetts Avenue, NW, Suite 615
Washington, DC 20036-1904
(202) 452-8097
www.nasi.org
nasi@nasi.org

National Center for Education Statistics
U.S. Department of Education
1990 K Street, NW
Washington, DC 20006
(202) 502-7300
http://nces.ed.gov

National Center for Health Statistics
6525 Belcrest Road
Hyattsville, MD 20782
(301) 458-4636
www.cdc.gov/nchs

National Center for Injury Prevention and Control
Office Of Communication Resources, Mail Stop K65
4770 Buford Highway, NE
Atlanta, GA 30341-3724
(770) 488-1506
www.cdc.gov/ncipc
ohcinfo@cdc.gov

National Clearinghouse for Alcohol and Drug Information
P.O. Box 2345
Rockville, MD 20847-2345
(301) 468-2600 or 1-800-729-6686
www.health.org

National Climatic Data Center
151 Patton Avenue
Asheville, NC 28801-5001
(828) 271-4800
http://lwf.ncdc.noaa.gov/oa/ncdc.html
ncdc.info@noaa.gov

National Collegiate Athletic Association
700 W. Washington Street
P.O. Box 6222
Indianapolis, IN 46206-6222
(317) 917-6222
www.ncaa.org

National Council on Compensation Insurance
901 Peninsula Corporate Circle
Boca Raton, FL 33487
(800) NCCI-123 (1-800-622-4123)
www.ncci.com

National Fire Protection Association
P.O. Box 9101
Batterymarch Park
Quincy, MA 02269-0910
(617) 770-3000 or 1-800-344-3555
www.nfpa.org
osds@nfpa.org

National Highway Traffic Safety Administration
U.S. Department of Transportation
400 7th Street, SW
Washington, DC 20590
(202) 366-0123 or 1-800-424-9393
www.nhtsa.dot.gov
    National Center for Statistics and Analysis (NRD-30)
    (202) 366-4198 or 1-800-934-8517
    NCSAweb@nhtsa.dot.gov

National Institute for Occupational Safety and Health
Clearinghouse for Occupational Safety and Health
    Information
4676 Columbia Parkway
Cincinnati, OH 45226
(800) 356-4674
www.cdc.gov/niosh
eidtechinfo@cdc.gov

National Spinal Cord Injury Association
6701 Democracy Boulevard, Suite 300-9
Bethesda, MD 20817
(301) 588-6959
www.spinalcord.org
nscia2@aol.com

National Sporting Goods Association
1601 Feehanville Drive, Suite 300
Mt. Prospect, IL 60056
(847) 296-6742
www.nsga.org
info@nsga.org

National Transportation Safety Board
490 L'Enfant Plaza East, SW
Washington, DC 20594
(202) 314-6000
www.ntsb.gov

Occupational Safety and Health Administration
U.S. Department of Labor
Office of Statistics
200 Constitution Avenue, NW
Washington, DC 20210
(800) 321-OSHA (6742)
www.osha.gov

Prevent Blindness America
500 E. Remington Road
Schaumburg, IL 60173
(800) 331-2020
www.preventblindness.org
info@preventblindness.org

Transportation Research Board
500 5th Street, NW
Washington, DC 20001
(202) 334-2934
www.nas.edu/trb

U.S. Coast Guard
2100 2nd Street, SW
Washington, DC 20593-0001
(800) 368-5647
www.uscgboating.org
uscginfoline@gcrm.com

U.S. Consumer Product Safety Commission
National Injury Information Clearinghouse
Washington, DC 20207-0001
(301) 504-0424
www.cpsc.gov
clearinghouse@cpsc.gov

World Health Organization
20, avenue Appia
CH-1211 Geneva 27
Switzerland
Phone: +41-22-791-2111
Fax: +41-22-791-0746
www.who.int
info@who.int

Accident is that occurrence in a sequence of events that produces unintended injury, death, or property damage. *Accident* refers to the event, not the result of the event (see *unintentional injury*).

Cases without lost workdays are cases that do not involve lost workdays but result in medical treatment other than first aid, restriction of work or motion, loss of consciousness, transfer to another job, or diagnosis of occupational illness.

Death from accident is a death that occurs within one year of the accident.

Disabling injury is an injury causing death, permanent disability, or any degree of temporary total disability beyond the day of the injury.

Fatal accident is an accident that results in one or more deaths within one year.

Home is a dwelling and its premises within the property lines including single-family dwellings and apartment houses, duplex dwellings, boarding and rooming houses, and seasonal cottages. Excluded from *home* are barracks, dormitories, and resident institutions.

Incidence rate, as defined by OSHA, is the number of occupational injuries and/or illnesses or lost workdays per 100 full-time employees. See formula on page 61.

Injury is physical harm or damage to the body resulting from an exchange, usually acute, of mechanical, chemical, thermal, or other environmental energy that exceeds the body's tolerance.

Lost workdays are those days on which, because of occupational injury or illness, the employee was away from work or limited to restricted work activity. *Days away from work* are those days on which the employee would have worked but could not. *Days of restricted work* activity are those days on which the employee was assigned to a temporary job, worked at a permanent job less than full time, or worked at a permanent job but could not perform all duties normally connected with it. The number of lost workdays (consecutive or not) does not include the day of injury or onset of illness or any days on which the employee would not have worked even though able to work.

Lost workday cases are cases that involve days away from work, days of restricted work activity, or both.

Motor vehicle is any mechanically or electrically powered device not operated on rails, upon which or by which any person or property may be transported upon a land highway. The load on a motor vehicle or trailer attached to it is considered part of the vehicle. Tractors and motorized machinery are included while self-propelled in transit or used for transportation. *Nonmotor vehicle* is any road vehicle other than a motor vehicle, such as a bicycle or animal-drawn vehicle, **except** a coaster wagon, child's sled, child's tricycle, child's carriage, and similar means of transportation; persons using these latter means of transportation are considered pedestrians.

Motor-vehicle accident is an unstabilized situation that includes at least one harmful event (injury or property damage) involving a motor vehicle in transport (in motion, in readiness for motion, or on a roadway but not parked in a designated parking area) that does not result from discharge of a firearm or explosive device and does not directly result from a cataclysm. [See Committee on Motor Vehicle Traffic Accident Classification (1997), *Manual on Classification of Motor Vehicle Traffic Accidents*, ANSI D16.1-1996, Itasca, IL: National Safety Council.]

Motor-vehicle traffic accident is a motor-vehicle accident that occurs on a trafficway—a way or place, any part of which is open to the use of the public for the purposes of vehicular traffic. *Motor-vehicle nontraffic accident* is any motor-vehicle accident that occurs entirely in any place other than a trafficway.

Nonfatal injury accident is an accident in which at least one person is injured and no injury results in death.

Occupational illness is any abnormal condition or disorder other than one resulting from an occupational injury caused by exposure to environmental factors associated with employment. It includes acute and chronic illnesses or diseases that may be caused by inhalation, absorption, ingestion, or direct contact. See also page 61.

Occupational injury is any injury such as a cut, fracture, sprain, amputation, etc., which results from a work accident or from a single instantaneous exposure in the work environment. See also page 61.

Pedalcycle is a vehicle propelled by human power and operated solely by pedals; excludes mopeds.

Pedestrian is any person involved in a motor-vehicle accident who is not in or upon a motor vehicle or nonmotor vehicle. Includes persons injured while using a coaster wagon, child's tricycle, roller skates, etc. Excludes persons boarding, alighting, jumping, or falling from a motor vehicle in transport who are considered occupants of the vehicle.

Permanent disability (or permanent impairment) includes any degree of permanent nonfatal injury. It includes any injury that results in the loss or complete loss of use of any part of the body or in any permanent impairment of functions of the body or a part thereof.

Property damage accident is an accident that results in property damage but in which no person is injured.

Public accident is any accident other than motor-vehicle that occurs in the public use of any premises. Includes deaths in recreation (swimming, hunting, etc.), in transportation except motor-vehicle, public buildings, etc., and from widespread natural disasters even though some may have happened on home premises. Excludes accidents to persons in the course of gainful employment.

Source of injury is the principal object such as tool, machine, or equipment involved in the accident and is usually the object inflicting injury or property damage. Also called agency or agent.

Temporary total disability is an injury that does not result in death or permanent disability but that renders the injured person unable to perform regular duties or activities on one or more full calendar days after the day of the injury.

Total cases include all work-related deaths and illnesses and those work-related injuries that result in loss of consciousness, restriction of work or motion, or transfer to another job, or require medical treatment other than first aid.

Unintentional injury is the preferred term for accidental injury in the public health community. It refers to the *result* of an accident.

Work hours are the total number of hours worked by all employees. They are usually compiled for various levels, such as an establishment, a company, or an industry. A work hour is the equivalent of one employee working one hour.

Work injuries (including occupational illnesses) are those that arise out of and in the course of gainful employment regardless of where the accident or exposure occurs. Excluded are work injuries to private household workers and injuries occurring in connection with farm chores that are classified as home injuries.

Workers are all persons gainfully employed, including owners, managers, other paid employees, the self-employed, and unpaid family workers but excluding private household workers.

Work/Motor-vehicle duplication includes *work injuries* that occur in *motor-vehicle accidents* (see definitions for work injuries and motor-vehicle accident on this page).

INDEX

The
HELEN OXENBURY
Nursery Collection

This edition especially produced for Borders Group, Inc., U.S.A.
2000 by Egmont Children's Books Limited
a division of Egmont Holding Limited
239 Kensington High Street, London W8 6SA

The Helen Oxenbury Nursery Story Book first published in Great Britain 1985
by William Heinemann Ltd and 1997 by Mammoth,
an imprint of Egmont Children's Books Limited.
Copyright © Helen Oxenbury 1985

The Helen Oxenbury Nursery Rhyme Book first published in Great Britain 1986
by William Heinemann Ltd and 1998 by Mammoth,
an imprint of Egmont Children's Books Limited.
Text copyright © Brian Alderson 1974, 1986
Illustrations copyright © Helen Oxenbury 1974, 1986

ISBN 0 434 80710 9

1 3 5 7 9 10 8 6 4 2

Printed in Dubai, U.A.E.

The
HELEN OXENBURY
Nursery Story Book

Contents

Goldilocks and the Three Bears

Once upon a time, there were three bears who lived together in their own little house in the wood. There was a great big father bear, a middle-sized mother bear and a little baby bear. They each had a special bowl for porridge, a special chair for sitting in, and a special bed to sleep in.

One morning the mother bear made their porridge for breakfast and poured it out into the great big bowl, the middle-sized bowl and the little baby bowl. But it was so hot the bears decided to go for a walk while it cooled.

Now a little girl called Goldilocks was walking in the woods that morning and she came across the bears' house. She knocked on the door and when there was no reply, she crept slowly in.

"Oh! Oh!" she cried when she saw the bowls of porridge. "I'm so hungry; I must have just one spoonful."

First she went to the great big bowl and took a taste. "Too hot!" she said.

Then she went to the middle-sized bowl and tried that porridge. "Too cold," she said.

Last she went to the little baby bowl. "Oh! Oh! Just right!" she cried, and she ate it all up, every bit.

Then Goldilocks saw the great big chair and climbed into it. "Too big," she said, and climbed down quickly.

Next she went to the middle-sized chair and sat down. "Too hard," she said.

Then she went quickly to the little baby chair. "It just fits," she said happily. But really the chair was too small for her and – CRACK – it broke, and down she tumbled.

Then she went into the next room where she saw three neat beds. First she climbed into the great big bed, but it was too high. Next she climbed into the middle-sized bed, but it was too low.

Then she saw the little baby bed. "Oh! Oh!" she cried. "This is just right." She got in, pulled up the covers, and went fast asleep.

Before long the three bears came home for their breakfast. First the great big bear went to eat his porridge.

He took one look and said in his great rough voice, "Somebody has been eating my porridge!"

Then the middle-sized bear looked into her bowl and said in her middle-sized voice, "And somebody has been eating my porridge, too!"

Finally the little baby bear went to his bowl. "Oh! Oh!" he cried in his little baby voice. "Somebody's been eating my porridge and has eaten it all up!"

After that, all three bears wanted to sit down. The great big bear went to his great big chair and saw that the cushion had been squashed down. "Somebody has been sitting in my chair," he cried in his great big voice.

Then the middle-sized mother bear went to her middle-sized chair and found her cushion on the floor. "Somebody has been sitting in my chair," she said in her middle-sized voice.

Then the little baby bear hurried to his chair. "Oh! Oh!" he cried in his little baby voice "Somebody's been sitting in my chair and broken it all to bits!"

The three bears, feeling very sad, went into the bedroom.

First the great big bear looked at his bed. "Somebody has been lying in my bed," he said in his great big voice.

Then the middle-sized bear saw her bed all rumpled up and she cried in her middle-sized voice, "Oh dear, somebody has been lying in my bed."

By this time the little baby bear had gone to his little baby bed and he cried, "Somebody has been lying in my bed, and she's still here!"

This time his little baby voice was so high and squeaky that Goldilocks woke up with a start and sat up. There on one side of the bed were the three bears all looking down at her.

Now Goldilocks did not know that they were kind bears

and she was very frightened. She screamed, jumped out of bed, ran to the open window and quickly climbed out. Then she ran home to her mother as fast as she possibly could.

As for the bears, they put things to rights, and since Goldilocks never came again, they lived happily ever after.

The Turnip

Once there was a man who lived with his wife and little boy in a cottage in the country. One morning in May the man planted some turnip seeds.

Before long little turnip leaves began to poke up through the brown earth. Then an odd thing happened. One turnip plant began to grow faster than all the rest. It grew and it grew and it grew.

"We must have that turnip for supper tonight," said the man.

So he tried to pull the big turnip out of the ground. He pulled and he pulled and he pulled. But the turnip stuck fast.

"Wife, wife," he called, "come and help me pull this great turnip."

His wife came running. Then she pulled the man, and the man pulled the turnip. Oh how hard they pulled! But the turnip stuck fast.

"Son, son," called his mother, "come and help us pull this big turnip out of the ground."

The little boy came running and took tight hold of his mother. Then the boy pulled his mother, his mother pulled his father, and his father pulled the turnip. But still it stuck fast.

Then the little boy whistled for his dog.

"Come and help us," the boy said.

So the dog pulled the boy, the boy pulled his mother, his mother pulled his father and his father pulled the turnip. But still it stuck fast.

Then the dog barked for the hen.

The hen came flying and grabbed tight hold of the dog's tail. Then she pulled the dog, the dog pulled the boy, the boy pulled his mother, his mother pulled his father, and his father pulled the turnip. But still the turnip stuck fast.

"Cluck, cluck, cluck!" cried the hen.

And the cock came flying to help. Then the cock pulled the hen, the hen pulled the dog, the dog pulled the boy, the boy pulled his mother, his mother pulled his father, his father pulled the turnip and . . .

Whoosh! . . . Up came the turnip out of the ground, and down, backwards, they all tumbled in a heap. But they weren't hurt a bit and just got up laughing.

Then they rolled the turnip into the house and the boy's mother cooked it for their supper. Everyone had all they could eat and still there was enough left over for the next day, and the next, and the day after that!

The Little Porridge Pot

There was once a little girl who lived in a village with her mother. They were very poor and things got worse and worse until one day they found that there was nothing left to eat.

"I'll go into the forest and see if I can find some berries," the little girl said. And off she went.

She had not gone far when she met a very old woman who smiled at her. "I know that you are a good little girl and that you and your mother are poor and hungry. Here is a little pot to take home. Whenever you say to it, 'Cook, little pot,' it will fill itself full of delicious steaming porridge. When you have had all you can eat, you must say, 'Enough, little pot,' and it will stop making porridge."

The little girl thanked the kind old woman and took the pot home to her mother. They were both so hungry that they could scarcely wait to say, "Cook, little pot."

At once the pot was full of porridge. Then, when they had eaten all they could, the little girl said, "Enough, little pot," and it was empty again.

From that day on, the little girl and her mother were never hungry anymore, and they lived very happily for a while.

But one day when the little girl was out her mother wanted some of that delicious porridge all for herself. Carefully, she got the pot down from the shelf and said the magic words, "Cook, little pot." In a moment the pot was full.

The little girl's mother ate as much as she wanted. Then, suddenly, she screamed.

"Oh dear! Oh dear! I can't remember how to make it stop!"

The porridge kept on coming and coming. It filled the little pot to the brim. It seeped over the top and down onto the table. Bubbling and steaming, it overflowed onto the floor. More and more kept coming. The porridge ran across the floor and out of the door and streamed down the street. It went into neighbours' gardens! And into

their houses! Finally, there was only one house in the whole village that wasn't filled with porridge!

"Oh! Oh! Oh!" all the villagers cried at once. "Whatever shall we do?"

At that very moment, the little girl came home, and seeing porridge everywhere, she cried, "Enough, little pot."

To everyone's relief, the porridge stopped coming. However, they all had to squeeze into the one house that had escaped and live there together until, at last, they could eat their way back to their own homes.

The Three Little Pigs

Once there were three little pigs who grew up and left their mother to find homes for themselves.

The first little pig set out, and before long he met a man with a bundle of straw.

"Please, Man," said the pig, "will you let me have that bundle of straw to build my house?"

''Yes, here, take it,'' said the kind man.

The little pig was very pleased and at once built himself a house of straw.

He had hardly moved in when a wolf came walking by, and, seeing the new house, knocked on the door.

''Little pig, little pig,'' he said, ''open up the door and let me in.''

Now the little pig's mother had warned him about strangers, so he said, ''No, not by the hair of my chinny-chin-chin, I'll not let you in.''

''Then I'll huff and I'll puff and I'll blow your house down!'' cried the wolf.

But the little pig went on saying, "No, not by the hair of my chinny-chin-chin, I'll not let you in."

So the old wolf huffed and he puffed and he blew the house down, and ate up the little pig.

The second little pig said good-bye to his mother and set out. Before long he met a man with a bundle of sticks.

"Please, Man," he said, "will you let me have that bundle of sticks to build my house?"

"Yes, you can have it. Here it is," said the kind man.

So the second little pig was very pleased and used the sticks to build himself a house. He had hardly moved in when the wolf came walking by and knocked at the door.

"Little pig, little pig," he said, "open up your door and let me in."

Now the second little pig remembered what his mother had told him, so he, too, said, "No, not by the hair of my chinny-chin-chin, I'll not let you in."

"Then I'll huff and I'll puff and I'll blow your house down!" cried the wolf.

But the little pig went on saying, "No, not by the hair of my chinny-chin-chin, I'll not let you in!"

So again, the old wolf huffed and he puffed, and he

huffed and he puffed. This time it was much harder work but, finally, down came the house and he ate up the second little pig.

Then, last of all, the third little pig set out and met a man with a load of bricks.

"Please, Man," he said, "will you let me have that load of bricks to build my house?"

"Yes, here they are – all for you," said the kind man.

The third little pig was very pleased, and built himself a brick house.

Again the wolf came along, and again he said, "Little pig, little pig, open your door and let me in."

But, like his brothers, the third little pig said, "No, not by the hair of my chinny-chin-chin, I'll not let you in."

"Then I'll huff and I'll puff and I'll blow your house down!" cried the wolf.

And when the third little pig wouldn't open the door, he huffed and he puffed, and he huffed and he puffed. Then he tried again but the brick house was so strong that he could not blow it down.

This made the wolf so angry that he jumped onto the roof of the little brick house and roared down the chimney, "I'm coming down to eat you up!"

The little pig had put a pot full of boiling water on the fire and now he took off the lid. Down the chimney tumbled the wolf and – SPLASH – he fell right into the pot.

Quickly, the little pig banged on the cover and boiled up the old wolf for his dinner.

And so the clever little pig lived happily ever after.

The Gingerbread Boy

There was once a woman who hadn't any children of her own and wanted one very much. One day she said to her husband, "I shall bake myself a nice gingerbread boy. That's what I shall do."

Her husband laughed at this idea but that very morning she mixed the dough and rolled it. Then she cut out a little boy shape with a smiling mouth and two currants for eyes. When she had popped him in the oven, she waited for him to bake and then she opened the door. Out jumped the gingerbread boy and ran away through the kitchen and right outside.

"Husband, husband," called the woman as she ran after the gingerbread boy.

The man dropped his spade when he heard his wife call and came running from the field.

But when the gingerbread boy saw the woman and the man chasing him, he only laughed, running faster and faster and shouting:

> *"Run, run, as fast as you can,*
> *You can't catch me,*
> *I'm the gingerbread man!"*

On he ran until he met a cow.

"Moo! Moo!" called the cow. "Stop! Stop! I want to eat you."

But the gingerbread boy only laughed and ran faster than ever, shouting, "I've run away from a woman and a man and now I'll run away from you!

"Run, run, as fast as you can,
You can't catch me,
I'm the gingerbread man!"

The cow chased after him but she was too fat and couldn't catch him. He raced on until he came to a horse.

"Neigh! Neigh!" snorted the horse. "You look good to eat. Stop and let me gobble you up."

But the gingerbread boy only laughed and shouted, "I've run away from a woman, a man, and a cow, and now I'll run away from you!

"Run, run, as fast as you can,
You can't catch me,
I'm the gingerbread man!"

The horse galloped after the gingerbread boy but couldn't catch him. He raced on faster and faster until he came to some farmers in a field.

"Ho! Ho!" they cried. "Stop! Stop! and let us have a bite."

But the gingerbread boy only laughed and shouted, "I've run away from a woman, a man, a cow, a horse, and now I'll run away from you!

"Run, run, as fast as you can,
You can't catch me,
I'm the gingerbread man!"

The men joined in the chase but no one could catch the
gingerbread boy. He raced far ahead until he came to a

river and had to stop. There he met a fox who wanted very much to eat him then and there, but he was afraid the clever gingerbread boy might escape.

So he said politely, "Do you want to cross the river?"

"Yes, please," said the gingerbread boy.

"Well, then, jump on my back and I'll swim across."

"Thank you," said the gingerbread boy; and he did just that.

When they were about halfway across, the fox said, "The water is deeper here. I think you'd better crawl up onto my neck."

"Thank you," said the gingerbread boy; and he did just that.

When they had gone three-quarters of the way across,

the fox said, "You'd better climb up onto my head. You can't be very comfortable there."

"Thank you," said the gingerbread boy; and he did just that.

"We're nearly there now," said the fox a moment later. "I think you'll be safer if you get onto my nice long nose."

"Thank you," said the gingerbread boy. But no sooner had he climbed onto the fox's nose than the fox threw back his head and SNAP! went his big mouth.

The gingerbread boy was half gone.

Then the fox did it again, SNAP!

The gingerbread boy was three-quarters gone.

The fox was having a very good time, and he did it again. SNAP!

The gingerbread boy was all gone.

And that was the end of the gingerbread boy who had been too clever for the woman, the man, the cow, the horse, and the farmers. But not clever enough for the fox.

Henny-Penny

One day when Henny-Penny was scratching about for corn in the farmyard, an acorn fell down from the oak tree and hit her on the head.

"Goodness gracious," she cried, "the sky is falling. I must go and tell the king."

So, off she went in a great hurry and soon she met Cocky-Locky.

''Where are you going?'' asked Cocky-Locky.

''I'm going to tell the king the sky is falling,'' said Henny-Penny.

''Can I come, too?'' asked Cocky-Locky.

''Yes, do,'' said Henny-Penny.

So off went Henny-Penny and Cocky-Locky to tell the king the sky was falling, and, before long, they met Ducky-Daddles.

''Where are you going?'' asked Ducky-Daddles.

''Oh, we're going to tell the king the sky is falling,'' said Henny-Penny and Cocky-Locky.

''Can I come, too?'' asked Ducky-Daddles.

''Yes, do,'' said Henny-Penny and Cocky-Locky.

So off went Henny-Penny, Cocky-Locky and Ducky-Daddles to tell the king the sky was falling and, before long, they met Goosey-Poosey.

''Where are you going?'' asked Goosey-Poosey.

''Oh, we're going to tell the king the sky is falling,'' said Henny-Penny, Cocky-Locky and Ducky-Daddles.

''Can I come, too?'' asked Goosey-Poosey.

''Yes, do,'' said Henny-Penny, Cocky-Locky and Ducky-Daddles.

So off went Henny-Penny, Cocky-Locky, Ducky-Daddles and Goosey-Poosey to tell the king the sky was falling and, before long, they met Turkey-Lurkey.

"Where are you going?" asked Turkey-Lurkey.

"Oh, we're going to tell the king the sky is falling," said Henny-Penny, Cocky-Locky, Ducky-Daddles and Goosey-Poosey.

"Can I come, too?" asked Turkey-Lurkey.

"Yes, do," said Henny-Penny, Cocky-Locky, Ducky-Daddles and Goosey-Poosey.

So off went Henny-Penny, Cocky-Locky, Ducky-Daddles, Goosey-Poosey and Turkey-Lurkey to tell the king the sky was falling.

They went along together, Henny-Penny, Cocky-Locky, Ducky-Daddles, Goosey-Poosey and Turkey-Lurkey – along and along, until they met Foxy-Woxy.

"Where are you going?" asked Foxy-Woxy.

"Oh, we're going to tell the king the sky is falling," said Henny-Penny, Cocky-Locky, Ducky-Daddles, Goosey-Poosey and Turkey-Lurkey.

"But you're not going the right way," said Foxy-Woxy. "I know the right way. Let me show you."

"Thank you," said Henny-Penny, Cocky-Locky, Ducky-Daddles, Goosey-Poosey and Turkey-Lurkey.

So off they all went with Foxy-Woxy leading the way, and, before long, they came to a dark hole. Now this was really the home of Foxy-Woxy but he said, "This is the shortest way to the king's palace. Follow me."

So Foxy-Woxy went a little way down the hole and waited for Henny-Penny, Cocky-Locky, Ducky-Daddles, Goosey-Poosey and Turkey-Lurkey.

First came Turkey-Lurkey.

"Snap!" Foxy-Woxy bit off Turkey-Lurkey's head.

Next came Goosey-Poosey.

"Snap!" Foxy-Woxy bit off Goosey-Poosey's head.

Next came Ducky-Daddles.

"Snap!" Foxy-Woxy bit off Ducky-Daddles's head.

Next came Cocky-Locky.

"Snap!" But this time Foxy-Woxy was getting tired and he missed, so that Cocky-Locky managed to call out to Henny-Penny, "Look out! Don't come!"

Henny-Penny heard Cocky-Locky and ran back home to the farmyard as fast as she could go. And that was why she never told the king the sky was falling.

The Elves and the Shoemaker

Once there was a shoemaker who lived with his wife in a little cottage. They were poor and he found it hard to earn enough money to live on.

Finally the day came when they had no money and only a crust of bread for supper. However, there was just enough leather left to make one pair of shoes. The shoemaker cut out the pieces carefully and put them on his workbench ready to sew together in the morning.

He woke early next day and went to his bench to make his last pair of shoes. But instead of the pieces of leather he had left the night before, he found a finished pair of shoes. They were more beautiful than any the shoemaker had ever made.

"Wife, wife!" he called excitedly. "Come and tell me if I'm dreaming!"

At this his wife came running and when she looked, she cried, "Oh, no, you aren't dreaming. The shoes are finished and . . . and . . . oh, so beautiful, too!"

While the shoemaker and his wife were turning the shoes around in their hands to see the fine stitches, a grand gentleman came in. He saw the lovely new shoes and wanted to buy them then and there. What is more, he paid the shoemaker so much for them that the shoemaker was able to buy leather for two more pairs. He also bought some fresh bread, cheese and other good food.

In the afternoon he cut out the new leather carefully and put the pieces on his workbench ready to sew together in the morning. Then he and his wife sat down

together for the best meal they had had for a long time. They went to bed very happy and slept soundly.

When they woke up next day, lo and behold, there were two new pairs of shoes, all sewn and shining on the

workbench. That same day the grand gentleman came to buy shoes for all his family and took both of the new pairs. The shoemaker was able to buy enough leather for four more pairs, and there was money left over, too.

Again on the third night the same thing happened and in the morning they woke up to find four new pairs of lovely shoes. Then more friends of the grand gentleman came and every pair was gone in a twinkling. This went on from day to day until the shoemaker and his wife were growing rich.

One morning the shoemaker's wife said, "We must try to find out who is being so kind so we can thank him."

"I know what we'll do," said the shoemaker. "Tonight we'll stay up and watch to see what happens."

So that night they hid themselves in a corner of the room and waited.

At midnight they heard the front door open and then they saw two little naked elves come dancing in. The elves sat down at once and began to sew so fast that, in only a few moments, there was a whole row of perfect new shoes and every single piece of leather had been used. Then the elves climbed down from the bench and ran out the door.

Next morning the shoemaker's wife said, "Now that we know who is helping us perhaps we can thank them in some way. I think they look cold without any clothes, poor things. I'm going to make them each a jacket and trousers and knit them some warm socks. It is getting colder every day and when the winter comes they will be frozen."

"What a good idea," said her husband, "and I will make them each a special pair of shoes."

They both set to work that very day but it took them some time because they had to stay awake many nights and watch to make sure of the right size. At last it was Christmas Eve and the clothes and the shoes were finished. The shoemaker and his wife laid them out carefully on the bench instead of the usual pieces of leather. Then they stayed awake and listened for their little friends to come.

When the clock struck twelve slow strokes, the elves came dancing in. At first when they climbed on the bench they couldn't understand what had happened. Then one of them held up a little jacket and they both cried out, "Oh, look! Look! These are clothes to wear and they will just fit us!"

It took only a moment to put everything on, and last of all, they found two little pointed caps. Everything fitted so perfectly that the two little elves danced and sang with delight.

Then out of the door they ran, and after that Christmas Eve, they never came again. But all now went well for the shoemaker and his wife. They were never poor again but lived happily ever after.

The Three Billy Goats Gruff

Once upon a time there were three Billy Goats. Their names were Big Billy Goat Gruff, Little Billy Goat Gruff and Baby Billy Goat Gruff.

They had lived all winter on a rocky hillside where no grass or flowers grew for them to eat. By the time spring came and the weather began to get warmer, they were thin and very hungry.

(54)

But over the bridge on the other side of the river the hillside wasn't rocky at all. There the grass was thick and green with delicious flowers growing in it.

"We must cross the bridge to the other side where we can find plenty to eat," said Big Billy Goat Gruff.

"But the wicked Troll who lives under the bridge won't let anyone cross," said Baby Billy Goat Gruff.

The Billy Goats Gruff were afraid to cross the bridge but it was the only way to reach the lovely grass. They grew hungrier and hungrier every day until one day they put their heads together and made a plan.

First Baby Billy Goat Gruff went down the hillside and started across the bridge.

"Who goes there?" cried the Troll.

"It's only me, Baby Billy Goat Gruff."

"I'll eat you up," screamed the Troll. "I eat anyone who dares to cross my bridge."

"But I'm so small I'm only a mouthful," said the littlest Billy Goat Gruff. "If you wait for my bigger brother, he'll be along in a few minutes."

"Oh, all right," said the Troll crossly.

So Baby Billy Goat Gruff went safely over the bridge.

Before long the next brother, Little Billy Goat Gruff, came to the bridge.

At once the Troll roared, "You can't cross my bridge. I'm going to eat you up!"

Little Billy Goat Gruff leaned over the side and called down to him, "I'm only a bit bigger than my baby brother and scarcely more than two mouthfuls. Wait for my big brother who will be coming along soon."

"Oh, very well then," said the Troll, "but I'm getting very hungry and I won't wait much longer."

Before the old Troll could change his mind, Little Billy Goat Gruff was across the bridge and away up the hill to join his brother.

It wasn't long before Big Billy Goat Gruff came down the hill and started to cross the bridge. At once the Troll jumped out from underneath and reached up to catch him. But Big Billy Goat Gruff was very strong and he butted the Troll hard with his great horns. He tossed him high in the air and then . . . splash ! . . . down . . . down he went, right into the middle of the river.

How Big Billy Goat laughed as he dashed across the bridge and up the hillside to join his two brothers.

(56)

Little Red Riding Hood

There was once a little girl whose mother made her a new cloak with a hood. It was a lovely red colour and she liked to wear it so much that everyone called her Little Red Riding Hood.

One day her mother said to her, "I want you to take this basket of cakes to your grandmother who is ill."

Little Red Riding Hood liked to walk through the woods to her grandmother's cottage and she quickly put on her cloak. As she was leaving, her mother said, ''Now remember, don't talk to any strangers on the way.''

But Little Red Riding Hood loved talking to people, and as she was walking along the path, she met a wolf.

''Good morning, Little Girl, where are you off to in your beautiful red cloak?'' said the wolf with a wicked smile.

Little Red Riding Hood put down her basket and said, ''I'm taking some cakes to my grandmother who's not very well.''

''Where does your grandmother live?'' asked the wolf.

''In the cottage at the end of this path,'' said Little Red Riding Hood.

Now the wolf was really very hungry and he wanted to eat up Little Red Riding Hood then and there. But he heard a woodcutter not far away and he ran off.

He went straight to the grandmother's cottage where he found the old woman sitting up in bed. Before she knew what was happening, he ate her up in one gulp. Then he put on the grandmother's nightdress and her nightcap, and climbed into her bed. He snuggled well

down under the bedclothes and tried to hide himself.

Before long, Little Red Riding Hood came to the door with her basket of cakes and knocked.

"Come in," said the wolf, trying to make his voice sound soft.

At first, when she went in, Little Red Riding Hood thought that her grandmother must have a bad cold.

She went over to the bed. "What big eyes you have, Grandmama," she said, as the wolf peered at her from under the nightcap.

"All the better to see you with, my dear," said the wolf.

"What big ears you have, Grandmama."

"All the better to hear you with, my dear," answered the wolf.

Then Little Red Riding Hood saw a long nose and a wide-open mouth. She wanted to scream but she said, very bravely, "What a big mouth you have, Grandmama."

At this the wolf opened his jaws wide. "All the better to eat you with!" he cried. And he jumped out of bed and ate up Little Red Riding Hood.

Just at that moment the woodcutter passed by the

cottage. Noticing that the door was open, he went inside. When he saw the wolf he quickly swung his axe and chopped off his head.

Little Red Riding Hood and then her grandmother stepped out, none the worse for their adventure.

Little Red Riding Hood thanked the woodcutter and ran home to tell her mother all that had happened. And after that day, she never, ever, spoke to strangers.

The Little Red Hen

Once there was a pretty, neat little house. Inside it lived a Cock, a Mouse and a Little Red Hen.

On another hill, not far away, was a very different little house. It had a door that wouldn't shut, windows that were dirty and broken, and the paint was peeling off. In this house lived a bad old mother Fox and her fierce young son.

One morning the mother Fox said, "On the hill over there you can see the house where the Cock, the Mouse and the Little Red Hen live. You and I haven't had very much to eat for a long time, and everyone in that house is very well fed and plump. They would make us a delicious dinner!"

The fierce young Fox was very hungry, so he got up at once and said, "I'll just find a sack. If you will get the big pot boiling, I'll go to that house on the hill and we'll have that Cock, that Mouse and that Little Red Hen for our dinner!"

Now on the very same morning the Little Red Hen got up early, as she always did, and went downstairs to get the breakfast. The Cock and the Mouse, who were lazy, did not come downstairs for some time.

"Who will get some sticks to light the fire?" asked the Little Red Hen.

"I won't," said the Cock.

"I won't," said the Mouse.

"Then I'll have to do it myself," said the Little Red Hen. So off she ran to get the sticks.

When she had the fire burning, she said, "Who will go

and get the kettle filled with water from the spring?"

"I won't," said the Cock again.

"I won't," said the Mouse again.

"Then I'll have to do it myself," said the Little Red Hen, and off she ran to fill the kettle.

While they were waiting for their breakfast, the Cock and the Mouse curled up in comfortable armchairs. Soon they were asleep again.

It was just at this time that the fierce young Fox came up the hill with his sack and peeped in at the window. He stepped back and knocked loudly at the door.

"Who can that be?" said the Mouse, half opening his eyes.

"Go and find out, if you want to know," said the Cock crossly.

''Perhaps it's the postman,'' said the Mouse to himself. So, without waiting to ask who it was, he lifted the latch and opened the door.

In rushed the big fierce Fox!

''Cock-a-doodle-do!'' screamed the Cock as he jumped onto the back of the armchair.

''Oh! Oh! Oh!'' squeaked the Mouse as he tried to run up the chimney.

But the Fox only laughed. He grabbed the Mouse by the tail and popped him into the sack. Then he caught the Cock and pushed him in the sack too.

Just at that moment, in came the Little Red Hen, carrying the heavy kettle of water from the spring. Before she knew what was happening, the Fox quickly snatched her up and put her into the sack with the others. Then he tied a string tightly around the opening. And, with the sack over his shoulder, he set off down the hill.

The Cock, the Mouse and the Little Red Hen were bumped together uncomfortably inside the sack.

The Cock said, ''Oh, I wish I hadn't been so cross!''

And the Mouse said, ''Oh, I wish I hadn't been so lazy!''

But the Little Red Hen said, "It's never too late to try again."

As the Fox trudged along with his heavy load, the sun grew very hot. Soon, he put the sack on the ground and sat down to rest. Before long he was fast asleep. Then, "Gr––umph . . . gr––mph," he began to snore. The noise was so loud that the Little Red Hen could hear him through the sack.

At once she took her scissors out of her apron pocket and cut a neat hole in the sack. Then out jumped: first the Mouse, then the Cock, and last, the Little Red Hen.

"Quick! Quick!" she whispered. "Who will come and help me get some stones?"

"I will," said the Cock.

"And I will," said the Mouse.

"Good," said the Little Red Hen.

Off they went together and each one brought back as big a rock as he could carry and put it into the sack. Then the Little Red Hen, who had a needle and thread in her pocket too, sewed up the hole very neatly.

When she had finished, the Little Red Hen, the Cock and the Mouse ran off home as fast as they could go. Once inside, they bolted the door and then helped each other to get the best breakfast they had ever had!

After some time, the Fox woke up. He lifted the sack onto his back and went slowly up the hill to his house.

He called out, "Mother! Guess what I've got in my sack!"

"Is it – can it be – the Little Red Hen?"

"It is – and the Cock – and the Mouse as well. They're very plump and heavy so they'll make us a splendid dinner."

His mother had the water all ready, boiling furiously in a pot over the fire. The Fox undid the string and emptied the sack straight into the pot.

Splash! Splash! Splash! In went the three heavy rocks and out came the boiling hot water, all over the fierce young Fox and his bad old mother. Oh, how sore and burned and angry they were!

Never again did those wicked foxes trouble the Cock, the Mouse and the Little Red Hen, who always kept their door locked, and lived happily ever after.

The HELEN OXENBURY *Nursery Rhyme Book*

Rhymes chosen by Brian Alderson

Girls and boys, come out to play,
The moon doth shine as bright as day;
Leave your supper, and leave your sleep,
And come with your playfellows into the street.
Come with a whoop, come with a call,
Come with a good will or not at all.
Up the ladder and down the wall,
A halfpenny roll will serve us all.
You find milk and I'll find flour,
And we'll have a pudding in half an hour.

A, B, C, tumble down D,
The cat's in the cupboard and can't see me.

Apple-pie, pudding and pancake,
All begins with an A.

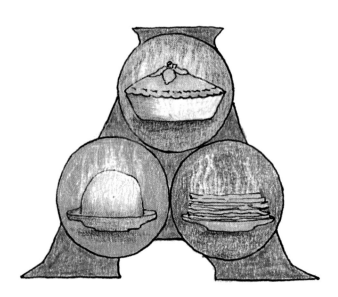

1, 2, 3, 4, 5!
I caught a hare alive;
6, 7, 8, 9, 10!
I let her go again.

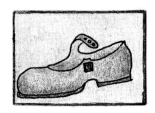

One, two,
Buckle my shoe;

Three, four,
Shut the door;

Five, six,
Pick up sticks;

Seven, eight,
Lay them straight;

Nine, ten,
A good fat hen;

Eleven, twelve,
Who will delve;

Thirteen, fourteen,
Maids a-courting;

Fifteen, sixteen,
Maids a-kissing;

Seventeen, eighteen,
Maids a-waiting;

Nineteen, twenty,
My stomach's empty.

When Jacky's a very good boy,
    He shall have cakes and custard;
When he does nothing but cry,
    He shall have nothing but mustard.

There was an old woman who lived in a shoe,
She had so many children she didn't know what to do;
She gave them some broth without any bread,
She whipped them all well and put them to bed.

Little Tommy Tittlemouse
Lived in a little house;

He caught fishes
In other men's ditches.

Solomon Grundy,
Born on a Monday,

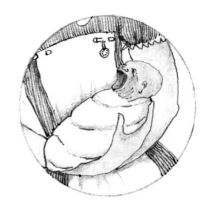

Christened on Tuesday,

Married on Wednesday,

Took ill on Thursday,

Worse on Friday,

Died on Saturday,

Buried on Sunday;

This is the end
Of Solomon Grundy.

Sing a song of sixpence,
  A pocket full of rye;
Four and twenty blackbirds
  Baked in a pie;

When the pie was opened
  The birds began to sing;
Wasn't that a dainty dish
  To set before the king?

The king was in his counting house
  Counting out his money;
The queen was in the parlour
  Eating bread and honey;

The maid was in the garden
  Hanging out the clothes,
There came a little blackbird,
  And snapped off her nose.

Jenny was so mad,
  She didn't know what to do;
She put her finger in her ear,
  And cracked it right in two.

Hey! diddle, diddle,
The cat and the fiddle,
The cow jumped over the moon;
The little dog laughed
To see the sport,
While the dish ran after the spoon.

Three blind mice, see how they run!
They all ran after the farmer's wife,
Who cut off their tails with the carving-knife,
Did ever you see such fools in your life?
                    Three blind mice.

Ding, dong, bell,
Pussy's in the well!
Who put her in?—
Little Tommy Lin.
Who pulled her out?—
Dog with long snout.
What a naughty boy was that
To drown poor pussy-cat,
Who never did any harm,
But kill'd the mice in his father's barn.

14

Tweedle-dum and Tweedle-dee
   Resolved to have a battle,
For Tweedle-dum said Tweedle-dee
   Had spoiled his nice new rattle.
Just then flew by a monstrous crow,
   As big as a tar barrel,
Which frightened both the heroes so,
   They quite forgot their quarrel.

When good king Arthur ruled this land,
He was a goodly king;
He stole three pecks of barley-meal,
To make a bag-pudding.

A bag-pudding the king did make,
And stuff'd it well with plums;
And in it put great lumps of fat,
As big as my two thumbs.

The king and queen did eat thereof,
And noblemen beside;
And what they could not eat that night,
The queen next morning fried.

Peter White will ne'er go right.
Would you know the reason why?
He follows his nose where'er he goes,
And that stands all awry.

Elsie Marley is grown so fine,
She won't get up to serve the swine,
But lies in bed till eight or nine,
And surely she does take her time.

And do you ken Elsie Marley, honey?
The wife who sells the barley, honey;
She won't get up to serve her swine,
And do you ken Elsie Marley, honey?

Little girl, little girl, where have you been?
Gathering roses to give to the queen.
Little girl, little girl, what gave she you?
She gave me a diamond as big as my shoe.

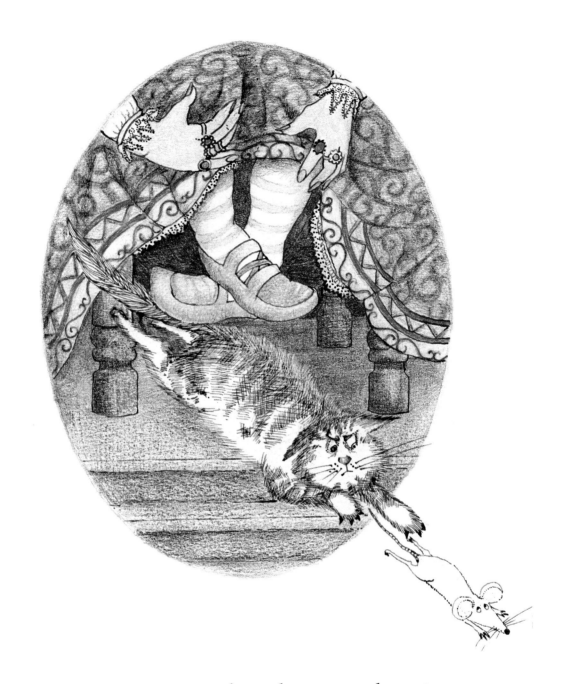

Pussy-cat, pussy-cat, where have you been?
I've been up to London to look at the queen.
Pussy-cat, pussy-cat, what did you there?
I frightened a little mouse under the chair.

The lion and the unicorn
    Were fighting for the crown;
The lion beat the unicorn
    All round the town.
Some gave them white bread,
    And some gave them brown;
Some gave them plum-cake,
    And sent them out of town.

Hector Protector was dressed all in green;
Hector Protector was sent to the Queen.
The Queen did not like him,
Nor more did the King:
So Hector Protector was sent back again.

24

Curly locks, curly locks, wilt thou be mine?
Thou shalt not wash dishes, nor yet feed the swine;
But sit on a cushion and sew a fine seam,
And feed upon strawberries, sugar, and cream.

Baa, baa, black sheep,
　　Have you any wool?
Yes, marry, have I,
　　Three bags full:

One for my master,
　　And one for my dame,
But none for the little boy
　　Who cries in the lane.

Rock-a-bye baby, thy cradle is green;
Father's a nobleman, mother's a queen;
And Betty's a lady, and wears a gold ring;
And Johnny's a drummer, and drums for the king.

I had a little husband,
      No bigger than my thumb,
I put him in a pint pot,
      And there I bid him drum.

I bought a little horse,
      That galloped up and down;
I bridled him, and saddled him,
      And sent him out of town.

I gave him some garters,
      To garter up his hose,
And a little handkerchief,
      To wipe his pretty nose.

As I was going up Pippen-hill,
    Pippen-hill was dirty,
There I met a pretty miss,
    And she dropped me a curtsey.

Little miss, pretty miss,
    Blessings light upon you!
If I had half-a-crown a day,
    I'd spend it all upon you.

Master I have, and I am his man,
　　Gallop a dreary dun;
Master I have, and I am his man,
And I'll get a wife as fast as I can;
With a heighly gaily gamberaily,
　　Higgledy piggledy, niggledy, niggledy,
　　Gallop a dreary dun.

I had a young man,
He was double-jointed,
When I kissed him,
He was disappointed.

When he died
I had another one,
God bless his little heart,
I found a better one.

If you sneeze on Monday, you sneeze for danger;
Sneeze on a Tuesday, kiss a stranger;
Sneeze on a Wednesday, sneeze for a letter;
Sneeze on a Thursday, something better;
Sneeze on a Friday, sneeze for sorrow;
Sneeze on a Saturday, see your sweetheart tomorrow.

See this pretty little girl of mine,
She brought me a penny and a bottle of wine.
A bottle of wine and a penny too,
See what my little girl can do.

The fair maid who, the first of May,
Goes to the fields at break of day,
And washes in dew from the hawthorn tree,
Will ever after handsome be.

On Saturday night
Shall be all my care,
To powder my locks
And curl my hair.

On Sunday morning
My love will come in,
When he will marry me
With a gold ring.

Needles and pins, needles and pins,
When a man marries his trouble begins.

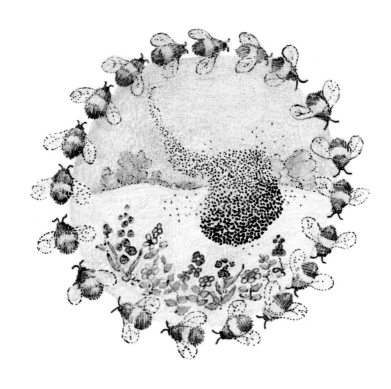

A swarm of bees in May
Is worth a load of hay;

A swarm of bees in June
Is worth a silver spoon;

A swarm of bees in July
Is not worth a fly.

There was a piper, he'd a cow;
    And he'd no hay to give her;
He took his pipes and played a tune,
    Consider, old cow, consider!

The cow considered very well,
    For she gave the piper a penny,
That he might play the tune again,
    Of corn rigs are bonnie!

What are little boys made of, made of,
What are little boys made of?
Snaps and snails and puppy-dogs' tails;
And that's what little boys are made of, made of.

What are little girls made of, made of,
What are little girls made of?
Sugar and spice, and all that's nice;
And that's what little girls are made of, made of.

Don't Care didn't care,
Don't Care was wild,
Don't Care stole plum and pear
Like any beggar's child.

Don't Care was made to care,
Don't Care was hung.
Don't Care was put in a pot
And boiled till he was done.

Little Tom Tucker
Sings for his supper;
What shall he eat?
White bread and butter.
How shall he cut it
Without e'er a knife?
How will he be married
Without e'er a wife?

Twelve huntsmen with horns and hounds,
Hunting over other men's grounds.

Eleven ships sailing o'er the main,
Some bound for France and some for Spain:
I wish them all safe home again:

Ten comets in the sky,
Some low and some high;

Nine peacocks in the air,
I wonder how they all come there,
I do not know, and do not care;

Eight joiners in joiner's hall,
Working with the tools and all;

Seven lobsters in a dish,
As fresh as any heart could wish;

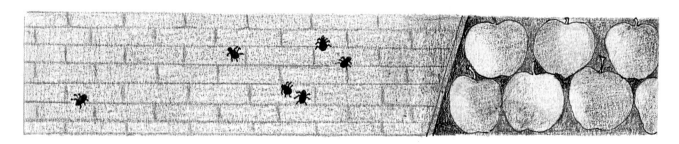

Six beetles against the wall,
Close by an old woman's apple stall;

Five puppies of our dog Ball,
Who daily for their breakfast call;

Four horses stuck in a bog;

Three monkeys tied to a clog;

Two pudding-ends would choke a dog;

With a gaping, wide-mouthed, waddling frog.

There was an old woman sat spinning,
And that's the first beginning;
    She had a calf,
    And that's half,
She took it by the tail,
And threw it over the wall,
And that's all.

Baby and I
Were baked in a pie,
The gravy was wonderful hot;
We had nothing to pay
To the baker that day,
And so we crept out of the pot.

I am a little beggar girl,
My mother she is dead,
My father is a drunkard
And won't give me no bread.
I look out of the window
To hear the organ play—
God bless my dear mother,
She's gone far away.

Little Polly Flinders
Sat among the cinders
Warming her pretty little toes.
Her mother came and caught her
And whipped her little daughter
For spoiling of her nice new clothes.

Jack Sprat could eat no fat,
    His wife could eat no lean;
And so, betwixt them both, you see,
    They licked the platter clean.

Eaper Weaper, chimbley sweeper,
Had a wife but couldn't keep her;
Had anovver, didn't love her,
Up the chimbley he did shove her.

Last night and the night before
Twenty-five robbers knocked at the door.
Johnny got up to let them in
And hit them on the head with a rolling pin.

Desperate Dan
The dirty old man
Washed his face
In a frying-pan;
Combed his hair
With the leg of a chair;
Desperate Dan
The dirty old man.

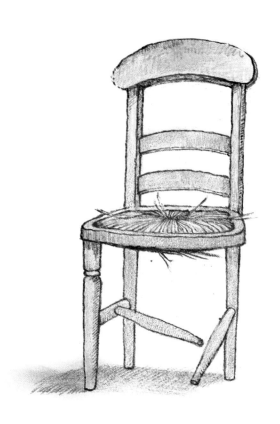

House to let,
Rent to pay,
Knock at the door
And run away.

Up and down Pie Street,
    The windows made of glass,
Call at Number Thirty-three,
    You'll see a pretty lass.

Her name is Annie Robinson,
    Catch her if you can,
She married Charlie Anderson,
    Before he was a man.

Bread and dripping all the week,
    Pig's head on Sunday,
Half a crown on Saturday night,
    A farthing left for Monday.

She only bought a bonnet-box,
    He only bought a ladle,
So when the little baby came
    It hadn't got no cradle.

Barber, barber, shave a pig,
How many hairs will make a wig?
''Four and twenty, that's enough,''
Give the barber a pinch of snuff.

Policeman, policeman, don't take me!
Take that man behind that tree!
I stole brass, he stole gold.
Policeman, policeman, don't take hold!

Who comes here?
  A grenadier.
What do you want?
  A pot of beer.
Where's your money?
  I've forgot.
Then get you gone
  You drunken sot!

Trip upon trenchers, and dance upon dishes,
My mother sent me for some barm, some barm;

She bid me tread lightly, and come again quickly,
For fear the young men should do me some harm.

Yet didn't you see, yet didn't you see,
What naughty tricks they put upon me:

They broke my pitcher,
And spilt the water,
And huffed my mother,
And chid her daughter,

And kissed my sister instead of me.

Rosemary green,
And lavender blue,
Thyme and sweet marjoram,
Hyssop and rue.

Gray goose and gander,
  Waft your wings together,
And carry the good king's daughter
  Over the one strand river.

A man of words and not of deeds,
Is like a garden full of weeds;
And when the weeds begin to grow,
It's like a garden full of snow;
And when the snow begins to fall,
It's like a bird upon the wall;
And when the bird away does fly,
It's like an eagle in the sky;
And when the sky begins to roar,
It's like a lion at the door;
And when the door begins to crack,
It's like a stick across your back;
And when your back begins to smart,
It's like a penknife in your heart;
And when your heart begins to bleed,
You're dead, and dead and dead indeed!

INDEX OF FIRST LINES